On top of his often scathing r
troopers were rampant, Johnston w
was coming . . . The biggest story of all was that exclusive interview with the most fascinating leader in Europe — and if Castle is right, the Hitler scoop cost 46-year-old Johnston his life . . .

Michael Platt
Calgary Sun

This book stands as a valuable asset for anyone interested in the military, newspaper, or general history of British Columbia in the early twentieth century . . . Colin Castle has undertaken a labour of love. The retired schoolteacher spent four years researching, transcribing, and writing the story of newspaperman Lukin 'Rufus' Johnston . . . He needs to be credited with preserving the story of this extraordinary character . . . For a time Rufus was in turn aide-de-camp to both General Arthur William Currie and General Sir Julian Byng, who later became Governor General of Canada. He was also tasked with taking future prime minister Winston Churchill out to "show him the sights" at Vimy Ridge. Castle has successfully captured in this work the extraordinary talent Rufus had for meeting and befriending important people . . .

Bruce Hodding
BC Studies, *December 2014*

Castle has drawn an account of pioneer life in Canada for a young British fellow, a bit of a dandy, who learned how to scrabble for a living. Rufus used what he learned to become an ace journalist, providing a sharp picture of the young province of BC, including accounts of travelling the Kettle Valley Railway and visiting Okanagan points by steamer. The book also gives a vital account of the First World War trenches . . . but emerging from those details and war horrors is a picture of a young man with an incredible enthusiasm for life.

Dorothy Brotherton
Westside Weekly, *Kelowna*

A revealing glimpse into the early world of BC newspapers. Following the fascinating life of reporter and *Province* editor Lukin Johnston, whose own story ends like a detective novel, we see both BC and Europe through the eyes of a remarkable and worldly British Columbian.

Dr. Henry Yu
Associate Professor of History
University of British Columbia

Lukin 'Rufus' Johnston is the perfect image of a late Victorian British schoolboy who conquered the Canadian West . . . and parlayed this dual patriotism into a respected, and ultimately thrilling, journalistic career in Western Europe during the 1930s.

Frances Clay Welwood
Author of Passing Through Missing Pages:
The Intriguing Story of Annie Garland Foster

Drawing extensively on Johnston's own diaries and family letters, Castle gives us a strong sense of what made Johnston tick, including his love for his wife, Bee, as well as interests such as Little Theatre. This is a comprehensive biography of a man who could have faded into the obscurity of history, even though he was a household name eight decades ago. It is also a real-life mystery.

Dave Obee
editor-in-chief
Times Colonist, *Victoria, BC*

Rufus

RUFUS

The Life of the Canadian Journalist who Interviewed Hitler

COLIN CASTLE

GRANVILLE ISLAND PUBLISHING

Library and Archives Canada Cataloguing in Publication

Castle, Colin, 1936–, author
Rufus : the life of the Canadian journalist who interviewed Hitler / Colin Castle.

Includes bibliographical references and index.
ISBN 978-1-926991-33-7 (pbk.)

1. Johnston, Lukin. 2. Journalists—Canada—Biography. 3. Foreign correspondents—Canada—Biography. 4. World War, 1914-1918—Canada—Biography. 5. Soldiers—Canada—Biography. I. Title.

PN4913.J64C38 2014 070.92 C2013-907881-9

Editor: Kyle Hawke
Cover and text designer: Omar Gallegos
Index consultant and proofreader: Renée Fossett
Maps design: Jamie Fischer

Granville Island Publishing Ltd.
212 – 1656 Duranleau St.
Vancouver, BC, Canada V6H 3S4

604-688-0320 / 1-877-688-0320
info@granvilleislandpublishing.com
www.granvilleislandpublishing.com

First published in May 2014
Second printing in 2015
Printed in Canada on recycled paper

To my dear wife Val, Rufus's granddaughter,
and my adviser, cheerleader and friend,
whose loving patience and forbearance
over three years have enabled me
to get the research done and the book written

Contents

Maps

Photographs

Family Good-luck Charm

Rufus's good-luck bagpiper, a lead soldier that his son Derek pressed upon him 'for good luck' at the end of his first leave in 1917. Rufus carried him faithfully, through all the perils of Passchendaele and the later battles of Amiens and Arras.

The battered little bagpiper would have an extended life. In World War II, Derek was in the Canadian navy and carried the little soldier with him. It was in his pocket the day HMS *Harvester*, the British destroyer to which he was temporarily assigned, was sunk by a U-Boat in the Atlantic. He managed to swim to a Carley float and was rescued. Probably for Bee's benefit, he always credited the bagpiper with keeping him safe.

Rufus's Lukin Family Tree

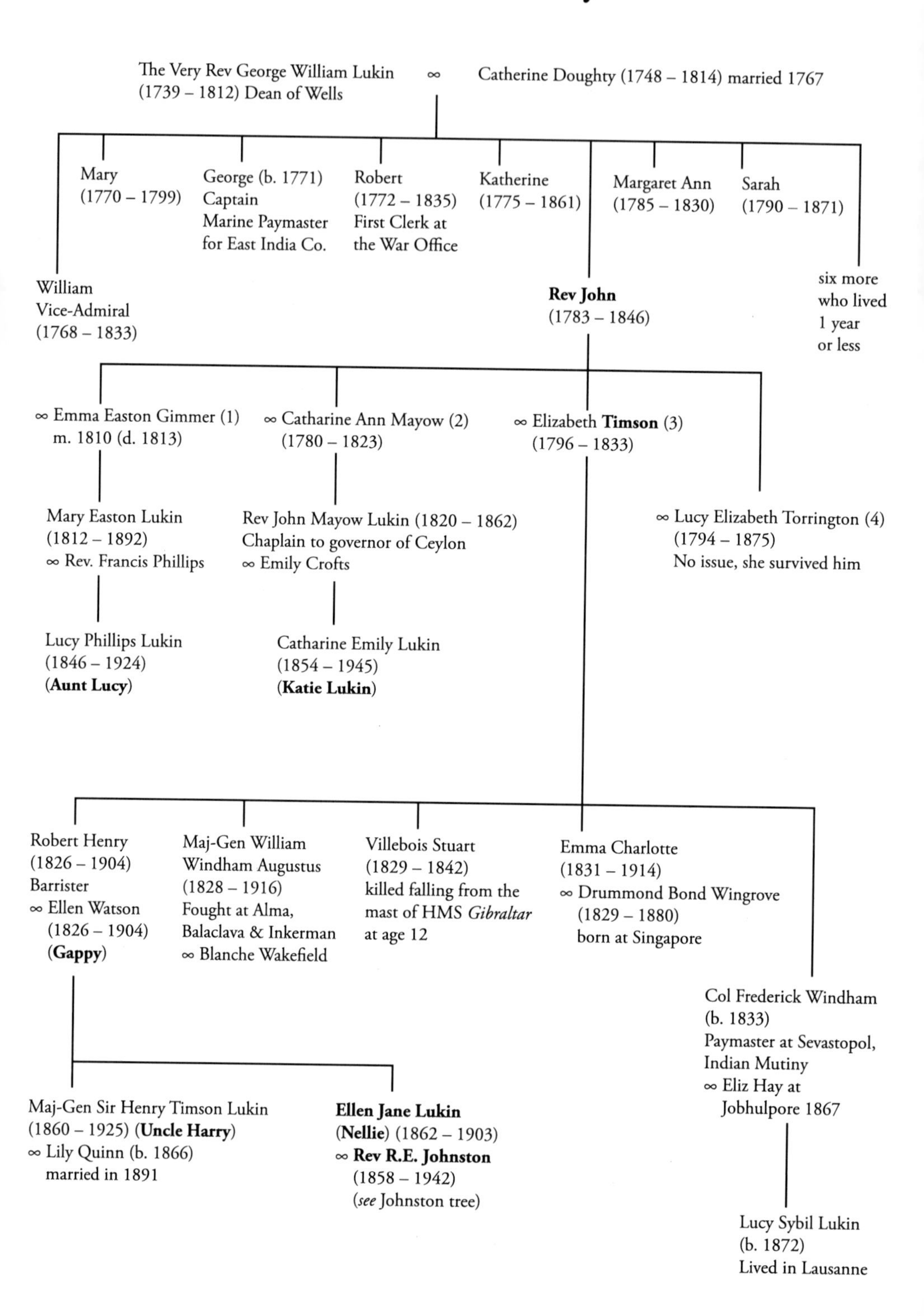

Rufus's Johnston Family Tree

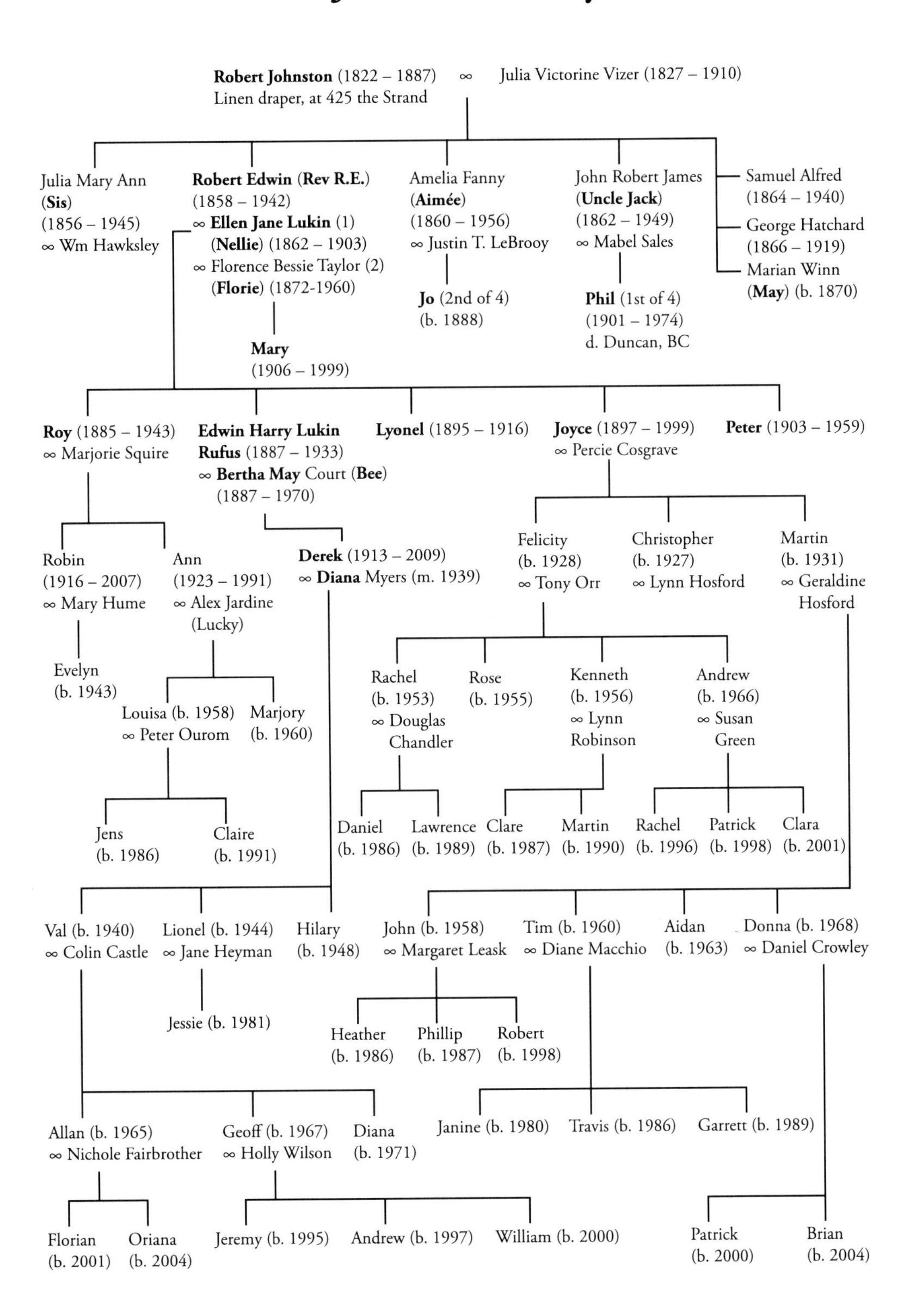

Foreword

I was never Colin Castle's best student. He once cut me from our high school debating team during a practice session before a big tournament. I had endeavoured to bluff my way through a speech, having failed to do any research or preparation beforehand. Colin taught me a valuable lesson that day; that glib charm will only get you so far. He saw no substitute for hard work, a lesson I have continually, vainly sought to disprove in the more than three decades since.

Colin was the best of teachers at our rural high school outside Kelowna on the west side of Okanagan Lake (rural no more — the fruit orchards have long since been paved over for suburban strip malls, condominiums and boutique wineries). His classroom lessons were enlivened by an erudite, Oxford-bred wit (how he came to be in our midst, we never knew), and that wit was augmented by an agreeably earthy sense of humour, on display in our more relaxed extra curricular work.

Our band of student debaters roamed much of the territory covered a half-century earlier by roving journalist Lukin "Rufus" Johnston. We borrowed a recreational vehicle from the family of a teammate for a tournament at a private boys school in Victoria. Colin drove while several of us sat at the table in back playing cards. On another occasion a convoy of teachers and students descended on Lethbridge, Alberta — a town you will come to know in this book as the setting for a low point in young Johnston's pre-journalism travels — for a model United Nations session that drew students from throughout western Canada. Lethbridge was a low point for me as well; I woke up in a motel room after the weekend to find that I had overslept, and my entire team had left, each carload thinking I was riding with someone else. The weekend UN session was perhaps too much fun for me, owing to the more lax Alberta drinking laws, and the elusive charms of a female delegate speaking for France. Colin will be just learning this as he reads these words. It fell to Colin to explain to my mother why I would arrive home a day later on a bus. My belated apologies, Colin.

I saw Colin occasionally in the years after high school, less frequently as I busied myself in Vancouver with work as a reporter and editor at *The Province* newspaper. Earlier this year, one of my old classmates put me back in touch with Colin. He was nearing the end of three years' work on this book about Lukin Johnston, a legendary *Province* reporter-editor of the 1920s and 1930s, and thought I might have something helpful to say about Johnston's time at the paper, from 80 years' distance.

I had the pleasure of a couple of telephone conversations with Colin, and discovered that the Castle wit was undiminished — he recalled a particularly pestilential suede jacket I wore throughout high school and beyond, and suggested the thing would have come if I whistled for it. I read his book and realized that his appetite for hard work was similarly enduring. His work here is thorough, enlightening and entertaining. At some point during our conversations, he sent me a note asking whether I might want to write a foreword for the book: "Most Forewords are pompous and overblown but I'm thinking of the opposite — something in your inimitable style, that nevertheless sounds reluctantly positive about both subject and author."

Here is where Colin and I part company — I can muster no reluctance about either subject or author. Colin came to the story of Lukin Johnston — known affectionately as Rufus to his friends and family — through his Canadian-born wife Val, who was the granddaughter Rufus would never know, owing to circumstances that form the book's central mystery. I will leave it to readers to discover that mystery for themselves in these pages.

Colin took on this book project as a labour of familial love, meant to give Rufus's grandchildren, great-grandchildren and great-great-grandchildren a full picture of their ancestor. But the resulting book should draw a much wider audience. Colin has taken Johnston's letters, diaries and published writings, added his own extensive research and insight, and crafted from that a meticulously detailed portrayal of one extraordinary man's life, from modest childhood in a British country vicarage at the turn of the last century, to his last trip as a veteran foreign correspondent criss-crossing Germany and central Europe in 1933, talking to power brokers, ordinary folk, and fellow journalists in a half-dozen countries.

Johnston, an extraordinarily prolific writer, filed regular dispatches on those travels to Canada's Southam newspaper chain, and would no doubt have followed that work with a book-length analysis of mid-1930s Europe under the looming shadow of fascism and war had he lived longer. His earlier work included books detailing his travels in his adopted home of British Columbia and in his native England.

In retelling Johnston's story, Colin Castle has also given us a vivid picture of Rufus's Canadian life and travels, from his arrival in Canada as a teen, his wanderings and various jobs — banker, farmer, cowboy, miner and finally reporter. Landscapes vividly depicted along the way include the desolation of Saskatchewan's Qu'Appelle Valley in a record cold winter, the rugged B.C. interior before highways, Okanagan Lake via steamboat, the oddly British enclave of Vancouver Island's Cowichan Valley, and the nascent city of Vancouver, still hemmed in by thick rainforest.

Johnston's front line service as an officer during the First World War is also brought starkly to life, with a soldier's-eye view of death and fighting at Vimy Ridge, Avion and Passchendaele.

Back in civilian life in the 1920s, he emerges as a major figure in the development and maturing of the newspaper scene in Vancouver and Canada. Self-taught but a remarkably quick study, he soon rose to the top of his chosen profession. His natural ease with people and his relentless curiosity, coupled with the experience gained in various pre-journalism fields, earned him the confidence of interview subjects that included workingmen, barons of industry, scoundrels, privates, generals, princes, presidents and prime ministers.

In recounting Johnston's decades in Vancouver, Colin has given us as well a rich portrait of Vancouver seen through Rufus's eyes. One of his first *Province* assignments as a tyro reporter before the First World War involved a trip to remotest Deep Cove on the north shore of Burrard Inlet, where a small development was being carved from the dark forest. I write this from my home in that very neighbourhood, now a 20-minute urban drive to downtown when traffic is light. When Rufus was looking to build a home for his own family in the 1920s, his attentions fell to Point Grey, where roads were just then being cut through the woods. The metropolis' limits have since sprawled southwards to Delta, north to Squamish and east past Langley and Mission.

As well, the newspaper and the metropolis it serves have changed in that white men from Britain no longer run things. Johnston's own youthful British chauvinism was tempered by his years in Canada and abroad. Judging from Rufus's later writings, I suspect that if he were to see today's *Province* newsroom, with its cosmopolitan mix of men and women from every continent, it would be a change that the erstwhile British public schoolboy would appreciate. Well, the sight of women journalists would give him pause. He was a man of his time, after all.

From a remove of eight decades, one can see that some things never change in the journalism racket. I can identify with Rufus's perennial inability to manage his finances, a common fault among those in the profession. The enthusiastic alcohol consumption also rings a bell. His work at its best vexed those in power, as the best journalism still does today, even as publishers then and now worry about keeping powerful advertisers. My current newspaper work involves features on entertainment and culture — where Rufus also spent some time in his career — but working across the newsroom are the Lukin Johnstons of our day, still doggedly irritating the comfortable. The tools have changed — video and the Internet now augment print on paper but the basic job is the same: get out there, get the story, and get back. Few ever did that better than Lukin "Rufus" Johnston.

Glen Schaefer
The Province
Vancouver

Preface

I have wanted to write *Rufus* since 1998 when I retired from teaching. It became a practical project, however, only after the death of Rufus's son Derek in 2009. In writing his own *Personal Memoir*, Derek felt he had done enough to satisfy the curiosity of family members about his father's life. It was clear to us all that he wanted no book written in his lifetime. Derek — and Bee before him — must have dreaded having to relive the misery of Rufus's sudden death, the inevitable consequence for them of any such attempt.

Nevertheless, the preparation and writing has taken four years — an unconscionably long time for which there are two main explanations. The first is the nature and volume of the most important sources — thirty years of family letters and seventeen years of Rufus's diaries. Almost all were hand-written, and although people wrote clearly a century ago, for such material to be accessible when writing the book it had first to be typed into computer files to make it retrievable by computer-search. The transcription itself took well over a year, a process not speeded by Rufus's preference for pencil, the blunter the better, for making diary entries.

The second reason for slow progress was the intense interest for me of everything I was reading and transcribing. For a history buff the temptation to explore each of Rufus's references to people, plays, and events was irresistible. I hope that this spontaneous research produced a more interesting story for readers — it certainly ate up the hours, and I had fun! If you add to that the slower pace at which we seventy-somethings work, remembering that we also like to smell the flowers, then four years seems more reasonable — a shorter time, I'm told, than the average student takes for a PhD.

I hope *Rufus* proves to be an enjoyable read for those who pick it up. It is not intended as more than that and the many references to the Vancouver *Daily Province* — a still-thriving newspaper for which Lukin Johnston wrote in sixteen of his twenty years as a journalist — are just parts of his life story. They are not an attempt to tell the *Province*'s story and I apologize to those associated with that paper who may find its treatment herein less complete or rigorous than they would have liked.

I have tried to resist the temptation to editorialize on points of history and have done so only when absolutely necessary. For some of the more significant people Rufus knew or met, I have included brief biographies in the end-notes as the least obtrusive way of providing such background. Outside sources are recognized in the end-notes; footnotes are reserved for explanations of the text. There is a short bibliography.

As Rufus's papers lay in Johnston family basements for eighty years, it seems a pity that this book was not written earlier, while the readers and admirers of Lukin Johnston, the journalist, were still in our midst. However, Derek had organized the papers into files and boxes, each with contents neatly described, and had had many of his father's letters typed. It is a fair assumption, therefore, that he expected this book to be written after his own death – possibly with his posthumous blessing.

I have many people to thank for their help in the research, writing, publication and marketing of *Rufus*. Top of the list is the late Derek Johnston himself, who so carefully preserved his father's effects. My wife Val, Derek's daughter and Rufus's granddaughter, has been my research partner. She typed all of Bee's letters and some of Rufus's, researched her grandmother's story, was a reliable interpreter of smudged pencil-writing and a provider of sensible advice. She has always encouraged me and has been selflessly tolerant of my irregular work habits and unpredictable moods. Our son Geoff Castle has given good advice and masterminded Rufus's sensational latter-day appearance on Twitter, while Jessie Johnston, our niece, talked me through the intricacies of creating and running a website and blog, followed by weekly chats about its further development. Kim Plumley, of Publicity Mavens, is ensuring that news of *Rufus*'s publication reaches those who matter. And last of all Glen Schaefer, *The Province*'s entertainment writer, the only person in BC with links both to the author and to the newspaper that taught Rufus his trade, was kind enough to write the Foreword to *Rufus*.

Finally there are the people at Granville Island Publishing: the boss, Jo Blackmore, who held the ring, persuaded me to cut the manuscript to publishable proportions, provided sensible advice, and talked me out of defeatist moods; copy-editor Kyle Hawke, who patiently coaxed this balky author to adopt commonly used punctuation standards and was always ready with good alternative wording; Renee Fossett, copy-editor and proofreader, whose experience and knowledge have saved me from committing too many horrors and whose advice was ever sound; Omar Gallegos, who has designed this pleasing book; and Jamie Fischer, who has converted my jottings into maps.

Colin Castle,
West Kelowna

CHAPTER 1

Generals, Barristers, Drapers and Priests

Edwin Harry Lukin Johnston was born with a halo of flaming red hair to Nellie Johnston and her husband Ted, on August the 8th, 1887. They lived in Surbiton, England, where Ted — more formally the Reverend Robert Edwin Johnston, M.A. — was an Anglican curate. He and Nellie, whose maiden name had been Ellen Jane Lukin, chose to call the baby, their second son, Harry.

As he became old enough to care about such things, young Harry may not have liked this name much but he liked 'Ginger' even less, the nickname bestowed upon him by his older brother Roy and gleefully picked up by every boy in the neighbourhood.

He was four when the family moved to Folkestone in Kent, whence the name Ginger followed him as closely as his shadow. One afternoon after they had been there for some time, he was with Nellie doing errands in town, when a group of soldiers from the barracks came swinging down the sidewalk towards them. One soldier, also with bright red hair, spotted Rufus as they passed.

"Hallo, young feller," the red-headed soldier said, cheekily ruffling the boy's unruly mop.

"What do they call you then, with all that red hair?"

"They call me 'Ginger'," Harry answered rather crossly. "And I hate it!"

"Ginger, eh?" said the soldier, "that's what they used to call me till I put a stop to it!"

The boy's interest suddenly awakened. "What do they call you now?" Harry demanded in his piping voice.

"Why, they call me Rufus like I tell 'em to," the soldier replied with a chuckle, running off after his pals.

"But what does 'Rufus' mean?" Harry called after him.

The soldier turned and hollered, "Why, red-haired, silly — like the king," before vanishing round the corner.

Harry remembered Miss Skidmore reading the story of the king William Rufus in the schoolroom. *Rufus! That's a fine name*, he thought. That day at family tea, after breathlessly recounting the afternoon's adventure, he announced, "No more Ginger! Everybody please call me Rufus, like the soldier!" At the time, Nellie may have smiled indulgently at this insistence, but her son's determination stayed with him and he would get his way — by the time he was six not only did she herself always refer to him in her diary as 'Rufus' but she sometimes shortened it to 'Rufie' — even to 'Rufe'!

Ted Johnston, or R.E. as he was referred to more formally, was an exceedingly sound man, as he revealed in his huge correspondence with his family. Most obviously, he was a man of faith — no placeman vicar he. His religious belief was the core of his being, and controlled his relationship with the world. This relationship comprised absolute honesty, a humility so complete that his own interests and comfort consistently took a back seat to those of others (of his children in particular), and a fatalism which ensured that his own fairly limited ambition would never raise enough steam actually to improve his circumstances.

Beyond faith, R.E. was a man of intellect who had enjoyed the university education that his children would do without. This was important for Rufus in many ways. His father, for example, seemed so well able to analyze his son's various distant situations over the years — a tall order from parochial Kent — that he was able to offer advice that was usually wise, sometimes followed, and often even sought. Beset by the needs of his children for relatively modest subsidies over the years, R.E. had the brains and ability to write and publish a number of books for which there was still a large captive market, thus supplementing his meagre church income. These included *The Eternal King and His Kingdom*, 1908, and the six volumes of the *Marden Manuals for the Graded Sunday School*, and the *Catechist's Manual*, all 1912. Excepting the last, these were written for children, in short sentences and simple language, full of compelling imagery and brimming with belief. They are totally charming. The manual for adults, practical and devoid of grandstanding asides, must have seemed a godsend to lay people charged with teaching Sunday School but with no idea where to begin. He also wrote a serious biography of his brother-in-law, Major General Sir Harry Lukin, published in 1929. He had access to Harry's papers after his death, of course, but for a man of the cloth to have written such a good book about soldiering was in itself remarkable.

Another of R.E.'s strengths was his financial competence. It fell to him not only to have to referee the disbursement of money from two different sources — the Johnston Trust and what was referred to as 'the Timson money' — but to ensure that no individual be permitted to borrow more than what was eventually coming to them from either, that they pay realistic interest on borrowings, and that they pay their premiums on their life policies on time.

The sums were not large but maintenance of interest from the funds affected his own financial survival and he waged a constant and successful battle with his sons' urgent requests and financial naïveté.

As a father, R.E. was kind and loyal, and to him fell the total care of his family when his beloved Nellie died in childbirth in 1903 at age 41. At the time, he had five children: 18-year-old Roy, 16-year-old Rufus, 8-year-old Lyonel, 6-year-old Joyce, and newborn Peter. A housekeeper-governess was absolutely necessary and so Florence Bessie Taylor, a long-time parishioner known to all as Florie, entered their world. Not being endowed with the tact necessary in the situation, unfortunately, Florie quickly got on the wrong side of Roy and Rufus, a breach that only widened when she and their father decided to marry in 1905 — they saw their father's second marriage as treason to their beloved mother. In spite of this sorry situation, R.E. managed to head off his sons' hostility by his example and, overtly at least, they remained polite to Florie. Through the worst of it all he seems to have criticized no one, been attentive and loving to all, and to have retained the devotion of his children, though their persisting dislike of Florie must have caused him much pain.

R.E.'s father provided his heirs with welcome commercial genes, not that these seem to have reached Rufus — commerce, or even the ability to avoid losses, never being his thing. Robert Johnston, the grandfather Rufus never met, was a linen draper who lived over his shop at 425, the Strand, in London. The 1861 census finds him prosperous enough to maintain a household of fourteen, including his wife Julia, his widowed mother, an unmarried sister, a cook, a housemaid, a nurse for his three children, and four draper's assistants. Grandfather Johnston died the year Rufus was born, but Rufus knew his grandmother Julia; she was often at the vicarage, was known as 'old Mrs Johnston', and lived to 83.

Of Nellie, we know much less because of her early death. She was a much-loved mother and, from her surviving Rough Diary[1], it is clear she devoted herself absolutely to her young family and the life of the parish. She may have had miscarriages in the eight years between the births of Rufus and Lyonel. We know that she lost Una Faith in 1902 and she died after giving birth to Peter in the following year.

On Nellie's side of the family, Lukin family pride in their ancient lineage limited their occupations to a few professions, and remarkable characters are clustered on the branches of the family tree. Nellie and her brother Harry were the children of Robert Henry Lukin, a barrister, and his wife Ellen Watson. Ellen died young, as her daughter Nellie would do. When Robert Henry died in 1904, he divided his estate between Harry (in South Africa) and the late Nellie's children, his grandchildren — thus providing the capital for the Johnston Trust in which Rufus and his siblings would share. Robert Henry, the grandpa they knew as Gappy, died when Rufus was 17.

Robert Henry's siblings were less useful to Rufus but infinitely more exciting to boast about. The lives of this brood personified the tragedy and triumph of the Victorian empire. There was Major General William Windham Augustus Lukin who fought in the Crimea, an artillery officer in the brutal battles of Alma, Balaclava and Inkerman, as well as at the siege of Sevastopol. His unfortunate brother Villebois Stuart Lukin joined the navy as a midshipman and was killed at Gibraltar at the age of 12 when he fell 100 feet from the rigging onto the deck of *HMS Formidable*. Their sister Emma Charlotte Lukin may have lived a humdrum life though she married the remarkably named Drummond Bond Wingrove, born at Singapore. Finally, Colonel Frederick Windham Lukin, a cautious individual, was paymaster at Sevastopol and married his wife Amy Hay at Jobhulpore, India.

We can look back to Nellie's great grandfather, the Very Rev George William Lukin, Dean of Wells. He and his wife Catherine had fourteen children — of these, six died as infants, two of their four surviving daughters lived into their eighties and the four surviving sons were so pleased with themselves that they had a picture painted of the group. They had their reasons, I suppose. The eldest, William Lukin, was a Vice Admiral; Captain George Lukin was the Marine paymaster for the East India Company in Bombay; and Robert Lukin became First Clerk at the War Office. The youngest, the Rev John Lukin (1783–1846), married four times and had seven children. He was Nellie's grandfather and his third wife, Elizabeth Timson, was her grandmother. With his previous wives, the Rev John was also the grandfather of her cousins Katie and Lucy.

Rufus's uncle Harry would be the Lukin relative with the most impact on his life, and his career was as remarkable as those of his forebears. In spite of being "mad keen on soldiering" and having attended a crammer, he failed to get into Sandhurst, Britain's school for career army officers. His long-time friend Col. Judd explained. "He found the examination too much for him — he was a slow thinker. However, he went through the Knightsbridge riding school and completed a short course on infantry drill at Chelsea Barracks." Thus prepared, he set off for South Africa and managed to wangle a commission in Bengough's Horse, a native unit operating with the 17th Lancers in the Zulu war of 1878–79.

He was wounded at Ulundi but later did sufficiently well to be gazetted a lieutenant in the Cape Mounted Rifles, the only permanent unit in the Cape Colony at the time. After taking part in further wars against the tribes, in 1893 he returned to Britain for courses in artillery and machine-guns. He married Lily Quinn of Fort Hare in 1891 when he was 31, she 25, but, sadly, they would remain childless. By the end of the Anglo-Boer War in 1902, he was Colonel of the CMR and in 1910, when the Union of South Africa was created, he was promoted to Brigadier General and appointed Inspector General of the Permanent Force — basically, the Union's top soldier. In Judd's opinion, "Being quite fearless he was particularly successful as a regimental or small column commander. [But] he had no experience of independent command over large forces and might fairly be described as the very best type of conventional soldier whose day probably passed with the cavalry and horse artillery." Nevertheless, in

World War I he defeated the Germans in South West Africa, later commanded the South African Brigade at Delville Wood in France and then took command of British 9th Division.[2]

Many of Rufus's ancestors were men of action, or of faith and words, who lived bravely in the face of difficulty and danger, while few made their living with numbers or through a technical skill. His own life would follow the example they had set.

Chapter 2
Childhood

"I should be very sorry to lose our little chorister, the 'Flaming Seraph' as we sometimes playfully but audaciously call him, for we like him very much."

Dean Farrar, 1900, on the possibility of Rufus having to leave the King's School.

Rufus was born in Surbiton where his father was curate at St Matthews. The family Bible gives their address as 5 Woodside, Tolworth, Surbiton, about 500 metres from the church. For his first eight years, his only sibling was his brother Roy, older by twenty-one months. Both enjoyed playing sports but Roy would develop into an exceptional athlete which compounded Rufus's early difficulties in keeping up. When not competing, they had great times together, especially when R.E. took them on expeditions. In later years these would be cycling holidays on the continent and so resourceful a man would surely have thought of others suitable for younger boys — maybe fishing or rowing on the Thames in Surbiton days, or climbing the Downs and walking along the cliffs after they moved to Folkestone because such things would delight the adult Rufus.

In 1891 their father had a promotion — to Priest-in-Charge of another new parish, on Cheriton Road outside Folkestone. As his church and vicarage were as yet unbuilt, temporarily they moved into Enbrook Manor on Risborough Lane, a large house that would serve as vicarage for four years. Rufus was four when he found himself in the nursery there. When the sweep came, of the many chimneys, he swept those of the nursery, kitchen, study and schoolroom only. As his younger sister Joyce later remembered, apart from the kitchen there was usually just one fire lit downstairs. On winter evenings Ted and Nellie would sit in the study, the children in the nursery until bedtime; once they were in bed, the many others in the house might use the nursery or the kitchen; or they would share the study. Nellie records that the "new sweep found a sackful of soot in the study chimney pot — a great blessing not to have the fire smoking", which suggests that in winter the study was the center of the house's life. There was no electric light and they carried candles to unheated bedrooms. Newcomers could easily get lost in the house at night, especially if they ran out of matches.*

Nellie, as the family and parish organizer, kept a *Rough Diary*. Unfortunately only the one for 1893 has survived and it provides much detail about Rufus's childhood. As life in the vicarage was as unchanging as the Lord's Prayer, one suspects, other years would have been similar though names might change and people grow older. In her diary, Nellie referred to Rufus and Roy as the 'Babes', even when 8 and 6. This habit was reinforced by the large number of teenagers living with them — either as boarders attending the High School, or as students in their own schoolroom. Either way, their fees kept Ted solvent. The house offered a loving, very Christian environment and Nellie became a surrogate mum to all. If anything, living in such a crowd actually improved the lives of Rufus and Roy — they had so many people willing to talk to them, play with them, help them play tennis or cricket, show them how to hold a golf club or a fishing rod or take them on expeditions. Thus Bijou, Nowell and Ronald, all teenagers, came with the family on holiday, to the circus, for a picnic and for a drive; the same gang plus Winnie stayed with the family for Christmas and Winnie twice took the boys up on the Downs on her own. At other times there were Frank, Kenneth, Eldred and Willie for company — on and off, a total of eight young people in the house over the year.

The boys, of course, were quite able to amuse themselves. They had a large lawn on which to play cricket in the summer months and, joy of joys, a grass tennis court too, where they developed a passion for the game. Nowell shared their love of sports and was down at 5:00 am in summer to help old Charlie cut the grass — with a push mower. Joyce — ten years younger than Rufus — remembers that "summer was never long enough for all our tennis and cricket." The adults also enjoyed tennis and Nellie mentions at least six tennis parties on their court that summer. As the boys had spent much of the winter of 1892-3 in bed, first with mumps, then with measles, topped off by pneumonia in Roy's case, Nellie was keen to keep them healthy over the next winter. When cricket and tennis ended in September, they were sent off (no doubt willingly) to the local gym every Saturday morning — weather permitting, as they had no 'conveyance' and would have to walk. All this physical activity had its costs: family legend records that Rufus suffered three green-stick fractures in early youth.

Because the manor house was such a warren, all and sundry could, and did, come to stay. In spite of the young people each having their own room, a room was kept all year for Nellie's brother Harry and his wife Lily — she stayed most of the year while Harry was taking courses; also, at different times,

---

* Nellie tells us in her *Rough Diary* for September 21: "Mr de H arrived. Poor man lost himself several times in this rambling house and was caught going into the Babies bathroom by K.S! And Mrs S also saw him groping and remarked "It is chilly" but never offered to help him out of his difficulty!"

combinations of the La Brooys (Ted's sister Aimée and husband), old Gappy (Nellie's father), old Mrs Johnston (Ted's widowed mother) and his sister May were staying in the house. Further, there was a cast of other adults living there: Miss Skidmore (Kitty), governess and teacher who took an invaluable share of parish duties; Mr. Roberts the cook; Mr. Rowlands and Mr. de Havilland, men of vague responsibilities who helped out but who may just have been paying lodgers. It was all a bit like Noah's Ark and their guests quickly absorbed the sharing spirit — for example, Lucy Lukin took Nowell to the theatre, and when she went to tea with a friend, took Winnie with her. Gappy went to Dover with Bijou and Kenneth, then to Canterbury with Ronald, Bijou and Roy and they "had a good tea." And Harry Lukin, back from one of his courses, introduced Roy and Rufus to the mysteries of golf, and later took Frank, Eldred and Willie out fishing — they caught eight between them. "Beautiful fish," he noted, mockingly, in his sister's diary, "Sole dabs, at least 2 ozs each!"

Nobody in that house was bored. In winter, as Joyce remembered, "evenings were always at home, except for a rare treat to a play or concert or parish event. Charades we played with enthusiasm. We were very content with reading, games (draughts, chess, patience and whist — under Dad's tuition!) — and handicrafts." They would sell these at a sale — there were several in 1893; and of course there was music, when they all sang and at which Rufus increasingly excelled as years passed, as he had a wonderful treble voice as a small boy. Amazingly, no member of the family played an instrument but Kitty Skidmore and Winnie played the piano and Winnie also sang. In 1893 there was no gramophone but after the family bought one they spent happy winter hours dancing — "very proper compared to today," 90-year-old Joyce remembered; "we danced the polka, waltz, foxtrot, gallup and lancers" around the dining room table. It was perhaps because Rufus did not share this experience that in later years he did not enjoy dancing — much to Bee's disappointment.

Nevertheless he was always an accomplished performer, as Mrs King, headmistress of the girls' school at Cheriton, recalled. "My recollection of Rufus is of a little chap of seven with vivid blue eyes and wearing a blue suit. At a village concert he was to recite a little poem, *The Silver-Plated Teapot.* He began gorgeously. At the end of verse two he calmly turned round to Miss Skidmore, his governess, who stood nervously in the wings, and said quite audibly: "What comes next, Skiddy?" He got the applause of the evening — I don't wonder, he was the delight of the parish."[3]

Rufus's and Roy's family life was affected by their parents being so engaged in parish work. Nellie who, with Winnie, had been to hear Miss Pankhurst when she visited Folkestone in February,[4] was involved in trying to improve the lives of the women and children. She personally sponsored a Mothers Meeting group, a Girls Club and the maintenance of its club house, a Temperance society, a Boys Bible class, a Church Lads brigade and possibly the church school — and was trying to raise money for them all. With Kitty Skidmore and occasionally Winnie and Ted, she shared weekly meeting duties for the groups — a big commitment. Volunteers helped, but the burden was constant. Rufus and Roy learned early to share their mum.

There were times when activities eased off — for a month in summer and another at Christmas. That did not mean that Ted, Nellie and their two boys could spend private time together, as families would do today. When they went to Sevenoaks in August the household consisted of Ted, Nellie, Kitty (who soon left), Bijou, Nowell, Ronald, Rufus, Roy, Alice and Ellen, to be joined within a day or so by old Mrs Johnston, Lily and Harry (though he soon left) — a party of thirteen, then eleven. On Christmas Day they were thirteen: Ted, Nellie, Roy, Rufus, Gappy, Harry, Lily, Winnie, Nowell, Ronald, Alice, Anne and Ellen. Although Alice, Anne and Ellen were domestics who helped to make it possible for the rest to be together, old man Noah would certainly have felt at home!

The family had no conveyance — no trap and definitely no automobile, though Joyce remembers country picnics with a donkey cart and bicycles, and being able to meet Lyonel on a donkey on his way home from school — but those memories were of Thanet after 1900. Old Mr Martin, the miller, who was also the churchwarden, used to love to take Roy and Rufus for rides in his cart[5] and Nellie would hire Mr Butler's 'cab' whenever a set of wheels was necessary. Thus when Bijou had been sick, she was sent to school and fetched by cab for a whole week; and occasionally in winter she would write "Social evening at Miss De La Mare's in Butler's cab" or "Winnie, Bijou and I went to a Social at the High School. Butler took us in the cab and fetched us." But Nellie cut the cabbie little slack — when Bijou had on a new dress, she commented that "Butler swaggered Bijou in"; and when he spoiled her arrangements she could be quite unforgiving: "Butler didn't wait at Radnor Park Station for Mrs Lukin [Lily] and Miss S [Kitty Skidmore] — old idiot!" On their holiday in Sevenoaks the family was delighted to have the use of a pony and trap thrown in. For several halcyon days their enthusiasm for driving in this contraption knew no bounds — with the predictable result: the poor old pony went lame and then they all did a great deal of walking! Fortunately, their friends the Hall-Halls lived nearby and Frank H-H, who had been one of their boarders, was happy to drive when necessary in the H-H trap.

Although never 'life in the fast lane', vicarage life had its moments for small boys. Even their mother's charitable efforts could put them on their mettle, as when Roy and Rufus, with Bijou to keep an eye on them, were put in charge of a table at a Temperance Society sale at Sandgate. The Folkestone *fête*, of course, was a much anticipated occasion: in 1893 the boys saw the local Cheriton lads win first prize for drill and band-playing; they were taken to the circus and in the evening there were fireworks. With so many observant adults around them, they could never hope to escape churchy things entirely; so I don't suppose Rufus minded when his mother took him to inspect progress on their new vicarage; nor when he and Roy went to Hythe on the train with Uncle Harry, even if it was to look at a new stained glass window in the church there. They would probably have preferred to have gone with him to the Army School of Musketry, where, on another occasion, he demonstrated a new-fangled machine gun to their bewildered father! There were also less welcome occasions, such as when Roy and Rufus were taken to tea at Mrs d'Altera's — but who knows, Mrs d'A may have had a reputation for sticky buns; or the one time in the year when they had their hair cut by a barber; or when the same barber shaved their heads during an epidemic of head-lice in the house; or even when his mother picked through their hair for fleas and dusted them with flea-powder; "caught 19 fleas," she recorded, "half of them off Frank."

1893 was Rufus's *annus horribilis* for infectious disease — chicken pox and whooping cough may have happened later and probably one at a time! But life at Enbrook Manor laid the foundation for a lifetime of playing tennis and other sports whenever and wherever he could. Likewise, tramping on the Downs near Folkestone, along with walks taken with his father on their summer holiday that year, established his love of hiking. The countryside was important to him even then, and would remain so. A few random memories survive of Rufus and Roy as boys. On one occasion, the pair of them found a great hiding place in an abandoned building along a road or street. From this vantage point they fired dried peas from peashooters at passing horses — with predictable reactions from the startled animals. On another occasion they tied up their housekeeper for a prank. And on a summer holiday at Yalden, near Maidstone, while their younger siblings were messing about in boats by the river, Roy and Rufus startled any witnesses there were by 'streaking' along the river bank — not an everyday occurrence in early 20th Century England![6]

Both boys began their schooling in the vicarage schoolroom. There they were taught by their father, but also, in 1893, by Kitty Skidmore. They received an excellent basic education, especially in languages, writing, history, geography and religion. Rufus wrote many letters that have survived and kept a diary for years. Even in the diary it is well-nigh impossible to detect errors of spelling or syntax. His vocabulary was enormous, he used words precisely, redundancies seldom occurred and his sentences were balanced — all this even in letters to his Dad. Similarly, the regularity of his handwriting makes it easily readable a hundred years later, in spite of his tolerance of blunt pencils. It was the best preparation imaginable for the career he eventually chose.

On 23 June 1895 Rufus's life changed substantially when his brother Lyonel was born. Then 7¾, Rufus had enjoyed the status of youngest child for as long as he could remember, with all the implied tolerance of his foibles. By 1895 he was old enough not to care too much about Lyonel usurping his role, but there must have been subtle changes in how he was treated by both parents. And Lyonel's arrival was a harbinger of even greater change: two years later, on 23 November 1897, Joyce was born and they all had a sister. For the next five years they were a family of six, although the older boys and their two younger siblings lived quite different lives, as by 1899 the older two were away at school for most of the year. But summers were happy family times and Joyce obviously hero-worshipped Roy and Rufus to an extent and gave them an audience for their occasional outrageous behaviour.

In 1897 he went as a boarder to the King's School Canterbury junior school, at first as a fee-paying student, though possibly his father paid less because he sang part-time in the cathedral choir. Still only 9 he was almost certainly homesick, but so collegial a fellow would have found his feet quickly and singing in the choir would have seemed like home. Eleven other boys started that May, most about his age. Two of these were the Montgomery brothers, Bernard and Donald, sons of the Bishop of Tasmania. They only stayed at King's a term but Rufus would have known them because Dean Farrar, the choirmaster, was also their grandfather. The Montgomerys were probably also in the choir and one imagines them, with Rufus, enjoying tea and crumpets with their grandfather. Regardless, Rufus (or the world) would come across them again: Bernard became 'Monty', the World War II Field Marshall; and Donald, older and less exalted, was called to the bar in BC in 1911 and he and Rufus would meet again.

THE LATE NINETIES WERE HARD TIMES and particularly for the priest-in-charge at Cheriton. During the summer of 1898 he could no longer see his way to paying Rufus's fees and wrote to Dean Farrar in hopes that he might win a choir scholarship. The Dean, who was most encouraging, obviously saw Rufus as a star. Although Mr Hodgson, the headmaster, thought that Rufus might win one on his own, Farrar assured R.E. that if not, he would provide one for him as a chorister. "If we could get his full services," the Dean wrote, "I think he would soon be a solo boy." The scholarship was duly provided and Rufus become a soloist. He was now spending part of his school-day at choir practice and services which part-time choristers did not.

Unfortunately, even with Rufus's fees taken care of, R.E. found himself in another jam in 1900, when Roy, too, was at King's. Once again he contacted the helpful Dean, this time with a request for consideration for a parish of his own where he would have a larger income as vicar. Farrar replied, in letters typed enthusiastically badly by himself. "I was sorry to receive your letter and I sincerely hope that it will not become necessary for you to remove your boys from the King's School. I should be very sorry to lose our little chorister, the 'Flaming Seraph' as we sometimes playfully but audaciously call him, for we like him very much."

Farrar promised to write to the Archbishop at once and a few days later reassured R.E. that he had also "spoken strongly" to the Bishop of Dover. He ended this second letter with a plea for R.E. not to remove the boys "without letting me know as I feel sure that we shall be able to arrange about one or both of them in one way or another." When the Archbishop soon afterwards offered R.E. the vicarage of St Peter's in Thanet, Farrar was overjoyed, as "this will, I trust, enable you to keep your dear boys at the King's School." Singlehandedly and unwittingly, the Flaming Seraph had done his father a pretty good turn.

His singing as a boy soprano in the Cathedral choir was out of the ordinary and earned him considerable local fame. But one suspects that what he liked about the school was the fraternity of which it had made him a member. KSC boys called each other by their surnames, something that didn't happen in the Cheriton vicarage. The education they received placed emphasis on old-fashioned Christian values like trust, honesty, loyalty, duty and hard work. It was assumed that the world needed them, that they would be the next leaders of Britain and its Empire. There was absolutely no sense that all of this, the Empire with its self-congratulation and divine assumptions, might possibly be found a little wanting in a Post-Darwin age where science and therefore merit were becoming increasingly important.

Such observations were for the future; in the here and now of 1897 Rufus was thoroughly comfortable with his school environment. He was an intelligent boy with a keen interest in people and the world, so he took naturally to the humanities — history, languages, geography, religion, literature (his favorite subject, according to Derek). Throughout his eight years at KSC, he spent a good part of his week singing, either in choir practice or in the great cathedral itself, all of which he enjoyed; and he had the opportunity to play various sports including rugby, cricket, tennis, field hockey, rowing and fives. In March 1904, at the annual sports-day, Rufus competed in long jump, putting the weight and the mile, though he didn't place in any of them. Above all, he used the opportunity that KSC provided to get to know a large number of people — a network of friends and acquaintances.

To Rufus, happy family life ended on 23 September 1903 when he was sixteen. School had just started but he had come home from Canterbury for the birth of another baby — R.E. may have had a premonition it would be a difficult birth because a child born to Nellie the previous year had lived only a week. That evening, however, when the baby, Peter, seemed to have arrived as expected, Rufus had gone out, as no doubt it had been suggested that he do. He came in late, considered saying goodnight to his mother but decided against it, not wanting to disturb her. For the rest of his life it was a decision he would bitterly regret because she died during the night. For him especially, her death was a devastating blow.

It is useful to consider what he didn't do at school: he took no great interest in science or mathematics for instance — at least, it was never mentioned or employed by him in later life;[7] he made one school team, the Fives Pair in 1904 and 1905, but did not make the team in the major sports of rugby, cricket or rowing, nor was he awarded School Colours; and he never reached the dizzy heights of the 6th Form. He did, of course, leave school in July 1905, two weeks before his 18th birthday, which was about a year younger than the average. Nevertheless, he is on record as having graduated summa cum laude in 1905, as had Roy in 1902 when he was still 16, so perhaps at KSC this phrase just meant '*without blotting his copybook.*'

Of his father's schooling Derek said: "He enjoyed his school days although he made no special mark, other than winning some cups in minor sports"[8] — a rather damning assessment had it not been true. It certainly fits the information above, all gleaned from the KSC Register. The 'minor sports' would include 'fives' (an esoteric game even within English public schools) and maybe squash — something he enjoyed playing later when opportunity offered. He seems to have had no enthusiasm for team games with all their razzmatazz, even as a boy. The team spirit that coaches try to instill was distasteful to him; he preferred sports that pitted individuals against each other — fives, squash, tennis and later golf — and at these he was competitive, hence his two years in a row on the Fives Pair.

What are we to make of this intelligent young man not reaching the 6th Form, the level at which most boys spent their last two years? The obvious answer is: because he would not be going to university, as R.E. could not afford to send him. For the same reason Roy had left school in 1902 and was commuting to London where he was articled to a solicitor — the only affordable route to a lawyer's qualification and one that would take him seven years. Understandably, it did not appeal to Rufus; he stayed at school until nearly 18 because he enjoyed it and because his tuition was paid by his choir scholarship. By that time he was the leading boy in the cathedral choir[9] and spent his last year in the Army Class; its members were 6th Form age, most headed for Sandhurst, though a few were like himself with other plans.[10]

For Rufus, some of the most memorable events in his childhood were summer holiday cycling trips with Roy and R.E. both before and after their mother died. There were at least two of these, one of them, anyway, to France. During 1904 Rufus and Roy made their way to Hanover, possibly by bicycle although it sounds a bit too far. There they saw or stayed with their much older cousin Lucy,[11] as she reminded Rufus later on. "Are you stronger now?" she wrote; "if you remember, in 1904 you were in very poor health." We can only speculate what that meant.

In the summer of 1905, two events marked the real end of his childhood. The first was his father's marriage to Florie which he found hugely disconcerting. R.E. could rationalize his decision however he liked — she was a single governess living in his house (what would people say!), he was lonely living on his own and needed a helpmate as a vicar, even that he loved her — but Rufus (and maybe Roy) was not buying it. It felt all wrong, and the end of the home in which he had grown up. Rationally, he understood perfectly: he still loved his father and was polite to Florie, as she was to him — even quite loving by the sounds of it, when, later on, she helped him pack for Canada. But he hated the turning of the page and had difficulty disguising his feelings.

The second event came when he left school in July, his future uncertain. Family convention required that he enter a profession. There was no immediate urgency but his pride demanded he solve the problem of how he would earn his living before the year was out. Immediately, he had two options. The first was to follow his father into Holy Orders; and the second, promoted by Uncle Harry, was to take a commission in the army. He felt duty bound at least to consider the possibility of Holy Orders and, although he probably decided against it quite early, he kept his father guessing for several months. Finally, when he was already making plans to go to Canada, he wrote to his father from Brighton in October. Regarding Holy Orders, he told him,"I do not think the calling is one for which I am fitted & I feel no strong desire to enter it; so that, I think, is out of the question." Which sounds definite enough, but he would nibble at the idea again, on and off, over the next few years.

The problem with the army was that it required a private income — because it was not possible for an officer to live on his pay. However, the Royal Marines, with their depot nearby at Deal, was also a possibility; Marine officers' pay was somewhat better and because they spent much of the year at sea with the navy, an officer could get by, even enjoy life, on a private income of £125 — 150 a year. To start with Uncle Harry was willing to provide such an allowance for him – but first he had to pass the entrance exam. When he failed this comprehensively, his second career option fizzled out with it — although, as with the Church, he would return to nibble at it. In the future, he would be relentless when pursuing career goals, but in 1905 that never happened because his heart was never in it with either option.

Instead, he had his eye on a girl for the first time — something that can upset a young fellow's ability to keep his priorities in line. The Canterbury Cricket Week, in late July or early August, is still the high point of the Kentish summer and a magnet for students. So it was understandable that he spent the last days of school, or possibly the first of his summer holiday, amid the bunting, brass bands and brouhaha at the Saint Lawrence cricket ground — watching cricket, yes, but also greeting friends, exchanging addresses with other KSC leavers and endlessly discussing plans. Around the ground were pitched large white canvas tents — for Kent County Cricket Club members, for the Buffs regimental band, for beer and sandwiches, for ladies only, and one of them for the Old Stagers, amateur actors — cricketers and others — who had put on a play at Cricket Week since 1851. They were doing so in 1905 and, as Rufus and his friends strolled by their rehearsal tent, some of the younger performers were taking a breather.

Greetings were exchanged, the groups mingled and he found himself talking to a young actress, Bertha Court, called Bee, who had left school several years before but was his own age. There and then, or maybe after her show that evening, or over the next day or two of the cricket week, they talked. Bee later told her granddaughter Val that she first met Rufus at a dance in Canterbury — which she thought had probably been a church social. She is unlikely to have got this wrong so the dance itself may have been part of Cricket Week. The more they learned about each other, especially about what they had in common — religious backgrounds and a growing and idealized desire for a new start 'in the colonies' — the stronger the chemistry between them grew. This first meeting may have been brief but when they parted they kept in touch.

Bee's upbringing had been much poorer than his own. William, her father, was a laborer and Frances, her mother, had never been to school. Things had been so hard at one time that they had entered a workhouse in order to feed the family. Frances was determined that her daughters, Bee and Ada, would do better. So, when she and William were unable to pay fees for the parish school, she enrolled them with the Sisters of Providence, French nuns who offered girls a free Roman Catholic education. And because Bee was talented and intelligent, by the time the nuns left Canterbury when she was 13, she could speak French, some German, could read and write English fluently and, thanks to elocution lessons, could speak it without a Kentish accent. She could also sing, act, play the piano and had a smattering of history and math. She had, in fact, been educated out of her background and could do better for herself than working in a shop, marrying young and wearing herself out raising a large family. And it was a fate she was desperate to escape.

Reality intruded soon enough. Rufus returned to St Peter's in Thanet where he must make a serious effort to deal with other people's ideas for his future. However, once the R.M. exam had come and gone, he began seriously to consider the new start that so appealed to Bee — and in which he had his father's support. Going to 'the colonies' in general soon morphed into emigration to Canada and the creation of a life for himself in a country where possibilities seemed endless and social barriers non-existent. And the better he came to know Bee, who encouraged his Canadian ambitions, the more eagerly he accepted the notion of emigration.

After that he had little time left in England. He wrote to R.E. in October from Brighton. "I am certainly for going out as soon as may be, as I think the winter out there will be far more useful to me than it would be here." He was trying to decide which shipping line to travel on. There was much to be done and R.E. wrote letters and laid out money to ensure that, once in Canada, his greenhorn son would have a farm to go to, where he could learn the skills he needed to succeed as a homesteader in the 'Last Best West'.*

And so it was, on 29 October 1905, that he came to Canterbury to say goodbye to Bee. In 1910 he reminded her in a letter that "five years ago last Sunday, we took a certain famous walk up St Martin's Hill, and you leaned over a certain famous gate, and then — I kissed you!! And you said: 'I did not tell you you might kiss me' and then — you kissed me back and thereby hangs the tale of YOU and I. After that epoch-making event, I might add, I went home

* 'The Last Best West', together with 'Homes for Millions', were slogans of the hugely successful advertising campaign launched by Clifford Sifton, Minister of the Interior under Wilfrid Laurier (1896-1911), to populate Canada's prairies with old world farmers.

and told Miss Gould, with whom I was staying, that I had been to a Penny Reading — but that is a detail!" From then on, in their own eighteen-year-old minds, they were betrothed — though it is unlikely they mentioned this to their families; instead, both promised to write and Rufus vowed to return for her — as soon as he could afford to.

Eight days later, on 7 November, he sailed from Liverpool aboard the CPR ship *Lake Manitoba.* As she steamed slowly out into the Mersey, he looked back to shore. He later recalled, "a band is playing the emigrants off. But for me there is one figure that stands out through the wet mist. On the wharf, straining his eyes through the ever-widening distance, is a clergyman past middle age, my father. In my pocket I have a bulky letter that he wrote to me through the last night. It voices all the pent up sorrow that such a parting meant for him."

But for Rufus, there was little sorrow — only excitement. His childhood, too, was vanishing into that mist — and he couldn't wait to take on the world.

Chapter 3
Off the Boat
Ontario, 1905–1906

"Dull work walking up and down a field all day with no one to talk to but a horse!"

Rufus, 22 April 1906

Rufus much enjoyed the Atlantic crossing, as one might expect. He turned out to be a good sailor, actually enjoyed the food they were given and seems not to have missed a trick. He was taking snapshots of the Irish coast, admiring the sunset, trading horror stories with deckhands about the fabulous Devil's Hole, having a riotous time playing deck billiards, then deck quoits and "ringing & skipping". When fellow second-class passengers discovered he was a singer, his life became a blur of popularity and he was "everlastingly badgered to sing," — fun at first, but it happened so often that he found himself having to refuse. It was probably the first time he had come across so many young people — most of them men – of less genteel upbringing than himself. It called for some mental adjustments. He was horrified, for instance, that his three cabin-mates "sleep in their pants, socks and shirts and refuse to have the port-hole open!" — so much so that he felt compelled to speak to the steward about it!

Once the new world was in sight, Rufus and his shipboard friend Lissom spent the day on deck drinking it in — rounding Cape Race and its snow-covered hills and enduring a day-long blizzard in the Gulf of St Lawrence, when "the snow cut our faces fearfully. There were lots of porpoises to be seen and a most lovely sunset, all purple and gold and glorious crimson. The air in this part of the world is perfectly lovely, quite different from anything I have experienced before, very clear and bracing. . . . Scenery grand [when approaching Quebec City] all mighty cliffs covered with snow and great pine forests." It was his first sight of 'The Great Lone Land'.

The next day, they tied up at Montreal. Rufus and his pal had decided to break their journey to see the sights, but their Pinocchio-like anticipation of a welcome was dashed by 'Foxes' and 'Cats' at every turn. While Lissom was

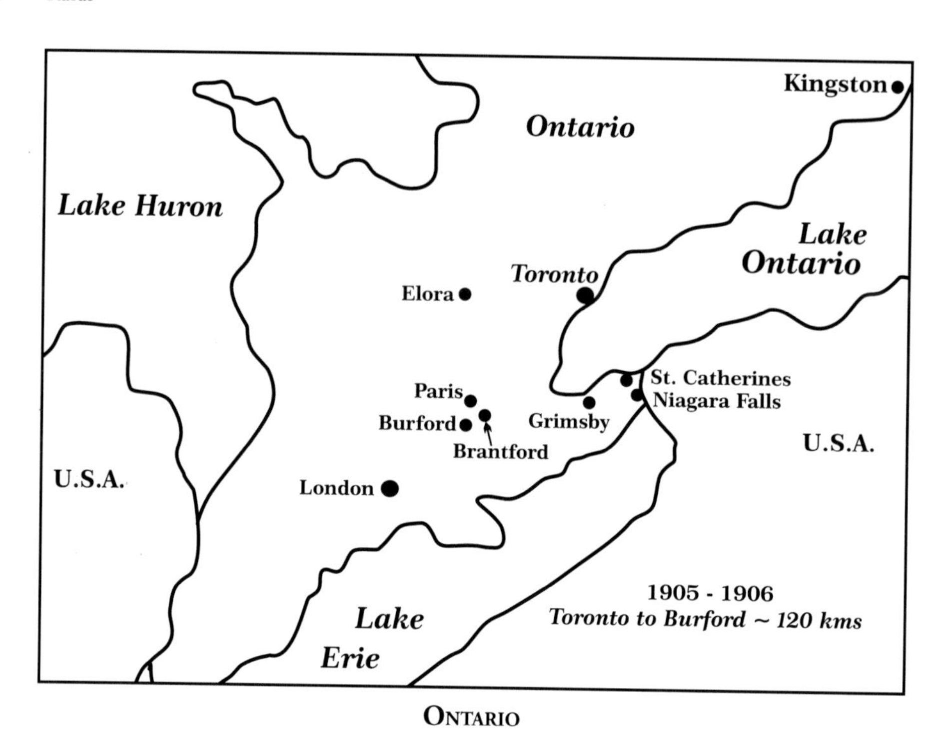

ONTARIO

negotiating the discovery of his lost luggage, Rufus, who had been be-friended on board by a Mrs Nash and her cute kiddie, was nobly looking after her as her husband had failed to meet her. Lissom, having found his luggage, reclaimed Rufus from this potential imbroglio but the pair of them, both desperately tired, tumbled straight into another. Over their faint protests, they were shoved into a cab by a very Fox-y gentleman, driven to the Albion hotel, a filthy dive "where everybody was very disagreeable and uncivil to us," and agreed to pay $1.50 (6 shillings sterling) each — for a shared room on the fifth floor.

Daylight had a calming effect and restored their faith: rebuffed by a 'Full Up' sign at the YMCA — recommended by a clergyman on the *Lake Manitoba* — they found a landlady who would rent them a room for half the Albion's price. Although she wouldn't feed them, she was "rippingly kind", allowed them hot baths "and treated us like a sort of mother" — treatment, one recalls, that Rufus had been lacking. They had time that November afternoon to explore Mount Royal, from which, as Rufus wrote, "you get the most wonderful view I have ever seen — of the city and river, etc. Then we walked onto the next hill and saw a most glorious sunset. As the hills were covered in snow and ice, it was a lovely sight." He had fully recovered his enthusiasm!

In Toronto, after a couple of days seeing the sights, the new friends parted — Lissom going north to a job arranged for him through family contacts, and Rufus traveling west to Mr Regy Gray's house at Burford, 60 kms beyond Hamilton. He imagined that Gray, with whom R.E. had been in contact, would have a job for him similar to Lissom's. In fact, as he would explain many years later, "I was being sold into slavery. I was going out to an Englishman in Ontario who was being paid a handsome sum to 'find me a job' on a farm. I think the sum was £50, so trustingly paid by my father. The scheme was this: My boss would go to a farmer – in my case a man called Tom Martin — and say to him: 'Tom, I have a good, husky green Englishman coming out. What will you give me for him?' And Tom would say: 'Well, Regy, if he's a husky lad, and quite green, I'll give you ten dollars a month for him for 6 months . . . or until he gets on to the game!' And so I was sold."

Poor Pinocchio, after two nights at the Grays' house, during which he found his host most amusing and "a rare good sportsman," he was taken to Tom Martin's farm near Paris, Ontario, with about $20 left in the world. Nothing was said about wages. Tom, who seemed very considerate of his greenness, told him to take it easy for a month or two and not to get up earlier than 6:30 for breakfast. Suspecting nothing, Rufus, of course, wanted to work extra hard in order to get wages as soon as he could. He wrote to his father, "I clean out the horse stables and cowsheds and drive the cattle out and do other odd jobs in the morning — such as driving loads of turnips into town. I've been plowing all day today. It is very easy to learn, or what they call a 'snap' here. I have not yet formed an opinion of the life out here; I can't say I'm in love with paddling in manure when I clean out the stables, but it has to be done and the plowing is all right."

But the dawning of the awful truth was not long postponed. As he later related, "In two weeks, during which time I had been several hours a day picking over rotten roots in a dark and rat-infested root-cellar below the barn, I felt that all was not correct. But I had only $20 and knew no-one in Canada except my slave-owner. So I had to tough it out while we killed pigs and scraped the bristles off them after immersing them in barrels of boiling water; and while we held a beefing bee and what-not from 6:00 am to 9:00 pm. I shared honors there with a poor Barnardo's girl who was disgracefully treated; and my final exit came when there was a row over this particular matter."

While scraping off bristles, Rufus had been planning escape and the arrival of the orphans' charity inspector gave him his chance. How he got himself and his belongings from the hilltop farm the 7 kms into Burford is not clear — maybe the charity inspector gave him a lift. Temporarily, he became "an out-of-work guest of the Rev Mr Leigh, vicar of Burford," and for his 'eats' washed bottles for a few days at the brewery in nearby Brantford. From there he retraced his steps to Toronto, which he reached with the temperature at -20° Fahrenheit, and put up at the Iroquois Hotel. As he had just $10 to his name, he decided it was time to play an ace. "I had a pocketful of introductions, one of which was from the Archbishop of Canterbury to Mr Edmund Osler of the Dominion Bank. I decided to see what he could do in the way of a job. I found a friend in old George Fowler, the hotel manager — and I needed one for Mr Osler was in Kingston and would not be back for some days, perhaps a

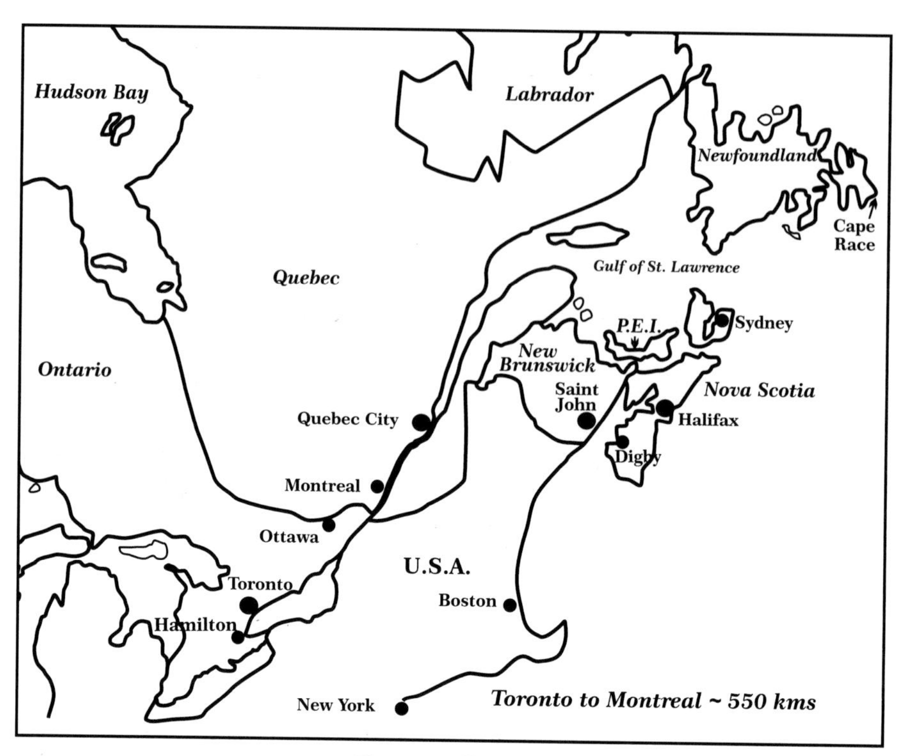

Eastern Canada

week or more. Fowler helped me get a job tending horses in some livery stables connected with the CPR freight sheds. I was flat broke but George Fowler fed me free for a week or more."

Clutching at straws, Rufus auditioned before the manager of the 1905 Broadway musical comedy *Dolly Dollars*. The man liked what he heard and offered him a job — if he would join the company in Chicago in a month's time! At that point the elusive Mr Osler returned. He saw Rufus and left him with the general manager, Mr Brough, who promised him a job — but then fell down dead in the bank that very day!

"So I took a job from a commission firm, peddling wire boot scrapers door to door in the dead of winter. I was to get 25 cents for each one I sold, but in five hungry days, sold only three." In desperation, he sold his revolver for $1 and, convinced he would never make a salesman, ditched his unsold brushes in a building site!

It was at this low point, as he was racking his brains for a new idea, that his problems were temporarily solved. He happened upon a Mr Waddell, a generous-hearted Irishman he had met on the *Lake Manitoba*. Waddell, who lived in Toronto, invited Rufus to his house, fed him and listened to his tale of woe. Then, when they had both agreed that a full belly was the first priority during an Ontario winter, he sent him to work for his friend John Hill, a farmer at Elora, near Fergus, who offered him no wages but would give him a warm place to sleep and his food in exchange for farm work. In spite of the appearance of being back to square one, Rufus was happy to accept the offer for the rest of the winter.

He found himself more or less running the farm for the much older John Hill — which, of course, was excellent experience, had he been set upon farming as a career. Hill was frequently away and Rufus just had to trust his hunches — there was nobody to consult. When the beef cattle wandered two miles into the bush, Rufus had to get them in before dark and took the dog with him. "It is a beastly job to get them in," he grumbled, "as they kick and butt and play the fool all the while." Having learned to plow for Tom Martin, by April he was seeding for John Hill. For a more romantic nature than his, the long spring days alone with horse and seed drill might have been idyllic. But to him it seemed "singularly dull work walking up and down a field all day with no one to talk to but a horse!" He found no task beyond him, even butchering hogs, and wrote that "things are going on pretty well with me just now as I get along first-rate with the family." However, lest his father believe him to be reconciled to farming, he added, "but it is a most ghastly dull affair, though I suppose pretty healthy."

The Hills knew that he hoped to go west when the summer came around and did their best to dissuade him. John Hill actually offered him wages — $5 a month plus bed and board — and proffered crumbling cigars (that Rufus smoked to avoid giving offense) if he would sign on until September. Mrs Hill, who seemed smitten by this tough young man with the flaming red hair, trailed him round the farm telling horror stories of the North-West. She failed to frighten him, of course, and in fact increased his wish to be gone. "She comes up to the barn and talks to me by the hour, hindering me from my work. She leaves all the stable doors open, one after another, so that the hens get in and its no end of a job to get them out! Heaven preserve me from farming all my life!"

In fact, in the few hours free time that he had, Rufus worked on his correspondence lifeline — with school-friends, family and probably Bee, although any letters to her from this time did not survive. He was in touch with two OKS's* in Saskatchewan: Ralph Marshall, three years older and homesteading, apparently successfully, and Phil Hawkes, his own age but who had left school early and was established somewhere in Saskatchewan. Both reported plenty of work opportunities and urged him to come west soon. He was also in touch with Walter Campbell — a year older, a King's Scholar who had qualified for Sandhurst but who had chosen to emigrate instead. Campbell had a job 50 miles away with the Canadian Bank of Commerce at Seaforth, Ontario – something that sounded wonderful to a young man who had had his fill of the great outdoors and of talking to a horse's rear end. For a while he was torn between leaving immediately for Saskatchewan — his first inclination

* OKS — Old King's School, acronym for alumni of King's School, Canterbury.

— and trying for a banking job in Ontario — strongly advocated by R.E. At the same time Uncle Harry was still offering an annual allowance if he would consider either the British or Canadian regular army — something that no longer appealed.

The balance was tipped when Campbell came to visit on an April weekend when he was on his own. They had a "ripping time talking over old times" and Rufus was persuaded to try his bank. Campbell seems to have been a much better advocate with the Bank of Commerce than Olson ever was with the Dominion. He persuaded his manager to support Rufus's application, which the manager then took to head office in Toronto. The upshot was an invitation to Rufus to visit Toronto in late April. He travelled there first-class and spent two nights in a hotel, all expenses paid. He took the precaution of using a general letter of introduction from the archbishop and, having passed a simple exam, was offered a post as a 'Junior' with free lodging in the St Catherines' branch, at $250 a year. Knowing that Campbell was getting $300, Rufus had the nerve to hold out for the higher figure, to which the bank immediately agreed, much to his surprise. He returned to Hills' farm to collect his belongings and within a couple of days was installed at St Catherines.

Rufus's new job was a triumph for networking, owed something to the good name of Archbishop Temple, but above all was a reward for his intelligence, courage and energy. He felt in control of his destiny again — a pleasant change after his experiences of the previous six months. And no sooner was he established in his comfortable room above the bank than he was planning for the future once more. Assuming bank life to be as good as Campbell's promises, he was contemplating a move in a year or two to the Hongkong & Shanghai Bank, "the best bank in the world," and wanting R.E. to research it for him.

It is not surprising however, considering his restless nature, that it took less than a month for the first cracks to appear in the facade of his 'high stool' contentment. The first bank responsibility that he really enjoyed was being sent out "in the mornings to go all over the town collecting drafts from the stores" — partly because he enjoyed chatting up the storekeepers, but also because by late May the weather was heating up. "I am thankful that I spend so much of my time out of doors and dread the time when I shall have to be shut up all day like the rest of the clerks."

However, he found work in the bank "not by any means as dull as I expected it to be . . . because you learn all about other people's business in no time." He also realized he was not entirely suited for bank work for more substantive reasons. "Campbell and myself are a good deal handicapped by the fact that we have no business education at all, whereas these Canadian fellows have nothing else . . . we are not nearly so smart at the work at first as they are." He consoled himself by recalling that they could use the adding machine — "a marvelous invention!" — for all big sums.

June brought news of the birth of Mary Eugenie Johnston to Florie and his father on May 22. In reply, Rufus mustered, "I was glad to hear of the arrival of the new sister and hope that both she and Florie are doing well," but could bring himself to say nothing more welcoming. June also brought warm weather and his room over the bank became hot and stuffy. So he and White, the ledger-keeper, bought a tent which they pitched for the summer in some woods, not far from the shore of Lake Ontario. To save money, they intended to live off the land. By rising at 5:45, they had time to cook breakfast, clean up the camp and take a tram the 5 or 6 kms to work. They caught sheepshead fish in the lake, snared rabbits and hoped to shoot pheasants. Everything was cooked in one pot over the fire and if it tasted bad they added curry — "not real curry but French mustard and canal water" — to take the taste away. They swam and rowed on the lake, canoed on the river and even managed some sailing. For a short while life was good, and Rufus enthused, "it is quite the Canadian life about which one reads in books." He must have spent much time travelling to and from camp because he was also singing several times a week at different functions, as well as earning extra money for singing in the choir at St George's church. When he sang at the Made in Canada Fair, the newspaper reported: "Mr Johnston, who has a rich full tenor voice, sang 'The Bedouin Love Song'. Noisy though it was, his clear true notes could be heard over the building."

As for sports, he had got to know the teachers at Ridley College where he regularly went to play tennis and cricket. Most of his social life was lived among those he considered gentlemen — namely, men educated at English public schools. For a newcomer to the New World it was an easy retreat into the familiar. Still, he was also happy to mix with 'real' Canadians and his reactions were unselfconscious and occasionally naïve. He once solemnly informed R.E. "They have very strange ideas in this country about introductions. For instance, during the past week I have been asked to three dances, two of them by people I had never set eyes on. I went to one of them and although I knew not a soul at the beginning, I seemed to have known everybody for years by the end of the evening. Such is Canadian hospitality; and it is certainly the best trait in the national character." However, when living with John Hill at Alma, he had been somewhat put out to discover that lumbermen working in Hill's woods were to stay in the house for a few nights — he dismissed them as "awful ruffians and dirty to a degree."

In spite of such attitudes — baggage from his schooling that he would gradually replace with a more catholic acceptance of people — for him the main advantage of banking over farming was its sociability. Instead of a lonely life among animals, this gregarious fellow was delighted to be back with his own kind — good, bad and ugly. As everybody visited the bank now and then, he constantly came in contact with people who had heard him sing, or who had heard of him and recognized his red hair. In this way he met the Rev Allan Ballard of Grimsby, Regy Gray's son-in-law, who invited him for the weekend. His introduction to the staff at Ridley College came through Drope, a teller, whose uncle was headmaster there and with whom he made his first visit. The headmaster was kind to him, and he was interested to hear that the man combined his school job with running a lucrative fruit orchard. He met several other fruit farmers, all young and English and who enjoyed the life. Also, within weeks of arriving, new friends from the bank had taken him to see Niagara Falls and to ride in the *Maid of the Mist* — a trip made possibly more exciting by the unpredictability of 1906 boat engines.

As he became busier and more involved in bank work however, he experienced no magic moment when it all clicked and became worthwhile. That was unlike him — his enthusiasm for new things generally caused him to start feeling 'ownership'. On this occasion, maybe it was the hierarchy of the bank that killed his interest — it was not the difficulty of the work, in spite of his initial misgivings, because he proved to be a 'fast study'. He did indeed get busier: he was up to 1:00 am one night balancing the books, having been given responsibility for two enormous ledgers — the Collection Book and the Cash Item Book. Even so, signs were accumulating that his mind was not focused on the unexciting business of looking after other people's money. As part of his responsibilities he had to send cashed cheques to their branches of origin to be cleared. "Unfortunately, I was not aware at that time that there is a town called London in Canada, and I therefore sent about $500 worth of cheques to London, England. This led to an unpleasant incident with the manager, but Connolly is a good-hearted soul."

The goodness of Mr Connolly's heart may have been more tested by another incident. As Rufus tells it, "one wet day we had decided to practice with the accountant's revolver against the day we might be held up. Most unfortunately, I sent a bullet ricocheting through the plate glass window of the manager's office!" Connolly was spared the necessity of deciding what to do about it, as Rufus was already working upon his own exit and no doubt keeping the 'good-hearted soul' informed.

By the middle of June 1906 he was beginning to hear again from Ralph Marshall in Qu'Appelle, who was willing to employ him over the winter. He seemed to have an answer for all of Rufus's objections: he would love farming in Saskatchewan — totally different from farming in Ontario; Ralph himself had thought he disliked farming, but life on the prairie had totally changed his view and nowadays wild horses couldn't drag him back into an office; instead of the juggling of Ontario farmers with marginal finances, he insisted that farming in Saskatchewan was "quite a reasonable undertaking, financially." At the same time, his friend White's family, who had never liked their son's choice of career, was encouraging him to accept Marshall's offer. It was all a bit overwhelming, and the pressure was increased by the imminent end of his three-month trial period at the bank, when his having to start paying "certain dues" would reduce his disposable income.

R.E., of course, was at first vehemently opposed to another move so soon. He had just allowed himself to relax about his prodigal offspring — for the time being safe from starvation with an adequate salary — when the alarm bells had started ringing again. He argued strongly in favor of a bird in the hand, but the siren song of those in the bush clearly had more influence with his son. At this point, instead of concentrating on his arguments, R.E. allowed himself to be tempted by foolish dreams of throwing up his living and transplanting his unwitting family to Ontario, in a country where the Anglican church was being pushed from centre stage and where, even if he could find a living, it would likely be more marginal than the one he had. Ironically, Rufus, although at first liking the idea, quickly understood the silliness of his father's suggestion and did a fine job of pointing out the practical problems — servants were unobtainable, it would be too much for Florie, the schools were co-ed and not of the same standard, etc. What was more, he had a talk with Ballard about R.E. 'parsoning' in Canada, and passed on his vehemently-held view that "to give up a good position in England to come out here would be madness." It was bird-in-the-hand redux and the old man gave up and, having done so, then supported Rufus's desire to leave the bank and go to Qu'Appelle!

How often does anybody make a rational decision — or are all so-called rational decisions in fact dictated by emotions of one sort or another and subsequently rationalized? This seems to have been the case here: Marshall's arguments and promises of bumper crops were accepted at face value while Rufus gave his own hard-earned experience on two Ontario farms little weight. Farming was restored to grace by the same person who had so recently written, "Heaven preserve me from farming all my life!" Having used the Rev. Ballard's argument to scotch his father's migratory plans, he seems not to have been terribly impressed by the same gentleman's warning to himself — that "if I go (to Saskatchewan) I must expect to get hammered pretty hard." Although he did not "expect to fall in love with it *right away*," the fact remained he was doing an odd thing — giving up a relatively secure situation in a new career after just three months' experience for an unknown situation in a career he had already written off, and in spite of the likelihood of getting 'hammered'!

However, by August 3 he had resolved these inconsistencies — at least, to his own satisfaction. Writing to R.E. just before leaving St Catherines, he announced he had been ". . . thinking seriously of taking Orders, and this, in part, is why I am going to the North-West; if I should take Orders, a year or two spent out there would give me a great advantage as a parson. It is a very rough life, and I am quite sure that a bit of knocking about would do me all the good in the world." The North-West as hairshirt — an argument straight from the Jesuit Relations! It had great merit: it would outflank his father's misgivings and, by turning necessity into virtue, it had made his decision 'rational'!

So at 8:00 am on 4 August 1906, he took the steamer up Lake Ontario to Toronto. After lunch with Mrs Nash, his needy friend from the *Lake Manitoba*, he left for the North-West on the CPR at 1:45, his journey largely paid for by money from his share of the Johnston Trust. It is hard to say whether he was shaking off the dust of Ontario or being drawn by the romance of the North-West — probably a bit of both.

Chapter 4
Pioneer Years
Saskatchewan, 1906–1909

"If I go to Saskatchewan, I must expect to get hammered pretty hard."

Warning to Rufus by the Rev Allan Ballard, Grimsby, Ontario, July 1906

Rufus was excited to be travelling west and all went well as far as Winnipeg, where he took a 14-hour layover. He had been working the OKS network and, in the vastness of the North-West with only the mail at his disposal, had managed to organize a reunion of four OKSs, including himself. The youngest, 18-year-old Sydney Brown, was a surprise — he had bumped into him on the train — but he had corresponded with Arthur Brown (no relation), 22, and Edward MacGachen (known as Mac Yorker), 23. All four were, or had been, in banking and Sydney hated it — which made two of them! Arthur had abandoned farming for a bank and would end up in Victoria as an accountant; Mac worked for the Bank of Montreal in Winnipeg, of which his father was the longtime manager. He had commuted annually to King's School, Canterbury, where he was a local celebrity: in 1899 he had received the Royal Humane Society's medal from Dean Farrar for saving three lives on the Lake of the Woods. Needless to say, they had a wonderful reunion dinner and the others put Rufus on his train at 10 pm.

The overnight journey to Qu'Appelle was fortunately brief as, according to him, "it was an awful experience." There were no sleepers and he travelled in a colonist car. "It was chock full of filthy emigrants," he told R.E., his heart full of Imperial scorn which life in Canada would soon moderate. "You sleep on bare boards, I shared mine with a beast of a Chinaman." In Rufus's defence, he was facing the reality of Clifford Sifton's 'stalwart peasants' policy,[13] and in western Canada in 1906 most would have shared his emotions about the Chinese.

None the worse for the experience, he was met by Ralph Marshall at Qu'Appelle. Once they reached his farm, it was immediately obvious that Marshall had been stretching the truth in his letters. In fact, their residence was

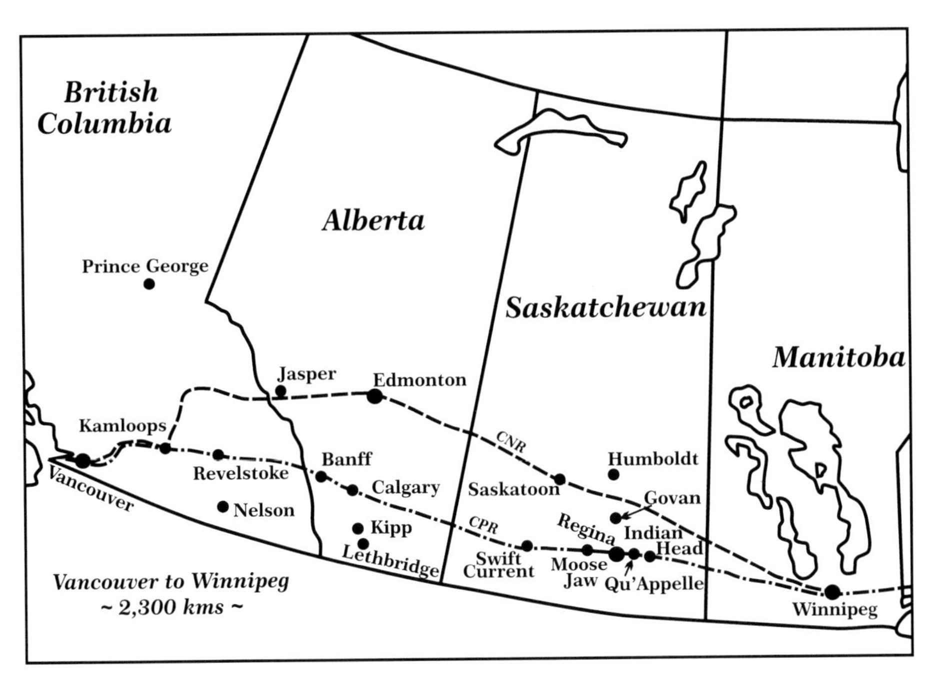

WESTERN CANADA

neither a log cabin, nor even a sod cabin — both of which could be rendered fairly weatherproof — but "a mud-plastered shack in the bluff country south of Qu'Appelle."[14] He was given a tour of the property on horseback: 320 acres overall with 145 under crop. "We ride a lot here," he confided to his father. There were a dozen horses, five milking cows, some steers, heifers and calves. The horses belonged to Pott, Ralph's partner, who was away in England having to choose between his wife and his Qu'Appelle property, so it was possible he would not return. Meanwhile, they were decidedly alone — 320 acres is a large chunk of landscape to live in the middle of. Between them, they had all the farm work to do, and must also cook for themselves. Though Rufus found the cooking "rather a bore," the immediate future looked busy: haying today, cutting wheat next week. It was decidedly not going to be an indoor occupation.

There follows a gap of four months — August to December 1906 — when no letter survives from him or R.E. By 23 December the work from the fall should have been done, the grain stored or sold and the livestock sold or hunkered down in the barn. In fact, as Rufus was later to admit, the first blizzard came down on them in late October, preventing them from getting in all the oats and green feed needed to feed their animals. That had not been their only problem: at some time in the fall they had both fallen sick "from drinking bad water," which sounds sinister. Whether typhoid or not, it had been serious enough for the doctor to bill Rufus $10 for his services — a large sum at the time. Meanwhile, their crop sales must have been minimal because, as he later admitted, they subsisted that whole, long winter on a diet of bannock and sardines. In spite of these misadventures, he and Marshall continued to get on well, and in fact were considering combining on a new homestead, though how Marshall's existing place figured in this was not explained.

By December, life had become one long round of parties in Qu'Appelle. Predictably, Rufus's singing voice was his passport to social success. He took part in the "willing workers show" in the Town Hall, as the star of the famous double sextet "Tell Me Pretty Maiden" from the musical *Floradora.* A chorus of six girls sang the female part while Rufus alone sang the male part of the duet (normally sung by six males). They were encored to the rafters and Rufus was still glowing with pleasure when he wrote. A few days after Christmas, he wrote again, describing his hectic schedule.

> *Monday night – I skated all evening.*
> *Tuesday – went to church & communion & out to dinner with the Dicksons [lawyer, future judge] in the evening.*
> *Wednesday – to a hockey match (on the ice) in the evening.*
> *Thursday – to a Christmas Tree and dance at the Town Hall.*
> *Friday – to an 'old-timers' hockey match – played with brooms and a football instead of sticks and 'puck'. Tonight, at last, I am taking a holiday.*
> *Tomorrow, Sunday – I go out to tea and then to church.*
> *Monday – to a swagger ball at the Town Hall where I have to sing.*
> *Tuesday – to a dinner party at the mayor's (Harvey, an Englishman).*
> *Then on Thursday is the Farmer's Ball which is a very sporting annual event. I am going to sing at the opening of a new Presbyterian Church on the 7th and at a Methodist concert on the 13th. We are very broad-minded here & as it seems to amuse the people, I sing in any sort of a church at all. I should like to come back and get a job in town here next winter if I can, as the people are most awfully hospitable and kind & 'life goes by with a song' here.*

It all sounded pretty frantic but the alternative was sitting at home, trying to keep warm and listening to the wind.

By 26 January 1907 the winter had set in in earnest. The temperature had been at -20°(F) for three weeks and he had spent $52 on a fur coat in order to be able to drive — a cloth coat gave no protection against the everlasting wind. He explained that the real value of $52 was £6 and not £10 (at the usual exchange rate of 5:1) though such an argument would likely not have cut much ice with 'good-hearted' Mr Connolly. He had been to Indian Head to see Qu'Appelle play hockey against that place — there had been a special on the CPR to take them the 10 miles across the prairie. He had really joined in the spirit of the event and both towns had gone mad over it. And because the bank manager wanted him to sing, he had been put up free. He had done more research into homesteading but had not yet chosen a district. Meanwhile, he wanted

R.E. to send off a box full of his pictures and bits and pieces of school stuff, also his carpet-making materials with the manual. Long winter evenings were proving hard to fill and they were reduced to "lying up in the field granaries on moonlight nights to shoot the hungry coyotes that swarmed that year,"[14] as he reminisced many years later.

By 3 February the winter was beginning to take a toll on his spirit. He described the wreckage of a rotary snowplow he had seen, which had crumpled when it charged a huge frozen drift. Trains were running two *days* late. And to make things more unpleasant, as he told R.E., he had had a case of 'la grippe'. "It is no sort of fun to get ill here. I have been laid up this week for a couple of days but am better now. Everything in our bedroom that can possibly freeze *is* frozen solid in the morning & although we get the room like an oven at night, the fire would not keep in till morning. As an example, last Sunday we 'lay in' till about 11.30 when Ralph jumped out and rushed for some furs to rub his nose with as it was frozen!! (absolute fact!)".

He expanded on the cold weather. They were suffering the worst winter in thirty years and, although he liked Qu'Appelle, he was having second thoughts about settling in such a cold place. In later years he added details about the situation that he had not liked to tell R.E. For example, while their animals became slowly weaker in their sod barn, Rufus and Marshall were suffering in their shack. Not only was their bedroom frozen, but the wind forced snow between the boards and formed drifts *inside*! Not surprisingly, the grass was looking greener over the mountains — people from Kamloops were in town, had been talking about fruit-farming and he was thinking seriously about it. But R.E. was not to get the idea that he was abandoning homesteading — far from it, he was just working on a scheme somebody had suggested whereby he might do both! If not in 1907, then maybe in 1908. One can imagine R.E. rolling his eyes and thinking anxiously about the shrinking pool of money that Rufus might call upon!

It would likely not have improved R.E.'s mood that Rufus added a list of what he would need to bring a homestead under the plow and make it habitable: a riding horse, a shack, provisions, a pony and buckboard, a sod stable and enough left over to pay for having the land broken (a team of his own, even oxen, would be unaffordable) and for bringing lumber from the railhead. It could all be done for $500, he thought, though it would not be a luxurious performance.

Rufus then talked about 'Old Henley', their next-door neighbour, an ex-government surveyor who knew the land of the North-West. Henley suggested: waiting for a survey that was nearly complete near Moose Jaw, then selecting a homestead and building a shack on it; and, while waiting for the railway to Lethbridge to be finished, working on a fruit farm in BC. To Rufus it sounded do-able — but for R.E, one imagines, the concept bred yet another nightmare. Anyway, he was no longer talking of partnering with Marshall, and Henley was going to scout out a site in the Moose Jaw district for him.

February, meanwhile, continued very cold with the odd short thaw. One of their cows became so weak that something desperate needed to be done to save her and the vet prescribed a diet of gentian and beer.[15] While Marshall went off to town to get the beer, Rufus was left trying to keep the wretched cow alive in the stable. Marshall returned many hours later, hopelessly intoxicated having drunk some of the beer in town and the rest on the way home. The cow died, and although they skinned her while she was still warm, they were besieged by wolves for the next four day, and it was too dark to shoot them. This was the only time that winter when he and Marshall quarrelled! Meanwhile, there continued to be little work to do, while the social calendar ticked along, with bridge at Harveys' one night and an invitation for Rufus to sing at an 'at home' on another.

By mid-month he was sounding better informed and more urgent about his fruit-farming idea and was now concerned that the ten acres of BC land he would need, worth $110 an acre in 1907, might cost up to $300 in a few years. He estimated he would need $1600 to start a fruit farm, plus $400 to keep him alive until he could sell fruit, a total of $2000 or £400. As he thought he had only £200 coming to him from the Trust (it was actually less as he had already received some of it), he suggested that he borrow Peter's share — the lad could not possibly need money for education for another 15 years, by which time a well-established Rufus would have returned it!

There is a two-month gap in the correspondence but it appears R.E. refused to let Rufus borrow Peter's money, though he sent him the balance of his own. When Rufus next wrote, he was in a hotel in Qu'Appelle, spending a few days building himself up. Apart from lingering malnutrition, he was now afflicted by rheumatism; and although he did not say as much, he had had to leave the farm to make way for Pott who was expected daily. His job with Marshall, despite earlier talk of bumper crops, had been a financial disaster: he had worked for eight months, had been paid for just one and Marshall owed him for the other seven. Considering the state of the latter's finances, there was little prospect of Rufus seeing any of it. However he looked at it, his situation bore out Ballard's prediction — he had indeed been "hammered."

Nevertheless, he remained optimistic. A few days of sunshine would see him right and, on the plus side, he was ten times stronger than he had been when he left England. Ten days after that and he was full of beans again — and of plans. He had solved his immediate problems by getting a job in Harvey's lumber yard at $40 a month. "Now that I've had a few days holiday," he told his father, "I feel in great form and quite settled now that I've got a good job." He had a new homesteading partner, Verini, who was also working in Qu'Appelle. Rufus had just had some excitement on a borrowed horse that had only once been saddled: the horse had tried to throw him and had set off at a gallop. He had stayed in the saddle and the animal had eventually calmed down but he declared his "bronco-busting days" officially over! In spite of that, he planned to ride out west right away, in search of cheap stuff for his homestead. Old Henley had been in touch from Moose Jaw and had advised him not to go down there for another two to three months — or until the survey maps had been drawn up.

By the end of April Rufus was enjoying his lumber yard job though also aware that Harvey was underpaying him — he claimed to be able to double his wages by switching companies. But for now he was gaining experience and he liked Harvey, who gave him other perks including lending him a horse. The job suited him well though he found it hard to control his prejudices and his temper. "My worst trouble comes from the Germans who can talk hardly any English. They always choose a cracked board and want 10 cents off the price. Yesterday I found it necessary to hit one in the stomach with a plank & he went and dealt with the other Lumber Co. forthwith."

By mid-May spring had still not really arrived: there were no buds on the trees and there had been a recent snowfall. This was the last straw for two citizens, who died as the snow fell — one of them the doctor whose bill Rufus had just paid. The whole town attended their funerals, held in the cemetery two miles out, and when each funeral was over, there had been a mad race to be the first rig back into town!

The end of May saw little change in his situation. Henley was still estimating another month before he need go and register his homestead. He himself was becoming more comfortable in his job and was frequently left to run the yard — a challenge for someone who found mathematics difficult and who now had no calculator to run to. "For instance a man came in and wanted me to figure out the requirements for a house 24 x 36, 2 storeys, etc. Well, this is no mean job when you consider that every board in the whole building has to be reckoned. Then in the middle of it 4 Germans and a French half-breed come in & of course demand to be served at once; putting everything out of my head & so losing the thread of the calculations. This constantly happens. Germans are the most bumptious swabs imaginable out here & require pretty straight and forcible talking to keep them in their place!!" His skills as a salesman were improving — forcible talk trumps swinging a plank!

But that was work: in his time off, by contrast, he was having fun. "I love the West," he enthused, "it's just great!" He had spent a whole Sunday on horseback exploring the countryside, leaving at 6.30 am, stopping for dinner at a farm and getting home at 5:30 pm. He was playing tennis regularly and was never at a loss for someone to go and see. The Harveys constantly asked him up to their house, had asked him up to their place on the lake and Mr Harvey liked to take him driving in his new car. What was more, he was involved in organizing the dance at the Town Hall being put on by the "Great Unmarried." He had now rented a room, which was cheaper than living at the hotel; he was batching for breakfast and lunch but, for the time being, still eating dinner at the hotel, in spite of their food being "very dear and very, very vile!"

Once again we lose sight of him — this time for six months. His next letter to his father, written on 10 November, came from a hundred miles to the northwest, halfway to Saskatoon. He began brightly: "Well here we are at Govan. It is a tiny place with about 100–150 men and six women in it, dumped out on the open prairie, not a tree within ten miles. It is only just a year old." Nevertheless, it boasted three lumber yards and Rufus was number two at the Beaver Lumber company's branch.[16] His immediate boss, Browne, had other business interests and the company was not happy with the amount of time he was devoting to their yard. In his optimistic way, Rufus was already anticipating Browne's departure together with his own promotion, including the raise he would receive! It looks as if delays in the homesteading survey had postponed his own departure from Harvey's. It being by then too late in the year to start a homestead, on 6 November Beaver hired him in either Regina or Moose Jaw and sent him north to Govan.[17] The trip north involved overnighting in Strasbourg, where he slept on one of four cots in a pub parlor measuring 10 x 12, with another man sleeping on the floor.

He was getting on well with Browne who hailed from Brantford, and they had discovered mutual friends. There were also men from Burford in town who knew Regy Gray, an example of how Rufus's constant networking helped him make friends in a new place. A month later, just before Christmas 1907, he wrote a more informative letter, but mostly about business. Their yard still had $7,000 in uncollected debt for lumber already delivered and that was after "having squared off over $3,000 worth in notes, mortgages, bills of sale, etc., but not much cash." Cash was hard to come by, thanks to the ruthless way elevator companies squeezed the farmers, who were then unable to pay their own bills. Beaver Lumber's solution was to bypass the elevators and ship carloads of farmers' grain in Beaver cars to Fort William — so the farmer could pay his lumber debts! It worked and they were still in business, but he was having to work hard and would be unlikely to have the very social Christmas he had enjoyed the previous year.

In answer to R.E.'s question, Rufus described the people of Govan as "almost all what you in England would call ruffians, and lots of them of the worst type and therefore very hard to deal with because one never knows who is honest and who is not. There are only two of what you in England would call educated gentlemen, Clancy [the bank manager] and Miall [the lawyer]." It is a wonderfully revealing description as it shows how the country is changing Rufus. He went on to puncture R.E.'s fantasies about the Wild West: although they only occasionally saw a Mountie — up from Strasbourg — nobody paid him any attention; as he explained "this is quite a peaceful, law-abiding settlement compared with most of its kind." Dullsville indeed!

By January 1908 he appeared to be forming a friendship and all-purpose partnership with Miall. "I sleep in my office and take meals in his and we exchange visits in the evening. The hotel is too expensive and too uncomfortable and the proprietor is a loathsome man." Rufus now claimed to be a cook and they took turns. The furniture in his bedroom, including the bed, was homemade and nobody could accuse him of extravagance! When asked about his hobbies, he self-righteously declared that as nobody in the North-West had time for anything that did not earn them money, his hobby had become just that — earning money.

At the end of January, as anticipated, Browne was fired and Rufus became 'cock o' the walk'. His amusements had become curling and watching hockey, both on Govan's new open air rink. He was getting a good many settlements of existing debts and a week later was claiming that money was beginning to loosen up a bit.

Miall, a lawyer and therefore some years older, was a friend in need — there being few others around with whom Rufus could relax and feel comfortable. With a good deal more experience, Miall appears to have attempted to lead him into business ventures, the first of which was ingenious: because both craved a daily bath, they had set up a public bathhouse and hired an unemployed barber to run it. Rufus claimed to be on the hook to the bank for no more than two months salary "if we go bump," but there was no chance of that happening as the bathhouse was always busy and they were making money.

A second scheme was still projected. This was for a grist mill to mill the farmer's grain and bypass the elevator companies. They planned to raise $6000 to build it and also somehow keep control of it. Luckily for Rufus, it almost certainly never got off the drawing board — incurring debts would have put paid to his plan to visit England and get engaged to Bee.[18] But his last words to R.E. in a letter of 11 February 1908 were: "of course, it's only a vague outline at present, but I haven't a doubt but that it will materialize this year, and if it does there's a pile of money in it."

This, his last surviving letter from Saskatchewan, was followed by eight months of silence. In January he had mentioned having "a cancellation in for an excellent homestead only three miles from town and I think it will materialize OK." When it became his, he registered it with some partners — necessary because he could not take time off from Beaver to work on the property without risking Browne's fate — and he would need the lumber yard income. By February he seemed well set up: his Beaver salary may have been as high as $75 a month, allowing him to save at least half. He was able not only to buy a ticket to England, but to finance a long stay.

We next catch sight of him on 9 October — just off the boat train and dining with Roy in London, England! He would be gone from Canada for 4½ months, from early October 1908 until late February 1909, and what follows is based on few clues. His first destination was his father's new vicarage at Marden, Kent, which he had not seen. He also had Mary, his new half-sister, to meet; now 2½ she was full of precocious questions. Furthermore, his younger siblings, Lyonel, Joyce, and Peter, took some getting to know again — they had been 10, 8 and 2 when he went away and were each three years older. They wanted Canadian songs and were an eager audience for his stories. R.E., of course, had plenty to talk to him about: apart from money matters that often preoccupied them, there was the topic of Holy Orders that he had so carelessly aired before departing for the North-West. Meanwhile, he made himself useful, helping with parish functions and singing in the choir. For all these things, a month was enough — the family had become used to him again, and he anxious to be about the real purpose of his trip.

This, of course, was to become engaged to Bee. It seems likely that when he first went away they wrote to each other often, though no letters survive. Meanwhile, her dream of a life with him in Canada kept her single while contemporaries were getting married all around her. To be free from family pressure to marry, she found a job as governess or nanny the other side of London at Harrow-on-the-Hill, a job that would have provided her with bed and board. But when his letters became less frequent, perhaps during that winter of 1906–7, she was unsure that he would ever come and, to please her mother, agreed to consider marrying a well-off Canterbury man. This may also have been her way of pressuring Rufus to come back for her, and if so, it certainly worked. And when, some time in 1908, he wrote to say he would finally be able to come in October, she was in the not-too-unpleasant situation of having to choose between suitors.

Years later, in one of his random anniversary musings, Rufus told R.E.: "9 November is the anniversary of the day I met Bertha* again in 1908 at Harrow-on-the-Hill." Nothing more — no hint as to how their meeting went. Probably Bee was a bit distant with him — she had every right to feel poorly treated, after all. And as she would have had few chances to get together with him while she was working, they arranged to meet again when she came to Canterbury for her Christmas holiday.

For another month Rufus's whereabouts are hazy but he was in Canterbury on Christmas Eve. He may have been there a while and would be back after Christmas. In a much later letter to Bee, he reminisced. "I shut my eyes and saw the old upstairs room at the Rose Hotel on a wintry morning when you came up there and Mrs Eddy played and I sang "Thora"**. And that made me think of all those days about Christmas 1908. Do you remember walking past Bunce's with your old headpiece in the air — on Christmas Eve — and I was standing in the door of the Rose. Then I dashed in and got my cap and caught you up on King's Bridge — and then we had a scene and I gave you your orders to marry me."

Was this their first meeting since their Harrow encounter? The 'scene' was no doubt about the man she was considering marrying and she later remembered that Rufus had said, "Now this won't do! You're going to marry *me*!"[19] Whatever the facts, we have the impression that nobody won the argument that evening, and that Rufus would have to work hard to get his way.

---

* He usually called her Bertha to his father — at least in the early days.

** "Thora's Song", or "Ashtaroth", was a popular romantic ballad by Adam Lindsay Gordon. It is a maiden's lament for her absent lover, beginning "We severed in early autumn," and every verse concludes "Thou comest not back again." This was so close to Bee's recent situation that it was probably their courtship song.

It sounds as if he was staying at the Rose — henceforth always their base in Canterbury. On Christmas morning, maybe late on Christmas Eve, he took a train the 35 miles to Marden with presents for his brothers and sisters. He spent Christmas with his family, but when the services were over, the turkey eaten and the last cracker pulled, he took the train back to Canterbury, with a vague promise to come back soon — vague, because he planned to stay there as long as it took.

Realizing, suddenly, that he would have to woo Bee all over again, he laid siege to her and they spent "all those days about Christmas" together. As the Rose had an upper room with a piano — the lounge "with electric light" of its advertisements — they could meet there, quite properly, talk interminably, play the piano and sing, all without their families being aware. His tales of the New World rekindled her wish to leave class-ridden England and soon they were enjoying each other's company and feeling the excitement they had felt back in 1905. Nobody talked about that other fellow any more, and doing things together began to feel . . . comfortable. And so it was that, some days after Christmas, they were at a dance and dancing together when he observed, rather matter of factly, "I think we should get married." To which she replied, "Oh, all right!"[20] And that was that, an unromantic climax to a most romantic week!

It was time to break the news to Bee's parents, William and Frances Court. Their permission was not strictly necessary as Bee was of age, but it would make life easier for her. Intending to impress, the next day Rufus went to call at #2 Whitstable Road, sporting the fine fur coat he had bought for $52 at the Bay trading post in Qu'Appelle, and which had saved his life in that terrible winter. In spite of its workaday origin the coat spelled success to William: his eyes lit up at sight of it, and he warmed to this young fellow who seemed to have done so well. But it was without enthusiasm that he and Frances consented to their engagement — and William extracted a promise not to marry until Rufus had held one job for six months at a wage on which he could marry.

Then they went to Marden to introduce Bee to the family and obtain R.E.'s blessing. From the start Bee hit it off with R.E. but he well knew the precarious state of his son's finances and, like the Courts, was far from enthusiastic about the idea of their marriage. The fact that the Courts were country people of little education, who inhabited a different social world from the churchy and privileged one in which Rufus had grown up, was another reason for his faint disapproval. Nevertheless, he wished them well.

From the tone of R.E.'s letters in 1909, he still considered Rufus too young to know his own mind and was certainly doing nothing to hurry things along. The faint mockery of his use of "Mrs Harry" to refer to Bee in a letter to Roy reeks of quiet disapproval of the whole business. It was Bee who felt the most urgency, as it was she who wanted to escape her present home situation. To that end, Rufus and she arranged, before he left, that she would soon come to Canada, where she would work until they were able to marry. Unfortunately, by the end of his stay, Rufus was unable to give her money for her ticket, so the 'when' was left open.

Which brings us to the last part of Rufus's English visit. Roy, having finished his articles, was a qualified lawyer. His younger brother's enthusiasm for Canada was infectious and Roy was keen to join him for a while, perhaps to share in a new venture, maybe just to see the world, but he expected to return to England. As for Rufus, he had found his four-month holiday much more expensive than planned — as he later told Uncle Harry, it had "crippled his finances somewhat seriously."[21] After so much time away, he would have no job awaiting him in Govan, but he did have his share in the homestead, to which he would return. As both of them would need money to get started (restarted, in Rufus's case) they managed to borrow a sizable sum from a Mr Hudson.[22] This gentleman had intended that his loan be used to start a fruit farm in BC. The condition was not committed to paper, the boys claimed not to have understood it, and although Roy used his share for that purpose, Rufus certainly did not.

There are no surviving letters from Rufus in 1909 and only two from R.E., one of which was to Roy. On 27 May 1909, he wrote Rufus a frustrating letter, full of politics with only a single line about his situation: "Do tell me about your Govan business, and whether you have got the money and the box." For R.E. to have written so little about Rufus's affairs was not usual and he clearly had no worries about him. "Your" business could refer to the bathhouse, or to Beaver Lumber if Rufus had gone back to work there, or even to the ranch (see below), although it is hard to square this with R.E. having no worries!

But whatever Rufus's actual situation when R.E. wrote to him, it very soon changed: at some time early in 1909 Rufus and his partners were living on their homestead, by then a ranch, near Govan. He had given up any job he may have had in order to concentrate on it but apparently it did not do well. Partly because it would mean fewer mouths to feed, Rufus left to take a job promised to him in Lethbridge, Alberta. Depending on how that job went, he planned to return to the ranch later, as he had money invested in it and his partners would be there. But fate decreed otherwise: the promised job evaporated, and when another cropped up he decided to stay in Lethbridge until he could afford to go back to Govan. In later years he claimed to have shovelled coal for a living and to have been an intermission singer in a movie theatre, and this may have been part of how he made a living that summer, fall and winter.

For the coal-shovelling job, there is the evidence of a story that Rufus often told and which Derek includes in his monograph. "One night, with the temperature many degrees below zero, there was a long line-up waiting to buy sacks of coal, which had first to be filled. A boy came to my father and asked if a sack of coal could be reserved for him because he wanted to see a hockey game that was on, which he would miss if he had to wait a long time. My father said this was not possible — the supply was limited and there might not be enough to go round. The boy decided to take his chance and see the game but when he returned all the coal was gone. My father heard later that the boy and his family had frozen to death that night."

There is another indication of what he was up to for three months over the winter of 1909–10. There survive two tiny photographs: the caption of the first one, of Rufus leaning against a small shack with a grain elevator in the background, reads "My shack at Kipp, Alta, winter 1909–10, 15m W of Lethbridge (3 months alone)"[23]; the caption of the other, of three men with a team of horses and a lumber wagon beside the same shack, reads "Fuller Bros unloading lumber at Kipp." Somehow he was making a living there, but exactly how is anybody's guess.

Meanwhile, Roy had done what Mr Hudson expected and had gone to Nelson, BC, where he invested his borrowed stake in a small fruit farm at Harrop on Kootenay Lake. He may also have invested money for Rufus, though it is more likely that his brother plowed all he had into the ranch. R.E. wrote to Roy, for circulation to Rufus, on 27 October 1909. Rufus was not with Roy at the time and we learn that the latter had planted fruit trees,[24] hoped to earn his first fruit income from strawberries in summer 1910 and meanwhile was looking for a winter job. As a complete newcomer he had done well. His father urged him to try to be first with a crop in the spring and heaped on advice about 'cloches' for early forcing, manure, irrigation, etc., etc. However, he also advised him to look out for his own interests and to feel free to leave Rufus and the fruit acreage if a legal opportunity opened up. "Mrs Harry", it seemed, (with no money yet from Rufus) was still at home and unlikely to come over until spring 1910 — and her mother had apparently been trying to persuade her to stay. He advised Rufus not to be angry about this, but to concentrate on providing inducements for her to come.

In due course, perhaps in February 1910, Rufus joined Roy at Harrop, where they spent the rest of the winter. He never returned to Govan and in 1911 was still trying to sell his stake.[25] The best evidence that he was in Harrop at all that winter is a piece of fiction he wrote, set on Kootenay Lake, entitled "Elinor Stanton's Secret". It shows familiarity with the region and, because it is fiction, was surely the product of a Rufus with nothing to do. There are two other clues: in 1911 he claimed to know Martin Burrell, the new Minister of Agriculture and ex-MLA for the Kootenays, with whom he and Roy had played tennis and cricket in Nelson and Grand Forks, evidence that he was in the area, on and off, until summer 1910.[26] Derek would later tell the story, accepted in the family, that "as soon as Roy and Rufus had harvested their strawberry crop,[27] they went into Nelson and spent all the money from the sales!" That this may even have been in late June is supported by the tennis and cricket. And, contrary to family mythology, it does not necessarily imply a disgraceful binge in Nelson: more likely, their income from this first crop was just enough to pay their winter bills. What Derek might have added is that they then abandoned the Harrop farm,[28] and by 25 September were living in Vancouver where both of them had jobs. It had taken Rufus nearly five years to cross Canada to British Columbia's west coast, but he was there to stay and henceforth it would be 'home'.

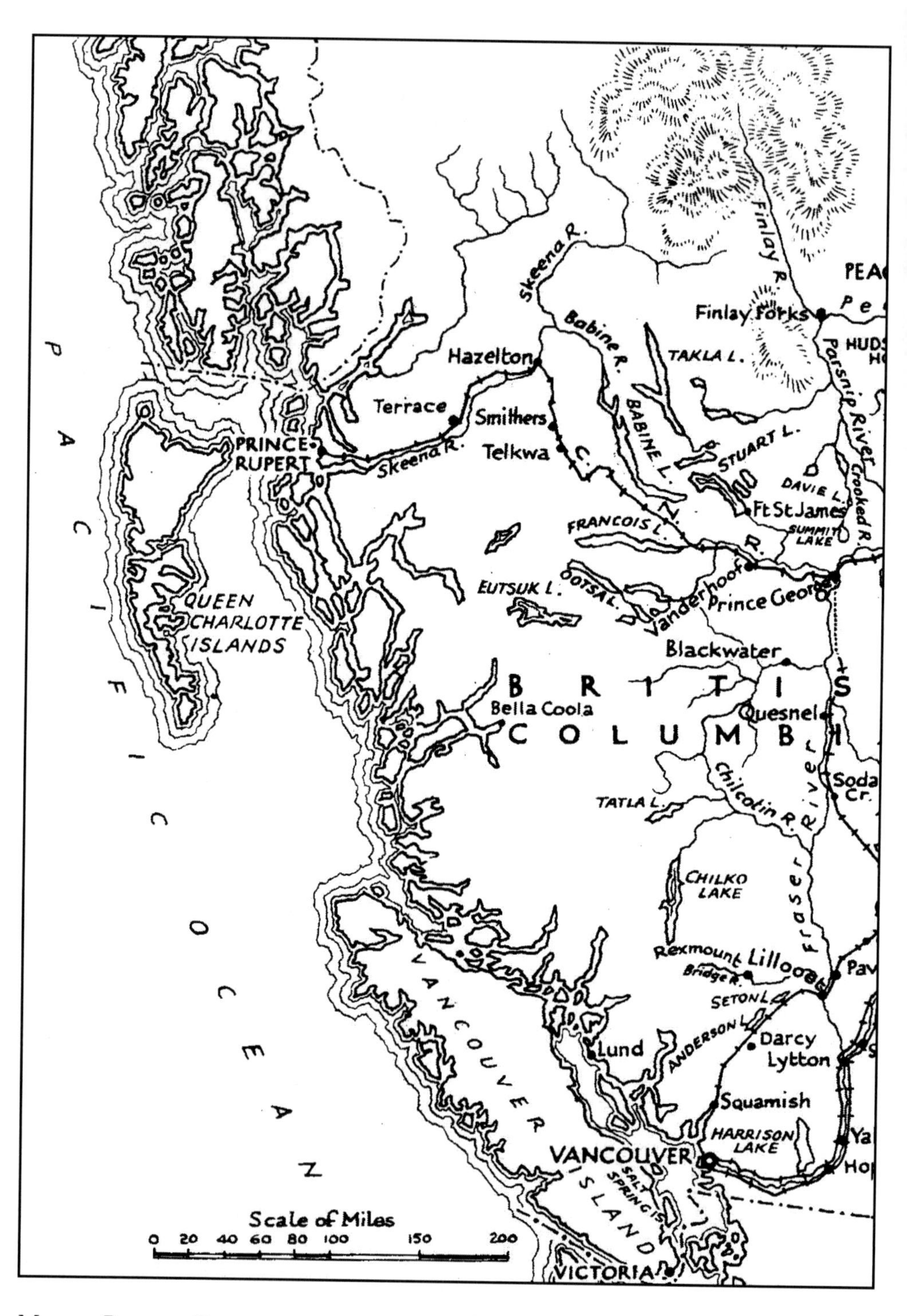

Map of British Columbia from the International Border to the 56th parallel of latitude

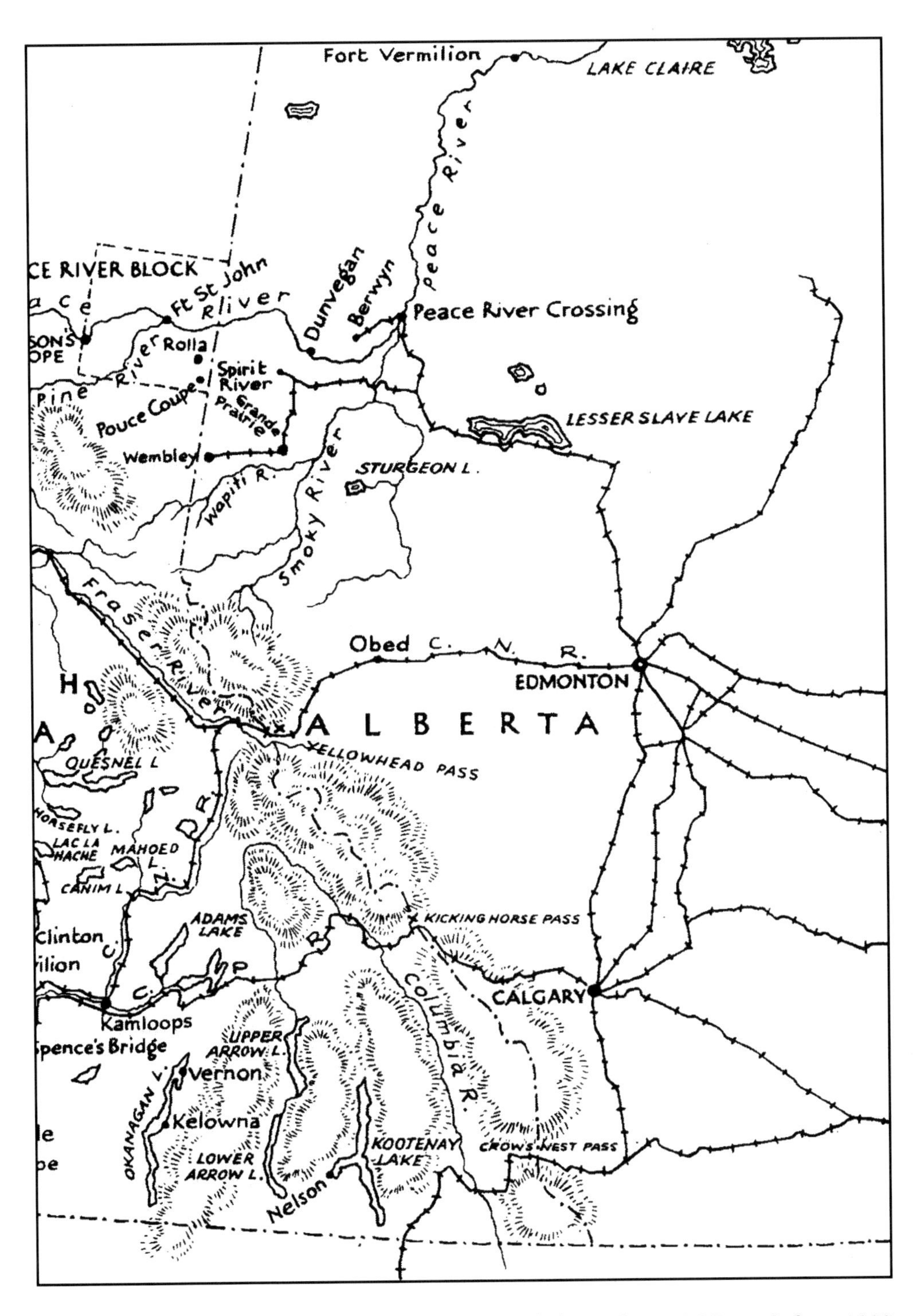

Taken from Rufus's book *Beyond the Rockies*, J.M.Dent & Sons,1929

Chapter 5
Journalist
Vancouver, 1910–1911

"I think I shall stick to journalism for good."

Rufus to R.E., Oct 1911

Rufus arrived in Vancouver for the first time in April 1910. A Nelson friend, probably a journalist himself, had seen his writing — maybe his "Elinor Stanton" story — and suggested he try journalism. He liked the idea and, straight off the train from the interior, went to the *Province* to ask for a job. "He was received very doubtfully by the city editor, who said: 'Well, let's see what you can do. There's a new real estate development out at Deep Cove — you see if you can get a story on it, and if it's any good, I'll give you a job.' My father found his way out to Deep Cove, but when he sought to interview the development manager, this man would only give an interview if my father bought a lot, and the cheapest was $40. This was about all the money my father had; however he bought the lot, had his interview, wrote the story and got the job."[29]

On 8 May he wrote to Bee from 578 Burrard St, Vancouver. He had been working as a journalist for a couple of weeks, was "enjoying the work immensely" and had had "nearly a column a day . . . in the paper all this week." He was already showing characteristic resourcefulness: when he had been late for the sermon of a well-known cleric on the occasion of the death of the king, he had asked the preacher for his notes, "but he had none! So I wrote what I thought he probably would have said and told him I would put it in as his sermon. He agreed. I think it is rather amusing — you'll see from it what the church lost when I did not become a parson."

No others of his 1910 letters have survived until one to R.E. on 25 September, but what Roy and he were up to is reasonably clear. They returned to Nelson in May, where they played cricket and tennis, harvested their strawberry crop and sold it. Surprisingly, Rufus was still employed by the *Province* during this time and remained so until the end of the year; he was presumably sending them articles on Kootenay life, and later from the Skeena Valley, to keep himself on their books, which suggests that from the start, although poorly paid, he was recognized as being out of the ordinary run of cub reporters — a 'keeper' in other words.

They left the Kootenays for good in late June or early July. They were broke again, of course, having paid their Nelson debts with the proceeds of the strawberry sales, and stayed in Vancouver only long enough to sign up for work on the Grand Trunk Pacific Railway, which was recruiting men to lay track in the remote Skeena Valley in northern BC. It was tough work in a rough environment and they lived in a company camp. The conditions were terrible and both of them became sick. Roy was seriously ill with typhoid and spent weeks in hospital, presumably back in Vancouver — long enough for his medical bills to consume all the proceeds when his Harrop property eventually sold. Rufus, with abscesses in his mouth, was less ill, and, to compensate for their sufferings, had found in the GTP a target for a series of exposés of the company's labour practices, on which he now considered himself an authority.

By 25 September they had been back from the Skeena long enough for both to have recovered. Rufus was furious that W.C. Nichol, owner of the *Province*, would not print his stuff on the GTP, castigating him for refusing to publish the views of the 'working man' on labour relations. He was just off to work, briefly, for the CNR, who were laying track somewhere east of New Westminster; he hoped that, if he were able to compare the two companies' work camps, Nichol might relent. He was having his eyes opened to the power of newspaper owners and not just Nichol; he could not get British papers to accept any article critical of conditions in Canada: he had had no luck with Northcliffe of *The Times* and wanted R.E. to sound out Phillips of the *Daily Express*.

At some point after he started at the *Province* he finally managed to send Bee enough money for a ticket. She sailed out of Liverpool aboard the *SS Canada* on 27 August 1910, reaching Montreal on 2 or 3 September. His father's advice had been good — and the price of her ticket had been the best form of persuasion. Though she was soon supporting herself in Montreal as housekeeper to a Miss Harriet Drake, she and Rufus still had many months of separation ahead of them if they were to keep their promise to her parents — and that job with a good enough salary was not yet on the horizon.

Looking back over his first six months with the *Province*, it is surprising that this 23-year-old neophyte seemed able to work for the paper when it suited him — also that he could bypass the editor and deal directly with Nichol, owner of the newspaper and an influential Vancouver citizen. The explanation lies with Nichol himself: he had bought the *Province* in 1901 and by 1910 had made it the most influential paper west of Winnipeg. When other business interests started to occupy him, he showed a knack for hiring good people to keep up the paper's prominence,[30] and Rufus had qualities he valued in his journalists:

resourcefulness, ambition, energy, enthusiasm and, above all, ability to write interesting stuff well. We can be sure that his Deep Cove piece contained journalistic bloopers, but it would also have been well-written — everything he ever wrote was well written. From Nichol's point of view, he was worth a gamble because "not 1% of reporters can write the King's English," as Rufus himself would later observe.[31]

He wrote again to his father in early October, sounding contrite about the chops and changes of his previous two years — as well he might. For not only had his enterprises failed spectacularly — with the single exception of Beaver Lumber — but he had invested all that was his from the Johnston Trust with only a slim chance of ever seeing any of it again, and had incurred a debt to Mr Hudson whose repayment would occupy his worry time for the foreseeable future; also, he owed money to R.E. himself, upon which his father was rightly charging him interest. Still, Rufus did not dwell on the details — after briefly mentioning his regret, he declared, "However, I think I shall stick to journalism for good — the only alternative would be taking Holy Orders and I do not think I shall do that in the end." As for his ambition in life: "It is not riches, I think, except as a means to an end. I think I want 'power', and I think a journalist at the top of the tree has enormous power — for good or evil."

In light of future events, this was prophetic, although at the time it probably brought little comfort to R.E. who had learned to treat such stated intentions with caution. Upon reflection, he could hardly take issue with his son's pursuit of the power to influence others — it is also sought by priests, after all — and he could only welcome the dramatic narrowing of the search for how he would earn his living. Now, if only he would just persist in his current choice!

Rufus, Roy, and Myers, an Eton & Balliol colleague at the *Province*, had moved into a flat at 1352 Bidwell Street. Rufus was never content with a 'job' in journalism: a 'job' filled his day with an editor's assignments but provided only a bare subsistence. From the beginning, he understood that to earn an income on which he might marry and live well, he must also be 'freelance', write pieces on controversial topics and offer them to all comers. So when Nichol preferred to shield the railway barons from the truth, Rufus offered his work on the GTP to *The Times* and *John Bull*. By 23 October he had also been approached by Lefroy, editor of *Canada*, a Toronto illustrated weekly. When he wanted to be named *Canada*'s special BC correspondent Lefroy asked for a couple of articles — a good thing — but also wanted him to drum up advertising — not such a good thing as he hated selling things and was bad at it. The extra work meant he needed to buy his own typewriter and, with Roy away on legal work for the CPR, he frequently worked until midnight.

He wrote again on 6 November. It was his lucky day: the anniversary of his sailing for Canada in 1905, of getting his job with Beaver Lumber in 1907 and now of being appointed BC representative for *Canada* weekly, which will bring him $50 a month. He had already had two articles accepted — on the Fraser River Mills, and an investigative piece on crooked practices at Fort George by the Natural Resources Company. He was starting research on the Dominion Sawmill Company, recently floated in Britain and rumoured to have concealed information in its prospectus. In other words, he was busy. In spite of this, he had found time to enjoy himself: he had seen Alla Nazimova in Ibsen's *A Doll's House* and also in *The Fairy Tale*. What was more, he had recently heard Bernice de Pasquali and Antonio Scotti at the Opera House. Boomtown Vancouver was on the west coast cultural circuit — something of which he would always take maximum advantage.

Rufus took a few days in Victoria at the end of November to drum up advertising in *Canada* by government departments and took the opportunity to interview premier McBride. It was one of the only occasions in his journalistic career when he admitted to having been nervous as the subject of his interview was the increasingly infamous Dominion Sawmill Co. The usually intrepid Rufus told R.E., "The price at which it was floated was outrageously high and the prospectus contains many misstatements. I have never yet undertaken work involving so much responsibility, and I must confess that the prospect somewhat appalls me as yet."

At about this time he decided to work full-time for *Canada* and to accept Lefroy's suggestion that he make a tour of the province to seek advertising. As this would take him out of town for weeks, he seems to have resigned his position with the *Province*. From Victoria he went to the Okanagan. A postcard from Kelowna indicated that his route would take him to Nelson and then to Prince Rupert. Not until 18 December did he finally come home to Vancouver, broke and discouraged. "The trip has been somewhat of a disaster, financially speaking. I knew I was taking a small chance, but had I known anything of advertising I should certainly not have taken it on at this time of year. No one has money available for advertising at the end of the year although in the spring I might have made good money."

Waiting for him in Vancouver was an offer from Lefroy of a better job, but in Toronto. He suspected Lefroy would withdraw it when he discovered how poorly he had done selling advertising, and this proved to be the case. He was now out of a job too, and lamented to R.E., "Six weeks ago, after eight months steady slogging on the *Daily Province*, I seemed on the verge of getting my foot on the second rung of the ladder! Now I am worse off — materially — than I was in May." By the beginning of January 1911 he was forced to make painful decisions. He still saw journalism as his future but a combination of his having left the *Province* for *Canada*, and the blowing of his savings on a gamble to make $500 in an advertising blitz with that paper, had ended in disaster.

It made for a gloomy Christmas but by the second week of 1911, as he described to R.E., he had found a temporary solution: ". . . an offer of a good post with the London & Lancashire Life Insurance Co. I might get back on to the *Daily Province* but the pay is so wretched that I really do not think it would be wise to take it on again. I must, if possible, do something to get ahead of the game & pay you what you have spent for me. Then, when I am several hundred dollars up, I can go back into journalism if I like, but just at present, I do not think I can afford to do it."

R.E. was beside himself with frustration when he received this letter and penned a long critique of Rufus's work history, basically accusing him of lacking perseverance — especially for having left the *Province* after only eight months. In this case Rufus was surely in the right. He had found his profession, journalism, but the wages for a job in journalism were so low that he would always be miserably poor were he to rely upon them. Eight months with the *Province* had taught him the basic tricks of the trade, but for someone with his ambition — with his investigative instincts and writing skill — it was reasonable to shoot for something better through regular freelance work. This life insurance job would provide him with just such an income base, allowing him in his spare time to send articles to a list of papers willing to take his material — and to pay him for it. Once he had established this wider market, he could afford to take a regular job with a newspaper again. As we shall see, events would justify his confidence.

Rufus and Roy spent their Christmas with a family called Sharp[32] who were known to R.E. Rufus no doubt had occasion to tell them of the events of his first year in BC. He had helped harvest a strawberry crop, held two jobs in journalism, worked on two railways, travelled the length and breadth of the province, visited all the main cities (small though some of them still were), was known to the premier and members of his cabinet, had made waves with articles on the hot topics of the day (including labour, race and corruption) — and yet was now considered a bit of a failure by his father!

1911 seemed always to have a surprise in store. He started his insurance job at the same time that he and Roy were ejected from their flat, only to find a much nicer one at 1627 Barclay St. The insurance job was turning out well, allowing him to discover unsuspected organizing abilities and giving him time to write on Reciprocity*, Prime Minister Laurier's electoral hot potato, which he criticized in detail as favouring "the interests" at the expense of BC lumber and agriculture. His Prince George article in *Canada* had stirred up plenty of comment and a local Vancouver 'rag', the *Saturday Sunset*, was throwing weekly stones at Lefroy's publication over it. Rufus was actually glad about this — the first time that *Canada* had taken a stand on anything — though it was ducking Reciprocity. By the middle of February he was bucked to be able to report that Lefroy wanted him to keep in touch in case opportunities cropped up — possibly in London. Rufus had said he was only interested in a good offer, so assumed that any that might come along would be acceptable. Ironically, Lefroy's first offer was indeed good — a repeat of his tour of BC, but in the spring when advertising war-chests would be replenished. Unfortunately, he could not accept without resigning from London & Lancashire, which he refused to do, but he was peeved that somebody else would now reap what he had sown at such personal cost.

---

* A limited free-trade arrangement with the USA.

Meanwhile, he continued to seek outlets for articles, and here *Canada* was useful. Lefroy took his Port Mann article — in which he was probably the first journalist to warn of the environmental risks of riverside industries for the fishery, one on Fort Qu'Appelle and another on developing the Fraser Valley. When *Canadian Finance* approached him in March, Rufus sent a series of three articles on the GTP on the Skeena River. By April, Myers and he, with a couple of others, were planning a weekend hike 38 miles into the mountains behind Hope to visit the Steamboat Mountain gold mine — whose shares were the object of the recent speculative investment bubble in Vancouver. They had to postpone the trip twice because of late snowmelt; consequently he and Myers, with a portable press all ready to ship to start a newspaper in Hope, were pipped at the post by a competitor — fortunately, as it would have been paid for by Myers and thus leave Rufus even deeper in debt. At the end of April they had to postpone a third time because one of their co-venturers, the contractor Dickie, had had a half-built Vancouver apartment house blown up by striking carpenters! In the meantime, however, Rufus managed to sell the Steamboat trip idea to Nichol, who paid him $25 up front for future articles on it. He also sold it to *BC Magazine*, which bought an article on Hope and promised him $15 for another on the mine.

The Steamboat Mountain[33] trip, when it happened, was an astonishing physical feat. Four city guys, looking like young gents out for a stroll in Rufus's pictures (though possibly taken on the previous 'recce' weekend), yomped 76 miles through mountainous country in mud, slush and, in some places, snow several feet deep, along the 'merest track' used by pack horses. They covered in two days a distance for which most people allowed four. Consequently, they arrived late both evenings at guest bunkhouses to find no bunks available: they had to sleep outside on balsam branches which were comfortable, but nightly frosts made even this an ordeal. Rufus was shocked by the poor treatment of packhorses along the trail, but not as deeply as he was when they put up at the 23 Mile guesthouse on the way back, to find the wife and daughter of the owner *wearing trousers*! The mine itself, a hole in the hill with a few miners using primitive equipment, didn't rate a mention in his letter to R.E. But he enthused, "as a test of endurance, that trip takes some beating." Good and bad, it was all grist for his mill, from which he drew full benefit in the days ahead.

In terms of personal satisfaction, the original outcome of their herculean efforts to sniff out wrong-doing at Steamboat was disappointing: neither of his sponsors had the stomach for publishing his allegations in the material he sent them, prompting these scornful comments to his father. "Lefroy sent back my article & photographs on this subject. He sent a very nice note with it saying that, as no attempt had been made over there to interest British capital & as the Coronation stuff kept them full up, etc., etc. I got it back two days after the smash was announced & every statement I made has been proved correct — and my warnings have been justified in every particular. The stuff about the claims was identical with that which I wrote for the *Province* after my visit to

Steamboat. Nichol cut out from my story all the warnings about the various claims 'because it would affect advertising returns'."

Finding himself comfortably off in an insurance job that taxed him little and left him time to write and think, Rufus was doing both with a vengeance. When he wrote to R.E., ideas, some wise, some hair-brained, flowed from his pen: one week it was the possibilities for a Western Press Association that consumed him, the next the need for white people to reach a live-and-let-live understanding with Chinese and Japanese people — he had suddenly realized the immorality and absurdity of the popular Asian Exclusion mania that had convulsed BC politics. Then he immersed himself in the wrongheadedness of sympathy strikes — socialist agitators were trying to start a general strike in support of the carpenters when there were a thousand unemployed willing to replace them — and next, it was the incompetence of Canadian civil servants.

By July both of them had worked themselves into a state of anxiety about the world situation and Rufus was concerned about an inevitable clash between Germany and Japan in South America! Neither seemed to anticipate serious trouble between Germany and Britain. Rufus wrote, "The Industrial problem is almost more complex than the international one to my mind. I think we must soon see the end of Socialism — I mean *practical* socialism as opposed to (or separate from) the theoretical socialism of the Fabians — and even the end of the power of Trade Unionism. They both start off with the basis that capital and labour are enemies — are opposed to one another. That is all wrong and the only solution — the only substitution — is cooperation, towards which many of the present movements seem to be tending."

He was aided and abetted by Sandy McLeod — a Balliol Rhodes Scholar from P.E.I. who had come to live with them in place of Myers — and Lionel Makovski, an older journalist friend. With these like-minded souls he spent considerable time chewing over such issues. He and Sandy even collected and analyzed speeches by Joe Chamberlain, Churchill, and Balfour over the last two British elections, in order to reach conclusions on the issue of mercantilism vs. free trade — turning Rufus into a free trader in the process. His summer of 1911, in fact, was turning into a seminar in public affairs, giving him an informal post-secondary education and a more complete worldview. It had other highlights too: he played plenty of tennis and won a tournament; he received two offers of promotion in the insurance world, both declined with thanks as they promised more responsibility but no more money. Privately he still rated insurance below banking as an occupation, even though he was becoming involved in the BC Underwriters Association.

But journalism remained his first love and two developments seemed to justify this in his eyes. First, and inevitably, the Steamboat bubble burst and Rufus wrote triumphantly to R.E.: "It has been proved that the chief claims were 'salted' with filings from US gold coins!" Of the refusal of Nichol to print his uncut material, he added, "That is an example of the sense of duty to the 'public' of a Western edition!! He would have gained enormously by making a great 'scoop' in publishing that story but he was simply afraid. Now I have the laugh over him — and he likes it not at all." No doubt Nichol — privately his most useful fan and guardian angel, had he but known — would have put it a little differently.

The second development would eventually force him to understand Nichol's point of view on such material as his Steamboat exposé. In late July, while on insurance business in Victoria, he was approached about the editorship of the *Cowichan Leader*. At the time, he was interested but noncommittal — he had to decide whether or not to stick with insurance for Bee's sake and made a startlingly good analysis of the conflict between his duty and his inclination. "The editorship," he wrote to his father, "would be worth $100 or $125 [a month] to start but would mean living in a small town up country. On the other hand if I stick here I shall get a Provincial Managership for some company or other sooner or later[34] and when I do, I shall make a fat thing of it. In the former case, it means comparative poverty and an interesting life — and in the latter case it means making money and a life that repels me. But in the latter case, it means being in a sound financial position in a year or so, which, after all, I think is my duty to aim at. For while I shall not marry until I can properly afford it, I want to get an assured position as soon as possible. It does not seem quite the same to suit myself when it means sacrificing Bertha's interests. She has a rotten time as it is and no doubt if I give up any journalistic ideas temporarily and do what seems my duty to her, Providence will direct the way back into the more interesting life later on, if she sees fit. It is rather a puzzle when you find your inclinations go strongly one way and your duty seems to lead the opposite way."

The weakness of this as a rational argument, of course, was to permit Providence any role at all. He often used 'godly' language when addressing his father but, after mailing the letter, may have said to himself: *Johnston, you idiot, if you miss this offer of an editorship — the very thing you've been hoping for and surely the best way to make your name — what guarantee would a fattening insurance manager with fading journalistic pretensions have of receiving another?*

Put like that, of course, what happened next was not a bit surprising — except perhaps to his father. A week later, he received a written invitation to come to Duncan to be interviewed for the editorship. He went, was interviewed — and accepted the job. On 11 August, he was writing to R.E. as though he had never previously mentioned the matter: "At the present moment I am Managing Editor of the *Cowichan Leader* — at least, I am to take up my duties here on Sept 1st."

Bee, meanwhile, the object of those smothered pangs of conscience, had been in Montreal since September 1910. In December Rufus had written to R.E. "Bertha tells me that she wrote a long letter to you soon after she came out but, as she got no answer, she supposes it went astray. Her address is: c/o Miss Drake, 639 City Hall Avenue, Montreal. Her work seems very hard and trying. I only hope I get this new position [with *Canada*] as it will mean a big step nearer a sound footing, when I shall be in a position to marry."

We know he did not get it, and Bee soldiered on until, rather casually, Rufus reported to his father on 25 April 1911: "Poor Bertha is in hospital — seems to have overworked!" She spent a month in that hospital, he later reported,[35] but when she came out her life improved drastically. Probably by arrangement between the two women, she left Harriet Drake to work for her sister, May Molson.[36] May's husband John Molson was a man of substance and manager of the Market and Harbours branch of Molsons Bank in Montreal. Their only child Margaret was turning six and her schooling and care were now entrusted to Bee. She had exchanged the drudgery of an overworked housekeeper (read 'general servant'), for a rewarding existence as Margaret's cherished governess. One of the only photographs of her as a single woman shows her strapping on snowshoes for a winter outing with the little girl.

In spite of Rufus's earlier analysis of her best interests, she was probably delighted to hear about the Duncan job. Most importantly, his income would finally be enough to get married on and that meant the end of the beginning. All that remained was a six-month wait. She left Montreal, finally, in February 1912 — to go back to Canterbury, collect her wits, say goodbye to her parents, and return to marry Rufus in April. She seems to have disliked her father more than a little and would have shed few tears over him. But she loved her mother and, as she did not expect to be back, would have found it hard to bid her farewell.

Chapter 6
Rural Editor
Duncan, 1911–1914

"I will be the boss here, or quit."

Rufus, 19 December 1912

Rufus arrived in Duncan towards the end of August 1911, ten days before he took over the *Cowichan Leader*. He had just turned 24 and had thought of himself as a journalist for just sixteen months. Nevertheless, in effect he had been headhunted for the job and the directors seem to have had few qualms about his appointment. It does seem extraordinary at first but the explanation is not hard to find. He had made plenty of waves for someone with so little experience. His article on shady practices by the Natural Resources Company at Fort George had produced a lively spat between newspapers; articles on the Steamboat bubble, on pollution of the Fraser, on the Dominion Sawmill Company or on Grand Trunk Pacific work-camps, all drew attention to the man behind them. From early days Nichol himself appreciated his talent for communicating complicated subjects simply and memorably, being happy to take his articles though he no longer worked at the *Province*. Nichol may have tipped the *Leader* directors; equally, they may already have been aware of him — he had publicized himself well enough and the BC newspaper world was a small one.

Later on, Rufus was dismissive about his early experiences in Canada, as was Derek who would contrast his own single-mindedness at the same age with his father's apparent lack of direction. Nevertheless, his wilderness years help explain his instant success as a journalist. What other young man, faced with writing an editorial in Duncan, BC, could call on so much understanding and experience of this huge country? He had worked on farms in Ontario, Saskatchewan, and British Columbia, could plow a field and sow and harvest a crop; he could handle cattle, goats and horses and could butcher hogs; he had lived westerners' hostility to eastern manufacturers; he had survived the

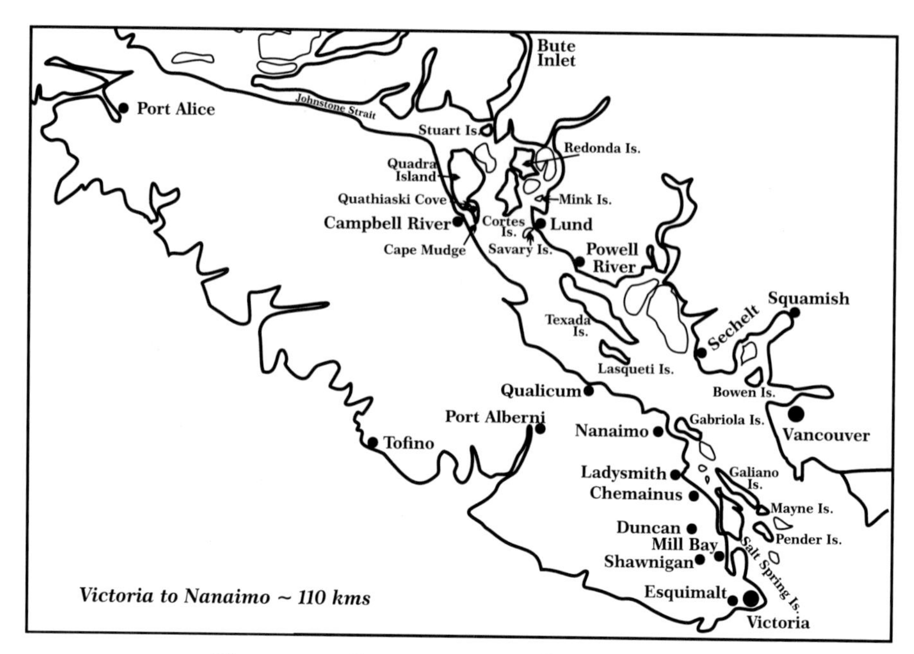

VANCOUVER ISLAND AND THE GULF ISLANDS

coldest prairie winter in decades; he knew the railways intimately, having ridden them, paid their freight rates and worked in their track-laying gangs; he had a basic understanding of retail lumber, banking and life insurance; he had seen the reality of Sifton's immigration policy, dealt with Germans, Ukrainians, and Chinese at close quarters and had ridden horses for a living on the great plains; he had homesteaded his own land and other people's; he had rubbed shoulders with the native people of many provinces; he was familiar with the main Canadian cities and had visited every region of BC. In fact, he knew more of the country than did most Canadians twice his age.

Before taking the job, Rufus described Duncan as ". . . the town of the district [of Cowichan] and the most delightful spot in all Canada. The district is entirely an agricultural one and the people are practically all English — mostly army or navy retired officers and a hard-working lot at that." That was part of the story, but the town itself had roots among the earliest immigrants to the district, who arrived aboard *HMS Hecate* in 1862. These people, including William Chalmers Duncan, were English farmers, not gentry, and remained distinct from the more recent, often better-off, arrivals. The district became economically viable after 1886 when the Esquimalt & Nanaimo Railroad connected it to Victoria and Nanaimo, and more diverse after the opening of the Lenora copper mine at nearby Mt Sicker in 1900 and of two more by 1902. When those mines closed by 1909, many of their Chinese miners came to live in Duncan.

For so small a settlement it had wide social distinctions. The wealthier English families, with their public school backgrounds, were known locally as

'Longstockings'[37]; they in turn, if provoked, would refer to the other whites as 'Mossbacks' or 'Shortstockings'. Then there was Chinatown, which had provided refuge for laid-off hard-rock miners after 1909. As well, the town was constricted by the encircling reserves of the Cowichan Indians. Its name was happenstance: the railway company named its station in the area after William Chalmers Duncan on whose land they had built it. The town grew around the station and remained unincorporated until 1912 when Duncan's son Kenneth became the first mayor. In 1911, 3,864 Europeans were living in the Cowichan census district, perhaps 1,500 of them in Duncan itself. It was definitely a small town but one with defined interests some half a century in the making. Rufus later claimed it to have been the only residential *district* in Western Canada at the time, and that it enjoyed more wealth per capita than any comparable district in Canada.[38]

Predictably, the newspaper existed because its residents, though a rural community, were relatively sophisticated and wanted one. A dozen local 'heavies', Ken Duncan amongst them, had put up the money to start the *Leader* and saw it as their newspaper. It was not going to be easy for an ambitious 24-year-old outsider to make the newspaper *his*, which of course was Rufus's intention — why else would he have taken the job? It was fortunate that his predecessor, Brettingham, had been no great shakes as a newspaperman and had made little effort — consequently, everybody wanted to see improvements and these would not be obstructed. As Rufus planned it, ". . . the great thing will be to make the newspaper hum for the first three months and then get my appointment made permanent at $125 instead of $100 — that is the understanding I have with them, provided I suit them."

The new broom could not wait to get started. By 26 August he had done a week's work in the *Leader* office already and had summed up the situation. "There are various things to be remedied. Expenses are too high and there is not enough job work coming in to the office to suit me. I want first of all to put the thing on a sound financial basis, so as to gain the thorough confidence of the directors. Then I shall be in a position to demand various changes and to improve the letterpress part of the paper . . . It is only a little rag, of course, but I want to make it the best of its kind in BC and to make the job department a really paying concern . . . It is ripping to be able to take a real interest in my work again . . . Thank Heaven to be out of Life Insurance for ever and aye!"[39]

His editorship started slap in the middle of the federal election campaign. No sooner was he into his office than he was receiving complaints that the paper carried no politics. After parrying a few of these, he had a brainwave: he met the secretaries of the Liberal and Conservative associations and offered ". . . to sell them half a page apiece, in each issue until the election, for the trifling consideration of $60. Then they could libel each other all they liked — after the style of the political parties of Eatonswill in David Copperfield. They both thought it a splendid idea . . . So we make money, everybody is pleased and I gain kudos all round."

But the fact of having so triumphantly expanded the newspaper brought its own problems. The day before the next issue found the Managing Editor, in all his glory, cycling the 20 miles to Ladysmith ". . . with the manuscript of the Liberal MP Ralph Smith's letter, returning the same night with 60 lbs. of type for the next day's issue. We had not enough type free from job work to do it in time unless I did this."

There were other ripples too: once the election was over, he wanted to avoid having to downsize from eight pages back to six. "So on Monday, I am going down to Victoria to try to scratch up some advertising contracts," this time, one hopes, in the comfort of the E&NR. Along with such small humiliations, his new job brought flattering perks. Premier Richard McBride dropped in for a chat one day, with the local MPP, Hayward, and the federal Tory candidate. Another day Ralph Smith brought in Templeman, federal Minister of Inland Revenue. After the election, Rufus would comment to R.E. that "poor old Templeman, who was licked in Victoria, is quite a useless old stick," but at the time was happy to talk to him. He and Hayward, however, subsequently developed a rather cautious friendship and Hayward would be instrumental in introducing him to the members of McBride`s government — which was most useful for Rufus, both in having such access and in becoming better known.

At the end of his third week, Rufus sounded happy with his progress. "My work goes on well and prospers. When I arrived the company had an overdraft of $684; today it was $322 and I have paid the men up to date and so won their good will. So far this month the work done in the office — job and advertising — is nearly twice what it was for the whole of last month." In order to reduce the overdraft even faster he had undertaken the printing of a catalogue for the local big store, Cowichan Merchants. "If it goes on all right it will just about bring us up square by 1 November." It all involved hard work and long hours — Rufus was staying with his friend Stanley Dick, who had 10 acres and kept chickens — and he had to ride 3½ miles on his bike to and from work. Nevertheless, he claimed to be happier than he had ever been in Canada — with one caveat. "So far I get on well with the people. But I rather dread those beastly dances and things in the winter to which I suppose one must go — I would far sooner come home and smoke and read after a long day."

It took just a month in his new position for him to start sounding like the derided W.C. Nichol. With no indication that he appreciated the irony, he told his father, "Unfortunately we, like practically every other newspaper in the world today, are more or less dependent on our advertisers for our living. Our advertisement list is naturally a small one and we cannot afford to risk offending a portion of the people thereon by taking sides too strongly in political battles. Therefore, at present at any rate, my business is to see that both sides have absolutely fair treatment at our hands." So much for having the laugh over his former employer!

For some time he felt his way cautiously in dealing with shareholders and directors. Of the twenty shareholders, five were directors and he met with them regularly. As the shareholders were politically divided, there was no pressure to hew to a particular line, though his middle-of-the-road course was making the paper a "roaring Liberal organ" in the minds of some Tories, accustomed to the partisanship of Brettingham who doubled as Conservative party secretary. After just a month in the job he could be philosophical about such critics — he certainly did not seem worried about them, observing that "there was never a man worth having who did not make *some* enemies." As for the directors, he liked them all — they approved of his financial policy and tried to help him however they could.

His first editorials were on topics likely to be popular. He encouraged the movement to incorporate Duncan, avoided election issues and drew attention to "the dangerous condition of the sidewalks on Station Street," the *Leader*'s address. Within a week or two he was trying humour. "We do not know the name of the owner of the cow — a Jersey we think — which slept the early part of the night of Saturday last in the middle of the road at the point where the Cowichan Lake road joins the main trunk road. Our dramatic critic . . . on a bicycle . . . discovered this fact rather suddenly. In fact he took a nasty toss over the back of the sleeping cow . . . He was not seriously hurt . . . but if cows are addicted to sleeping in the middle of the road, the owners ought to be compelled to place revolving lights on their backs."

In early October he hired another man in the print shop for the extra advertising and job notices, and was making minor changes to improve the printing machinery. His friend Hayward, a shareholder and a member of McBride's cabinet, had suggested making the *Leader* a Tory organ again if he wanted it to make money. Rufus heard him out politely but was beginning to understand the opportunities for expanding the business, both as newspaper and printshop, and considered such expansions a more desirable way of doing so.

At a directors' meeting later in the month he could report the overdraft paid off, all debts paid, and a reasonable credit balance at the bank. It was quite a turnaround in seven weeks and won him general approval. Pushing his advantage, he went on to suggest that they update the printing machinery and pay for it by increasing the capital. The directors swallowed that too and suggested he buy shares himself, so that they could appoint him Managing Director instead of Managing Editor. It all sounded positive and there seemed little doubt that his temporary appointment would become permanent when the three months were up. His editorials were still crowd-pleasers. It being long before freedom from discrimination was considered anybody's right, he launched into an appeal for the moving of the Cowichan band from their riverside reserve — "The progress of this town and district is retarded by the existence of this reserve at our very doors," he fumed. Soon afterwards he started a series of attacks on the CPR; the company owned the E&NR and was locally considered to offer poor, unsanitary, and unsafe service.

Rufus, however, with his many personal debts, was in no position to be buying shares on his own account. He needed a significant raise but, without realizing it, was making this unlikely to happen. Yes, the business would one day make much more money thanks to new machinery and a list of other improvements he would suggest; but he needed the directors to raise his salary *now* — so that he could comfortably marry. But by increasing the capital, upon which dividends must be paid, in addition to having to sell enough advertising, print-jobs and newspapers to pay for all the new stuff not covered by the increased capital, he was repeatedly postponing the day when he might expect such a raise.

November 1911 saw his expansion plans starting to take shape. He spent a weekend in Victoria looking at printing machinery, the new shares went on sale and were snapped up within a day, he had nearly a whole new plant on order, and there was more advertising coming in than he knew what to do with. It was a humming little business and the future looked bright. His confidence was reflected in a thoroughly researched analysis in editorials of the pros and cons of incorporation, followed by a rather headmasterly pep-talk on the vice of being late. "Within the last few weeks it has been our business to attend at least three functions in the town. Not one of these started within 35 minutes of the stated time . . . This town has a reputation on the mainland for being an extraordinarily slack place . . . It is poor business and bad form . . . It would be an excellent thing if at the next concert or meeting the doors were locked five minutes after the tabled time and none admitted after that time."

Rufus, with no ties apart from his work, made the most of his last days of bachelorhood. Stanley Dick introduced him to the great outdoors of the Cowichan Valley. They would cycle over to Maple Bay to swim, which seemed to him an enchanted spot. "The water is a deep, deep blue and clear as crystal. We roamed about the shore and bathed in a pool a good twenty feet deep with white sand, where you could see . . . purple starfish on the bottom." Or they went fishing — on one occasion landing a seven-pound salmon that Rufus found very exciting. In November he and his cousin Jo LeBrooy, who was working in Chemainus, had a day's shooting with Dick and four friends, between them slaughtering 23 pheasants, 4 quail, and a grouse. As the days shortened, the Longstocking social scene picked up. There was a dance at the Hassals', to whose house they had an eerie seven-mile drive through the forest without lights, an experience he enjoyed more than the dance. Later there was a party at the Sunderlands' where he was amazed that adults played Christmas games although there was only one child there — a very Longstocking affair that he nevertheless enjoyed.

Rufus felt secure enough to start planning his wedding to Bee, who was still patiently awaiting word in Montreal. Although by late 1911 she was living in comfortable surroundings, he wanted to bring their wedding forward for her sake — to put an end to her having to work at all. When his father argued for delaying "this matrimonial business," Rufus summarized why it was a good idea. First of all, he claimed, he could now afford to marry: he was earning $25–$30 a month from freelance work on top of his $125 salary. Secondly, journalism was definitely his vocation and an editorship, together with freelance income, was *the* most desirable situation within journalism — a position with a city paper would be the same financially and provide less secure employment. The main aim, he considered, was to become better known in the next few years, from which more freelance work — and income — would follow. And thirdly, a director was willing to lend him the money to buy a lot and build a house.

It sounded good but he had a worrying tendency to put a positive gloss on awkward facts — for example, that he would have "two *whole* years" to repay "as rent" the $1,000 that he would need to buy a lot and build a five-room bungalow. On a monthly income of $155 maximum ($1,860 p.a.), it was an impossibility of course. He was really saying *It will be a problem later that I don't want to think about.**

The letter in which he laid this all out was written on 14 December 1911 and his father henceforth accepted the inevitable. Bee and Rufus set their wedding date for 11 April 1912, the preliminaries began to take their course and he bought a one-acre lot at Somenos, 1¼ miles out of town. With a good carpenter as his builder, their house started taking shape in February with Rufus, whenever he could find time, working on it too. Meanwhile, he spent Christmas with Roy in Vancouver, and on his return to Duncan found it in a social whirl, with invitations every night to events he did not enjoy — but to which he felt obliged to go.

There was a rather explosive event just after Christmas — a visit from a furious H.E. Beasley, Island Superintendent of the CPR, who had come up from Victoria "especially to storm at me" and who was incensed about his attacks on the railway for various misdemeanors, including how it shipped milk from the Cowichan Creamery. "What annoys him is that I have taken care that every CPR official in authority, from Sir Thomas Shaughnessy down, shall read my tirades. I have been sending a marked copy of each issue to all the highest officials and friend Beasley is getting into trouble." Probably taken aback by his youth, Beasley called him an "insolent cub" and said he "wanted thrashing". Rufus had the confidence to take such rantings in stride without overreacting — he just offered to clear the copy room so they could settle it man-to-man — which must have been deflating for the angry official. He had also sent copies of his paper to the Medical Commissions in Vancouver and Victoria, both of which were investigating the pure milk question — "my remarks are to be brought before the Milk Commission next week," he crowed. In his words, he had "got them going," and as he had wanted, was definitely becoming known.

With the new year he adopted an aggressive mission statement for the newspaper's masthead, couplets by an obscure American Supreme Court judge,[40] the first of which read:

* In his monograph on his father Derek observed that he "was always rather casual and over-confident — a bad combination — about money matters" P.7.

HERE SHALL THE PRESS THE PEOPLE'S RIGHT MAINTAIN,
UNAWED BY INFLUENCE AND UNBRIBED BY GAIN.

At the same time he introduced photography, starting on 4 January with an undistinguished snap of the new Duncan hospital. For the next month or two the upcoming incorporation was the only news in the town. The *Leader* reported a visit to Victoria by a deputation of Duncanites, heaped praise on Hayward for his efforts to speed the process, and on 28 March, triumphantly reported the inauguration of the city with a group photo of "The First Mayor and Council of the City of Duncan" and a fine portrait of "His Worship the Mayor, Kenneth F. Duncan, Esq." As the paper told the story, ". . . after supper the band [on a borrowed flatbed truck] turned out to do honour to the new mayor and council and a tour of the town was made with stops at all the hotels and places of interest. The crowd, which numbered more than 100 people, was addressed by the mayor and aldermen [travelling in two borrowed motors] at the different stopping points . . . While on the way the band discoursed sweet music . . . on the return journey the procession stopped in front of the office of the *Cowichan Leader* and more cheers were given and the procession broke up after the singing of 'God Save the King'." A rustic bacchanal if ever there was!

Meanwhile the house was progressing, slowly, because of the need to clear the bush and then because it rained incessantly, yet Rufus, facing a two-month countdown as February rolled around, was eternally optimistic. His letters in March are full of everything in the world except the house and only on the 21st, exactly four weeks before his rescheduled wedding, now 18 April, does he concede that "the house is (still!) progressing slowly . . . The plumbing is being done at the moment. This is about the most expensive item of the lot." Fortunately, his carpenter was not just an ex-contractor from the old country but also a neighbour. He, too, was determined to get the job done well and on time, to encourage imitators in the neighbourhood where every new house pushed up property values.

Bee's progress towards her wedding was long, complicated, and eventually timed to perfection. She sailed from Montreal on *Empress of Ireland* on 23 February, arriving in Liverpool about 1 March. She spent a month in England — mostly with her parents, who had moved to #1 Ivy Lane, Canterbury, but for some of the time with R.E. at Marden. She was ill while in Kent but had otherwise been busy with wedding preparations. At the end of March she sailed back to Montreal, probably overnighted at St Catherine's Street with the Molsons, then took the train for Vancouver, arriving on 15 April. Roy met her, introduced her to the Squire sisters, Marjory and Agnes, who dined with them and probably put Bee up for the night. He completed his part of the plot on the morning of the 16th by putting her on the boat for Victoria. There on the wharf, at 5:45 pm — after a second separation of just over two years — Rufus met her.

Of their meeting, he later recalled, ". . . you were wearing your old purple straw hat and blue suit." What Bee remembered were his first words: "Well, my child, I thought you were never coming!" And as Rufus also remembered: "Then we went over to the dear old Empress — and had our first dinner together for years — how lovely it all was!" Presumably they spent the night there — in emphatically separate rooms.

In the morning they took the E&NR to Duncan, where Stanley Dick, Rufus's friend and landlord, met them and drove them to the house of Major and Mrs Hodgins. These kind people, with their three children, had agreed to allow Bee to observe the proprieties by putting her up for the night of 17 April. On the 18th, she arrived at the tiny church of St Mary the Virgin at Somenos on the arm of Stanley Dick, who would give her away. The *Leader* tells us that "she was dressed in white with a large picture hat"[41] and they were married by the Rev F. Granville Christmas — universally known as Father Christmas — with Roy as best man. As Rufus told R.E., ". . . on the day all the local celebrities turned up and the church was packed . . . The service was quite beautiful. The church was decorated by some kind neighbours and the choir insisted on turning out and singing a couple of hymns and a psalm."

The reception was put on by Mrs Hodgins in Stanley Dick's house, where Rufus had been living during his last bachelor months. "Roy proposed our health in the approved manner." As the invitation list had grown to sixty guests, it must have been quite a party. Unfortunately there are no photographs of the occasion — Rufus reminisced in a much-later letter to Father Christmas[42] about "silly old Milledge's ghastly error in making a hash of the wedding group photograph." That must have been very disappointing — there being nothing like photographs to persuade skeptical family an ocean away that their secret suspicions of improper shenanigans in the colonies were unfounded.*

A real honeymoon was not in the cards financially and the few days they did manage were full of business appointments. A friend, Rothwell[43], drove the newlyweds over the Malahat to Victoria on the evening of the 18th and they spent their wedding night (Thursday) at the Empress. "We went over to Vancouver the next day," Rufus explained to R.E., "and stayed there till Monday morning. We saw a good deal of Roy and Marjory and she and Bee like each other much." Things might have been pretty difficult if they had not: Rufus had previously told his father that he had "a lot of business to attend to [in Vancouver] and it is the only excuse I shall get to get away for a few days for a long time." Round one in the match between romantic hero and workaholic had definitely gone the wrong way. But at least, from the very beginning, Bee could have no further illusions about what she was up against.

She gives us a snapshot of Rufus soon after their marriage. In a letter to R.E. in June 1912 she told him, "I found Rufus just a little older — with a determined and sometimes rather severe expression. In character he is a lot

* 18th April 1912 was also the day that *Carpathia* docked in New York with the *Titanic* survivors. Until then most news of the sinking of Titanic on the 15th had been speculative and would have been the topic at the reception.

older; much of the old impetuosity is gone — he has more strength of will and far more patience than he used to have . . . He works very hard — the paper is going ahead wonderfully. He is very popular here and I believe he is very happy just now!" Clearly the early struggles at the *Cowichan Leader* had forced him to focus his mind, which had matured him. It was the first job he had had from which he could not just walk away — especially once they had decided to get married. She may not have realized the part she herself played in his popularity; as he had predicted, being married had made it much easier for him to socialize with the locals.

For a couple so atypical of their community, they did well for wedding presents and managed to furnish their house — the upside of having all those people in the church. R.E. probably gave them the best present — and one that he could probably ill afford: he forgave Rufus his trespasses and wiped the slate clean with a formal receipt for £20, "being repayment of monies advanced on his behalf to this date." Uncle Harry came up with £10. Bee arrived in BC laden with good things from Kent, for which she had sent out a circular thank-you letter before she left, with a promise to write again "as soon as I have seen Rufie." And the newspaper's directors "weighed in rather handsomely with a set of dining room furniture."

Once Bee had written letters to all those kind people, she was faced with the problem of making a life for herself in her new situation. Her workaholic husband was out all day — they were too far from town for him to come home for lunch — so she had many hours to fill and gardening was not her thing. She had, of course, to tackle the housework and the cooking, which were duties she endured but did not enjoy and were certainly not a full-time occupation. The weekend after their honeymoon, she spent the day sewing curtains while Rufus was hacking away at the backyard wilderness. 'Adam delving while Eve span' made an idyllic image for a letter home, but was not going to be a way of life if she could help it.

Two problems with their hastily-built love-nest soon emerged and the first was the more disconcerting. According to family legend, Bee so strongly disapproved of the pit-toilet that was their only loo that she would walk daily into Duncan to use the facilities at the Tzouhalem Hotel, and people along her route were said to check their clocks by her passing. It was the toniest hotel in town and a Longstocking resort of choice where, after a few weeks, she would meet friends and maybe be brought home by one, as they all had motorcars or horse-drawn traps.

The second problem concerned their distance from town. Although their house, named St Stephen's, was only 1¼ miles from the centre, even this was too far, both in summer and in winter. In summer the enemy was dust. "Pulverized by horse hooves and cartwheels, adulterated by the feces of dogs, cows, chickens, horses and indiscreet humans, the rich topsoil swept, in a talc-fine powder, from the unpaved streets into the homes and businesses." To go into town Bee must walk through it and in the process become as filthy as the streets. In winter, "Cowichan rains turned dust to slurry. The same unappealing ingredients mixed with rainwater in boot-deep pools . . . Passing carts squirted the green-brown liquid onto storefronts and anybody who happened to be nearby."[44] Bee could no more walk in it than Rufus could ride his bike.

What Bee needed was friends and, fortunately, she was good at making them. Their wedding reception had been a good start, of course, followed by a party for the young couple given by Jane Hayward[45] the next weekend. Bee hit it off at once with her hostess — who at 46 was four years older than her husband William, the MPP — and soon had the makings of a social life with Longstocking women a good bit older than herself. To that end they spent the 24 May weekend in town, watching and playing cricket — it would have rung bells for them although Duncan was hardly Canterbury. Still, everybody came to watch and to meet Bee, who had a wonderful time; Rufus played cricket and also had a good day as he made 47. This was the only recorded time he played cricket in Duncan — although he is in the 1912 club picture, looking desperately keen to belong but feeling just a bit out of it.

When she wrote to R.E. in July, Bee mentioned recently socializing with three older families who were important to their lives in Duncan. Herbert Clogstoun, OBE, was 56 and a retired Indian civil servant. In his heyday he had administered 100,000 people and 'advised' the Maharaj Rana of Dholpur.[46] His first wife had died in India, he had remarried in 1909, bought 79 acres beside Quamichan Lake in Cowichan and had built the house that later became the Quamichan Inn[47]. Beatrice Clogstoun, his wife, was younger and became a friend of Bee's. David Pearce Sunderland was 54 and had been a captain in the 4th Hussars in India. His wife Mabel was ten years younger and their children ranged from 13 to 20. Clive Phillipps-Wolley was 58, extremely wealthy and lived in an enormous house called The Grange. He had been British consul in the Crimea, a barrister, a British army captain, a big game hunter and also ranked among Canada's top half-dozen contemporary writers. His wife Janie, now in her forties, had married him when she was 16 and also became one of Bee's friends.

Rufus reported her away for a weekend in August, and in September she went with a friend to Victoria to shop and had a puncture on the Malahat on the way home. She and Rufus were repeatedly asked over to people's houses and friends visited them regularly. Part of the reason for this welcome activity may have been that Bee was by then unmistakably pregnant. As she was also often feeling unwell, in early October Rufus was a grass widower while she stayed with Jane Hayward for a few days. Friends were going out of their way to look after her which made both of their lives easier.

This was timely, for Rufus's life had been becoming more complicated. As his confidence grew, he had taken a more combative line in editorials and sooner or later was bound to run afoul of the mayor, as local newspapers will do from time to time. In early November he criticized city council for some small dereliction and 'his worship' reacted with fury. In addition to being mayor,

Duncan was a *Leader* shareholder and chairman of the directors but when he ordered him to write a follow-up piece at his direction Rufus refused to do so. Recklessly defiant, he wrote to R.E.: "either I'll be the No.1 man or I'll move on!" The next week's paper appeared without his retraction, and the next, and the one after that. He believed he had the support of the other directors, which must have been the case because there followed a six-week cold war between Station Street and City Hall during which his bookkeeper, William Macaulay, insisted on reporting to Duncan rather than to Rufus. The fact that he kept his job meanwhile indicates that most directors recognized, in spite of the fireworks, that he was doing a good job of growing their investment and putting them on the map.

Peace eventually returned at a mid-December meeting. Rufus had trumpeted defiance beforehand but must have moderated his tone as he later reported the air had been cleared and he had been assured that Macaulay would soon retire. In spite of appearances, Duncan was no bully. Though a big man with wide shoulders, he was described as doe-eyed and reticent and best defined by what he was *not*: noisy, brash, volatile, or extroverted. His power came from his name and his membership in the Masons, who were big in the valley. He probably enjoyed their confrontation even less than Rufus did. As for the distrusted Macaulay, the "dour Scot" was also a wizard with figures. Though loyal to Duncan, he was no fifth columnist and was still with the *Leader* a year later — by which time Rufus would even refer to him as his "excellent bookkeeper."

There was another more worrisome happening in their joint lives at this time — treated later on as a joke, but nobody was laughing in 1912. One time when Bee was away, Rufus was enticed into a high-stakes poker game at the Cowichan Country Club and lost $485, nearly four times the monthly salary on which they were scraping by. He confessed his transgression to Bee, no doubt to shrieks of dismay as their baby was due in a month or two, but the incident had good consequences: Bee took charge of their finances, and Rufus never played poker again — except for penny stakes. Both decisions served them well.

As 1912 drew to a close, their life was full of activity between Bee's bouts of not feeling well. They took two trips to Victoria for a couple of days each time, in each case mixing business with pleasure — the story of their early married life. Happily, they were not without family contacts. A business opportunity took them to Vancouver for a couple of days where they saw Roy, his fiancée Marjory Squire, Marjory's sister Agnes and her boyfriend Harold Jardine. Rufus thought Jardine — Roy's close friend and a pal of Stanley Dick's — a "dear good chap." Soon afterwards Harold and Agnes had Sunday lunch with them in Duncan, where her brother Bill was one of their neighbours. They also exchanged visits with Jo LeBrooy, Rufus's Chemainus cousin. She was about Bee's age and a governess and would bring her charge to tea on several occasions.

Both of them became involved in the Duncan Amateur Dramatic Society's Christmas play, Rufus as chairman of the committee and Bee, unable to perform, in charge of supper, helped by three or four friends. The event was

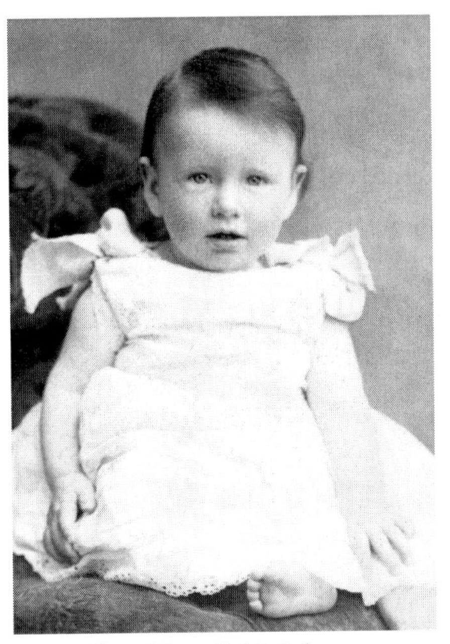
Edwin Harry Lukin Johnston (Rufus), 1888

Nellie Lukin, Rufus's mother

Johnston family before Rufus sailed for Canada, 1905; standing: Rufus, Roy; seated: R.E., Peter, Joyce, Lyonel

Bee, 1903 — aged 16

Rufus at their camp on Lake Ontario near St Catherines,
drawn by White, the ledger-keeper, 1906

Rufus and his shack at Kipp, Alberta,
where he spent "three months alone" in the winter of 1909-10

Rufus, behind, and a friend on the Steamboat Mountain trail, 1911

Rufus, portrait, 1911

W.C. Nichol, owner of the *Province*, later Lt. Governor of BC, who twice hired Rufus (courtesy City of Vancouver Archives)

Duncan Cricket club, 1912
Rufus top left, W.H. Hayward with cap, waistcoat, sixth from the left

Rufus at work at the *Cowichan Leader*, Duncan, 1913

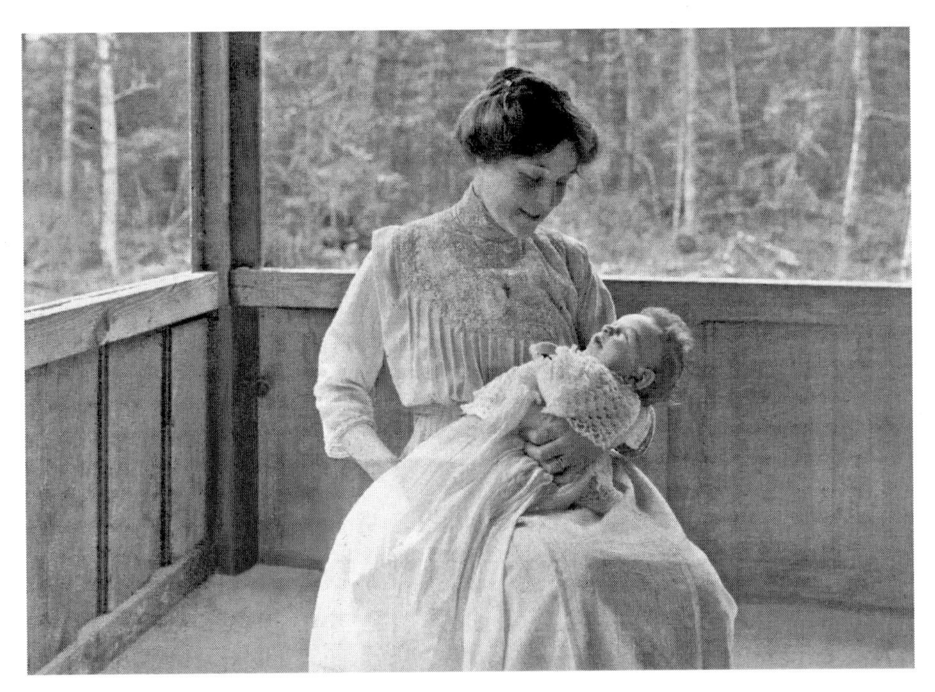

Bee with Derek aged 2 months, at St Stephen's, April 20, 1913

St Stephen's, Rufus's and Bee's house in Duncan, April 1913

Mayor Kenneth Duncan, 31, Agnes Duncan, 20, 1912 (*Cowichan Leader* photo)

The men of the family during R.E's visit to Linden Cottage, Victoria, May 31, 1914
back: R.E., Derek; front: Roy, Lyonel, Rufus

a great success, said to be the best ever, so both felt pleased with themselves at their first Christmas, which they spent alone together. As Bee told R.E., "we started to cook our Christmas dinner. Our charlady had given us a duck — and I had a pudding sent out from England last year. There was great excitement while the bird was in the oven — we had to look at it every five minutes — and the cat and dog sat round the stove sniffing wonderingly. About half-past three everything was ready — I had to stay out of the sitting room while Rufie laid the table. (He thinks he's an artist at this sort of thing.) It really looked ever so pretty — I wish you had all been there. The only thing we lacked was a carver! I took it to the Hall for cutting up sandwiches and it mysteriously disappeared — our knives all come from the fifteen-cent store and they absolutely refused to assist in dissecting duck — so Rufie had to use a razor!! Afterwards we just slacked — its the first holiday Rufie has had without having something to do. We didn't even wash up that day!"

Rufus was back at work on Boxing Day when the *Leader* next appeared. This issue was 10 pages thick, along with a special Christmas section of 25 pages which had been months in preparation. It showcased local businesses and for it he had drummed up sales and advertisers in Victoria. The front page had an elegant new appearance, with the city's elk's-head crest set in a wide scroll. And there was more to come. On 30 January 1913, with Bee due any day and when most fathers-to-be would have been keeping a low profile, the *Leader* proclaimed on its editorial page, for the first time: "E.H. Lukin Johnston, Managing Editor". The message was plain: he was the boss. He had chosen to interpret new-found peace at the *Leader* as a victory and his editorials would reflect it.

In case there was any doubt, in this issue he picked fights with the *Vancouver Sun*, the *Daily Colonist* and Premier McBride. In the *Sun*'s case he delivered an Imperial rocket for quibbling over the cost of training militia. As for the *Colonist* he lampooned its owner, J.S.H. (Sam) Matson, for accepting $75,000 from the BC government, for "services rendered" in connection with the acquisition of the Songhees reserve in Victoria Harbour. He suggested it "seems a lot of money for the services of Mr Matson" and assumed he would be dividing the money among "several persons" - also for services rendered. He goes on: "We are therefore anxiously awaiting an official announcement concerning these divisions of the booty because we confidently expect that the government . . .

will recognize . . . the yeoman service which the *Cowichan Leader* has at all times rendered to the present administration. If we could afford it we should publish a full-page portrait of Sir Richard McBride and his colleagues, but pending definite information as to the disposal of their $75,000 we have not yet given the order for the cuts." He wondered whether it wasn't a little selfish to make such a big present to an already wealthy man, and concluded, "Why not help out an organ like the *Cowichan Leader* which has ever been ready to come to the aid of the government when it finds itself in difficulties over the purchase of an Indian Reserve, or any other such knotty problem?"

It was a witty piece of self-promotion and character assassination by innuendo; it highlighted the coziness between the *Colonist* and the Tories and subtly reminded the premier that Duncan had also asked to have an Indian reserve moved. But it was reckless journalism under the circumstances.

Derek arrived nine days later on 8 February in Duncan hospital. Roy wired: "Derek Johnston: glad you've come and are a man. How is poor old father?" No mention of Bee, who was actually better off in hospital than she would have been at home — where she would have been isolated with a baby. After a month's advertising, Rufus finally managed to hire a girl to look after her at $30 a month and Bee and Derek came home in early March after an extended stay. Rufus was up to his ears in debt, what with doctors' fees, hospital charges and now his hired help, a Miss Laidlaw, who turned out to be worth every penny. He was so stretched he was unable to repay R.E. for covering a bill for him — probably an insurance premium. As he wrote to Uncle Harry, Derek's arrival had been "rather an anxious time for me and I am most mightily glad now that it is all over." Their son was baptized on 18 April 1913, their first anniversary, by Father Christmas in St Mary's, Somenos. There were three godparents — Clive Phillipps-Wolley, Herbert Clogstoun and Mrs Saxton-White — all older than Bee and Rufus, but immeasurably wealthier and well able to raise Derek in the event of their unexpected demise.

However, Rufus already had another problem, though a pleasant one: just as Bee returned from hospital, his eighteen-year-old brother Lyonel arrived. He was a charming lad and Bee took to him at once, as did the infant Derek. At first she found another man around the place useful but Rufus had to get him started in a career and they had no need of another mouth to feed. Over the last couple of years, Rufus, Roy and R.E. had been debating Lyonel's best option for when he left school: R.E. wanted to send him to Japan, Roy advised starting him with a London lawyer as he had done, and Rufus thought he should come to Canada. When he consulted Bill Squire, who had been brought up in Tokyo and would later live and work there, he advised strongly against R.E.'s plan because the Japanese did not want whites in their country.

This carried the day; now Lyonel was in Duncan and Rufus had to get him settled. Two surveyor friends agreed to take him on if he passed his preliminary exam in a month's time, so he continued to live with them while doing a minimum of three hours studying a day. Counting Miss Laidlaw, for a while they were a family of five, but when Lyonel passed his exam he was immediately hired by a surveyor and disappeared into the bush — emerging only occasionally for a weekend. Rufus was to look after his money and keep an eye on his spending — the fox in charge of the henhouse, as it were — and although Lyonel was sensible and frugal it was a responsibility he did not need.

Meanwhile, Rufus had renewed his campaign against Matson at the *Colonist*. In March he accused him of misrepresenting a speech by Hayward, of "garbling" Hayward's words — suggesting that he had allowed personal spite or partisan zeal to blind him to his duties to the public. As the year progressed, he adopted other crusading causes, but expended most effort on the Oriental Question, a topical hot potato. In support of Alderman Smithe's motion at city council, he supported a ban on Orientals, especially Japanese, being allowed to own land. He made a strong case for their complete exclusion, supporting his arguments, learnedly, with recent Japanese history. The most frequent subject for his editorials was the related question of indentured Oriental labour which he continued to support although the idea was at the furthest extreme of right-wing politics. His views no doubt reflected those of the company he kept in Duncan and it is good to remember that he was still only 26. This was the same Rufus who had written, in May 1911 before he came to Duncan, "We cannot be allowed to stifle a race of people because they happen to be yellow!" When the Royal Commission on Labour visited Duncan in November 1913, he made a presentation supporting indentured labour and another witness argued the same issue in its starkest terms when he observed: "The Chinaman is a slave in his own country — why shouldn't he be a slave to us?" Fortunately, the commissioners, who had found support for the idea in BC to be limited to the Cowichan Valley and to Ashcroft, rejected it as being "abhorrent to all feelings of humanity!"[48]

Other causes he championed included the enforcement of rules against bad drivers, imperial defence, returning the Bible to schools, and combating socialism. Later in the year he became less gentle in his treatment of Duncan's city council. In March he was after them to speed up new regulations for plumbing and sewerage before the hot weather; in April he was calling for them to contribute to the building of a new agricultural hall; in May he was urging council to petition the Royal Commission for help in moving the Cowichan reserves. In July he really went after them for failing to sprinkle the streets (to keep the dust down) in the hot weather — it appears council had just forgotten and had then put the job out to tender instead of hiring somebody, anybody, temporarily. "Delays of this sort, in a matter so urgent, are annoying," Rufus fumed, "and appear to be totally unnecessary."

Journalism of this sort can be an ivory tower exercise — until somebody retaliates and the real world bites back. For most of the year Ken Duncan appears to have taken the Leader's criticism in stride but by early December he had had enough. He had "flown up in the air" again and Rufus was moved to tell R.E., "I am aware that by speaking straight out on local matters and by refusing to be coerced to say this, that and the other by threats of various sorts, I have made myself powerful, and, incidentally, spiteful enemies here." He did not specify precisely what he meant.

Meanwhile, his situation had changed twice. By June his accumulated debts had become intolerable and he had no hope of receiving further capital funds — though he had expected to receive "$400 from the Beaver people" in Govan* in December 1911, his letters are silent as to whether this was actually paid. So he applied a radical solution: he sold their house at a low price in order to pay off other debts, then bought it back with a private loan of $3,000, to be paid off at $50 a month. Having paid $250 cash and $50 a month for 6 months, by December he had reduced the principal by $550. "Now," he told R.E., "I must begin to pay off other small debts and part of the original sum borrowed before April last year", *i.e.*, before they got married, which presumably included his 1909 debt to Hudson.

The second change was more unexpected. When in Victoria in September, he had had lunch with the reviled Sam Matson — at the latter's invitation one assumes. He told R.E. only that "it was very friendly and interested me much." However, a month later he beseeched his father not to mention Matson to Hayward, who was visiting England and was expected at Marden. "They are more or less deadly enemies," he explained, "and it would be *very annoying* if he knew of my transactions with M . . . It is best to let him imagine that the money I have in it came from home — or Timbuctoo — but not from a local source."

It looks as if Matson, most surprisingly for someone whose morality and honesty were frequently and publicly questioned by Rufus, had lent him $1,000, and possibly more, to enable him to buy *Leader* shares. Why had he done so? Because Matson discovered during their lunch that Rufus wanted to buy the *Leader* but had no money, nor any hope of any. So he offered to lend him $1,000 — ostensibly to make a start on buying up the shares, but, as he had just discovered that Rufus could never hope to raise enough to buy a majority, it was in fact to shut him up! Once Rufus was in his debt, he would have to consider his benefactor's reaction before unleashing another tirade.

Rufus explained to R.E., "He asks no say in anything. I don't know what I should do if he were to direct me to write what I did not believe. If I refused he might injure me by letting his interest in the company be known (and thus Rufus's apparent hypocrisy) — and if he liked to be really nasty it might result in my exit." He was beginning to realize he had accepted 'thirty pieces of silver'.

At home, Bee managed well with baby Derek after the wonderful Miss Laidlaw left in July. She had been wise to make friends with established older women and they came through with offers of hospitality, transport and (crucially) babysitting. She could also leave Derek with her cleaning lady, Mary,

---

* This was payment for his share either in the ranch in which he invested in 1909 or in the mysterious Govan business to which his father referred in a letter of May 1909 — more likely the latter.

who doted upon him. Once on their own, Bee and Derek spent a week with Jane Hayward, then a few days with Beatrice Clogstoun. It probably helped that Derek was an easy baby who smiled on demand and who had seen enough people in his short life that he was content to be left with comparative strangers, both short-term and long. Indeed, he seems to have enjoyed their attentions as it happened often and was never an issue.

For the rest of the year there were plenty of tea-parties, visits, picnics and regattas (at Maple Bay or Salt Spring) with a varied cast. This included cousin Jo LeBrooy and her employer's family; Lyonel, occasionally, for the weekend; Roy and Marjory, who had married in April and moved to Victoria in the fall; Mrs Matson, with whom Bee and Derek went to stay just two weeks after Rufus's famous lunch and whom he was already describing as "a dear woman"; and various journalist chums from apartment-sharing days, including Lionel Makovski and Hugh Savage. Amidst this agenda, he and Bee managed several trips to Vancouver and Victoria (once without Derek), and a two-week holiday in October, spending one week with the Haywards and the other with the Clogstouns. It seemed as if people couldn't get enough of them. And when opportunity offered, Rufus slipped away for a night or two at Lyonel's camp, in a vain but enjoyable attempt to bag a deer. Though job and marriage had clipped his wings, he relished the Cowichan Valley still, though perhaps no longer with his previous zest. "Duncan in the late summer of 1911 was beautiful," he later reminisced, "it was prosperous, it was gay. In short, it was one of the most delightful residential districts to be found anywhere — a district unique in all Canada."

By December 1913 Rufus's career as editor of the *Leader* was drawing to its inevitable conclusion. When, early in the month, he upset mayor Duncan again he seemed suddenly to realize that he might have provoked too many people too often and that this might have consequences. As Henry puts it in *Small City*, "such high-octane journalism is ultimately unsustainable in a small town — Johnston's successful muckraking was his own undoing." On the surface their life continued along its customary path. Because of the impassable condition of the roads, Rufus, Bee and Derek moved into a hotel in Duncan for the month before Christmas. This made it possible for them to see each other during the day and also made it easier for Bee to get to rehearsals for the annual Christmas play. No more supper committee for her — this year she had the lead in Piñero's *The Schoolmistress*.

They moved back home for Christmas, where Lyonel joined them. He had been laid off for the winter and, in January, Rufus managed to find him temporary work, with board & lodging, until he was rehired by a surveyor in the spring. Of their Christmas, Rufus told R.E., "We had our Christmas dinner on Christmas Eve instead of the day, because the Haywards very kindly asked us over there for their dinner, etc. Bee & Lyonel decorated the dining-room with Chinese lanterns & streamers. We went over to the Haywards in the afternoon of Christmas day. Miss Hayward [Violet, their 23-year old daughter] drove Bee & Baby, and Lyonel & I walked. After dinner there, which was very jolly, 14 of us altogether, Bee & Lyonel went across the road to the Chisholms' Xmas party [young bachelor brothers] — charades & dancing, while I stayed & played Bridge with Hayward, Major Hodgins & a man named Nonè. We all enjoyed it much as we stayed the night out there & Baby was so good. Next day, both Bee & Mrs Hayward were very seedy. Bee is only just fit again." Bee explained in a postscript, "I'm afraid I got overtired — and then goose & dancing finished me."

The final incident at the *Leader* occurred in January 1914 while Bee was busy with her play. Rufus, as we have seen, enjoyed portraying McBride's government as cozy with business and marginally corrupt. He got wind of a group of Victoria businessmen who had bought property at Cowichan Lake and were lobbying the government to build a road there from Duncan. He was indignant at such a suggested use of tax money, because only private investors, not taxpayers, would benefit from opening up the lake. What his research had not told him, however, was that the ubiquitous Matson was one of those investors, all of whom were furious at the *Leader*'s public excoriation of their plans. Matson had learned to keep a regular eye on the Duncan newspaper and decided it was time to act: in the middle of January, he offered Rufus a job as News Editor at the *Daily Colonist* in Victoria — an opportunity, he knew, that Rufus could not refuse. Had he done so, Matson was in a position to insist, as both of them well knew, though nothing was said by the wily Sam. It suited him to let Rufus believe he had been headhunted — which he seems to have done, as he told his father that Phillipps-Wolley had recommended him.

For Matson it was quite a coup: he had gained an excellent writer with editorial skills, and had silenced an embarrassing critic in so doing, thus earning the gratitude of cronies, including Premier McBride. There is a possibility that the plot was deeper and *Leader* directors were in cahoots with him — or, if not, that they, too, were glad to be shot of Rufus: for, as the latter told his father, he had been treated by them in the terms of his departure "in about as mean and parsimonious a manner as one can imagine."

He could take one consolation from his precipitate exit: his friend Hugh Savage, whom he had recommended, was appointed editor in his place. A skilled journalist but without his own restless ambition, Savage was the ideal small-town editor. He would hold the post until 1957 and turn the *Leader* into the excellent newspaper that Rufus imagined it could be.

Cartoon of Rufus with pram, 1913, by Vasco Loureiro

CHAPTER 7
City News Editor
Victoria, 1914–1916

"Two of us are a sufficient offering."

R.E., 18 March 1915

Rufus had never admired the *Colonist*, having told R.E. in March 1912 that its owner, Matson, "deals largely in real estate and uses the paper to further his own ends without any regard for the interests of the public." He assumed him to be "a man without any principles whatever" and accused Lugrin, that newspaper's editor, of being equally unprincipled and "one of the worst rogues unhung." Twenty-two months later, on 28 January 1914, he announced to the same correspondent that he was going to work for them and gave his opinion that "the *Colonist* is certainly the best and most influential paper in BC, if not in western Canada . . ." How his tune had changed! He went on: "The Editor is nominally over the News Editor, but the latter has full charge of all news in the paper and the make-up of it." Or so he hoped.

However, the proof of the pudding was still a week or two away — he was due to start his new job 16 February and in the meantime he and Bee had time to pack up their belongings and ship them to Victoria. They were not too sorry to leave St Stephen's, their little house in the woods. A fortnight earlier Rufus had written: "I do so wish I could sell and move into Duncan — it is too much for Bee here in the winter." Now that his wish had been partly granted, his only regret was leaving the garden he had wrested from the bush. "We have worked so hard to make it nice for you in the summer," he had told R.E., who would be arriving for a visit in May.* "I have planted quite a number of rose trees and hundreds of bulbs." Also, the death of Satan, their much loved little terrier,

* This trip had been at the top of R.E.'s agenda since the departure of Lyonel for BC. It was also a reconnaissance as he was secretly still toying with the idea of finding a clerical opportunity in Canada — and moving his whole family.

made the house seem suddenly empty — when he was hit by a car, Rufus even published a dog obituary.

Bee was not well — had not been completely right since Derek's arrival. The doctor had diagnosed shingles — a painful, stress-related condition — and one might have expected it to be made worse by the worry of moving house and the pressure of her leading role in the play. The opposite seems to have occurred and these may even have assisted her recovery: she looked forward to living in a city again, particularly as they would be joining Roy and Marjory there; and acting was as compelling to her as a whiff of scandal to Rufus. Determined not to let the move interfere with her performances, she arranged to stay with Jane Hayward after Rufus had gone and to join him in Victoria later. Meanwhile, as both would be busy, they "farmed out" master Derek to Mary for a week or two — "until we get a house and get properly settled." They never knew how lucky they were that their one-year-old just accepted this.

Roy had found a bungalow for them, which they went to Victoria to see. Maybe this was too small because they rented 1217 St Patrick Street instead, a house in Oak Bay — 2½ miles to the *Colonist*, 500 yards from Oak Bay Beach and a bit further from shops — whence Rufus planned to cycle to work. There was plenty of room for their furniture and, with three bedrooms, room for R.E. when he came in May. It seemed ideal and it was only after he started work that problems with the location became obvious. His workday ran from 6 pm until 2:30 am — but he also had a daily editorial meeting at 12:45 pm. Add half an hour each way for cycling and his time at home would be pretty short — though at first he assumed he could find ways around this problem. Meanwhile, Bee arrived on 21 February, fresh from thespian triumphs, eager to start life in a house with indoor plumbing and, once she had collected Derek, to resume family life. Like Rufus, at first she was "in love with the house," found nothing amiss and was eagerly planning R.E.'s room.

Rufus, however, was soon working sixteen hours a day, partly because his midday meeting would extend into the afternoon, making it impractical to go home and return by 6 pm. This job was infinitely more stressful than editing the *Leader*: the pressure was daily rather than weekly and, with Matson a hands-off owner and Lugrin, the editor, living up to his reputation, morale was low and the performance of reporters and staff poor. "Last night," he groaned on 15 March, "was the worst I have had." The telegraph editor had been drunk and there was a shortage of copy. Booze was always a problem — a reporter had been fired for being drunk the previous week; the reason that Rufus's own job had been vacant was because his predecessor had fallen 25 feet out of a window when under the influence; and that morning he had had to sack the female social reporter for the same reason. It was not a happy workplace, though Matson seemed pleased with his work and insisted the paper was improving.

Rufus and Bee knew nobody in Victoria apart from Roy and Marjory and could expect no safety net of friends to rally round as in Duncan. Within a week or two they had admitted their mistake in taking the house. Rufus wrote, "We find it much too far out of town. I spend several hours going and coming each day and not only is it very hard for me, but it means that poor Bee spends nearly all the day and night alone. Both of us were getting into a bad state — what with the lack of sleep and the everlasting work of it. So, much to our regret, we have decided to move as soon as may be." Bee and Derek were soon living in a boarding house near the centre of town whence she could more easily look for a better place. Rufus took his meals with them but still slept at St Patrick Street.

Cheering them up at this gloomy time, the review of *The Schoolmistress* in the *Cowichan Leader* was glowing in its praise of Bee. "As Miss Dyott in the title role, Mrs Lukin Johnston is to be highly commended. She has more than the average endowment of dramatic ability and her beautiful enunciation might serve as a model for many who tread the professional stage. To her talent, allied to that of Mr Barrington Foote as the impecunious aristocrat, much of the success of the production was due."

A second reason to smile came when Bee found a small house that they both liked and one-third the distance from town. This was 'Linden Cottage' at 1041 Linden Avenue. For a while they were desperately busy trying to balance a second move with Rufus going to work every day, but they managed it and were comfortable in their new place by the time R.E. arrived.

At this point the flow of letters ceased and it is more difficult to reconstruct their lives. Rufus was able to handle the 1.3 kms up and down Fort Street to the *Colonist* with relative ease, especially as it was a downhill ride to work, approximately the same distance he had ridden in Duncan, and Fort Street was paved. His 12:45 pm meeting was still a problem but solutions would have turned up — perhaps by conducting the meeting by phone, by keeping it short or even by the *Colonist* paying for a cab — a possibility, as Sam Matson, in spite of his devious ways, had a reputation for treating his workers well.[49] Morale would surely have improved with Rufus as part of the equation. If he had the right to fire delinquents, presumably he could also hire good reporters — at least until the war started when hiring became impossible. Bee, too, would have had a better life. She had a buggy for Derek* and could trundle him to Fort Street shops. She would have had Rufus home (though fast asleep) until lunchtime, and again in the afternoon. After an early dinner together, she would still be alone in the evening, but this was manageable as they had a telephone. For the situation to become more than bearable, they needed to make friends and we can be sure that this most sociable couple did not take long.

We know little about R.E.'s visit except that its timing was miraculous in all sorts of ways. He sailed from Liverpool on 8 May 1914, reached Montreal on the 14th and arrived in Vancouver on about the 20th. He spent two months in BC, partly with Roy and partly with Rufus, and left for home from Vancouver on 18 July. While in Victoria he had three sons with him for part of the time and there is a famous picture of the "men of the family", including Derek,

---

* It was the last item she advertised for sale before leaving for England in May 1916.

taken on the steps of Linden Cottage on the afternoon of 31 May, Whitsunday. He later reminded Rufus in a letter, "we went to the early celebration at the cathedral — Roy, Marjory, you and Lyonel; in the afternoon we took many snapshots on the steps of your house and all had supper there."

The next day, June 1, Lyonel left for the north with a survey crew on the GTP steamer *Prince Rupert*. R.E. continued, "On June 21 . . . I did gardening in your little garden & played with Derek, & in the evening we went to Pantages and saw that most absurd man with hugely long arms with which he cuddled himself — do you remember?" He made the most of his few days with Lyonel. ". . . tramping about those very hot streets buying his kit — it cost so much that I could only manage to give him $10 for his pocket." He also visited Duncan and likely stayed with the Haywards or the Phillipps-Wolleys, as he had recently had visits from both men when they were in England.

For much of the rest of June, thanks to his photo album, we know that Rufus took Bee, Derek, and R.E. on a Union Steamships vessel up the coast to Alaska and back, calling at isolated mines, whaling stations and the tiny port of Prince Rupert. Maybe it was while Bee was on this trip that she became ill again, an illness that overshadowed the last part of the old man's stay. He left for Montreal with the unsettling knowledge she was about to undergo an operation and was much relieved at Rufus's wire in Montreal that all had gone well and that she was recovering. She wrote a short poem about it, published by the *Colonist*, 26 July:

The Operation
Is it only a week ago since I prayed to Thee for aid?
As the night grew less, the morn drew near and, O God, I was afraid.
Then through the Shadowed Valley back to the light again.
My soul was cheered, dear ones were near, but ah! the agony and pain.
Thy pleading form before me, nurse with her touch and smile,
each soothed my spirit, calmed my fear and bade me rest awhile.
Now to Thee with grateful thanks I lift my heart above,
As on the air a voice I hear whispering 'God is Love'."

It sounds as if the surgeon had made a painful incision but we can only speculate as to his reasons for doing so.* Her fears were reasonable — at the time no operation was routine. R.E. wrote from the train and again from his hotel in Montreal before boarding his ship. His concerns were about Bee, of course, and he was most thankful for them having given him a good time. But he was also wrestling with Roy's request for £50 each for himself and Rufus from the Timson money in the Johnston Trust. He emphasized that this trust was intended to benefit all the children equally and that the pair of them had

* In later years Bee had two further operations for un-named gynecological conditions — probably also the problem here.

already had £300 more than they were entitled to — which was unfair to the others. Nevertheless he agreed to ask the Trustee, Mr Woods, for the money, on the understanding that it be repaid, with interest at 4½%. He confessed to being worried by Rufus's money troubles.

R.E.'s Atlantic crossing was uneventful. But as the ship approached Southampton on the evening of 4 August, to their astonishment, watchers on board saw all the lights go out on ships in the port. Their own ship had no radio and those on board had had no news of the events of the past few days. So when the pilot came aboard, he was surrounded by passengers asking him what it meant. He answered with a single word: "WAR!"

The outbreak of war was at first greeted with disbelief in much of Canada. But the death of Lt-Cmdr Clive Phillipps-Wolley and the sinking of his ship, *HMS Hogue*, on 22 September shattered any illusions to which Rufus and Bee may have been clinging. This officer was not only the first Canadian killed in the war, but the only son of Derek's godfather Clive P-W and the father of a third Clive P-W, a solemn little boy shown playing with Derek in a 1914 snapshot. The Lt-Cmdr's father had recently visited R.E. in Marden and had been associated with Rufus in the Duncan branch of the Navy League. That the first Canadian casualty should have been his son was both cruel and devastating.

Of the three Canadian Johnston brothers, Rufus was the only one not to leap into uniform. Roy tried to enlist in Victoria but was rejected on medical grounds. He and Marjory then left for Britain in the hope of being able to join up there. His Squire in-laws were instrumental in procuring a commission for him and he was gazetted 2nd Lieutenant with the 3rd battalion of the Dorsetshire Regiment on 30 December 1914 — by which time he had already been some months in uniform. He and Marjory were living in Wyke Regis, Dorset, where his battalion was training.

Lyonel's enlistment was more dramatic. When news of war eventually reached his survey camp in the wilds of northern BC, he and his friend Joe Mason trekked two days with a native guide through the bush to the nearest telegraph office, there to offer their services for the first Canadian contingent. However, by the time their survey party returned to Victoria, the first Canadian troops had sailed, so they joined a militia battalion, the 50th Gordon Highlanders, and Lyonel signed his attestation paper on 7 November 1914. Rufus and Bee provided him with a home-base while he was training in BC and he would have been with them for Christmas. He remained in Victoria until February 1915, then left for England with the 30th Battalion and by 15 March was at Shornecliffe Camp in Kent.

Meanwhile Roy's regiment expected to go to the front by the end of March. R.E. had procured an excellent Webley revolver for him (courtesy his more worldly uncle, Justin LeBrooy), a luminous compass, waterproof trench stockings, field glasses and anything else he could think of. By April Roy was a platoon commander at the front near Bethune and would remain there for several months, though his war would be a short one. Gas was first used by the Germans that spring in that section of the front and may have been the cause of his being invalided home — which he must have been by August because his son, Robin, was born in April 1916. Only in November 1915 did Rufus hear from R.E. that Roy had a home posting, was still feeling "seedy" and had been ordered to continue "doing nothing" by a Medical Board. He was still "far from well" the following April.

By contrast, Lyonel's military career was meteoric and tragic. After reports of the use of gas at Ypres, R.E., Florie, Joyce, and the vicarage servants worked nearly all night making homemade gas-masks of War Office pattern for Lyonel and the men in his barrack room, which reached the men before they left Shornecliffe. They shipped out on 2 May 1915, with Lyonel's platoon going as reinforcements for the 7th Battalion of the Leinster Regiment. Before leaving, he wrote a chirpy and poignant little letter to "My dear Ginger and Bee", asking them to send his trunk to Marden — "as, if I am wounded or anything like that, I will have no clothes to wear." He ended "hope to see you again someday with any luck. From your loving brother Lyonel." He was still a private, though one who stood out from his peers: at Shornecliffe he had been attached to central Brigade office as orderly to the officer in charge of embarkation and had had an interesting time carrying messages to generals and other authorities. In his father's opinion, "he has wonderfully developed and gives the impression of a keen, thoroughly reliable soldier."

Rufus and Bee, of course, were still in Victoria. He could not consider enlisting with a convalescent wife but, as Bee regained her health, he decided it was his duty to do so — in spite of active discouragement from the family. Uncle Harry, from his campaign HQ in German S.W. Africa (now Namibia), took the time to advise him that as long as there were enough single men willing and able to go into the firing line, there was no necessity for those with married ties to do so. R.E., with one son at the front and a second about to go, begged him to agree "that two of us are a sufficient offering." Both must have realized their efforts were likely in vain, for Rufus — as romantic an imperialist as ever breathed — must eventually heed the call. The timing probably dictated by the state of their finances, it took more than a year: on 8 November 1915 he enlisted in the 88th Battalion, the Victoria Fusiliers, was "appointed to commissioned rank" and shown as 'Lieutenant' on his Officers' Declaration paper agreeing to serve overseas.

By that time much had changed. From the start Lyonel had been in the thick of the fighting: with the 7th battalion of the Leinsters he fought at Givenchy ten days after landing in France, and at Festubert a few weeks later. Between those two battles he took a minute to send a pro-forma army postcard to his brother, in which the writer might only delete statements that did not apply before signing it. The surviving message, dated 11 June 1915, read: "I am quite well. Letter follows at first opportunity. I have received no letter from you for a long time."

Tactics were still primitive and casualties huge — 3,000 for the Canadian division in the two encounters. In such circumstances leaders emerge and on 20 August Private L. Johnston was gazetted 2nd Lieutenant in the parent British regiment, the Prince of Wales Leinster Regiment (Royal Canadians), as a platoon commander in the 2nd Battalion's 'A' company. He would lead his platoon in a series of actions in late 1915 before being granted eight days home leave before Christmas.

Rufus and Bee, having researched the possibility of a military pension for Bee while she was on her own, decided that if Rufus was going to Europe, they would all go. There was nobody they could ask in Victoria to look after their belongings in their absence, so on 26 October 1915 the contents of Linden Cottage — including, among a long list of other treasures, a "very fine upright piano by Chickering," "a Columbia Grafonola with 40 records," a large number of books, a Gentleman's Bicycle and a coop full of chickens — were sold at public auction. It must have been especially heartbreaking for Bee, who would have felt most keenly the heavy heartache in parting from their treasures. They moved into rooms at 'the Aberdeen' on McClure Street, close to the centre of Victoria; Rufus gave this as his address when he enlisted and it was where Bee and Derek lived until they all left for England.

Meanwhile, the 88th still needed a hundred men to fill the ranks and Lieutenant Johnston, former News Editor at the *Colonist*, was an obvious choice to recruit them. He seems to have run recruiting offices in both Victoria and Vancouver and to have filled the newspapers with notices. At the same time he was taking courses in machine-guns and musketry and learning his new trade.

Their life in British Columbia soon came to an end: in April Bee put a sad little notice in the *Colonist* advertising for sale Derek's bed, mattress and baby buggy; on 20 May Rufus left with the 88th on the CPR for Montreal, then aboard *SS Olympic* for England; and at about the same time Bee and Derek also left — first for Montreal and then New York. They sailed for England on 27 May on *SS Alaunia* and landed at Falmouth on 4 June, but not before Bee, ever the compulsive performer, had entertained the passengers at the ship's mid-Atlantic concert, in the spirit of 'damn the torpedoes'.

She and Derek may have been met by R.E., but in due course they made their way to Marden — and no doubt also to Canterbury to see her mother. Rufus, who was training at nearby Otterpool Camp, was reunited with wife and son when he arrived for a three-day leave on 18 June. He took the opportunity to write a lighthearted 21st birthday letter to Lyonel, in which he said, among other things, "By Jove, we do love this place. They are all so deliciously kind, and Boody* simply has the time of his life. He plays in the hayfield with the chickens all day long . . . I'm afraid it will be some time before I can catch up to your exalted rank, but if you will consent to be interviewed by a very humble

* Derek's nickname.

— and equally ignorant — subaltern, I will certainly try to look you up when I come over."

As the senior surviving officer, Lyonel had found himself in command of 'A' company in February 1916, and the situation was formalized on the 4th by his promotion to Temporary Captain, though he was not yet 21. His father's assessment of him as a soldier before he went to France seems to have been accurate, because shortly after that he received a nomination from the Commander in Chief for a permanent commission.

On 21 June Rufus had hardly returned to camp when he received a wire from his father:

"Lyonel dangerously wounded today."

This was followed next day by two others:

"Our dear Lyonel died of wounds yesterday." And later,

"Memorial service on Sunday. Come if possible."

During a quiet time in his part of the line Lyonel had been doing his job, visiting the men in his company's exposed forward positions, when he had been shot through the back of the head by a German sniper. Rufus's letter had never reached him and a month later was 'returned to sender', bearing various official stamps and the penciled inscriptions: "Killed," and "Died of wounds," signed: "J.H. Poole, Lt, OC 'C' company, 2nd Leinsters".

It can not have been much consolation to R.E. when he received a letter from the divisional commander, Major General Capper, who wrote of Lyonel: "A good officer and a great loss, not only to the battalion, but to the Army. It is rather heart-breaking to lose men like him in this sit-down form of warfare." His battalion commander, Lt Col Orpen-Palmer, also wrote: "He was beloved and respected by all, was a most gallant lad and had risen fast in the Army . . . I personally have lost a dear friend and my best company commander." He could hardly have been better appreciated — senior officers rarely write such things.

One can only imagine the grief in the Marden vicarage. Rufus, until that time loath to consider that he owed it to his father to avoid heroics, was finally convinced. Of R.E.'s three older sons — so keen to go to war such a short time ago — Lyonel was dead, Roy an invalid and he, Rufus, in imminent danger of sharing their fate. He accepted that his father was right — that "two of us are a sufficient offering" — and that he owed it to him, and to Bee and Derek, to seek an alternative to being an infantry platoon commander. It was a difficult thing to swallow for such an honourable man.

While he was on Salisbury Plain training with his battalion, he had a humiliating experience. Officers had to take an equitation course but could avoid it by passing a riding test. Rufus and his friend Stanley Dick were keen to avoid the course, but while he, with his prairie experience, was confident of passing the test, Dick, a novice, needed a little help. So they bribed the groom to provide Dick with the most docile animal while Rufus agreed to take whatever came, which turned out to be a strong and skittish beast. All went well until the examiner signalled a change of pace by cracking his whip. Dick's animal broke into the required trot while Rufus's took off across Salisbury Plain as if pursued by the whole German army. In spite of his bronco-busting experience, he was unable to regain control until rescued by a squadron of Hussars! Consequently he failed, much to his chagrin — while Dick passed.[50]

When he went away, Bee and Derek remained at Marden. Derek was a good child, not given to outrageous behaviour. The burden on his grandparents would also have been slight as Bee could pay for their board thanks to Rufus's wages. On 22 November the battalion left for France. As he went, Rufus sent her a letter, written on board *SS Olympic*, in which he summarized her financial position should he be killed — presumably they had talked about it and the letter was a reminder.

She would receive a pension of $37 a month plus a one-time separation allowance of two months pay ($40). He also carried $500 life insurance with the Clergy Mutual Life company. His father was his executor and would help her arrange payment of this. He also anticipated that she would receive his share of Uncle Harry's estate — reckoned to be considerable — and when she did, she might consider paying some of his debts which he listed under two headings: those that needed to be paid, at least in part; and those that he had no intention of paying but about which she had better know.

Under the first heading he listed $18.75 owing to St Joseph's Hospital, $50 of the $125 owing to Dr Ridewood, $25 of the $40 owed to Dr Wasson — "I don't think you would be justified in paying a greater proportion of the two latter debts as both doctors are well-off." Under the second heading he listed $431 ("alleged") to Parry* ("they cannot by any means collect this sum from you and you should not pay one penny of it — they have had their pound of flesh out of us!"); £100 to Mr Hudson** ("I will leave a letter for Mr Hudson"); and his unnamed debt to Matson ("who knows full well that in the event of my death, the amount owing to him will not be paid."). He ends by urging her not to pay a penny to anybody until after her own health is taken care of. Poor Rufus — he dreaded writing this letter, and no wonder. He would be leaving a wife with little income and the possibility of being hounded by creditors. No wonder Derek would later dismiss his father's approach to financial matters as a blend of approximation and optimism.

Meanwhile his uncle, General Harry Lukin, had become a star in a dark military sky. He had done a good job in S.W. Africa, taking the German surrender on 9 July 1915, and was appointed to command the South African contingent for the war in France. Known to the South African public as the 'Little General' and to his troops as 'Tim', he had seen more military action than any South African officer. After two months training in England, the brigade had been sent to strengthen the British army in Egypt, where it routed

---

* Maybe Arthur Norman Parry of Cowichan listed in the 1911 census — which might represent the balance left on the Duncan house, or on Rufus's poker debt from 1912.

** His fruit farming loan from 1909.

the pro-Turkish Senussis at Aqqaqia in February 1916. Once in France they were attached to British 9th (Scottish) Division (henceforth called 'the Jocks and the Springboks').

General Lukin, unlike his Canadian counterpart Currie, had to obey orders as his brigade was paid and maintained by British taxpayers — a bad bargain. When the battle of the Somme began in July 1916, he could do little other than watch as his Springboks were blown to smithereens in a forlorn attempt to take and hold an impossible position in Delville Wood. Over five days his 3,155 officers and men were reduced to 619 fit for duty. The general was devastated. "When the survivors of the Brigade paraded before him, Lukin took the parade with uncovered head and eyes not free from tears."[51]

But he had done his duty and his reward came soon after Rufus arrived at the front: in December 1916 he became GOC 9th Division.

Chapter 8
Platoon Subaltern
France, 1916–1917

"I cannot tell you how I long to get down to real work instead of this endless loafing."

Rufus, Dec 31 1916

From the moment Rufus reached Southampton with his draft for the 16th Battalion, he began bumping into friends — from Victoria, from Cowichan, even friends of Lyonel's. He began to feel at home in spite of the surroundings and dined with Sholto Gillespie, a young friend from Victoria, before boarding the transport for Le Havre. Crossing the Channel was unpleasant — there was nowhere to lie and nobody slept — "but we must get used to that," he commented philosophically. Once ashore, he and his draft were in the army's hands as they moved by train, gradually, from Le Havre to the front near Vimy Ridge. When they stopped in Rouen, he took a bath at the Hôtel de la Poste where, many years earlier, he had stayed with Roy and R.E. on a cycling holiday.

His first day with the 16th must have seemed like a scene from a war movie. Having 'detrained' at Aubigny-en-Artois, they waited for daylight at the station, then walked 8 kms to the battalion transport lines at Petit Servins. There they were fed and directed to battalion HQ at Carency, to which they also walked — another 8 kms. They reported and were assigned to platoons, Rufus to #1 Platoon. His company commander was John Hart, a friend from the 88th in Victoria, and that evening Hart took him to watch the explosion of a mine under the German trenches on the ridge. The big bang occurred on schedule at 9:50 pm and Rufus noted in his diary, "quite a big strafe* for ¾ hr. — baptism of fire, though a mile behind the line."

In his letter to Bee he was surprisingly explicit. "It was not a very big 'show' but to an amateur like myself it was wonderful. The mine went off with a terrific

* Artillery bombardment, though also used informally to mean 'tear a strip off.'

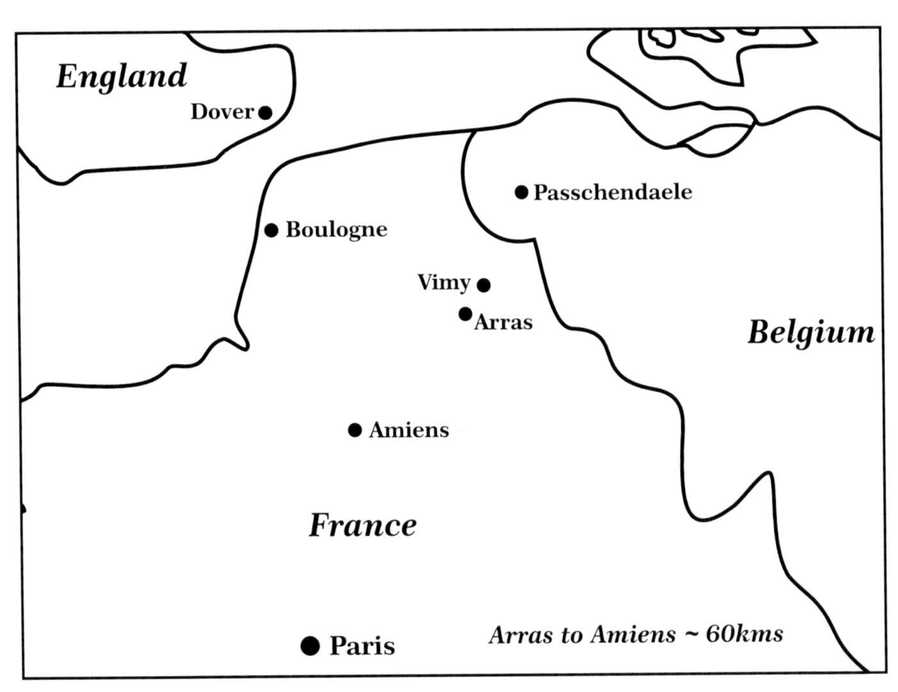

WESTERN FRONT

roar and at the same instant the whole air and earth trembled with the crack and roar of guns . . . The skyline where Fritz is was a blaze of light. He sent up star shells and SOS signals galore. In a minute bullets from his machine-guns were zipping all round. To my amazement, I was not a bit scared! I always imagined I should be scared stiff when first under fire and was asking myself continually why I wasn't. It was so interesting that one had no time to be frightened." He sounds excited, and as if he was enjoying himself!

He shared a dugout with Hart, the cellar of a demolished house that doubled as Company HQ. In the daytime it seemed habitable enough, especially with its stove. But at night it shared the universal problems of dugouts — rats and mice. They decided they must come down the chimney when the fire went out, but they were everywhere inside, even crawling over recumbent humans. Rufus's chocolate bar, safely stashed on a high shelf, disappeared without trace during the night.

During the next few days Rufus caught up with sleep, got to know his men, had time to write letters and to look up nearby friends — including W.H. Hayward, now 45, still the sitting MPP for Cowichan but about to go home after serving with the Pioneers. On 30 November, however, the 16th took over a section of the front line for four days. Rufus tried to reassure Bee ". . . you need have no anxiety, darling — it is so quiet here and there will be little danger. Nevertheless, I shall be glad to get the first effort over so as to begin to feel my feet."

He wrote again about midnight on the second night of their stint. Company HQ (which he shared still) was a sandbag shelter on the steep side of a quarry. The Huns had shelled the quarry on and off during the day, but now only an occasional machine gun swept the parapet. Subalterns did three hours on and six off, and his duties included visiting all sentries in the trenches and, after dark, the men in listening posts out in No Man's Land. His description was vivid. "It is a weird feeling at first, when you find yourself standing on top of your parapet as you go out — and Fritz sends up a star shell. You stand stock still — and think that everyone for ten miles must see you — but they don't. Do you remember Bairnsfather's picture?[52] It is so true. I go on again at 1 am — till 4 am. Everything is comparatively quiet and there is little to do — except try and keep warm. The mud is fearful and one's feet get dreadfully cold. The rats are simply amazing. They are everywhere. You step on them as you stumble along the trenches, and in the dugouts they are coming from every hole and corner. I do not like rats!" He ended the letter the next day at noon. "Just come off another relief. All OK, very tired. Am going to try and sleep for a few hours."

On 4 December he wrote again. "I wrote you a few hours ago, telling you I was going out on a detached post. By the Providence of God I have just returned. I will tell you about it. The said detached post lies 200 yards from our left flank on the side of a valley. Fritz is on three sides of you. There is no communication trench to the position and you have to go out over No Man's Land — swept at intervals by machine gun fire. We started out just after 'stand-to' at 5:15 pm and, after falling a hundred times into shell holes and disused trenches, arrived without casualties. I then placed my three bombing posts. I had a working party report to me at 8:30 — all but two were men just out tonight from England and they were scared stiff after the trip from the quarry. All went well until they had to leave at 12:00 midnight. I went out with them to start them off and had no sooner returned than Master Fritz let loose with his machine-guns. I heard one of the men call out: 'I am hit!' I called out to the corporal in charge and the man came back. When we had ripped up his shirt we found that the buckle of his braces, immediately over his heart, had been shot away — but he was only 'shocked'. They went ahead then, and we left at about 4:35 for the quarry. There was a mist, but Fritz knew we were about to move and, just as we 'stood-to', ready to move, he cut loose again. No-one was hurt and, with the guide in front of me, we started over ground hopelessly cut up by shell holes, etc. As we went over the crest of the hill he sent up starshells from both sides and we had to 'freeze' three or four times. Next he opened up on us with machine-guns and we 'flopped', but eventually arrived safely without a casualty. I looked back a dozen times on the trail, to see a dozen shadowy figures trailing out behind. When starshells went up — it seemed we must all be mowed down, so clearly were we outlined — but luck was with us and here we are. I chose to take that job — because I wanted the experience. It has turned out OK and I am glad I did. It was certainly the most eerie experience I have ever had."

Rufus's conscience had compelled him to experience these perils before he would agree to visit General Currie, 1st Division commander, with a view to applying for a job as a staff officer — generally considered safer than serving as a platoon commander. As it transpired, it would be easier to arrange than he knew. He wrote in his diary, "I was with Hughes, and we met Gen. Currie. He knew Hughes and stopped and spoke to him. He looked hard at me and said: 'I know your face — what is your name?' When I told him he said: 'Oh, you're Lukin Johnston[53]; why have you not been to see me before?' I told him I wanted to go to the front line before I came to him. He said: 'Come and see me at 2:30 today.'" When he did so, they chatted for more than an hour and the general promised to attach him to a brigade staff when the 16th went into divisional training before Christmas.

Armies being what they are, his posting took a little longer than that. After a week in billets and some necessary training, the battalion went into reserve for a few days and Rufus was occupied bringing up supplies or repairing trenches with working parties. Then they were back into the line for another tour. This time Master Fritz's artillery shelled their trenches constantly but Rufus's account is laconic, leaving the reader's imagination to fill in details:

Dec 17 – "First day, heavy shelling in afternoon"
Dec 18 – "Nothing particular. More shelling;"
Dec 19 – "Ditto. Trench smashed up."
Dec 20 – "Strafe in afternoon – trench all smashed in again."
Dec 21 – "Strafing began at 12:00. Big shells all along Souchez valley. A few whizz-bangs Cairns unwell. 54th relieved us at about 12:45. Heavy shelling as we moved out. No losses in platoon."*

During one of those days under shellfire, Rufus had an appalling experience that he later described to his father in a letter. "There was a 'show' on, and I was officer on duty in the front line. I walked along the trench, smoking a cigarette, I think, a thing I never do except under difficult circumstances, trying to be unconcerned but thinking all the time of my wife and boy and you. I spoke to some of the men 'standing-to' at the parapet — trying to encourage them. Among them — on sentry duty — was a youngster I had had occasion to 'strafe' a day or two before. He was kneeling on the fire-step, occasionally squinting over. In this position he could not possibly keep a proper look-out so I had to order him to stand up and look over the parapet. I waited for him to obey and, seeing that he was scared stiff, got up beside him and looked over. I was also

* A small-calibre German shell that travelled so fast that the whizzing sound of its flight was heard only an instant before the bang of its explosion.

very frightened, but much more afraid to appear a coward before my men than of a bullet. When I got down the boy stood up and did his job. Some hours later I was on my way up a communication trench at dawn, coming up to 'stand-to', and a stretcher pushed by me in the trench. I asked the bearer who it was. He said he didn't know, but turned back the blanket over the face . . . It was the boy I had spoken to. Oh, it's horrible, and the horror of it eats my heart all the time. One's fear is a curious sort of impersonal fear. As a rule one feels sorry for other people under fire — not realizing that you yourself are in danger. Instances like that I have described happen to all of us every day."

In the middle of all this he wrote a Christmas letter to Derek, aged 3¾. First he described how dirty he was, something that appealed to small boys. Then he described his dugout as "quite a long way under the ground, the roof kept up by pillars and posts. In the corner the cook is lying huddled up asleep by the brazier. When I came in he made me a nice hot cup of Oxo . . . It is strange to me that when shells and rifles are banging everywhere, so few people, comparatively, get hurt. Yesterday Daddy and his sergeant were talking in a trench when, suddenly, three great big shells called coalboxes — because they make lots of black smoke — burst within a few yards — luckily, just around the corner. We got covered with mud but that was all. One of my corporals was not so lucky — he was wounded and is now safe in England, I expect. It is very cold here now. There are oceans of mud and it freezes on your boots — till you almost want to shriek with the numbing pain. But it doesn't last long — and we're all in the same boat and all cheery . . . Kiss mummy for me and have a happy Christmas, both of you."

It is a clever and sensitive piece of writing to an anxious little boy. He was too old to be kept in the dark so Rufus gently introduced him to the dirt, discomfort, and danger of his daddy's life, with enough reality to satisfy his curiosity and his love of things-that-go-bang, but not enough to frighten him.

After being relieved, the battalion marched — a mere 24 kms! — to billets behind the lines at Maisnil. No sooner were they settled than Rufus got word that Uncle Harry, now GOC British 9th Division, was sending a car to bring him to his HQ for Christmas. For Rufus it meant two days living in a château instead of a dugout, sleeping between sheets, eating three cooked meals a day and sitting beside a fire in the evening. For the two men, it meant actually getting to know each other as grown-ups — Harry having last seen him as a small boy. They talked at length about Nellie — his mother and Harry's sister — arguably the most important person in both their lives. Harry enjoyed hearing Rufus talk about his childhood and of his adult life with Bee and Derek. But that was only one side of the holiday; the general's professionalism allowed no real relaxation. On Christmas Day he and Rufus toured his division, in the trenches, on foot — talking to the men, "wishing them all the compliments of the season — in his queer, brusque way," and making sure that they'd had their Christmas pudding. They were at it until 2 pm, when the Germans sent their contribution to a merry Christmas — an afternoon strafe.

As Rufus described it to Bee, "a big Hun shell burst not far away and between him and me a chunk of iron 6 inches long landed. It was so hot I could not pick it up at first . . . He says Aunt Lily should not be told of this little incident. It often happens, of course, but was closer than usual!" Poor Bee was thought to be proof against such fears, one assumes. Before Rufus returned to his battalion they also talked about Currie's promise — by then overdue — and Harry promised to arrange something should Currie fail to deliver. Needless to say, after this experience Rufus completely changed his opinion of the man. Where he had, until recently, considered him an irritating and stingy elderly relative, he now admired him and appreciated his kindness.

28 December 1916 was a miserable winter day with heavy rain. As there was no sign of activity in their part of the front, in an uncharacteristic move for the military, the CO cancelled all parades — creating for those not on duty the equivalent of a 'snow day' for school kids. It was an opportunity for a little normality and Rufus, with McGowan, Hart, and Cornell, walked to Bruay to dine at L'hôtel Serniclet — the best fare Bruay had to offer. Afterwards, with some of that battalion's officers, they went to a pantomime put on by the 14th battalion. It made it feel just a little more like Christmas.

Rufus spent part of January 1917 with 50 soldiers on a range practicing musketry, part on other training, and the last ten days with the battalion in support just behind the front line. Apart from a couple of working parties repairing trenches, he passed much of the time playing bridge with very little to do. He found the boredom of being on duty with nothing to do — loafing, as he called it — intolerable. He filled the time by seeking out friends in nearby battalions and it was while he was talking to one of these that "a big Minnie* burst close by," as he wrote in his diary, "and a piece of shrapnel knocked my pipe out of my mouth." It also chipped two of his teeth — his most significant war-damage to date.

The weather had cleared up and he gave Bee a description of an aerial battle. "As soon as a Fritz machine comes our way, you can follow its track — even though it may be too high to see it at once — by the little white clouds caused by bursting shrapnel. Against the clear blue sky it is a wonderfully beautiful sight. Yesterday a Fritz machine was brought down by two of ours — and later one of ours suddenly burst into flame and fell — you could actually see the poor man fall headlong out of his machine — from 10,000 feet!"

He had two other bits of news: he had a new batman — Private Gould, from Worcestershire, a most excellent person — who would stick with him through thick and thin — and a story to tell: "Did I tell you about our rat with asthma? Locally known as Archibald, he has a most extraordinary sort of wheeze. The cook chased him all round the dugout with a bayonet the other day. The beggar took refuge in a sleeping bag — and then got away."

* Trench mortar bomb — the mortar that fired it was called a *Minenwerfer*.

As it turned out, the division commander was as good as his word, even if he was a month late. On 28 January Rufus was woken by a runner — he was to report to 3rd Brigade HQ immediately. He felt so relieved that he went back to sleep for two hours and finally arrived at Brigade at 10:30. While he was waiting, he bumped into General Currie who was visiting. "He was very pleasant," Rufus told Bee, "asked me what I was doing, etc. He told the brigade major he wanted me to be given lots of work."

Chapter 9
Staff Captain 'I'
France, 1917

"When things looked blackest our 'buzzer' was smashed by shellfire and the signal man killed. Four runners whom I sent back with reports were killed and we were entirely cut off from Brigade HQ for hours."

Rufus's *War Book*, Passchendaele, 27 October 1917

Rufus's reaction to staff work was enthusiastic."The first real day's work since I have been in France. I enjoyed every minute of it. I am going to love this work. It is extremely interesting and all the staff are decent fellows." It was a good start but the flipside of 'no more loafing' was that his hours would be brutally long. The work varied in his first month. He started with the Quartermaster's ('Q') branch, dealing with gas defences at Calonne. While there he visited the Leinsters and met Plowman and Liston, two of Lyonel's subalterns. Next he was attached to the Brigade Major's (BM) office and worked on preparing courts-martial. In one case a soldier charged with desertion was making a fool of himself, ". . . making it certain he would be shot if he rambled on. So I offered to act as 'prisoner's friend'. I took him on one side and he told me, half weeping all the time, that shells affected his nerves, etc., etc. He thought he was going to be shot for certain and told me a lot of stuff about his family affairs — half mad with terror all the time. I got him off the desertion charge but he was convicted, of course, on a minor charge and got a pretty stiff sentence. He thanked me over and again afterwards."

In his last week he was with the Intelligence, or 'I', branch. Three staff officers were away and he discovered that being a 'learner' meant being a repository for established officers' unwanted jobs. Thus, as well as being 'acting' Staff Captain 'I', he was 'acting' orderly officer in charge of brigade subalterns and 'acting' Mess President. Furthermore, the fact that two of the absentees were on leave meant that Rufus's own chances of leave in the near future had evaporated. He consoled himself, and Bee, with the thought that "it shows they have some confidence in me as there is another attached officer here, who is several weeks senior to me, and they have passed him over."

As acting Staff Captain 'I' he was up in the front line every day, visiting the three battalion HQs and their observation posts, and was therefore in danger, "but not nearly to the same extent as one is on regular duty in the line," he told Bee. It was a good line for calming her fears but, because he had to be constantly on the move — even during bombardments when most front-line officers and men took cover — it was only partly true. During the week, he rode to Béthune in a motorcycle sidecar, a form of transportation he would get used to. It was a lovely day, Béthune was still a lovely old town and Rufus, a connoisseur of churches everywhere, stole a few moments from the war to enjoy the ancient stained glass in the church windows.*

At this time Bee was brightly urging him to try out a code that her doctor and his son (who was at the front) were using to beat the censor. Rufus would then be able to tell her where he was! He was horrified, and explained to her, "You see, to do that is now a court-martial offence, and officers are put on their honour not to do so . . . I went to a lecture the other day about censorship and secret service and you simply wouldn't believe how cunning the enemy is." At the very least, he would have jeopardized his budding staff career.

His probationary month had gone well and on 22 February 1917 he was posted to Canadian Corps HQ where General Byng was still GOC.** Within a few days he was writing approvingly of his new situation to Bee."This place simply wriggles with 'high-brows' in the military world. My dreams used to be bounded by 'the Brigade', but here a brigade is a mere pawn. I can handle generals and people quite reasonably well."

He had a little more difficulty with horses: he borrowed one from the stables, in spite of the groom warning him that it might try to bolt, which is exactly what it did. Rufus was ready for it, however, managed to remain more or less in control, did his shopping in the town and returned the nag. But "he nearly tore my arms out and I'm still stiff from it," he complained.

He had imagined his new boss, Byng's chief of staff Brigadier Radcliffe, as "a grey-haired old crank" and was delighted when he turned out to be "a ripping chap" of 43 and very charming. But he noticed that all Byng's staff, apart from himself, had won their spurs the hard way: Radcliffe had a DSO, Major Linton and Capt Heron, a DSO *and* an MC, while Major Chalmers and Capt Talbot Papineau had an MC — on the face of it an intimidating bunch of heroes to work with, though he seems to have taken it in stride. While in Radcliffe's office, he noticed a letter from Uncle Harry on the desk. He gathered that it had just arrived and concluded that he had therefore made it to Corps HQ on the strength of a good report from 1st Division — that is to say, on his own merits. Nevertheless, he was much impressed by Uncle Harry's kindness in writing right away. He ended his letter to Bee with "Cheer up, things are looking very

* Destroyed by German guns, along with the rest of the town, in March 1918. The stump of the church is now a restaurant.

** General Officer Commanding.

bright now." He must have had a hint of what was coming because, in spite of his earlier gloom, his first leave came through within days.

The remarkable thing about going on leave was its almost-peacetime normality. There was none of the military red tape and delay of his arrival — he simply cadged a ride with another officer for the 90 kms to Boulogne. As it snowed the whole way, they missed the morning boat by five minutes. That was disappointing but, after a leisurely lunch, he caught the afternoon boat and reached Victoria Station in London at 8 pm, where Bee met him. The pair of them took a five-minute walk to the Wilton Hotel where they dined and spent the night. They had no Derek to worry about as Bee had sensibly left him at their lodgings in Sidcup, near the house of Rufus's Uncle Jack.

At Rufus's request, Bee had choreographed his leave. They spent six of the ten nights at the Wilton, a fortunate choice because the weather was foul: snow, rain, and hail. That first morning they did very little, but after lunch caught a train to Sidcup where Boody, with their landlady Miss Holland, was waiting on the platform for his daddy. After a 'father and son' afternoon at Bee's lodgings, they visited Uncle Jack then brought Boody with them back to London.

The next three days were at Marden with R.E. Maybe by happenstance, Florie was away, allowing Rufus to have several long, late chats with his father. Joyce (19), Peter (14), and Mary (10) were at home. Rufus spent one wet afternoon playing a huge game of soldiers with the younger two — though it was remarkable he felt able to do so. Eventually they left for Canterbury to visit Bee's parents. By contrast, they spent only an hour or two with them and Bee seems to have seen it as a duty call, though she must surely have visited them on previous occasions since her return to England.

Afterwards, they went to the cathedral, stayed the night at the Rose and returned to London. They experimented with taking Boody to shows, and he dutifully sat through the matinée of *Theodore & Co.*, a musical by Ivor Novello and Jerome Kern. When his verdict was 'thumbs down', they found a nice person at the hotel to look after him while they went to *Romance!* that evening. Bee had planned one desperately social day, as Rufus reported in his diary. "Winnie Crosslegh met us at the Trocadero for lunch. I went on to see Florie in Hampstead and met Bee, Derek, and Winnie at Aunt Lily's later. Roy met us at the Wilton Hotel and we all went to dine at Hatchetts. Then Roy went back to Guildford and Win, Bee and I went to *Chu Chin Chow* at His Majesty's — a splendid show" — all while, presumably, the same nice person had been minding Boody.

With two days remaining, they took him back to Miss Holland in Sidcup, returned to London and that night went to *The Aristocrat* at the St James's Theatre, a rather grim play about the French Revolution. They kept to themselves on the last day, did a little shopping and went to bed early. Back in uniform in the morning, Rufus kissed Bee goodbye, grabbed some toast and caught the 7 am troop-train from Victoria — where the world still seemed sane. As the train gathered speed, ten days of condensed normality ended: by lunchtime he was in

Boulogne and by dinnertime back at Canadian Corps HQ — where the world was definitely mad. It was as if he had never been away.

No sooner had he got back than Talbot Papineau, the SC 'I'* left for a conference and he found himself desk-bound, picking up much of Papineau's work and unable to get up the line. Two days later, when he had to go the 7 kms to Bruay, he borrowed Papineau's horse. He should have known better — it was a spirited one-man thoroughbred, accustomed to being talked to in French. He wrote in his war diary, "Papineau's horse ran away with me to Bruay aerodrome — I was all in by the time he stopped."

He had been having stomach trouble, at times verging on dysentery, for some time before his leave. He had had the same problem occasionally when at the *Colonist* and MOs** he had seen in France had no idea what was wrong. Within three days of his return his old trouble was back. "It did not, of course, get quite right in England," he wrote, "but now it is rotten again". The MO suspected appendicitis but Rufus was refusing to have an operation before June when, all being well, he should be getting his captaincy. Bee too had a lingering problem with pains in her side which also sounded like appendicitis and Rufus commented "What a couple of crocks we are!" However, though both of them were unwell, at the time neither was really ill.

THE FOUR DIVISIONS OF THE CORPS were preparing to attack Vimy Ridge and things were heating up. When Papineau returned after a week, Rufus was able to escape the office and get up the line with Major Chalmers. They walked miles in the trenches, seeking out battalion COs, visiting brigade and divisional HQs. Their days took on a mess-crawling pattern: thus on 29 March he lunched in the 16th Battalion mess and had tea at the 3rd Brigade mess — both in 1st Division. The wonderful thing about his roving assignment was his near-certainty of meeting old friends every day. On 29 March, for instance, he met Little Rae from 'the lads' house' in Vancouver in 1910–11 — he used to appear in frock coat, top hat and eye-glass on Sundays — now a highly regarded colonel and DSO; also, Cy Peck, colonel of the 16th, who would win a VC in 1918; and "young Montgomery"[54] from King's School, with whom he "had quite a confab." He visited the 16th as often as he could. He knew most of the officers, some being good friends from Victoria days, others newer acquaintances like Joe Mason.

Rufus does not tell us what going 'up the line' involved but we can make assumptions. Crucial to the success of the upcoming operation was pinpointing the German guns, and therefore being able to eliminate them before the attacking Canadians came out of the tunnels. All front-line battalions had observation posts (OPs) whose main task was to pinpoint gun flashes and map them accurately. This information must be collected and reported to Corps

* Staff Captain (Intelligence).

** Medical Officer.

HQ for transmission to the gunners. Rufus might be interviewing battalion intelligence officers, visiting OPs — even siting them. He had also to gather information about the enemy from patrol reports, especially about the condition of the barbed wire in front of the German trenches.

His problem was to find enough hours in the day. As a learner he was low man on the staff totem and still getting "the thick end of the stick all the time" — having to accept extra work as the price of a future posting. Not only were his days long — often starting before dawn — but he was regularly on night duty, which was never uneventful. In his 29 March letter he was hoping, wistfully, that "one will . . . get an occasional full night's sleep and meals at something like Christian hours" when eventually assigned to a divisional or brigade HQ. As it was, he was always short of sleep, which must have contributed to his internal problems.

By 2 April the tempo of the gunfire was increasing noticeably. Rufus, who was up the line every day the week before the battle, was both fascinated and appalled. On 4 April he wrote, "Everywhere is distinctly unhealthy just now . . . the everlasting thunder of hundreds of guns goes on day and night. I don't know what the Somme was like but we have twice the guns here — massed in serried ranks. From a hill I have to cross sometimes, I can see for miles the bursting of our shells in the German lines, and the flash of our guns as they spit continually. Its all very grand but very horrible."

On his rounds on 8 April, the eve of the battle, he sat in a disused trench eating his lunch "in comparative comfort, munching on bread and cheese while the air overhead fairly sizzled with our shells and the ground occasionally quaked with bursting shells not far off. One gets used to it in some wonderful way — but I hate it all."

The next morning, April 9, the fronts of the tunnels were blown out just before dawn at 5:30. Men poured from the entrances, fanned out across No Man's Land and advanced slowly uphill, helped forward by a freezing gale that drove wet snow into the Germans' faces. The shells of the barrage were bursting just fifty metres ahead of the advancing troops, who must maintain the same speed. Currie, himself an artilleryman, had urged the infantry to 'lean into' the barrage, to follow it "as closely as a horse follows its filled nosebag!" This 'creeping barrage' was a key to his system. It called for great skill from the gunners, but it kept the Germans' heads down. The barbed wire protecting their trenches had been destroyed by shells with proximity fuses, and by the time the stunned defenders realized the barrage had passed, the Canadians were on top of them. Most Germans in the first line surrendered. If they chose to fight, they were at a huge disadvantage — down in a trench while soldiers with grenades were above them.

Hundreds of prisoners were disarmed and ordered to march to the Canadian lines — escorts could not be spared so a prod with a bayonet got them moving in the right direction. A few men stayed behind to deal with holdouts and the advance went on, with the attackers still keeping pace with the barrage. As it got lighter and they were fired on by machine-guns in the second line, they had new solutions: throwing smoke grenades to conceal themselves from the gunners, the attackers divided, some keeping the gunners' heads down with rifle fire, while others worked round the flank to silence them with grenades.

By noon the battle was over and the last Germans were scrambling down through the trees on the eastern slope. The crest of the ridge had been so chewed up by Canadian guns that one soldier remembered that "it looked like a rich plum pudding before it goes to the boiling!" Except for the Pimple, a strong-point still held by the Prussian Guard, the ridge was in Canadian hands. It had been taken "on a timetable", as a London newspaper told its readers. When 4th Division took the Pimple the following day, Byng observed ironically,"Poor old Prussian Guard, *what* a mouthful to swallow, being beaten to hell by what they called 'untrained colonial levies'!" General Ludendorff, the German Chief of Staff, had been confident of being able to hold the ridge and was considerably disconcerted. It was a famous victory for Byng's and Currie's common-sense approach to war.

Rufus wrote to Bee the day after the battle and, as it was already all over the papers, could write more frankly. He had spent 9 April at Corps HQ, helping to keep the GOC updated on the progress made. "The show has gone wonderfully well, including the 3rd Army show to the south of us, it is the biggest victory the British army has ever had. It was exciting enough here all day, where we heard everything from all parts of the front. The sight when our barrage opened up at 5:30 was perfectly wonderful. From where I was, you could see everything as the infantry advanced. Of course, we have had fairly heavy losses but nothing to what the Somme cost us. They say our artillery was twice as great as down there. The poor old 16th suffered worse than any battalion in the whole army, I'm afraid — one officer in my company was killed and one wounded. Today [10 April] I have been over to the old German trenches . . . — they must have had an awful time. Most of the fight is knocked out of them for the moment though no doubt they will counter-attack heavily in a day or two. You will understand that we have had night and day work and it still continues . . . I am very tired, darling, so forgive a dull letter."

In fact the barrage on the German trenches during the week before April 9 had been so intense that prisoners described it as the 'week of suffering'. Rufus, once his elation had passed, would discover the meaning of Wellington's lament — "nothing except a battle lost can be half so melancholy as a battle won." In his next letter, written on the 12th, he described the extent of the casualties suffered by the officers of the 16th. "Our losses give one rather a shock . . . Gordon Tupper, Campbell and Bevan (both of my company), McGowan (one of my best friends) and several others, all killed — Rietchel of Victoria also; John Hope and a number of others wounded . . . I suppose the price has to be paid — but it is rather appalling." The final list would also include Cornell, and among the wounded Scroggie, Floyd, S. Johnson, Rietchel, Kirkham, Joe Mason, and D. Clelland. He felt the loss deeply, especially as he had so enjoyed dropping in on them whenever he could, but his comment was surprisingly muted.

In the same letter he expanded upon the condition of the ridge. "The battlefield simply beggars description — it is horrible beyond all words. There is not a square yard which is not a shell-hole. The old German trenches simply do not exist — it is like being at sea — all around you destruction, horror and desolation. To add to it all, it was snowing hard all the while I was out and was intensely cold." In the days after the battle, when the front line had moved to the east side of the ridge, the state of the ground caused real problems. In his war diary he wrote, ". . . the continued rain and lack of roads made transportation extremely difficult. Each day I went up to the neighbourhood of Les Tilleuls crossroads to check up working parties on roads. There were about 4,000 men employed from all units." A few days later he added, "Not only is this weather hindering operations seriously, but it is making awful hardships for both men and horses. It is ghastly to see the place simply littered with dead horses." The mood was rather mixed. For those concentrating on the bigger picture, there was hope that the Germans were on the run. Rufus wrote to Bee on 13 April. "The Boche is retiring as fast as he can go, and we are after him. Surely it cannot go on much longer. It seems such madness for he *must* know he is beaten." But there was also gloom. In the same letter he mentioned that "Today I was up in the line with my old battalion — there are dreadful gaps among the officers and they are all rather in the dumps."

For him and for the survivors of the 16th, newly-learned coping skills would soon temper both emotions. The Germans were not about to fold their tent — as they would soon demonstrate when they repelled a major attack by the Corps on 3 May; and as for their grievous losses, the survivors learned not to grieve too much for there would be many more to mourn — they had a war to win and they had to get on with it. As if to make the point, in the 3 May action, only 1st Division succeeded in taking its objective, Fresnoy, while the other divisions were back where they started; in that battle the 16th lost two more officers — Macintosh and Bobby Powell of Victoria, another of Rufus's friends. He himself seems quickly to have developed the mental toughness to find silver linings.

On 16 April he had "a rather a wonderful day," meeting five men he knew from the Island, or in one case, from the machine-gun course. "Kilpatrick, Brakspear (Bevan's son in law), Bridgman, Clifton, 'Mike' McKenzie — the funny one — rather a lot for one day, wasn't it?" Two days later, he recalled, "I was making my way home across what was the old German line when I met a man and asked him the way somewhere. He stared and I stared — and it was Gladney! You never saw such an object as he was — 3 days beard, etc., and we were both wet to the skin." Later he met Barker, an OKS who was in a heavy battery with Madge, another OKS, and he promised to go and visit them. However, pleasant encounters could not lessen his exhaustion. He described his day: "I left at 6:15 this morning without breakfast, walked 10 miles or more in the rain and had nothing to eat until 3 pm. Tonight I am on-duty in the office and that means no sleep."

By this time he had established his credentials as a staff officer. The report he received on 24 April read "this officer is doing very good work and shows marked ability" and Radcliffe had recommended him for "staff employ." There was discussion about his next step but no decision. He could not yet sport red tabs but did get the occasional perk: on 4 May he was assigned to take Stewart Lyon[55], a Canadian AP correspondent, on a tour of the Somme in the journalist's car. He showed Lyon the battlefield and was then able to check other things off his 'to do' list. They hunted for, and found, the grave of Rupert Howard, a friend from Vancouver days, as well as a cross in memory of "Lieut Howard and NCOs and men of 16 Cdn Scottish who fell 4th and 7th Sept 1916". Rufus arranged to have the grave fenced and looked after and asked Bee to let Mrs Howard know all this. Then they called on Uncle Harry at 9th Division HQ — in a railway cutting east of Blangy. Uncle Harry was pleased to see him, while Rufus found his uncle older, but reasoned that he had a hard time lately (9th Division had done well in the Vimy operation, but to the south).

Possibly because it would be more difficult keeping in touch once he had left Corps, he paid seven social calls to the 16th between May 6 and May 26, doing what he could to help them cope with their dreadful losses. The weather had finally turned hot and he tried to make his rounds up the line in the early morning when it was cooler and, as he impressed upon Bee, also safer. There was plenty of activity in May as the Germans were clearly determined to lose no further ground and counter-attacked, sometimes successfully, whenever they lost trenches to an assault. This all meant little sleep for Rufus who was frequently on night duty.

Occasionally he ran into shelling on his rounds — on 14 May, for example, he made this laconic entry."Breakfast at 10 am with 7th Brigade. Got heavily shelled in Bois de la Chaudière. Lunch at 3rd Division, back at 4 pm." The next day, 15 May, he wangled a day's leave, plus a car from 'Q' branch, to go to Bailleul to find Lyonel's grave. He took a friend with him and they found the grave in the British military cemetery without much difficulty, marked only by a little cross with an aluminum name tag. Rufus ordered a bigger cross, made of wood and painted, from a local carpenter. Then they went to the No.2 Casualty Clearing Station, Rue du Collège, where Lyonel died, but the matron there in June 1916 had left and there was nobody who remembered him. Before driving home, Rufus bought lace for Bee and a lace handkerchief for Joyce, and they dined at the officers' club.

His time at Corps was celebrity-studded. His friend and mentor, Talbot Papineau, was no ordinary Canadian. Grandson of Louis-Joseph Papineau, leader of the Patriotes rebels in 1837 in Quebec, he was strongly tipped to succeed Laurier as leader of Canada's Liberal Party. Prince Arthur of Connaught, referred to as 'P.A.' by Rufus, joined the Corps as an extra staff officer — a genial and inoffensive royal with whom he was soon on friendly terms. He was on comfortable terms with the Corps commander, General Sir Julian Byng, whose temporary ADC he would be in late May, and also with General Currie.

He had also met Field Marshall Sir Douglas Haig on one or two occasions: one day he was busy studying a map in the general staff office when Byng entered with Haig. Rufus's back was to the door and he replied to the visitors' "Good afternoon" without looking round. When he finally did, he scrambled to his feet when he recognized Byng but did not recognize the other officer. "This is one of my learners," Byng told him and before Rufus could collect his wits, the officer was shaking his hand. "My name is Haig," he said, "what is yours?" while Byng's eyes twinkled merrily at his discomfiture.[56] Finally, when Winston Churchill visited Corps on 2 June, it was Rufus who was tagged to take him up the Ridge and 'show him the sights'.

Towards the end of May the GSO1 said to Rufus, "General Radcliffe tells me that it would be a very good arrangement for you to become Corps Staff Captain — how would that appeal to you?" It would mean staying permanently at Corps HQ, replacing Talbot Papineau, who had decided to go back to his regiment. It appealed to Rufus very much, of course, and he said so, reporting to Bee, "So there it stands, but it seems fairly certain that I shall get it — only, in this business, they never do anything without yards of red tape and fiddling about."

It was not to be, however. Instead, on 6 June he heard he would be going to 9th Brigade as Staff Captain 'I'. His captaincy would be gazetted in two or three weeks and until then, he cautioned, nobody was to write to him as 'Captain' — just to be on the safe side.

Financially, too, life was looking up. A captain's pay was $6.25 a day, $187.50 a month. With Bee's separation allowance their total monthly income became $237.50. He was bucked by this and excited about another possibility — that once at 9th Brigade as SC 'I', he would be a candidate for a six-week staff training course at Cambridge — Chalmers had just returned from this and would do what he could to get him accepted. He wrote a bubbling letter to Bee, telling her about a list of warlike bric-à-brac he was sending for safekeeping. This included a German knobkerry[57], a heavy loaded club studded with nails. "I am getting Gould [a metalworker by trade] to engrave the 16th's crest on 2 sides of a shell case and leave the rest just plain," he wrote — adding, with male naïveté: "think what topping vases they will make!" He was also sending her a birthday parcel containing a little brass pan or ashtray, a paper knife, and the two long strips of the Valenciennes lace he had bought in Bailleul.

Meanwhile, on 20 May Rufus had received a disturbing letter from Bee, who was finding Florie unfriendly to say the least. He was furious that this was preventing her and Derek from spending time at Marden. "I perfectly sympathize with you," he insisted, "and I *detest* Florie — for a jealous, poisonous old cat." It was an over-the-top response; no doubt already feeling stressed, he had 'flown up in the air' when he read her tale of woe — as he was wont to do. Later he would moderate his uncompromising attitude, although, in his reply, he asked Bee to plan his approaching leave without a visit to Marden; he wanted her to invite R.E. to stay with them at the Wilton and to invite Roy and Marjorie to lunch, if necessary promising to pay their fares — Roy was still generally unwell and being paid very little in an army desk job.

His diary for May and June 1917 recorded several defeats — seldom mentioned nowadays — suffered by one or another of the four Canadian divisions. Amongst these, on 10 May we hear that "4th Division lost trenches they captured yesterday." And after having taken La Coulotte on the previous night, on 3 June he recorded that "4th Division driven out of all new positions and back to old line."

Rufus was constantly on the go up the line — one day to the 3rd Division front line, the next to 4th Division, usually with Heron or Chalmers as he was technically still a learner. But Prince Arthur was pulling his weight and he was happy that "PA" was also doing his share of night duty — so often his own lot. It may be significant that it was on the 4th Division front that he spent most of his time in May — possibly doing what he could to assist with siting OPs and improving their intelligence gathering on their immediate opposite numbers.

His June 9 diary speaks of the appointment that was to change this indifferent record. It reads: "Sir Julian Byng left for 3rd Army at Albert. Currie came to take command of Corps *temporarily*." Until then the recently knighted Currie had been GOC 1st Division, the Corps' most successful unit, and the brains behind the victory at Vimy. It would be under his command, soon made permanent, that the Corps would earn its great reputation. For the last few days of Byng's tenure Rufus had been 'sort of' acting as his ADC while the genuine article was on leave. They seem to have hit it off because, when Rufus eventually bid him farewell, Byng said, "Goodbye my boy, the best of luck and be sure to come and look me up whenever you get a chance."

Currie he knew better, though it seems only by repute — it would have been hard for any Victoria newspaper reader not to have heard of either of them.[58] They discovered in conversation that both had been corresponding with 'old Dr Campbell' of Victoria — though Currie no longer did so after the old man published one of his letters.

On 14 June Rufus said his own farewells and joined 9th Brigade (3rd Division) at Villers-au-Bois as Staff Captain 'I'. He already knew and liked the GOC, Brigadier-General F.W. Hill, DSO; his staff colleagues were Capt. R.W. Stayner, MC, Brigade Major, and Capt. B.W. Browne, Staff Captain 'Q', once of the 16th, like himself. And he now had a learner of his own, Capt. Creason.

As SC 'I' of a brigade in the front line he was in the action more than he had been at Corps. The first morning he was up at 3 am to go up the line before 'stand-to' with Stayner and Creason. It was the same the following morning and he spent most of the day at OPs — the brigade OP in the morning and battalion OPs in the afternoon. The third day was similar and on his fourth day he and Creason were out very early, locating the left flank of the brigade for an assault that went out at 4 am. We hear no more about that action — presumably a raid — but the brigade was relieved later in the day so the pressure was off for a while. Rufus casually mentions a walk with General Hill in the afternoon to see Colonel Ralston, CO 85th Battalion (later to be King's Minister of Defence), "but the road was being shelled so we came back another way."

A sign, perhaps, of the Corps being under new management was a meeting to discuss operations of the brigade's four battalion CO's the following day — a very civilian and pragmatic approach to improving performance. Rufus took the opportunity of the lull before the next storm to slip away for a night with Uncle Harry at 3rd Army. He says nothing about the older man — who no doubt appreciated his nephew's visit — but for Rufus it was absolutely worthwhile, if only because he slept a whole night between sheets in a bed with springs — and in a château. It may have seemed a little less worthwhile in the morning when the price of such a good night's sleep turned out to be joining the general on a full inspection of the South African Brigade.

Back home at 9th Brigade there were other signs of the new broom: for the upcoming attack on Avion, the brigade "practiced barrages" — advancing slowly behind a simulated one. They practiced the actual attack over taped trenches in the afternoon, which went off well. Next day they did the whole thing again, this time in front of Currie himself. The attack, when it went in a few days later, went like clockwork. Another sign of the new broom was the brigade's light casualties; it implies that they had as many guns supporting them as the generals could scrounge; that the gunners had been able to locate all the German guns thanks to their control of Vimy Ridge; and that they had had a good counter-battery shoot before the first zero-hour. All of this bore the mark of Currie.

Rufus's war diary (with additions from his regular diary) reads:

June 28
"2:30 am – Zero for attack on Avion. 43rd Batallion attacked on left, 58th in centre and 52nd on right. I established Brigade Report Centre with 52nd Battalion HQ in "Piano" dugout under railway in Bois de la Chaudière (T.7.D.9. – Map D). All objectives of first phase gained, with 70 prisoners. Very light casualties.
7:10 pm – Attacked again and pushed our line halfway through village. Spent night at Brigade Report Centre."

June 29
"A few hours rest. All round line at Avion into posts of 43rd. Heavy shelling of Avion trench and railway. Called in at 3 Company HQ in line; took runner from Qu'Appelle, Andrew, with me."

June 30
"Easier day."

The war diary offers an explanatory note about the battle; it was fought over part-rural, part-urban country full of coal mines where "the fighting was made very difficult by the number of villages and mineshafts everywhere. The slag heap at Fosse 4 was the scene of several hard-fought 'scraps'." His diaries and letters contain none of the exclamations of amazement and horror that filled his writing about Vimy Ridge — after eight months in France he had seen it all. In fact, he does not tell us the half of it. For instance, the Staff Captain 'I' had been responsible for taping the practice areas he talks about. Later, during the attack, his task was to keep General Hill constantly informed of the position of, and the problems faced by, each of the three battalions, which he could best do from his Brigade Report Centre. Moreover, as soon as the battalions reached their objectives, he had to be in the front line, re-establishing OPs. And although he spent the night at the Brigade Report Centre, it is unlikely that he slept — there would have been too much going on. Only during daylight hours did he get his "few hours rest". The brigade was relieved on 2 July and Rufus was able to go on leave on the 4th. He had earned it.

It would be a memorable leave as things turned out — including the six-week staff course at Cambridge, he would be away from the trenches for nine whole weeks, though this time the war followed him to Kent: two days after reaching England, he and his family witnessed an air raid in progress from Uncle Jack's garden at Sidcup, when 'Boche' aircraft flew overhead, bound to or from London,[59] And the news from the war was always with them — Ypres, St Julien, and Hill 70 in August, the Russian debacle in early September.

Rufus's leave started at the Wilton Hotel, as before, though Bee let him find his own way and he surprised her eating lunch. Again, she had been busy making arrangements. That evening they went to their first play of the leave, *His Excellency the Governor*, at the New Theatre. Next day, after a lazy morning, they had lunch with Roy at the Troc, then went to Sidcup where Bee had left Derek with Miss Holland. They themselves stayed with Uncle Jack and the following evening, Saturday, having been joined by Roy, Marjorie, and the infant Robin, all took the train to Marden. They found Aunt Lily had preceded them so there was quite a house party, making it easier for Rufus to surf over his feelings about Florie. They spent all of Sunday at the vicarage, Rufus no doubt helping R.E. with the services, and on Monday morning left for Brighton, where Bee had chosen the Old Ship Inn as their new base — a hotel on the seafront with an unobstructed view of the promenade, the beach, and the sea. It was an inspired choice and Boody loved it. This was hardly surprising — this 'deprived' youngster's absentee father had turned up out of the blue and, in five wonderful days, treated him to building sandcastles, going out in a boat, riding a donkey, visiting the pier, relishing the 'oompas' of a brass band, and visiting the aquarium. It beat the heck out of life in suburban Sidcup.

At the end of the week they packed up and went to Cambridge. Rufus was expected to live in Clare College during the course and Bee and Derek had a place provided for them in a university hostel of some sort. This would never do, and by Sunday afternoon they had found the Kenmare, a lodging house at 74 Trumpington Street, a few minutes walk from Clare. Later, they bumped into Kenneth Dickson and his wife. An OKS a year younger than Rufus, Dickson was also on the course. The two couples liked each other and would get together often during their six-week stay; better still, Mrs D seemed happy, as people usually were, occasionally to look after the sociable Derek.

Rufus's hours varied — some days he was involved in a 'scheme' outside Cambridge and returned late. Most days, however, he made time for his family in the afternoons: this meant hitting the books on Sunday mornings to fit in all the things he wanted to do — course work, family outings, croquet or bridge or a movie with Bee, or a few hard games of tennis against men. There were memorable happenings. There was a Sunday picnic in a punt far up the river. It rained hard in the afternoon and they got drenched but nevertheless had a lovely time, and Boody — a four-year-old liability in a punt — really enjoyed himself. There was the hot evening after a game of croquet when Rufus and Bee took out a punt to cool off. All went well until Bee lost the pole in the growing darkness — and we're left to imagine how that ended. There was the afternoon service in King's College chapel, the last before the choir's holidays, to which Rufus took his father and Bee. With summer sun filtering through ancient glass and the soloist's voice soaring to the vault, even ex-chorister Rufus was moved to scribble in his diary: "beautiful singing."

To make up for their foreshortened stay at Marden, R.E. had come to Cambridge for a week and they took a room for him at Kenmare. Rufus usually slept there only on Saturday night but he did so a couple of other nights that week — with or without permission from the powers that be — so that he and his father might enjoy the late-night yarns they loved. They saw a good deal of the Dicksons, sometimes dining with them, once at the Red Lion at Grantchester, at other times playing bridge. One afternoon Kenneth Dickson invited Rufus over to meet John Deighton's sister — which Rufus was glad to do, as John, their OKS contemporary and an army doctor, had been killed at the Somme. Rufus and Bee had few opportunities to sneak off and dine at the Red Lion together — mainly because he had too much to do. And the six-week course was over all too soon after the sort of summer in that lovely old town that neither of them dreamed they would ever spend. "We found Cambridge terribly relaxing," he remembered.

There were ten days of leave remaining before he was due back at 9th Brigade and he was determined to waste not a minute. However, before they could retreat to Brighton they had visits to make. They spent a night at the Wilton, where they left Boody sleeping while they dined at the Troc and went to *Billeted*, "a pleasantly trivial comedy of errors" according to *Punch* but "a very good show" in Rufus's opinion and necessary light relief. The next day they all caught a train to Canterbury to visit Bee's parents, whom they saw that evening and again the following afternoon, though on neither occasion did they stay very long — in the same afternoon they also tried to see Mr Hodgson, Rufus's headmaster, and a Miss Featherstone. Both were away, unfortunately, so they caught an evening train to Marden for an overnight visit before returning to the Old Ship.

In spite of a windy start, Brighton lived up to expectations. During the week they found a new base for Bee and Derek with Mrs Brett Linton at 37 Brunswick Place, Hove, to which she would return once Rufus had gone back. Unsurprisingly, their hotel was booked solid for the weekend of 1 & 2 September — there were no rooms to be had anywhere — so, reluctantly, they returned to the Wilton, spent Saturday afternoon seeing the Canadian Pictures[60], an interesting but grim exhibition, and later consoled themselves at the long-running silly comedy *A Little Bit of Fluff* at the Criterion, which Rufus found "quite amusing but awful rot." Sunday, their last day together, they collected Bee's things from Sidcup, briefly saw Uncle George, dined quietly at the Wilton and walked along the embankment to Chelsea Bridge in the moonlight. Monday morning, 3 September, saw Rufus in uniform and on the boat train to Folkestone. There he found chaos and confusion: mines in the channel, sailings cancelled, an unexpected overnight stay at Marden and a long yarn with his father. Tuesday he was really gone: after a bathe at Boulogne, the last gasp of normality, he caught a ride with a general and was back at the war by nightfall.

He was not best pleased. "Here I am back in this beastly messy country where none of the pens are fit to use!" he wrote petulantly from Boulogne, but the mood lasted only until he reached brigade. Once there, he found himself acting as Brigade Major for the two weeks of Stayner's leave. This called for everything he had learned at Cambridge: as acting BM he was expected to produce plans for the brigade's imminent attack on Mericourt — that, and to see that Creason's work as acting Staff Captain 'I' was well done, including laying out taped practice areas and the establishment of OPs. To compound his difficulties, the brigade was in the line and would not be relieved until 17 September. His diary entries were scanty or overlooked entirely and the two letters he wrote at this time were brief. However, he rose to the challenge: within two days he had put together a 'provisional scheme of operations'. He told Bee on the 13th that, though very busy, he loved the work and actually wished he could stick to this job. He was able to get up the line most days though he was otherwise desk-bound. And he was sleeping better — his friend Browne's batman had borrowed a French cat and dog to destroy the rats' nest under the floorboards of their shared dugout.

During his last week as BM the brigade was out of the line and practiced daily over tapes; and on the last day Rufus fine-tuned and rewrote his operational plan. General Hill was pleased with the result, which he communicated to General Radcliffe. By the 24th Stayner was back as BM and Rufus as SC 'I', responsible for arranging co-operation with the new tank corps and the RFC. He and the new SC 'Q', Leighton — a colleague from Corps HQ who had replaced Browne — spent a day on horseback visiting OPs at the front, during which they survived being "heavily shelled" at a road junction through which they were passing. On another day they attended a tank demonstration. Rufus, always enthusiastic about new ideas, liked the CO of the tank battalion, "which will be with us [in the attack on Mericourt] — at least one Company of them. Good show, most hospitable people — lunch there and they sent us home in a car."

At this time, he told Bee, "I am going up in an aeroplane — not for fun, because that would possibly be risking one's neck unnecessarily — but I'm ordered to go for a certain purpose. I'm rather excited as I've never been 'up' before." A P.S. at the top of the page reads: "I'm back — and quite enjoyed the experience — it was almost like being in a motor car." Understatement notwithstanding, it must have been exciting and a bit frightening: after all, it was only eight years since Blériot crossed the English Channel.

In the first week of October rehearsals for the Mericourt operation became more complicated. Tankers and fliers joined them in exercises over tapes and General Currie himself came to inspect progress. Everything was set to go when, suddenly, Corps put the operation on hold. Rufus must have felt some disappointment after all his effort, but no doubt he shared the general relief — it was all about killing and being killed, after all. There followed a few days of relative relaxation when he had more time to write. He asked Bee to tell Boody that the tin soldier, a Highlander he had pressed on his father when they said goodbye, now stood guard on his bedside table; and he sympathized with her for their separation being harder on her than on himself. His hardship, he wrote, was "nothing to the tense waiting and loneliness you women have"; in spite of danger and fatigue, he had, after all, the companionship of the mess, plus a batman and a groom and horses. It was a perceptive insight for a husband and father of that time. Bee pressed her advantage. In her next letter she hoped he would not be upset to hear that she had been seeing a bit of Charlie Illsley, a friend of his based near Hove and whom they had both seen there in August. Rufus took it in stride: "Of course I don't mind," he insisted. "I should be a pig if I wanted to deny you a little pleasure like that." He seemed more exercised by Derek's misdeeds: "what a little monkey that child of yours is to go and pull the wallpaper off!"

MEANWHILE, GREAT EVENTS IMPENDED and the brief calm was about to be shattered. The British had been battering away at the German front near Ypres since July and by mid-October had been fought to a standstill in a moonscape of mud and water below Passchendaele Ridge — some 90 kms northeast of the Canadians. Rufus's diary had been filled with news of recent British attacks near Ypres, complete with prisoner counts. None had been decisive and finally, on 12 October, their first great attempt to seize Passchendaele Ridge had been thrown back in costly failure. The next day, in spite of Currie's refusal to involve his Corps in these killing fields, and over his continuing protests, Haig ordered the Canadians to relieve the exhausted Anzac and British divisions on the Passchendaele front and to drive the Germans from the ridge above. Currie agreed only when Haig told him that failure to produce a victory could have dire results, maybe even a French collapse.*

The brigade had anticipated the order from the day Mericourt was cancelled. It came on 9 October and Rufus wrote that they would be moving north on the 14th. By the 10th they were already on the move, if only towards the railhead, and Rufus was writing to Bee. "Here we are, trekking about this god-forsaken country in the mud and filth — never dry." Movement of any sort was a staff officer's nightmare, of course, because they had to organize it and he was feeling grumpy. Otherwise his morale was good. The next day, with his chum Leighton, he had made the move in his preferred way — cross-country on horseback. "Ripping day and ride," he wrote, "lunch at Béthonsart — v good." For those who spoke the language and knew where to look, the 'god-forsaken country' had its compensations. He was also asking Bee for books, preferably sixpenny editions as kit had been cut to a minimum. His choice: novels by best-selling author Maud Diver, yarns foreshadowing the future TV series Jewel in the Crown. Said also to be royal favourites, her sentimental page-turners offered front-line readers escape into the myth-world of the Raj.

On 14 October, the 9th Brigade 'entrained' at Tincques at 6 pm. It was cold, there was no heat in the train, and they crawled around northern France to cover the 70 kms to Godewaersvelde where they arrived at 4:30 am — 10½ hours later. The brigade was billeted 5 kms away at Caëstre. The following evening Rufus wrote to Bee. "Such a 36 hours have just passed! I never remember being so 'done in' as I am at the moment. I have been on certain duties — can't tell you more — which kept me up for 24 hours on end. I got a billet at 6 am, to bed at 6.45, promising myself twelve hours rest. But my window looks onto the cobbled main street of this town and in addition to the ordinary traffic, there seemed to be half a dozen Australian bands proceeding by. Anyhow, I got no sleep!"

The following day, 16 October, after a good night's sleep at last, he drove through Steenworde, Abeele, Poperinghe, and the shattered remains of Ypres with General Hill and Stayner. At Poperinghe they studied a model of the front at 2nd Anzac Brigade HQ. Then they went up the line to visit the HQs of 1st and 4th New Zealand Battalions at Banks Farm** and the Capitol respectively. The disastrous first battle for Passchendaele had been fought just four days earlier and the signs were everywhere — the countryside in a terrible state and hundreds of dead were still lying where they had fallen. To make things more

---

* The French army had been weakened by mutinies and was in no condition to resist a German attack; a continued offensive at Passchendaele was therefore necessary to keep them fully occupied.

** Abraham Heights, Hamburg, Banks Farm, the Capitol and all other named locations which are clearly not villages or towns were captured German-built concrete pillboxes. Unfortunately the Germans knew where they were — exactly — though they were strong enough to withstand direct hits from heavy shells.

unpleasant, the Germans, anticipating another attack, were keeping the line under constant shellfire. And it was raining — heavily.

During the next few days Rufus got ever closer to the action. In cooperation with the New Zealanders the brigade would soon relieve, he was locating and setting up OPs and assigning observers, in preparation for the Canadian attack scheduled for 26 October. After three days of this he wrote to Bee on the 19th from Wieltje, Belgium. "My hat — during the last 72 hours I've seen more of modern war and its horrors and hardships than in all the months past. Strangely enough I have been as happy as may be . . . for I have been extremely busy. Where I am now, the battlefield simply beggars description — the Somme isn't in it with this. The area is simply miles upon miles of shell-torn swamp — hundreds of dead still out — while the gunfire beats to bits anything heretofore missed! Incidentally, Gothas seem plentiful — yesterday we had a fleet of 18 — with any number of smaller planes — over our camp. I am up here with my Brigade Intelligence section — and the 8th Brigade SC 'I' is here too — Capt Younger, a brave, cheery chap. I also have scout sections [observers] from all our battalions. Last night we were in a tent but it was too 'unhealthy' so now we are in a sort of shelter in an old trench. Gould and Younger's batman have made it quite cozy. I am very well, in spite of wet feet and clothes and lack of sleep. The din is so terrific most nights that one can't sleep much."

He made it sound quite bearable, what with his 'cozy' shelter and the Gothas as picturesque background, but the reality was harsher, as his diary records.

> *Oct 18*
> *Moved up to near Wieltje crossroads. Got tents for observers. Met them and got camp fixed up. Boche bombed and shelled camp during day slightly. Back about 6 pm. Very noisy night and cold in tent.*
>
> *Oct 19*
> *Very hard at it each day up forward – locating OPs etc. Up line with Major McAvity to ABRAHAM Heights and then with Cooper and Barr to HAMBURG OP – an awful trip. General Hill, Stayner, Col. Grant, and Col. Genet up, also Gen. Elmsley. Got OPs approx located – a good day. We moved into bivvies in an old trench.**

On subsequent days preparations for the great battle continued and, as no letters survive for the next ten days, our only source is his diary. The 8th and 9th Brigades' OPs were operational before the brigades themselves had taken over the line which sounds unusual — 9th Brigade only moved into the line to relieve 4th New Zealand Brigade on the 22nd. Nevertheless Rufus records:

* Which means they crammed their tents into the trench — marginally less perilous but still not underground.

Oct 20
Went up to Abraham Heights OP about 12:45 pm – heavy shelling near OP. One of 8th Brigade observers badly wounded. Wrote Dad. Gothas dropped any number of bombs between 7:30 and 10 pm.

Oct 21
*Destructive shoots began by our heavies [artillery]. Observing shoots from now on. Up with Wallis to Hamburg, Waterloo, Abraham Heights. Back at about 4:30 pm. Heavy shelling all day. Parties sent up at night to Hamburg and Abraham Heights to construct OPs – wiring parties up to wire them. Brigade HQ moved to X Camp outside Ypres. Gothas over while I was there and got a lot of the 43rd Battalion men close by. V busy day. Whole party sent to Hamburg – except one – wiped out last night – Walker, my runner, badly wounded.** *

From then until the night of the 26th Rufus would sleep where he could.

Oct 22
5th Army 'show' to north at 5:25 am [planned as a diversion]. Great bombardment. Moved up to Banks Farm at night. Conference of COs at 7 pm. V crowded – slept on the table. Rained hard at night. Relieved 4th New Zealand Brigade.

Oct 23
Brigade HQ moved up to the Capitol – I went forward to Abraham Hts in the afternoon. Quarters in pillbox – very crowded but better than Banks.

Oct 24
Up line in am to KOREK etc. Liaison with Heavies [artillery] not very satisfactory. Capitol pretty heavily strafed in the afternoon [possibly 'friendly fire']. Fleet of 17 Gothas and many scouts over bombing about noon – wonderful sight. 12 or more [bombs] dropped close here. Divisional commander and Gen Radcliffe up at noon. One of our planes crashed near Korek about 11 am – pilot killed. Mix-up over working party for machine-guns, etc.

Oct 25
Up to Waterloo [his Brigade Report Centre] in morning to get decision on state of enemy wire [on whether wire had been sufficiently cut by shellfire]. Lot of short shooting [by Canadian artillery] into Marsh Bottom – shoot stopped. Much confusion all round with Division.

---

* He died the next day.

Smithe – scout officer of 58th – when laying tapes on far side of Ravebeeke, got 5 prisoners of 3rd Bavarian Infantry Regiment who were advanced party of relief and were lost. [He had no alternative but to take them on with his revolver – had they escaped they would have reported the location of the 58th battalion start line for the next day. He got an MC for this.]"

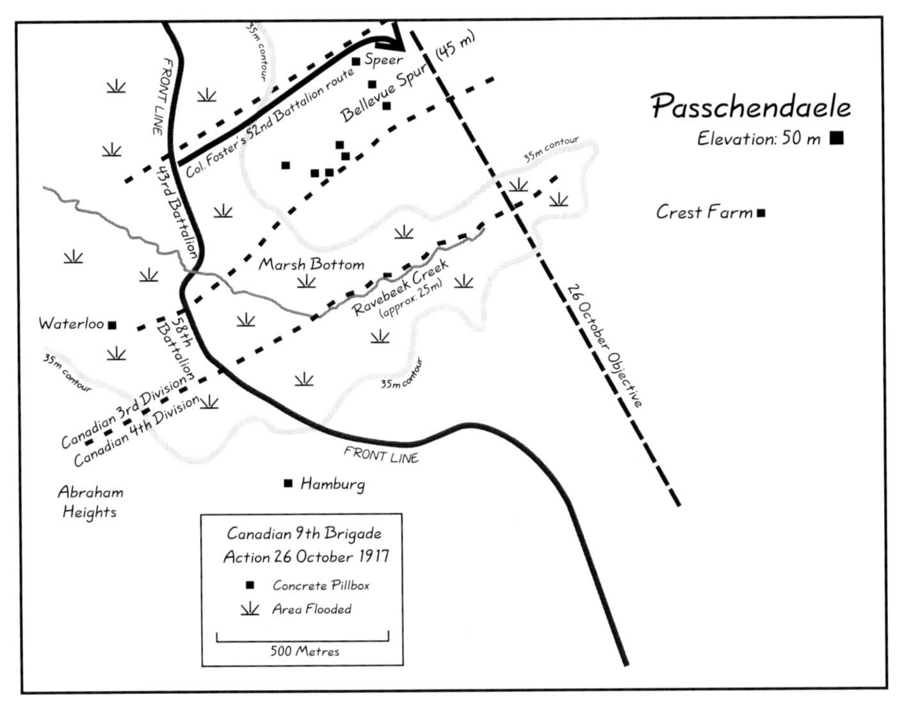

PASSCHENDAELE, 9TH BRIGADE ACTION, 26 OCTOBER, 1917

Everything so far had been preliminary to the Second Battle of Passchendaele which would open on the morning of the 26th. Of its four stages the most important was the first and it would be a "near run thing", as he described in his *War Book*: "To the 9th Brigade fell the task of capturing the key to Passchendaele Ridge, the Bellevue Spur. This is a steep knoll with very heavy wire defences, crowned with a number of concrete pillboxes. It was commanded also from the south by the Hun positions at Crest Farm and was strongly held by Bavarian troops. In the initial stages of the 9th Brigade attack it looked for a time as though we were in for a bad reverse. The two attacking battalions, the 43rd on the left and the 58th on the right, were severely checked half an hour after Zero. Lieutenant R. Shankland of the 43rd (later awarded the VC) and 20 men of the 43rd hung on to the crest of the spur and undoubtedly saved the situation. Lt. Col. W.W. Foster[61] of the 52nd battalion, which was in support, arrived about 10 am with 2 companies of his battalion. With great skill and daring (he was awarded the DSO) he led his men round to the north of the spur and eventually captured it with the six pillboxes and 150 prisoners. I was finally sent up to Bellevue in the afternoon to reconnoitre our line and went round the posts with Captain T. O'Kelly of the 52nd who was given the VC later for his work . . . I reconnoitred his new line and sent back a rough map. The runner was killed in sight of me and the sketch lost."

Rufus's diary describes how these events unfolded for him that day.

> *Oct 26*
> *Up to Waterloo with Methot [his French-Canadian runner]) at 2:30 am. Zero at 5:40 am. All OK till 6:15 am. Then 43rd Battalion on the left and 58th Battalion on the right retired over Bellevue spur. Very black until about 11:30 am when Col Foster of 52nd Battalion arrived. 1 Company of 52nd Battalion then moved round to the left behind Speer and cleaned things up with 150 prisoners. Col Foster – and Shankland of 43rd Battalion who hung onto Speer – saved what looked like a disaster. Waterloo [where he spent most of the day] had 5 direct hits, very heavy shelling and 43rd and 58th Battalions were badly cut up. BM [Stayner] came up about 3:30 pm. I went up to Bellevue with Methot at 3:30 and reconnoitred. Home [to Brigade HQ, Camp X] with BM by about 7:00 – all in. Brigade OP shelled – Barr wounded (VC subsequently).*

Lieutenant Robert Shankland was the hero of the day. His platoon, originally of 40 men, captured and held Speer, a concrete pillbox at the top of the spur (Rufus's map shows eight pillboxes within the battalion's boundaries) and the area around it. When 43rd Battalion was driven back by machine-gun fire from the flank, Shankland hung on to Speer and was joined by stragglers from other units. After driving off counter-attacks, in which his platoon suffered many casualties, Shankland temporarily handed over command, went back to 43rd Battalion HQ with a plan for an attack to take the spur, and then returned to his platoon. The subsequent attack was led by Colonel Foster, as described above. By mid-afternoon 9th Brigade seemed sufficiently established on Bellevue Spur for Rufus to be sent up there to see for himself and record the precise location of the new front line held by the brigade, and to report back. As 4th Division, meanwhile, had also reached its objectives, stage one of Currie's plan had been accomplished.

The real horror of the situation inside Waterloo on the 26th was described by Rufus in his letter to Bee the following day. "We have been taking part in this terrific fighting in front of Passchendaele. I think that now, if it ever becomes necessary to put it to the test(!), hell's torments can have no new terrors for me. My job, of course, necessitates me being mixed up in the mess when there is anything on and I can tell you that I have never experienced anything in my life so ghastly as these last 48 hours. You know well enough that I am no hero, but I had to steel myself to it. Late in the day [at 3:30 pm in his diary] — after we had

had 10 hours of the severest fighting, I got the message to which I am becoming used and which always begins: "the GOC directs that a staff officer be sent up to reconnoitre, etc." So out I went. Well, probably no-one has seen more heavy shelling than there was on that afternoon. I knew where I had to go so I got my good brave French-Canadian runner (the other one, Walker, had both legs broken last week) and said: "Come on, Methot!" and away we went. I can confess to you . . . that I gritted my teeth and thought of nothing but my two darlings waiting for me at home. As we went, and shells and death and frightful crashes were all round us, with mud up to our knees, I prayed a hundred times for courage and wisdom to carry on. We were out in that hell for an hour and a half and I never expected to get back alive. My Brigade report centre was in a pillbox [Waterloo Farm] in which also were two Battalion HQs and the advanced dressing station. It was simply jammed all day and night and all the time the wounded — horribly mutilated — were coming in. My telephone wires to Brigade were broken a dozen times and I had to rely on pigeons and runners to get word back. It is all a horrible nightmare . . . I am on night duty tonight — it is 3:20 am and I am so tired — Gould is just making hot tea outside!"

In his *War Book* Rufus gave a 'de-pigeoned' postscript to the situation inside Waterloo. "When things looked blackest our "buzzer" [ground wire] was smashed by shellfire and the signal man killed. Four runners whom I sent back with reports were killed and we were entirely cut off from brigade HQ for hours." In retrospect, 26 October 1917 was, without a doubt, Rufus's worst day of the war — certainly the one when he was the longest in mortal danger.

In the next few days things became calmer for him personally. He sent Creason, his learner, up the line the morning after the battle while he slept until 9:00 — the boot was on *his* foot at last. He spent the day writing up the narrative of operations, more or less alone at Brigade HQ, while everybody else was up the line. The trade-off was that he had to take the night shift at Waterloo — a long one, during which he was able to write to Bee, snatch just one hour's sleep at 8:30 am on the 28th and was not relieved until 3:30 pm the next day. He and Creason were "heavily shelled" as they left the line but he slept well that night at Wieltje and the 29th was an easy day, the brigade having been replaced in the line by 7th Brigade. 9th Brigade had taken a tremendous hammering on the 26th and General Hill visited each battalion during their ten-day rest period to congratulate the men on their courage and performance. Rufus realized that, although, as Staff Captain 'I', he had been less in harm's way than a battalion officer of his rank, he was nevertheless just as lucky to be alive and in one piece. It followed, if he wanted to spare his father the loss of a second son, that he would be wise to request a transfer to 'Q' branch. And, as with most big decisions in his life, he did something about it at the first opportunity.

When 3rd Division crossed the start line for stage two of Currie's plan, at 5:30 am on 30 October, 9th Brigade was not with them. Rufus noted in his diary that the operation did not go well, though most of the objectives were reached and the predictable counter-attacks successfully beaten off. His view was coloured, perhaps, by personal loss. As he wrote to Bee, "rotten news last night — Papineau was killed in the attack on Oct 30th. I really feel it a lot — you remember he was at Corps for months with me. Then he went back to his battalion, the PPCLI[62], partly, no doubt, his own fault and partly at his own wish. He was devoted to his mother — a widow whose only child he was — she lived next-door to Aunt Lily in Queen's Gate. Poor old Pap was so full of life and what a career in politics he was going to make after the war. Three whole years, nearly, he had been out here and was the first Canadian to win the MC. Another thing — my personal runner, Walker — you will remember he was badly wounded on Oct 25th — has died of wounds. Such a fine, brave fellow. My own runner now — one Methot — is recommended for the M.M. and I jolly well hope he gets it. Sometimes I wonder how long human endurance can stand this strain. It is a marvel to me, many times a day when in the line, that the men don't simply refuse to carry on — it is all so horrible."

On 5 November Rufus tried to catch General Farmar (Radcliffe's replacement) at Corps to request a transfer to 'Q'. Farmar was out so instead, he had a long session about it with General Hill, his GOC, which must have been hard for him. The next day, 6 November, his diary makes no mention of the successful conclusion of Currie's stage three. That day, 1st and 2nd Divisions captured 90% of Passchendaele Ridge, a job that 1st Division would complete on the 10th. After that, they rested. 9th Brigade was headed back into the line, apparently attached temporarily to 1st Division. His diary recorded the events of the next four days.

Nov 11
"Up the line – 7th Battalion HQ at Mosselmarkt – a perfect shambles. 10th & 5th Battalions' & South Wales Borderers' (SWB) HQs all in Meetcheele pillbox. Met Col Ormond (Dangerous Dan)[63] of 10th for first time at Meetcheele. You could only crouch in his filthy pillbox and on the floor was a dead, disemboweled man of the SWB whom it had been impossible to move. 8th Battalion HQ in Bellevue. Heavy shelling on road all day. In to Waterloo on the way back, but Brigade is to go to the Capitol again so I went there. On night duty. Handled guides at Waterloo and got back to HQ about 10:30 pm. Winslow from 2nd Brigade with me – saw Herridge."

Nov 12
"Nothing exciting happened. Heavy artillery fire all day."

Nov 13
"Creason up line in am. Boche attempted a counterattack at 4:35 pm and failed. Terrific shelling all day long. I was sent up to Meetcheele at 6:15 pm – rough trip – got back to brigade at 11:15 pm."

Nov 14
"Relief at night by 7th Brigade. I handed over to Le Sneur at 3:15 pm and walked out with Jacobi. Got shelled at Wieltje corner – some pretty close ones. Stayed night at brigade transport lines – quite tired out. Tremendous shelling of Gravenstafel road all day."

He was not too tired out to write to Bee, however. "By Jove we've had a strenuous trip this time. The funny old Boche thought he'd like to retake Passchendaele yesterday afternoon [the 13th], so he made a counter-attack at dusk. He did no business at all and must have lost very heavily. All day long he plastered us with heavies and everything else and put over gas about 4 pm. At 6 pm things looked a bit obscure so, of course, I was sent up to clear up the situation. It was black as ink and you can't use your flashlight up forward. So I staggered along with my runners — falling into shell-holes full of water every few minutes — blinded now and then with the flash of the guns. As we were going up the last spur, they put down a barrage on the road again and things looked and felt a bit "jumpy" for a time. But we got there OK. We got back at 11:30 — but the BM said my report was valuable. So it was worth it . . . Tell Sonny his bagpiper is still going strong and has seen some stirring times."

His letter reflects the confidence the Canadians now had in their dealings with the Germans. It sounds as if they never doubted the outcome of the counter-attack and the reason was plain: Currie took the time — sometimes a week — to concentrate artillery and stockpile ammunition before contemplating an attack — hence the four stages in his capture of Passchendaele Ridge. The huge firepower protected his attackers and was a devastating answer to counter-attacks — all possible routes for which had already been ranged in. The battle they had just fought, curiously, had presented the Germans with all the artillery advantages: it was a given that the Canadians would use the pillboxes for their headquarters; and the coordinates of pillboxes, trenches, and roads in an area they had recently controlled were accurately known to German gunners, yet they allowed the Canadians to move at will and themselves to be outgunned.

With 9th Brigade still based in Brandhoek, Belgium, on 15 November Rufus had ridden into Poperinghe with a friend where they had had lunch and done some shopping before returning to brigade about 4:30 pm. "Got strafed on return to brigade" he noted in his diary — which may mean by German shellfire but was more likely by an unhappy BM. Possibly as a direct result he found himself in charge of loading the entire brigade onto buses the following day — something he had not organized himself and which was a nightmare of confusion: ". . . imagine 100 buses, jammed full of men, all going to different places, on a pitch dark night on a road you have never seen before! It was some picnic!"

The buses eventually took them 100 kms southwest into France, ending up in billets in a group of villages west of Béthune. From the sound of his letter to Bee on 17 November it was all worth it. "Tonight, I have the queerest — and one of the most comfy — billets I have ever been in. It is a Home for Indigent and Diseased Old Men and Women . . . , run by three funny old Sisters of Mercy. They cannot do enough for us — I have a large room with a stove . . . & Gould a tiny room next door. He, of course, expected to sleep on the floor but they have put a mattress on the floor because it was *trop dure*!" The Sisters brought Rufus breakfast in bed on the 18th and again on the 19th — a fellow could get used to it!

Both days he had long rides through peaceful countryside: the first day with Kinnelly, his groom — they had lunch together in Lillers; and the next day round the battalions billeted in various villages with Leighton, before going to lunch [in a "good château"] with the heroic Col. Foster of the 52nd with whom he had recently played bridge a couple of times. It was all very pleasant. The brigade stayed put for the rest of the month and the only serious activity was a mysterious training scheme for which he was responsible. Officers, and presumably men, were going on leave — he himself had a leave warrant in his pocket for early December. His horse Nell was shod and misbehaved herself, giving him a bit of trouble, and the weather remained late-November-ish but never particularly cold.

He wrote to Bee on the 28th. The previous night, he reported, he had experienced his worst-ever bout of diarrhea, the third in a fortnight, though between bouts he was fit and well. And he had sad news: Jimmy Hewitt, late Sporting Editor of the *Province*, had been killed — and Rufus realized he had chatted with him on the day it had happened. Also McIntyre, a predecessor as News Editor of the *Colonist* and later deputy minister of fisheries — and he had also talked to him recently, in Ypres. "One gets rather oppressed with these continual losses — to talk to a man you know well one minute, and then to hear he is dead the next, is always a bit of a shock." He ended on a cheerful note. "The bagpiper is so excited about seeing Derek that he simply won't stop playing. He has no end of things to tell Derek for he has been in my pocket through all the hard and dangerous times."

His career as Staff Captain 'I' would soon reach a tidy conclusion. On 2 December he was ordered to report to 2nd Brigade as Staff Captain 'Q', which he did at 4:30 pm the following day. However, as another officer was temporarily covering SC 'Q' duties, by 9:30 pm he had permission to go on leave himself. His career as Staff Captain 'Q' would have to wait a while; in the meantime he had other fish to fry.

Chapter 10
Staff Captain 'Q'
France, 1918

"Upon my word, this man would drive a saint to drink. I will go on as long as I can — but soon something will crack — I shall either go to hospital or get fired!"

Rufus to Bee about General Loomis, 16 April 1918

On the way home Rufus spent a day cooling his heels in Boulogne and Bee finally met him at Victoria on 5 December. This leave would follow their established pattern: dinner at the Troc, a show — *Maid of the Mountains* at Daly's — and a night at the Wilton. They spent a couple of days with R.E. and Florie at Marden, a night in Canterbury to see Bee's mum and dad, and then went to Hove. There Rufus finally caught up with Boody — in bed with a cold and being looked after by Bee's landlady. They spent eight days in Hove, finding plenty to do even though it was winter, and returned to the Wilton for the last three — including a 24-hour extension to sort out a dental problem.

In Brighton, Rufus took Boody to the pier on the few warm days. They all walked on the front, spread their patronage around the tea shops, restaurants and watering holes while taking in everything the local theatres had to offer — *The Three Daughters of Monsieur Dupont* at the Theatre Royal, the anti-war American movie *Civilization*, and whatever romps were playing at the Hippodrome and the Palladium. Back in London, they took Joyce, who stayed a night with them, to J.M. Barrie's *Dear Brutus*, which Rufus liked. They went without Derek to *Arlette*, a French 'operette' which Rufus thought poor; and on his last afternoon they made their second visit to *Chu Chin Chow* — which Boody loved. The war intruded once: there was an air raid while they were dining at the Wilton before taking Joyce to the theatre. There was general consternation, but nothing worse, when the nosecone of an anti-aircraft shell came through the kitchen roof. The 'old soldier' of the party was a bit put out when they then had trouble getting to the theatre on account of a mere air-raid!

Back in France, after the customary cobbled-together journey, Rufus found himself among heroes once again: of the staff at 2nd Brigade HQ, consisting of Brig Gen F.O.W. Loomis (GOC but on leave in Canada), Lt Col W.M. Prower (acting GOC), Major J.P. McKenzie, (BM), and Major S.S. Burnham (SC 'I') — every one of them had a DSO. Only the Orderly Officer, Capt D. Ives, and Rufus's learner, Capt R.H. Winslow, were undecorated. As the front was quiet, many officers were on leave, or about to go, allowing him to get the hang of his new job relatively undisturbed. His references to it for the rest of December are confined to grumbles about late battalion ration states. But he was responsible for much more than that — everything that was consumed, in fact, from ammunition to fuel, to picks and shovels, to barbed wire and corrugated iron for the trenches, to trains for men going on leave, to the vehicles in the transport lines, to finding and allocating billets whenever the brigade moved, to the provision of clean clothes and baths — even the organization of seasonal athletic competitions. It required enormous attention to detail and a tidy mind to do it well and newspaper editing was probably no bad apprenticeship. Rufus admitted to being nervous starting a new job, so it helped that nothing much was going on. He did not yet know it, but he would have to work harder, go longer without sleep on a regular basis, and be under greater personal pressure as Staff Captain 'Q' than he had ever been as Staff Captain 'I'. And when his biggest test came in August 1918, when the Corps was advancing miles every day, he would be as much in danger as he had ever been at the battle for Bellevue Spur. It would be no soft option.

When he arrived, the brigade was billeted in villages near Bruay-la-Buissière, northwest of Arras. In early January the order came to move in a week's time to Château de la Haie outside Carency, 16 kms SE, and it was his job to get them there. He spent a day visiting his opposite number in the brigade they were replacing — not much fun, as he told Bee. "I had an uncommonly cold trip in a ramshackle old sidecar on roads which were like glass all the way. I was perished with cold when I got back."

Next morning he ordered a bus to take himself and a few officers per battalion to look over the available billets. After that, it was just a matter of calling the Corps Light Railway Officer, who ran the Corps' own railway, to arrange train transport for 5,000 men and it was done. On 7 January he was "up at 6:30 am and to Barlin to entrain the whole brigade. Went very well and all battalions got away on time and satisfied. Came on last train and reached Château de la Haie about 1 pm. Very busy in afternoon — round to battalions arranging baths and fuel."

Things seldom run that smoothly — probably beginner's luck, but it impressed General Embury who had replaced Prower on 1 January and would be GOC until Loomis got back. A Regina barrister, Embury had been to both Victoria and Duncan — they discovered mutual friends and Rufus expected to like him.

The brigade went into the line on 21 January and spent the rest of the month near Hill 70, rotating battalions in and out of the line. In preparation, the brigade had moved closer to the action and Rufus had toured the cluster of villages near Bully-les-Mines to find billets for the four battalions and the other components. Once again he travelled by sidecar although it was a "very bad day, heavy rain" and he "got soaked through." When the brigade was in the line, even rear areas were in range of German guns and were regularly visited by harassing fire. It was ignored but casualties happened — on 24 January Rufus recorded, "Archer, adjutant of the 8th Battalion, killed this afternoon by a Minnie shortly after leaving my office."

Otherwise, coal and baths were his main preoccupation for the month. Battalion quartermasters collected daily coal allowances from the brigade 'dump', but when a sudden cold snap hit on 9 January, Rufus found the cupboard almost bare. His diary read, "out all day rustling fuel" but pickings were slim, apparently, because the battalion coal allowance that day was a bone-chilling 10 bags. In the morning he rushed over to Corps, where he knew the 'Q' department from learner days, to demand more. Not surprisingly he got results: without comment he noted in the diary — "each battalion 40 bags of coal," and he remained a good provider until the weather improved.

Baths were not so simple. 1917 French farms boasted neither baths nor serious drains so an SC 'Q' had to provide temporary bathhouses with rows of portable tubs filled by hosepipe from a mobile water-heating vehicle and drained by more hose pipes into ditches or creeks. Battalions were allocated days at these bathhouses, through which the men paraded to wash off the squalor of the trenches. Rufus recorded their days in his diary, one suspects as a 'reminder to self'. Thus on 2 February his entry read: "5th Battalion bathing at Le Brebis; 8th Battalion bathing at Heudin; 10th Battalion bathing at Sains-en-Gobelle," and the next day, "Trench Mortar Battery, brigade HQ bathing at Le Brebis." Of all the brigade's officers, it was serendipitous that it should be Rufus, with his Saskatchewan experience in both delivering coal and supplying baths, whose duty it now became!

By the beginning of February he was back in the saddle. His 2 February diary entry reads: "Out riding most of the day — to 7th and 10th at Fosse 10, to 8th and Div'n at Brocquement, thence to 5th and 8th transport lines at Fosse 2." — probably 20–30 kms. In fact, he did so much riding that he must have become quite competent — in the April staff photograph, he is the only one wearing breeches and a cutaway jacket. Nevertheless, he continued to relate minor horsey mishaps, such as when a frisky animal he was riding reared up at the roar of a passing motorcycle. He handled the rearing up all right but, as the horse came down, a low telephone wire snagged him under the chin and dragged him out of the saddle. He was lucky not to be decapitated but complained only of a swollen throat for a couple of days.

Although 'Q' work became routine and therefore to some extent tedious, he remained engaged by it. One reason was his tendency to perfectionism; another was the opportunity to run into friends from being constantly on the move. Many a day he either chanced upon someone he knew or went out of his way to look one up. He enjoyed hearing the news from Duncan or Victoria and would pass on what he learned to Bee. As an example, in February 1918 there were eight such encounters, including Colonel Foster of the 52nd, Hart of the 16th, Col O'Gilvie & 'Old Major Critchley' (both from Victoria), Barclay of the 88th, Skinner of the 16th, Leighton (from 9th Brigade staff) and Prince Arthur. Comrades from the 88th or 16th always had a special place in his friendships.

The brigade remained in quiet sections of the line throughout February and towards the end was livening things up by raiding the enemy. This added to his work as he was responsible for providing raiding equipment — ladders, flares, and Lewis-gun slings,* the last of which would cause him trouble. From the beginning of March he was also involved in making the physical arrangements for courts martial — one of which resulted in a man being shot, a most disturbing event. The officer in charge had trouble with the firing squad, no doubt because such draconian discipline did not sit well with Canada's volunteer soldiers.

He was convinced the war would soon be over and predicted to Bee on 8 March — accurately as it turned out — that peace negotiations would be under way within eight months. Accordingly, he was already thinking about peacetime jobs. A friend, Roberts, had arranged a post-war job with Lord Beaverbrook, the Canadian who owned the English *Daily Express* among other newspapers. He knew Beaverbrook well and thought he could arrange an interview for Rufus too. He was asking Bee's approval because it would mean working in England, possibly the last thing she would want him to do. If she approved of his idea, characteristically he would want the interview during his upcoming leave. Another friend, Griffiths, had been pulling his leg, calling him "the luckiest man in France". In his opinion, "I seem only to decide I want a certain job and I get it. Well, I want a job with Beaverbrook — and I mean to land one," leaving her in no doubt as to how he hoped she would answer.

Two unrelated events brought this quite pleasant part of his SC 'Q' career to an end. The first was the return of General Loomis on 16 March. Rufus was scheduled for his own leave beginning late on the 17th and his diary entry for that day neatly summarized the impending change in his work environment. "Up line from 10 am to 6 pm. First session with General Loomis — very tedious!" He left brigade at 6:30 pm, and spent the night at the officers' club where Embury came down to say goodbye. The following day he left for England and, eventually, Brighton. He was there on 21 March when the second event occurred: as he wrote in his diary, "Huns attacked on 50 mile front Arras to Cambrai." Life for 2nd Brigade's SC 'Q' would never be the same.

In the meantime, however, he had a precious leave to enjoy. He met Bee at the Wilton after a night with his father at Marden. They went to *The Boy* at the Adelphi — a lighthearted musical featuring a new phenomenon, the 'flapper' — which they greatly enjoyed. Then off to Brighton next afternoon, where

* An early light machine-gun, so heavy that an advancing soldier needed a sling to take its weight.

Derek, with babysitter Maria, met his father on the platform. The Germans were rolling over Gough's 5th Army at that very moment but, when he heard of it, Rufus refused to let it spoil his leave. He had long been convinced that allied victory was the only possible outcome of the present insanity, which the Kaiser's offensive, he suspected, would at worst just delay. So they did all the things it was possible to do in a foggy seaside town in March — including twice taking Boody to hear the band on the pier. He had graduated to being taken to 'the pictures' and to a show at the Grand Theatre and was also big enough for walks on the front. But most seaside delights were out of season and, when his parents were 'seeking for further amusement' for him, he was happy to be farmed out to Maria or Mrs Wellman — even going willingly to church without protest. Bee had lived at #3 Holland Road, Hove, since before Christmas and had a number of friends for Rufus to meet. Otherwise they just lazed the days away, played Halma, downed the newly fashionable 'cocktails' before lunch — or before dining at the Old Ship, took in the slim offerings of off-season Brighton theatres and enjoyed the comfort Bee had created in her rented snuggery.

When the anticipated telegram arrived, at 12:30 pm on 27 March, it just said: "REJOIN". Rufus was in no hurry to do so; he anticipated chaos at the ports and spent the rest of the day with Bee and Boody, not setting off for London until late the following morning. He lunched with Uncle Harry (on leave himself) and Aunt Lily before catching an afternoon train to Folkestone.[64] He knew there were tough times ahead and wrote to Bee the next day from 2nd Brigade, having arrived at 3:15 am and slept for two hours in a chair. "So much to be done that I had to get up," he told her. In his War Diary he later wrote, "While I was away 1st Division was continually on the move between Hill 70 and Pas en Artois and back again. They marched 37 miles in one 24 hours but did no actual fighting. We are the flying counter-attack division of the army and are GHQ troops for the moment."

The first week in April was one of continuous to-ing and fro-ing by the brigade, culminating on the 7th when Rufus made this despairing entry: "A day of endless confusion. Orders cancelled and recancelled." The following day he managed to write about it to Bee. "Yesterday I had orders: "you will move rear brigade HQ and all transport, details, etc. to Hautes Avesnes,* to be clear of Berneville by 4 pm." I did not know where Hautes Avesnes was but found it on a map, got on my horse and proceeded to look round. It was 15 miles away. The move was over by 12:30. We marched — that is, I rode — in a blinding hail storm. Today I was up at 5:30 and got a lift on an ambulance — hell was too played out to take me after the double trip of 15 miles each way yesterday, Hautes Avesnes to Berneville. I went round the line and saw all my dumps, had an hour's business with the General and walked home — 7 miles. I need not tell you that I am 'all in' tonight. But I am happy because everything went OK and the GOC seemed pleased with the arrangements for once in a way."

* The underlined names were left blank in his actual letter for censorship reasons.

This was his first indication that Loomis was difficult to work for, although he had evidently been having difficulties since he got back. These continued through the following week and soon reached a crisis — at least, in his own mind. On 10 April he noted in his diary: "GOC had bad liver or something today — and I am, consequently, fed up." But this was nothing compared to what happened on the 16th, when he recorded, "GOC very difficult — got an hour's strafing about petty details in front of the Sergeant Major and Sergeant Hogben. Very fed up in consequence."

In a letter to Bee it sounded even worse, and he exclaimed, "Upon my word, this man would drive a saint to drink. I will go on as long as I can — but soon something will crack — I shall either go to hospital or get fired!" When he felt calmer, he pursued less drastic options. On the 18th he ran into General Farmar, Assistant Quartermaster General at Corps, whom he knew and liked and who handled appointments. After describing the problem, he asked for a transfer. Surprisingly — this was an army at war, after all — Farmar had been most understanding, said that he knew Loomis was hard to deal with and had agreed to arrange a transfer for him. Rufus felt encouraged — without waiting for Farmar's move, he asked Loomis for permission to apply to be sent on loan to the Imperials. Loomis was "not interested," period, but was willing to recommend him for transfer to Division HQ staff. Which left Rufus wondering whether Loomis might not think him useless after all, but just wanted to get rid of him! Taking no chances, on 22 April he grasped at another straw and, in response to an appeal, sent in his name to be considered for attachment to the French.

Rufus never summarized the problem but two things stand out: Loomis was an inconsiderate bully, prone to making unreasonable demands on his staff while indulging in rude and humiliating outbursts against them; and he was a micro-manager who interfered in the detail of his staff's work, then often changed his mind, thus doubling their extra work. An example of the latter occurred on 8 May. Rufus had billeted the Trench Mortar Battalion at Denier and Loomis had ordered them moved to Rullecourt. After Rufus had spent much of the day carrying this out, Loomis then cancelled the change at night. They were out of the line and there was no military justification — but Rufus could not argue with orders.

Nevertheless, although he suffered further annoyances at the GOC's hands, from this time things began to improve. The same day as the billeting fiasco, he had circulated a summary of his arrangements for games and amusements while the brigade was out of the line, including a schedule of baseball and football games between the four battalions over four days, plus five days of movies and band concerts. Perhaps to his own surprise, he noted, "this made quite a hit with the GOC." He sent a copy of the amusement programme to Bee, explaining that it was just one part of his job and had taken a huge amount of work when he had ten thousand other things to attend to. But he had found it very rewarding to see the pleasure that the programme gave. He added:

"I simply love my work — of course, it never ends. I am up at 7:00, not done till 11 pm. Today at 4:20 I had a meeting of battalion quartermasters. It was over about 6 pm. Then I had to rush to a tiny hamlet about 5 miles off to arrange about baths and clean clothing for all the men."

It may have been his enthusiasm that the general sensed and, if so, it did the trick. On 21 May he confessed, "Everything is going much more smoothly the last few weeks and the GOC seems to approve more of me. Major McMillan, DSO — my 'Q' learner — is a great comfort. He is 44 and such a dear — you would love him. He never gets flurried, is always the same courteous, sympathetic old chap. Just the man I need with my fly-up-in-the-air temperament." Sandy McMillan had arrived in the middle of April. Although fourteen years older, he and Rufus became fast friends — one of the few men, of the thousands he knew, to whom he referred routinely by his first name. Sandy seems to have been a calm type and no doubt Rufus was right about his influence on him.

Loomis is recognized by military historians to have been one of Canada's most creative First World War generals. He was "known for his mercurial temper, stern character, and hard-driving but competent generalship," a man "who never publicly removed his 'mask of command' during or after the war."[65] It was Rufus's misfortune to have to work for him and it may have been significant to their relationship that both had red hair and a fiery temper.[66] Reading between the lines, either in December 1917 or March 1918 the general formed a poor first impression of Rufus, who made life tolerable for himself again by managing — unwittingly — to impress the general with his program of sports and amusements, mentioned previously. In spite of himself, Loomis then re-evaluated his SC 'Q'. This happened about 8 May and thereafter, despite periodic eruptions of his boss's temper, Rufus could begin once more to enjoy his work.

The war, meanwhile, raged on. The Germans, having concentrated their whole force on the western front in the wake of Russia's collapse, since 21 March had been hurling it at the British and the French, hoping to break their will to continue — of the British in particular — before American numbers could tip the scales against them. Apart from sometimes acting as a strategic reserve, the Canadian Corps had not been involved and, when it did take its place in the line, the Germans left it alone. In spite of many demoralizing retreats elsewhere, Rufus remained optimistic, constantly reassuring Bee that things would turn out well. On 17 April, for example, he told his diary: "It is said that the Boche has in all 240 divisions of which 207 have now been thrown into the big battles. Foch's great striking force is being held until it is certain the whole of the Hun reserves have been used up." It was a morale-building concept, no doubt picked up on the staff grapevine, and it is interesting that he made no mention of American troops, except in disdain when his buddy Leighton was sent to the States as a trench mortar instructor, "entirely because they want to get rid of him," as he told Bee. "The blighter is leaving today en route to America at $10 a day — such is the reward of incompetence." He was evidently not expecting great things from Leighton's students.

Rufus expanded on his concept of allied strategy in a letter on 20 April: "The news is better from the north, isn't it? I only hope there is an end to this retiring. With us it's a question simply of hanging on — we know pretty accurately just what reserves the Hun still has in hand. When he has thrown the last of them into the struggle — then will be the time for us to strike with our reserves, untouched as yet. The great thing is that we must avoid these small shows, I think. We want to go one better than the Hun and do the thing in grand style — and then we shall win. He is running a great big bluff . . . You need have no great concern at the moment. We have busted about all over this end of France in the last few weeks but you will see in the papers when we do anything really exciting."

Meanwhile his ascetic GOC still cast a shadow across mess social life, as Rufus described. "Today at tea there was quite a jolly crowd in the place. Then in came our friend — and everyone simply froze!"

'Busting about', unfortunately, made billeting his constant occupation. This took him many miles on his mare Nell across spring countryside, beautiful in spite of the war. One day he met Corporal Harcourt Sunderland[67] from the Trench Mortar Battalion, on a bike, and they chatted about Duncan where they had known each other well. He also met Collins, Lyonel's surveying pal from Duncan. It was all very civilized and normal. Inevitably, he also had another horsey adventure, as he confessed. "Today my blessed old mare ran away from me, we were jogging quietly along when an enormous 12" Naval gun on a railway mounting went off and scared the life out of her. I'm not surprised, for the din was simply terrific."

At the time, 2nd Brigade HQ occupied a lovely château at Étrun, the one-time country seat of the Bishop of Arras. On a day there when the sun was shining and there was little work to do, Rufus went into the church for a while and then walked by the river — moments of sweet escape from the tumult and the tragedies.

In the middle of May he again challenged Bee's pessimism. By then he was willing to credit the Americans with their numbers, at least, and pointed out they were arriving at 120,000 a month while German losses since March could not have been fewer than those of the Allies. Every week the war went on, he believed, made ultimate victory more certain. Meanwhile the brigade was still 'busting about' and every week he had a new château to clean out and make habitable.

The 5th of June found him in an unfamiliar role, accompanying his cantankerous boss to a meeting with General Macdonell, GOC 1st Division, as a sort of prisoner's friend. Obviously, his own relations with Loomis had improved out of all recognition. As he described the problem, his boss had been exceedingly rude to two senior 'Q' officers at Division. "I have to go with him to the Divisional Commander and it is to come to a showdown. I hate this eternal friction — there is no need for it as, personally, I get on excellently with them all — but you can understand how very difficult things get at times. It is a pity because the old man undoubtedly has good points. He'll back you up and stick up for his staff against all comers and I must say that nowadays he is very nice to me in every way — we get on like smoke."

In further defence of Loomis he risked some honest introspection, admitting "I'm a fiery old stick. No-one ever likes me at first — I get into my shell and people say what a stuck-up ass I am. Well, I've thawed now in this brigade and if I'm not exactly the popular hero of the moment, at least everybody is glad to see me and the battalions constantly ask me to drop in for a meal, etc." As an afterthought, he asked: "Did you see that old Loomis got a CB?" and went on, rather wistfully: "Some day, perhaps, I'll get a ribbon of some sort — Leighton, as SC 'Q', 9th Brigade, got a DSO."

Instead, he suddenly became ill. For the rest of June, he suffered badly from a worse form of his usual stomach problems while the MO also diagnosed 'inflammatory muscular rheumatism' of his back muscles. He was in such pain he couldn't ride his horse. He wrote to Bee on 16 June. "My inside is in a simply appalling state — and what with that and my back I've had no proper sleep for more than a week." Many of the staff had also been ill, including Loomis — and such a martinet would have had to have been *really* ill to have taken to his bed, which he did for twenty-four hours. Perhaps it allowed him to sympathize with his SC 'Q' — without being asked, he recommended him for immediate special leave to get fit.

Somehow Rufus got himself to Boulogne. In his diary he wrote, "Feeling like death with a high temperature. Got leave to cross on today's boat — a day early — and reached Marden at 7 pm. Went to bed at once and appreciated all their kindness very much." He had sixteen days leave ahead of him, enough to do the trick — more or less. At least it would enable him to function through the crucial month of August, during which things would be much changed for the brigade and its SC 'Q', who had a vital role to play. The next morning he felt better, well enough, at least, to take his leave of R.E. and the solicitous Florie. He went to London, met Bee, and spent a couple of days getting her to a specialist — who wanted an X-ray of her insides — and trying to negotiate a home posting for himself at Argyll House,* on the grounds that Bee was not well. They found time, of course, for dinner at the Troc and a show at the Coliseum before going 'home' to Brighton.

There they both consulted a mysterious Major Thompson at the hospital. This gentleman provided Bee with the required X-rays and informed Rufus that he had colitis and needed up to six weeks in hospital, which was not helpful in the circumstances. Nature, however, lent a hand and by 4 July he was well enough to have people in for bridge. Derek may have been disappointed when his dad was not up to making sandcastles, but his dad *did* take him to the

* The Canadian Expeditionary Force's London HQ.

beach a couple of times, *and* for an excursion to Lewes Castle *and* onto the pier *and* to the pictures *and* to tea at Boots — *and* to teashops reserved for 'special occasions'. They had a day with Grandpa, who came over from Marden, and went to a children's service on Sunday. So the lad was far from forgotten though they sometimes made use of minders. Rufus got plenty of rest and in the evenings they went to plays or played bridge.

Before he returned to France, they spent a couple of nights at the Wilton and took Derek, by special request, to *Chu Chin Chow* for the second time, their third. Rufus visited Argyll House, found his posting request had been turned down, ran an errand for the GOC — picking up paraphernalia for his CB — and "thence," according to his diary, "to catch 2:15 staff train at Charing Cross." He reached 2nd Brigade just after midnight and the next morning, as he told Bee, "the GOC and the rest seemed quite pleased to see me back." The brigade moved into the line and he spent all morning touring the battalions with the GOC and the BM. Later, his war restarted with a bang when the Arras–Lens road was shelled a hundred yards from brigade HQ.

His return coincided with great changes in his life. On a personal level he had decided, on account of Bee's health and his own, to ask Loomis to recommend him for a UK posting. It speaks to Loomis's growing respect for him that he did so without demur — Rufus noted with satisfaction that the GOC's letter left brigade HQ "on the 1st run" on 15 July.

The second change was initiated by the Germans. On that day his diary read, "Hun attacked yesterday on 50-mile front," and two days later, "Hun attack seems to have penetrated about 2½ miles west of Rheims and been stopped there, and entirely east of Rheims." It was their last gasp; Ludendorff's great offensive — that had shortened his leave four months before — had finally ground to a halt. There followed ten days of business as usual, but by the end of July the decision had been made: the Corps would be part of the great hammer blow planned to descend on the German army on 8 August — a blow that would ultimately destroy it.

During the waiting Loomis's relations with his staff reached new lows. Maybe because he knew big things were about to happen, he became more difficult than ever. He and Rufus twice clashed over Lewis-gun slings, the importance of which the SC 'Q' seemed slow to understand — maybe because he had been too long out of the 'I' business.

As he wrote to Bee on 20 July, "I am not blind now to his many good points but, by Jove, he is a beast to work for. Every single officer and clerk here has been on the verge of the 'jumps' lately. 2 nights ago — when I had been out forward from 7 am to 4 pm — he had me got out of bed at 12:30 am to ask some trivial question — I *was* hostile. Never mind, it's good for me to learn to keep my temper and, after all, he can't take back those recommendations which, by now, should be well on the way to England."

In the middle of this kerfuffle, who should arrive at the front but the very civilian figure of W. C. Nichol, owner of the Vancouver *Daily Province*. No doubt, as BC's leading news proprietor, he was hoping for a privileged scoop from the Corps commander; but he also spent considerable time within range of the German guns talking to Captain Johnston about his post-war plans. While the middle of Arras, where brigade HQ was located, was being shelled and there were casualties in the Grande Place, Nichol was inviting him to renew his connection with the *Province*. As both he and Bee longed to get back to Victoria, Rufus was non-committal. He told Nichol he had no wish to do any more reporting — just writing. Undeterred, Nichol invited him to come and see him when he got back — a comforting offer for a soon-to-be-unemployed officer to receive in the last months of the war, despite his loftier ambitions.

For a day he also found himself acting as catering consultant and event organizer. The circus came to town in the form of Minister of Militia General Mewburn, Minister of Marine & Fisheries Colonel Ballantyne,[68] the Corps Commander, the Division Commander, commander at Montreal General Wilson and Arras commandant Colonel Hastings, together with their many minions. Loomis wanted to put on the dog and to Rufus fell the task of feeding them a *haute cuisine* lunch in the St Sauveur caves, the only safe place in, or rather under, town. All went well — the brass ate their fill while German shells were starting fires in the Rue des Capucins above. The re-awakening journalist in Rufus had been dying to work a room like that, but unfortunately, as he noted in his diary: "I had lunch before the rest — no room."

Loomis had planned a big raid on enemy trenches for the 26th , hence the fuss about Lewis-gun slings. For days before, Rufus was kept busy with these and other preparations, and on the night of 25 July, as he told his diary, he "went to bed at 11:15 pm, saying to Sandy what a monotonous old war it was on this front. Had just put out the light when a heavy bomb fell a few yards behind the house and another, heavier, across the street. Our room was filled with smoke and flying debris — not a soul hurt. The house opposite, within 20 yards of the GOCs room, completely blown inwards and the one at the rear also demolished. Then at 3:45 am Paget came and gave a gas alarm and we all trooped down to the mess underground for an hour. No monotony about last night!" At 9 pm the next day, the raid duly took place, involving 400 men from two battalions. They created enough death and destruction across the way to ensure there was little monotony over there either.

On the 27th, Rufus noted "everybody is taking it easy," and that level of activity continued for two days. He took advantage of the lull to see the amiable General Farmar at Corps HQ about his upcoming duty in England. He stumbled into General Currie's mess by mistake, excused himself, found Farmar and extracted from him a promise to write a personal letter to England about his case. Nobody ever accused Rufus of just waiting for things to happen. Meanwhile Major Herridge, the BM, had also fallen foul of the GOC and on the 30th Rufus found himself accompanying him to 1st Division HQ, where he too was to be paraded before General Macdonell. They had to wait two hours before this happened but the outcome remains unrecorded — eclipsed by orders for a sudden move, destination unknown.

Instantly, Rufus was totally engaged. It was the beginning of the endgame. The orders were for the brigade (along with the whole Corps) to move secretly at night from the front line near Arras to an undisclosed final destination. He did know their immediate destination — the village of Izel-lès-Hameau, 20 kms to the west — and it was his job to move there by rail the four infantry battalions, the trench-mortar battalion and brigade HQ, a considerable item itself. The two battalions in support, and therefore out of the line, were 'entrained' by Rufus and Sandy during the small hours of 1 August. The 31st had been stiflingly hot and he had spent it clearing out files and making arrangements. Once it was dark and movements were invisible to eyes in the sky, he was off to see 8th Battalion entrained behind the citadel. All went smoothly — both men and trains being on time for once. Then he reconnoitred the place of entrainment for 10th Battalion before snatching an hour or two's sleep. At 12:45 am he was out again, seeing to their entraining, but this time things went slowly — the first train got away at 2 am instead of 1:30 and the last not until 3:12. Worryingly, there were many aircraft about but the moon was just a sliver so they could have learned little.

There was a dramatic atmosphere of secrecy about this move. Each member of the Corps was issued with a slip to paste into his pay-book.

> KEEP YOUR MOUTH SHUT! *The success of any operation we carry out depends chiefly on surprise.* DO NOT TALK — When you know that your unit is making preparations for an attack, don't talk about them to men in other units or to strangers, and keep your mouth shut, especially in public places. Do not be inquisitive about what other units are doing; if you hear or see anything, keep it to yourself. If you hear anyone else talking about operations, stop him at once. *The success of the operations and the lives of your Comrades depend upon your* SILENCE. If you ever should have the misfortune to be taken prisoner, *don't give the enemy any information beyond your rank and name.* In answer to all other questions you need only say '*I cannot answer.*' He cannot compel you to give any other information. He may use threats. He will respect you if your courage, patriotism and self-control do not fail. Every word you say may cause the death of one of your comrades. Either after or before you are openly examined *Germans, disguised as British officers or men,* will be sent among you or will await you in the cages or quarters or hospital to which you are taken. Germans will be placed where they can overhear what you say without being seen by you. DO NOT BE TAKEN IN BY ANY OF THESE TRICKS.

The seriousness of the wording and its implications made a great impression — everybody, and especially the staff, just put their heads down and got on with their job.

The next few days were desperate times for those responsible for movements. 5th and 7th Battalions, still in the line, were relieved on 1 August. That night Rufus and Sandy were due to entrain them, along with the Trench Mortar Battalion. The infantry got away all right but the Trench Mortar Battalion never showed up, although Rufus waited until 3 am. Leaving them to fend for themselves, he caught a ride to a different entraining point, hopped a train moving another brigade, somehow scrounged a car at their destination, located billets for his brigade in and around Izel-lès-Hameau, and then went to guide in the first two battalions, the 10th and 8th, who were marching from the railhead. On 2 August he did no travelling but was constantly busy, meeting the 5th and 7th Battalions and arranging baths for most of the brigade. All this, while both he and the elements of the brigade were on the move.

By 3 August they were far enough behind the front to be able to move by day. Leaving the entraining to Sandy, Rufus, along with brigade HQ, left for their next destination at 5:30 pm. The train meandered through the French countryside, at first north east to Étaples, then, after an hour sitting at Noyelles-sur-mer, south through Abbeville to Senarpont, 40 kms west of Amiens, where they arrived at 4:30 am — 11 hours for a journey of 220 kms.

4 August was a long, frustrating day. He began it with a wonderful 17-km cross-country ride to their new brigade HQ at Aumont. Then he went out to meet the battalions in their assigned villages. By 6 pm he had seen the 5th and 7th settled and was out on horseback, looking in vain for the 8th and 10th. Eventually he borrowed an ambulance to look for them. He got to bed at 3 am and, as the brigade was being allowed to rest for the battle ahead, managed seven hours sleep.

On 5 August he went forward to reconnoitre the new transport lines at Boves, a front-line village some way east of Amiens. This took all day and he was not back until 10 pm. In spite of the hour, he had little sleep that night — the secret orders had been opened and staff officers, and maybe senior battalion officers, knew that the brigade would be attacking from a start line in Gentilles Wood, outside Boves. For those in the know there were enormous amounts of preparations to make and sleep became a luxury.

On the 6th, orders arrived for the move to the front line and for the upcoming operation. Rufus's understated diary entry summarizes the pressure under which he was working.

Orders for move and operation very late in arriving from Division. GOC and I went up in afternoon and took the orders for move to units – arriving back at Aumont at 6 pm. Embusing very satisfactory despite short notice. I went up in ambulance and met all [battalion] quartermasters on the road to give them information [about supplies of food, ammunition, etc. once the operation had begun – final objectives were 6 or 7 kms beyond the start line] Tremendous crush

> *of transport on roads – tanks by scores, etc. Slept an hour on floor of Town Major's office in Boves and then McDonnell woke me and I walked 4 miles back to see about transport line.*

His entry for the 7th is even terser:

> *Saw Doc Lee in morning and got some binding medicine. Very, very tired. Up to McGoven's [supplies] dump in morning with Templeman. Have now had probably ten hours real sleep this week. Moved at night into Gentilles Wood – and slept in a bivvy with McGoven at his dump. Great difficulty in getting people equipped, bombs not to be had, however all OK by 1 am. Weather has now cleared.*

Nevertheless, he took the time for a quick word to Bee. "Tell Boody that his piper, wounded at Passchendaele, has now been wounded a second time in the battle of Amiens [left blank in the original])! This time both his legs are broken but he is still 'carrying on'."

August 8, the first day of the Battle of Amiens, was a momentous day: it saw the Canadian Corps roll up the Germans facing them, advancing 6 kms and forcing Rufus to improvise frantically with food and ammunition supplies for the advancing 2nd Brigade troops — General Ludendorff later declared it

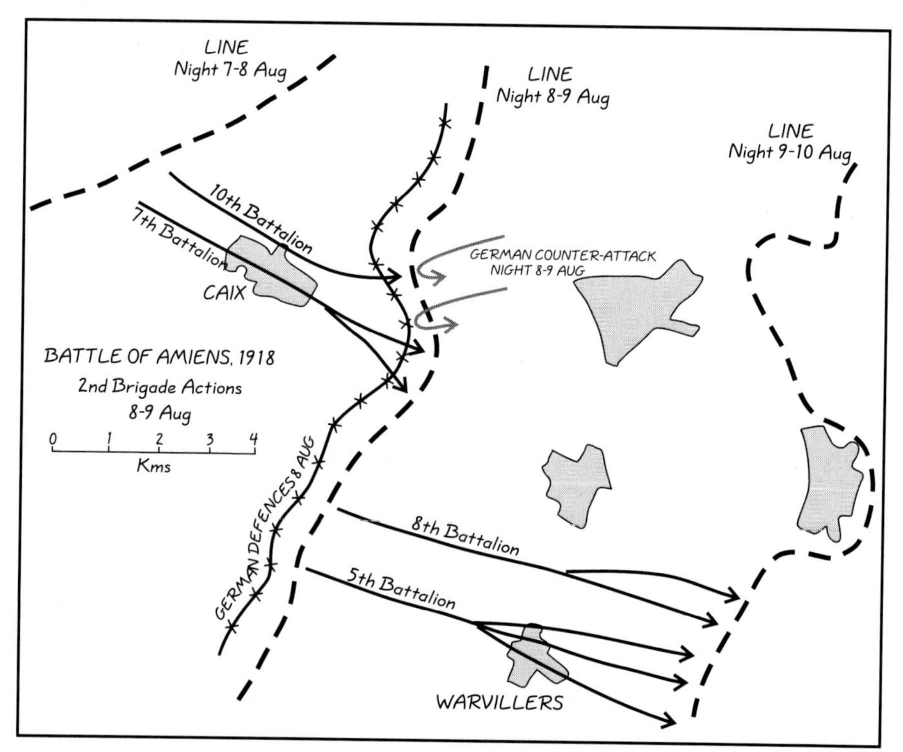

Amiens, 2nd Brigade Action, 8 & 9 August, 1918

"the Black Day of the German Army!" When he made his report to the Kaiser, that gentleman asserted: "The war can no longer be won!" All this, and it was also Rufus's 31st birthday. For him the day had arrived too soon. His diary read:

> *Aug 8*
> *Zero at 4:20 am. GOC, etc., moved forward to various places during the day and at night were at W. 25. d central [a map reference], an old Hun regimental HQ. I was busy moving transport, etc., and joined HQ about 5 pm. Found new show on for the morning, so had to rush back by horse and by car to get Trench Mortar Battalion as supply tanks fell down. Show a huge success. All objectives taken on 20-mile front by French 2 Corps on right, Canadian Corps and Australian Corps on left. 2,000 p.o.w.'s in this division. Slept in tent at Gentilles. 7th and 10th attacked – had to take bombs etc up to 10th at night."*[69]

His activities during the day are illuminated by a pair of battlefield messages that survive — both to a Captain Dudley, presumably in charge of brigade transport lines. The first one reads:

> Capt Dudley: The new transport lines are not nearly far enough forward in view of today's operations. Have location reconnoitred in neighbourhood of V.23 or 24 [squares on the map] and move them up tonight if possible or early tomorrow. Advise brigade supply officer of new location and also 'Q' branch.

The second one is an urgent order for munitions:

> Capt Dudley, MC, MM.:
> Ref previous message [not the one above], This was a rush order. Including what I have already asked for, we need the following, with a view to operations immediately: 300,000 SAA [rifle, Lewis-gun ammunition]; 250,000 MG, SAA [machine-gun ammunition in belts]; 3,000 No 23 RG or 3,000 No 36 RG [grenades to be fired from a rifle]; 1,000 No 27 RG; 800 Ground Flares [for illuminating No Man's Land]; 1,200 Verey lights 1" white [signal flares, fired from a pistol]; 300 Verey lights 1" red; 300 Verey lights 1" green; 200 Verey lights No 32 (RRR) SOS; 200 Verey lights No 32 (GGG); 600 shovels, 600 picks, 6,000 sandbags, [for digging temporary trenches at objective]; 2,000 Webley ammunition [.45 mm for revolvers]; 500 Colt ammunition [.45mm for revolvers]; 500 tracer SAA [phosphorus-based bullets for indicating targets]; 800 TMC and rings [trench mortar bombs and propellant rings]; We must have lorries to bring this up. I am coming back shortly and will meet you on the road or at new transport lines.
> Signed: Lukin Johnston, Capt., Staff Captain 2CIB, 4:20 pm."

The battle continued on 9 August, the "new show on for the morning" that Rufus had mentioned. His diary reads:

> *Aug 9*
> *Left with transport at 4 am to V. 22. d. [map reference] I reached HQ at 9:30 am – Z is 10 am. 5th and 8th Battalions attacked without tanks or artillery. Both had heavy losses: 8th Battalion – Major Raddell and 7 other officers killed and 400 OR casualties, 9 officers wounded; 5th Battalion – Major Crawford, Major Pyman and Padre Madden wounded. We advanced 5 miles and took about 600 p.o.w.'s. HQ moved to hospital south of Caix with all transport moved later to Mill Farm. I went up at night – Div GOC and Colonels Parsons and Browne there, etc., lost the way, with Cowley, on way back to hospital and got back at 3 am. Bombed at night."*

The battle continued into a third day but operations for the 11th were cancelled and all concerned had time to catch their breath and sleep. The main business of that day was a battle post-mortem, a two-hour conference involving staff officers and battalion commanding officers, quartermasters and transport officers, to profit from lessons learned about how to do this new mobile warfare.

In his *War Book* Rufus offered his own summary of the importance of the battle just ended:

> *The action in which the Canadian Corps took part east of Amiens on 8 August was one of a series of hammer blows which continued really until the resistance of the enemy was completely broken. The outstanding feature of the Canadian Corps' action was the speed of the move of approximately 35,000 men from the Arras front to Amiens – 40 miles away – and the secrecy with which it was accomplished. To deceive the enemy, one battalion of 2nd Division and one battalion of 4th Division were sent up to the line in Belgium with instructions to let the Hun get identifications from them. It was a great surprise to the enemy, therefore, to find himself attacked at Amiens by Canadians.*
>
> *The kind of fighting was quite new to Canadians. It was real open fighting. Much doubt was expressed by even Canadians themselves as to whether our system of transport. and our inexperienced staff officers would be found equal to the new conditions, of which they had had no taste before. The results speak for themselves. Captured transport helped to solve this problem. As soon as an action started the whole transport of the brigade was also on the road, following up as close as possible. Through all the battles at Amiens and Arras there was never any shortage of food, nor did the transport or ammunition supply fail.*

> *In one other respect was the fighting new. When we left Arras on 31 July, no one – except possibly the GOC and I don't think even he – knew where we were going. No map was given out until the day previous to attack. The result was absolute secrecy, an impossibility under the old system.*

As S.C. 'Q' Rufus had the unenviable task of collecting and writing up recommendations for honours and awards. To his surprise he found Loomis had recommended him for an MC. The citation read:

> *Recommendation for Military Cross — Capt. Johnston, Staff Captain 'Q', 2 CIB.* For conspicuous gallantry in the attack on the Amiens Defence System east of Amiens on August 8th and 9th 1918.
>
> During the advance of August 8th and 9th, when this brigade, on succeeding days, fought their way to their 6,000 yard and 7,000 yard objectives, the work of this officer was of the highest order. His care before the attack, in equipping the assault troops, and his skill and courage in personally superintending the supply of munitions during the course of the action, is responsible, in a considerable degree, for the great success which this brigade attained. On the night of August 9th, when the 7th and 10th Canadian Infantry Battalions were holding their final objective in the Amiens Defence System, east of Amiens, being heavily counter-attacked; and when the supply of S.A.A. [bullets] and bombs was depleted, Captain Johnston personally organized, and led forward, parties carrying munitions, and himself saw to their safe delivery at different points along the front line. During that time the enemy artillery was bombarding CAIX and the area east of it and his machine-guns were sweeping the approaches to our forward positions. Captain Johnston's task was a hazardous one, but one that he carried out successfully without regard to his own personal safety.
>
> Brig-Gen Loomis, 2 CIB.

On the 11th he had the time to write a quick note to Bee. "As the papers have now gone in, I can tell you that the General has recommended me for the MC. Of course, in a way it is all rot. I am no hero. I have tried to do my little job and with good success — everyone has been well fed and they've had ammunition, etc., under all conditions — sometimes very difficult times too. But beyond this I have done nothing particular. Don't talk about it until it comes out officially in a week or two. We are having very hard times still — but we are beating the old Hun very badly just here. My hardest job has been to keep all the transport, etc. and supplies of munitions up with the advances. It is a wonderful show — successful beyond our dreams. But of course he will hit back hard any time now and *then* will come our real test . . . I am so glad about IT! I've never had much chance to 'show 'em' until now!" There can be little doubt that he was a bit of a hero, for his activities that day impressed so severe a critic of his staff as Loomis. Rufus himself clearly felt he had earned it, and was exultant that he would be able to hold his head up in the company of much-decorated colleagues.

In the few days after the battle the Germans made life deadly and uncomfortable for the victorious Canadians by frequently shelling their own recent headquarters, messes, transport lines and other sites from which they had been ejected, now occupied by Canadians. 2nd Brigade HQ was in the château at Warvillers where Rufus's room was "in a sort of heavy concrete place". It was just as well — on successive days he noted "heavy bombing at night and all night," "grounds of château shelled for a couple of hours in am and got a few men in the horse lines," and "pretty consistent shelling all round here all night — with very heavy stuff." Against this background Rufus spent most of his time until 14 August working on Honours & Awards, on that day noting, "Busy as can be from 8 am finishing up H&A, a tremendous work," after having worked on it the previous night until 1 am.

Consequently it was more than disappointing for him to have to write in his diary on 31 August, "Decorations [among Loomis's staff] announced as follows: Herridge bar to MC, ditto Woods and Young; Templeman MC; Gilson bar to DSO, McDonald ditto, Saunders DSO; Self ???!" The reason for his own omission was said to have been his apparent conflict of interest. Although the recommendations bore the GOC's signature, he, Rufus, had prepared the documents and his name appeared as having done so. According to Derek, this was why his recommendation was turned down: some officer further up the chain of command decided that submitting one's own name was 'not cricket'. It might also have been rejected because of the discrepancy in the dates, noted earlier. Rufus would have to settle for a Mention in Dispatches — recognition, certainly, but hardly the hoped-for chance to 'show 'em'.

2nd Brigade was still in the trenches southeast of Amiens when Haig decided to move the Canadian Corps back to Arras as secretly as they had left it. 2nd and 3rd Divisions moved first, once more by night, and attacked the German defensive line near Neuville-Vitasse on 26 August. This was the first of a series of German defensive lines, one covering the next, intended as an impregnable northern anchor for their famous Hindenburg (or Siegfried) Line. 1st Division, meanwhile, of which 2nd Brigade was part, was just arriving in the Arras area having spent the nights of August 21–23 marching west and then north around Amiens and the night of August 24 in trains and buses en route to Arras. Every day, while the men were resting after a night's march, or after a bus or train journey, Rufus preceded them, arranging billets or bivvy sites. It was a hectic daily struggle in which he was increasingly handicapped by his health — his dysentery-like complaint giving him no peace night or day, leaving him feeling weak and exhausted. He was to be replaced by a Major Murray Greene but until the major arrived he was still in harness. As he put it on the 29th,

"I stayed in bed all day but all Q work comes to me still so it's not much good trying to get fit here."

Planning was impossible. Thus on 25 August everything seemed under control when he went to bed — but he woke to the news that everything had changed. There were fresh orders from division. Suddenly he was busing the brigade to Louez, meeting them at the debusing point and staying there until 3 am on the 27th to ensure that all busloads had been accounted for and assigned to billets — 5th Battalion at Anzin, 7th in Arras, 8th at Saint-Aubain, 10th at Sainte-Catherine, Trench Mortars with the 8th and 10th and Brigade HQ at Louez. Sick man though he was, by this time he was very good at his job and the troops got their rest.

By 31st August the worst of his bout was over. It was a well-timed relief as that day 1st and 4th Divisions were relieving the 2nd and 3rd and he went forward with the brigade when it moved into the line to establish a temporary brigade transport depot. The Corps had been in action since the 26th but news had been scarce — he knew only that 3rd Division had broken the first German line and had been two miles east of Monchy le Preux on the 27th. In the following days 2nd and 3rd Divisions had done their jobs well and by the 31st were still further east and facing the formidable Drocourt–Quéant line. This would be 2nd Brigade's first objective on September 2. Rufus slept the night of the 31st in a bivvy at a forward location with 7th battalion. For what would be his last active duty assignment, he had to be prepared for a dawn attack on the 2nd, which meant having all brigade transport on the road and ready to roll.

It was not to be quite that simple, of course — a day is a long time in a war. At 6 pm on the 1st the Germans counter-attacked the position held by 5th Battalion. Although the battalion beat them off, fighting continued until 2 am and they needed to be resupplied — just three hours before Zero at 5 am. Nevertheless, by 4 am Rufus had done the re-supply and the transport was still ready for Zero. The attack jumped off on time and, once more following the barrage "as closely as a horse follows its filled nosebag", 7th Battalion was the first unit to break the formidable Drocourt–Quéant line. Rufus followed as closely as he could with the transport; he "took them to Wancourt and then along the east side of the Cherisy-Vis en Artois valley," on a road parallel to the D–Q line on the old allied side. Later, after the brigade had also broken through the main German support position, the Buissy Switch line, he would write in his diary, ". . . up to advanced HQ. Visited 10th Battalion in rear of Cagnicourt [8 kms east of their start line] late in the day and left brigade HQ at night. Major Murray Greene relieved me."

It had been an astonishing day — as Rufus noted. "Battle a huge success with few casualties. 1500 prisoners in by 4 pm for 1st Division. Said to be 30,000 p.o.w.'s today." In fact, the day's results would be even more momentous — as Hindenburg himself wrote, "On September 2 a fresh hostile attack overran our lines once and for all on the great Arras—Cambrai road and compelled us to bring the whole front back to the Siegfried Line.[70] For the sake of economizing

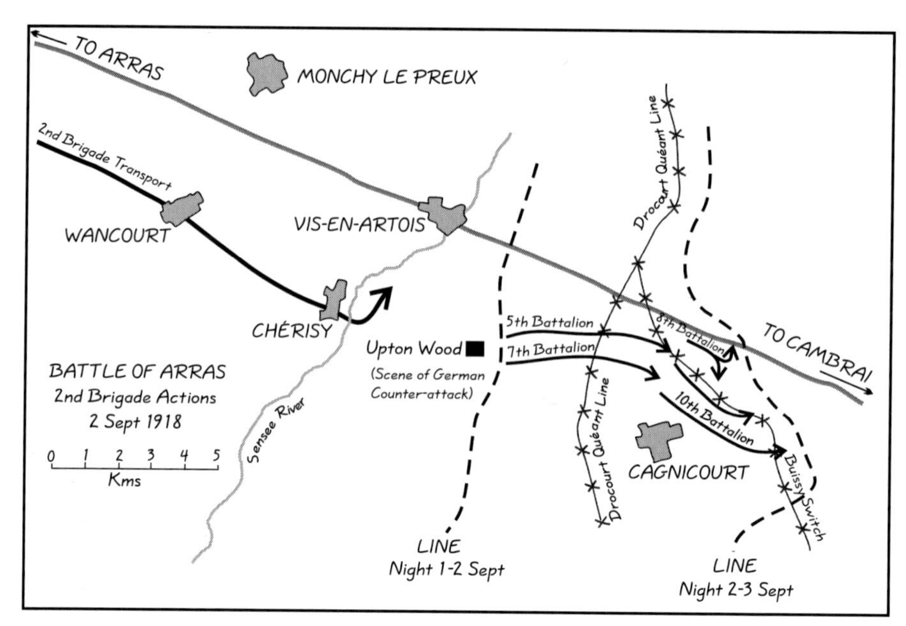

Arras, 2nd Brigade Action, 2 September, 1918

men, we simultaneously evacuated the salient north of the Lys." At a single stroke, the Canadian Corps had forced the Germans to relinquish virtually all the ground they had won during the first half of 1918.[71] For his last day with 2nd Brigade, it had been a pretty special one.

He does not tell us where he slept that night but no doubt he slept well. Next day he went to chase up a car at 1st Division's rear HQ and by chance ran into Generals Currie and Embury. Having bid those gentlemen a genuinely fond farewell — certainly so in the case of Embury — he was driven some of the way to the coast but completed the journey "on an empty supply train engine and, after various vicissitudes, reached Boulogne at 6:15 am on 4 September." He crossed to England on the 10 am boat. As he left Boulogne he may have reflected sadly on recent news that had affected him deeply: just before Amiens, Kenneth Myers — fellow journalist, Vancouver flatmate, and Steamboat Mountain companion — had died from wounds.

There were some final rumblings in the matter of his disappointment over medals. Soon after he returned to England he had a letter from Harry Lukin, then commanding 64th Division in Norwich, glad of Rufus's tour in England to "give his constitution a chance" and congratulating him on his promotion to major. The general continued, "It is a damned shame your fine work in August, and at other times, was not recognized by a DSO or MC — never mind, it may come along later. Anyhow, your promotion shows you have done good work."

Uncle Harry's disciplined unwillingness to rock the boat over this was not shared by R.E., who apparently spent the winter of 1918–19 seething over the injustice of Rufus's lot. In April he could no longer restrain his impulse to *do* something and fired off a letter to General Loomis. After introducing himself, he wrote, "after the advance of August 8th–9th 1918 you sent forward a very strong recommendation that he should receive the Military Cross. He has never received it. He had been previously recommended, after Passchendaele, when serving as Staff Captain on the 9th Brigade, for the DSO and for the MC but received nothing. He is, I believe the only officer on the staff of 2nd Brigade who has received no recognition for his services — of their value you are the best judge . . . My son has no knowledge that I am writing to you . . . but it seems to me that you ought at least to be made aware of the treatment that he has received and of the refusal to recognize your own strong recommendation."

Two months later R.E. received an answer. The general had been promoted to command 3rd Division soon after Rufus left France, which he did successfully until he left the service at the end of the war. A civilian once more and living in Montreal, as soon as he caught up with R.E.'s letter, he replied: "I am afraid there are many similar cases to your son's. All that I can do is to assure you that everything has been done which I can do in this matter. I have received several communications from Major Johnston and have matters still in hand . . . it would be very unsoldierly-like for me to make any radical objection to the decision of higher authority. I want to assure you, however, that I have great esteem for your son and appreciated his services very much indeed. The work he did while under me was of a very high order. He has my strong support and sincere friendship."

In spite of the strong echoes of Uncle Harry's letter, the obvious sincerity of his last three sentences must have made both R.E. and Rufus feel much better. The general's offer of friendship was equally welcome and, whenever he was in Montreal in the years to come, Rufus would drop in 'for a yarn'.

Chapter 11
Sufficient Sacrifice
England and home, 1918–1919

"They can't give back that young life, but they still have 'eyes to weep with'. Make them weep!"

Rufus in the *Daily Mail*, 10 October 1918

After reuniting with Bee and Derek at the Wilton as usual, Rufus's immediate need was to sleep, long and deeply. This he did, oblivious to traffic noises, until well into the following morning. Awake once again, there were things he must do before he could really relax: proving to himself, for example, that he could never have been a salesman by hawking books and a tapestry — all from France — around dealers in the ancient City of London, and being measured for a new uniform and a new pair of leather leggings. There were also shows to see — the popular musical *Box o' Tricks* at the Hippodrome and *Telling the Tale*, a new American musical with songs by Cole Porter at the Ambassadors. But when he had done all that, he had the delicious prospect of a week and a half doing as little as possible in Brighton, that half-remembered paradise beyond the sound of the guns where he might, from time to time, let the wounded Highlander tell Derek his stories or perhaps, now and then, take him on the pier. He and Bee played bridge a few times, took Derek to *The Lilac Domino*, a silly operetta, and went to church, twice, on Sunday. He spent the second weekend of his leave at Marden with his father. Then, on Monday the 16th, looking smart but a little awkward in the uniform he had picked up on the way, reported to Canadian base Witley, near Milford in Surrey.

For the time being, their separation continued — Bee remaining in Brighton with Derek while he lived at Boro Farm, the Witley officers' mess — but he would soon start looking for a family house. He was taking over the job of Deputy Assistant Adjutant General, or DAAG,[72] from a Major Benjamin, and this officer spent a couple of days introducing him to the battalion staff of the 9th, 11th and 17th reserve battalions, among the others that may also have been there. One of the more pleasing things about his new job was that the

GOC, Brigadier-General F.W. Hill, was his old friend from 9th brigade. They had a long yarn the day after he arrived and seem to have co-existed comfortably throughout his time at Witley; the general, with his wife and daughter, came to dine at Boro Farm a couple of times and he and Rufus frequently played bridge.

Once he had taken stock of his surroundings, and having had time to reflect on the impact of the war's tragedies and brutalities upon his own family, Rufus had a clear understanding of where to lay blame. As the war reached its inevitable conclusion across the Channel, he became consumed with loathing for 'the Hun' and by an unsentimental zeal to see that he paid. With this emotion ruling him, he wrote an article for the *Daily Mail*: "Make Them Pay!" by a Canadian soldier.[73]

> No-one could call me bloodthirsty. I am the most peaceable of men, I am not vindictive and I think I may say that I seldom harbour ill-feelings in my heart. But – I loathe the Hun. Why? I'll tell you.
>
> * * *
>
> Outside a pretty little bungalow in a tree-bordered street in Victoria, BC, hangs a red flag. There is a sale on. That was my home. People are inside there bargaining for our little household treasures. Cautious housewives are fingering carpets and curtains and appraising their value. A fat old dealer is trying to convince his pal that my priceless Sheffield plate soup tureen is not genuine. There is a man carrying away my child's cot. I have no home now. All the little store of books I treasured so is gone. My wife is living in a boarding house and the youngster has no nursery now. We've sold up so that I may join the -th Battalion. The Hun must pay me for that – must make what reparations can be made for breaking up my home; for all the heavy heartaches we had in parting from our treasures.
>
> * * *
>
> I am standing in the British military cemetery at Bailleul. It is June 1917. I have found what I sought. A simple mound with a little plain wooden cross at the head of it. My younger brother lies here. Five years ago he came out to British Columbia to me – as fine a lad as you could meet. He had just left school. A clean, wholesome product of an English public-school. In 1914 he left his job – surveying – and enlisted. He served eight months as a private in France, got a commission, and, within four months, his company. Two days before his 21st birthday – in June 1916 – he was going round the line at "stand-to". A sniper's bullet hit him square in the forehead – the next day they brought him here. It was a Hun's hand that pulled that trigger. Do you suppose I'll meet a Hun again when peace comes, without a haunting feeling that the hand I shook in greeting might be the hand that pulled that trigger? They can't give back that young life, but they still have "eyes to weep with". Make them weep!

* * *

An old man is walking slowly up and down the lawn in the garden of a beautiful old Kentish vicarage. It is a still summer night. Hardly a sound you would say. But the old man stops and listens. He can just hear a distant rumble – far, far away to the south. "The guns in France or Belgium" he would tell you. Day and night he is listening, listening for that distant rumble. He is my father. Four years ago I did not consider him on the border of old age. But three years of sorrow and ever-present anxiety, first for two sons and now for one only, have changed him. They have deepened the furrows in his cheeks, have turned his hair to silver, taken all the joy of life from his eyes. He is only one of millions. The Huns cannot make the old man young again, cannot restore the boy they stole from him. But even their brutal instincts can be made to realize how all decent people loathe a murderer. Make them feel it!

(*Daily Mail*, Thursday, October 10, 1918.)

It is a remarkable piece, punchy and persuasive. Its sentiment was widely shared by people in France, Britain, and Canada. But it was uncharacteristic of him to write such a thing, conflicting, as it did, with his own generous attitude towards former enemies in years to come. He may have regretted having written it — we do not know. Still, his article made its contribution to forming public opinion, a political force that ensured a vindictive Peace and an impotent League — both of which would later trouble him greatly.

The Canadian base at Witley trained green troops fresh off the boat from home, and, when they were ready, dispatched them to France in weekly drafts of about 600. The training was constant and exhausting and the men gave little trouble. That started later, once the war was over, or nearly so, and the camp full of idle conscripts who just wanted to go home. While the war lasted, in spite of the odd spot of bother, Rufus was never busy by 2nd Brigade standards; on the two occasions he took a weekend pass to Brighton, he travelled at lunchtime on Friday and caught a Monday morning train back. He had a weekly half-day, a very British luxury, and he and other officers seemed to travel to London with little excuse. A monthly membership at the local golf club helped him pass the time and he seemed restricted only by a duty roster that often kept him in the office on Sunday.

In October he and Bee, perhaps expecting the war to last until spring, decided to rent a house. No sooner decided than acted upon. Bee came up from Brighton, Rufus met her at the station, they looked at one house — and decided to take it. Leaving Rufus to complete the rental process, Bee went back to Brighton and arranged to return — with Derek and their few possessions — on moving-in day, set for the second Monday in November. This happened to be the 11th, the day on which their world went happily mad. Rufus's diary reads:

> *Nov 8*
> *Peace delegates from Huns meet Marshal Foch.*

When this news caused rumblings at the base, the DAAG took prudent precautions and his diary continues:

> *Nov 9*
> *Lovely day. Supposed to be my half-day – but busy all afternoon. Increase of police unofficially sanctioned. Kaiser (and Crown Prince) abdicated and fled to Holland.*

On Sunday the 10th he was on duty in the office. In spite of that, even he was unprepared for Monday's news:

> *Nov 11*
> *Armistice signed at 5 am and hostilities ceased at 11 am. Up to town by 12:13. London simply mad. Met Bee and Derek at Victoria at 5:15. To Wilton, thence by taxi to Criterion, later to Piccadilly, RAC Club, and finally had dinner at [Lyon's Corner House on] Coventry [Street][74] – very cheerful, etc. Enormous, mad crowds everywhere in London and all business at a standstill."*

After a night at the Wilton in which nobody slept much, they left London next day on an after-lunch train and "found the house in a pretty bad pickle." Leaving Bee and Derek to make of it what they could, Rufus reached his office in late afternoon where a much worse pickle awaited him: the troops in the camp, as their way of celebrating, had raided 'Tin Town' — the civilian shops on the base — and in spite of his "prudent precautions", had gutted many shops and done thousands of pounds worth of damage. As DAAG, it was his pigeon and within 24 hours he had assembled and set in motion a Court of Inquiry into the 'Tin Town riot'.

This event was just the most public in a stream of similar ones that would create most of the DAAG's work from then on. With every day that passed the frustration of soldiers still at Witley grew, often exploding into mayhem, and his job was to keep a lid on things. The situation was made worse by Spanish flu, about which posterity has heard so much but which seemed to him less a threat to life than an inconvenience, and one that increased the soldiers' boredom by official overreaction. On 25 October, for example, new rules from on high limited mingling with the general public as a precaution against transmitting flu. That day, he had to cancel a soldiers' dance, presumably because of the rules against mixing. Whether for the same reason, or simply as a reaction to rumbles with the locals, on the 21st he had to put Godalming out of bounds to soldiers, and the Red Lion at Milford on the 30th.

Anticipation that the war would soon be over had been building through the autumn as Germany's support system crumbled. Soldiers in reserve battalions, most of them by that time reluctant conscripts, couldn't fail to be affected when Bulgaria surrendered at the end of September, or when Turkey capitulated a month later, followed immediately by the break-up of Austria-Hungary. Every new desertion of Germany by an ally reduced the recruits' willingness to obey orders. At the same time, since the Russian Revolution of the previous year, politicians and generals had been anxiously looking for Bolshevists behind every strike or demonstration. This applied equally to the September railway strike and the Tin Town riot. The powers-that-be were nervous and there was pressure on Rufus to do what he could to stop the wheels falling off the bus.

When 12 prisoners escaped from the guardroom of a reserve battalion, Rufus suddenly became very active — inspecting battalion guards and guardrooms with the Assistant Provost Marshall, the top military policeman. When he found plenty to complain about in guardroom after guardroom, he tried a radical remedy: he replaced the guard details, until then assigned daily from among their unmotivated, rookie comrades, with details drawn from recovering veterans at the 1st Canadian Convalescent Depot. This seems to have worked and the subject disappeared from his diary. More bothersome was a string of canteen robberies in November and December, no doubt committed by conscripts with interrupted criminal careers, but such small-time crooks could safely be left to the military police.

Bee was anxious to return to British Columbia, as was Rufus — in spite of his earlier notion of working for Beaverbrook. However, he was doing little to bring it about and, instead, wrote a long, gloomy letter to R.E. predicting a Bolshevist tidal wave submerging Britain and Europe. Taken aback by this uncharacteristic alarmism, R.E replied at once, pouring cold water on the idea. "No, no," he objected, Rufus must revisit his history — pessimists had made such predictions in 1789 and 1848 but England and its monarchy had survived. He wisely advised him to see Bolshevism as being like 'flu — not everybody catches it, and most of those who do, recover. Instead, he urged him to worry about the present — and to write to Lord Northcliffe.

It was good advice and it galvanized Rufus. The next day he went to London, not to see Northcliffe,[75] but to inquire at Argyll House about returning to BC as soon as possible. R.E., who had decided to reinforce his letter in person, also came to London. Father and son, with Uncle Jack, lunched together and visited Parliament, after which R.E. came for a night in their new house at Milford. The following day — a little blearily, after one of his customary late nights with Rufus — R.E. caught the train back to Marden and Rufus sprang into action. He cabled Nichol in Vancouver, agreeing to return to the *Province*; he wrote to Lord Northcliffe, proposing himself as *The Times*' 'own correspondent' in Vancouver; and he bought a puppy, immediately named Sato. Only the puppy purchase seems odd — he and Bee were, after all, planning to leave the country. The weekend followed — a pleasant evening with General Hill and family and, for Rufus, a Sunday raking leaves and burning them in a garden they would soon abandon. No mention of Sato being taken for a walk but decisions were being made by man and dog. On Monday morning Northcliffe replied — he was interested and wanted to see Rufus in London. Sato, on the other hand, apparently was not: he had voted with his paws and disappeared, probably upsetting Derek and maybe Bee, but greatly simplifying their immediate future.

For ten days life went on — there was an increasing number of Canadian military social events to attend, while Rufus ensured due process for ne'er-do-wells — though things were now calmer. Then came 5 December, another action day. He went to London for his meeting with Northcliffe. After three quarters of an hour listening to the great man — who believed that Canada's ultimate destiny was union with the USA — he was duly anointed *The Times'* Vancouver correspondent. Rufus and Bee lunched together, then she went to see an unspecified specialist for her second appointment in as many days, while he went to Argyll House to apply for 'home discharge' from the army, a move that may have fast-tracked their passage because he was given a sailing date for 21 December, just over two weeks hence. Such preferential treatment may also have been because he was paying for their passage — thanks to the handsome pay and allowances of a major and member of the Staff.[76] The next morning he gave their landlord two weeks notice on a house they had been living in for less than a month.

When Rufus visited Argyll House a week later, Major Bosworth (Officer i/c Ocean and Rail Transport, but in peacetime Chairman of Canadian Pacific Ocean Services) suggested waiting until after Christmas — when they could travel on CP's *Empress of Asia* on a repositioning voyage direct to Vancouver via that new wonder of the world, the Panama Canal. For two not-very-well people it was not a difficult choice: a three-week sea voyage, half in tropical waters, must have been a wonderful prospect even on a liner fitted as a troopship. However, these new travel arrangements had to be confirmed and the clock was ticking.

Rufus had taken a week's leave starting on 18 December — to allow them to get out of the house and say goodbye to family. It was still uncertain how they would be going home while they were packing up on the 19th, but they took the train to London and this time stayed at the Golden Cross Hotel on the Strand, nearly opposite Charing Cross station. All the excitement of the times and the season flooded through their window: there was a huge crowd on the Strand, come to see Sir Douglas Haig and his Army commanders, including Byng, emerge from the station and drive slowly along the Strand below their window on their way to meet the king at the palace. Among the throng of ADCs and staff officers Rufus recognized friends and colleagues.

The next day, 20 December, Bosworth confirmed their Panama trip, so, feeling relaxed about their immediate future, Rufus and Bee took the train to

Canterbury to take leave of Bee's mother and father. Derek, then nearly six, remembered them from this visit as two little old people — and it would be the last time he saw them. In truth, the Courts lost a daughter when Bee married Rufus, just as R.E. had gained one. Although Bee had been in England for two years and five months, it seems possible that she had seen her parents only when she went with Rufus on his leaves. This time they made two visits: once in the afternoon with Derek for a cup of tea, and a second time without Derek after dinner. Although the feelings of all parties were understandable, the situation was profoundly sad. As they usually did when in Canterbury, Rufus and Bee stayed and dined at the Rose. The following morning, they visited the cathedral and the King's School, where Rufus saw Hodgson, his headmaster, Helmore, his music master, and the vergers, all of whom filled him with memories of his days in the choir. They even visited Miss Gould with whom Rufus had lodged when he was courting Bee.

It was Saturday afternoon when they travelled up the line to Marden to spend the weekend. Marjorie was there with Robin, but it was really all about R.E. saying goodbye to the son of whom he was now so proud, and his 'daughter' and grandson, both of whom he loved dearly. Rufus and Bee were most dutiful about their churchgoing — together to the early service, while Rufus read the lessons morning and evening, by bicycle lamp the second time because the gas was off. After supper, when Rufus expected a long chat with his father, he nearly exploded with frustration when "Florie and the rest did not budge till 10:45!" As a result, refusing to be denied, father and son were very late to bed.

They left early next morning, though Rufus and R.E. were plotting to meet again before they sailed — now to be 2 January, as they discovered that morning. After dropping their bags at the Golden Cross they had rather a grand day — tea with Uncle Harry and Aunt Lily at 2 Queen's Gate Place, "a very cheery time" according to Rufus, dinner at Hatchett's and afterwards to the Savoy, presumably to hear the band, watch the dancers and maybe dance themselves. The next day, Christmas Eve, they returned to rented rooms in Milford. He was on duty between Christmas and New Year — his final contribution to the army — allowing staff less lucky or less enterprising than himself to take time off. These officers would likely be stuck there for the foreseeable future, after all, keeping the lid on increasingly restless troops at what was seen as a godforsaken posting. Nevertheless, Rufus's little family had a happy Christmas together in their rooms: "an excellent Xmas dinner — fowl, pudding, etc." But all staff work landed on his desk for those few days and he did what he could — even inspecting the 500 men needed for lining the streets when President Wilson[77] came to the Guildhall. Not until Sunday the 29th did he bid farewell to General Hill.

Three days of semi-tearful pandemonium followed. Both Rufus and Bee had important loose ends to tie up: he managed to catch up with Lefroy (editor of *Canada*), had an interview with Long, his immediate boss at *The Times*, and picked up a suit from a tailor; she saw her specialist for the third time in the month, spent time with her longtime friend Winnie Croslegh and also with a Miss Nito, who came to London expressly to see her and stayed overnight. Roy appeared three times over a couple of days, and R.E., with Uncle Jack, joined them and Roy for a merry lunch at the Troc. R.E. joined them again for tea at Lyons Corner House that afternoon and turned up next morning at BC House where Rufus had business with the Agent General. "Dad came and sat there a while," Rufus noted rather sadly. R.E. had lunch with Uncle Harry but tea with Rufus again.

Maybe at his father's suggestion, that afternoon Rufus had been to the office of the *London Gazette*[78] in the faint hope there might be news of his MC; predictably, it was in vain — as he noted in his diary, "nothing for me!" In fact, he had received some recognition in *The Times* the previous day. Under the heading "Mentions in Dispatches, Overseas Forces, R.A.F. and US Troops", this notice appeared: "War Office, December 31. The following is a continuation of Sir D. Haig's dispatch of November 8, submitting names deserving of special recognition: Canadian Forces, Commands and Staff." In an alphabetical list Rufus's name appears: "Johnston, Capt. E.H.L., Manitoba R."[79] Ironically, three names lower is "Loomis, Maj-Gen. F.O.W., CB, CMG, DSO, Quebec R!"

That evening, their last in England, while Bee bade Miss Nito farewell at Victoria, Rufus was saying his last goodbye to his father at Charing Cross. They could not be sure they would see each other again, making this the hardest of their many leave-takings for the old man — to lose his successful prodigal and his happy little family again, so soon after they had courageously navigated the dangers of the war, seemed cruel.

On 2 January Rufus, Bee, and Derek caught the special train from Euston and were aboard *Empress of Asia* in Liverpool by 3:30 pm. They sailed at 5 pm, along with 100 officers and 1,200 soldiers. Rufus made no mention of other families so they may have been the only one. Bee was going home to British Columbia with a question mark hanging over her own health. Rufus's diary since his return from France abounds with cryptic entries on the subject, such as that for September 11: "Bee not well and in bed when I got home." Not counting coughs and colds there had been similar entries on October 28, November 1, and December 9 and 13 — culminating in three recent visits to a London specialist. Rufus, of course, found it impossible to discuss 'women's complaints' in his diary, to the extent of not even mentioning the doctor's specialty. It seems likely that her ailment was gynecological for which the solution, eventually, would be surgery. Meanwhile, she was frequently 'under the weather' and spent many a Sunday morning resting and being pampered by him — he would bring her breakfast in bed as a treat.

Rufus, meanwhile, had been enduring the rumbling affliction in his insides which flared up occasionally and never quite went away. It had made his life difficult in France — completely disabling him, for example, in the crucial week before the Battle of Amiens — and was the reason General Loomis agreed to sign his application for a posting in England. During calm periods it remained manageable and it made sense, therefore, to return to British Columbia before seeking his discharge so he could be treated in a military hospital.

More immediately they had a three-week voyage to enjoy — though the 'enjoyment' took a while arriving for some. On the first day out the seas were rough enough to keep Bee in her bunk and make Derek seasick, though Rufus was already relishing the surviving luxuries of the ship and lost seven shillings playing bridge. For the next couple of days the ship was driving into a full gale which delayed the patients' recovery, so not until the fourth day did they start to appreciate their surroundings. By this time Rufus had had several sessions with the skipper and, having heard his tales of wartime adventures, was already planning articles. The situation was ideal for reminiscence journalism and Rufus took advantage of it to write articles for *The Times*. On day six the weather was warm enough to have cold-climate types scrambling for their least uncomfortable attire. Young Derek, confident on his new sea legs, wanted to spend his time with the soldiers at the lowerdeck pool. He escaped from his cabin by climbing out of a window, made his way below and may have been having an even better time than his bridge-playing parents — until he fell off a hatch near the pool and banged his head. The escapade brought an end to the bridge game — and to his freedom; the following day "Private Davis came to look after" him.

Fortunately for Derek, a much more thrilling amusement lay in store. With phenomenally bad timing, the Panama Canal had opened eleven days after the British declaration of war in 1914. Having spent its first four years as a US Navy shortcut, it hoped now to attract the world's shipping and especially the great liners. Judging by the reception given the *Empress of Asia*, her 68-foot width made her the beamiest ship to have passed through the locks so far — the liner *Kroonland* having previously held that honour. Rufus's diary recorded the fuss that was made of them.

Jan 14
We reached Colon at 6 am. Went ashore at 9:30. Took the 11 o'clock train to Panama (2 hrs). We were entertained – with the Captain and about 20 others – by the Red Cross to lunch, etc. We went in a car all over the place with Judge George A. Conolly, US Commissioner for Panama Land Claims. Most delightful people. He took us through old Panama, Ancon, and Amador to the Administrative Building at Balboa where I saw John Collins, Editor of the Canal Record *– thence to Conolly's home, lovely view. He would not let us spend a penny. We had a gorgeous and most interesting time. Back at Colon 7 pm, dined on the ship and shopped in Colon. Before and after dinner to shops and dance at lovely George Washington Hotel overlooking the sea.*

Jan 15
We left Colon at 7 am. We passed through Gatun lock into Gatun Lake

by 10 am. Crowds of troops, white and nigger, at lockside, throwing bananas and oranges at us. A deputation of ladies, etc., from the Red Cross, and the British Minister to Panama, Sir Claude Mallett, came on board at Miraflores lock and stayed on the ship until the pilot left near Taboga Island.*

It was the high point of the trip; thereafter each day was cooler and, in spite of being in sight of land much of the time, bridge-playing became more obsessive — on several days all morning and all evening. Everybody was looking forward to the concert on the 21st and when it flopped — "very dull" in Rufus's words — he and Bee decided to do something about it. Another concert was announced for the 23rd, in aid of the Vancouver Seamen's Home, and in that time "Bee wrote and acted a sketch with Capt Freedman which went very well. I sang and we gave a BC Quartet which won a prize of a bottle of whiskey."

Once in home waters, the ship remained anchored off William Head for a frustrating four hours before docking in Victoria. Rufus and Bee, with Derek, thrilled to be back in the town they thought of as home, rushed ashore to dine. Their meal took longer than expected and, when they got back to the wharf, they found the *Empress* had sailed without them! They scrambled to catch the old CPR steamer and, after an uncomfortable night, arrived in Vancouver early enough to be waiting on the dock when the great ship, dressed overall with flags and bunting,[80] tied up to a noisy welcome.

Instantly Rufus was all business. While Bee and Derek spent the morning packing and preparing to land once more, he had called at the *Province*, seen Nichol and firmed up his terms of employment — $175 a month, to start as soon as he was healthy and out of the army; amazingly, he seemed delighted by these terms. After lunch they got settled temporarily at the Dominion Hotel and, next day, discovered Mrs Cornish's boarding house, downtown at 1110 Melville Street, where they arranged a longer-term stay for Bee and Derek while Rufus was in hospital. As long as he remained, technically, a soldier, he would receive his major's pay — which took all the worry out of their immediate future.

That evening, still all business, Rufus caught the night boat back to Victoria. Top of his list was to settle things with Matson, his most recent civilian employer. In spite of Bee's love of Victoria, they realized that his year-and-a-half as News Editor at the *Colonist* had been much more stressful for them both than his job at the *Leader* had ever been, and was thus the last kind of job he should be returning to in his present state of health. Matson proved frustratingly elusive, however, and Rufus's search consumed the better part of two days before he caught up with him on the telephone. He broke the news that he would be working for Nichol and, to Rufus's surprise, Matson

* Rufus's use of this word in his diary would have seemed normal to Canadians at the time.

"was very cordial and nice." Much relieved, he tracked down their steamer trunks, forwarded them to Vancouver, then submitted himself to a medical board for a physical. The doctors declared his condition D3, which he must have expected as he recorded it without comment. After meeting an array of Island friends at the club, one of whom had been kind enough to give him a bed while he was in town, he returned to Vancouver.

To be told you are D3 at anything is deflating — what remains of one's confidence tends to dissipate quickly and it certainly seems to have had that effect on Rufus. There were still a few days until he was due at the Fairmont Military Hospital but, instead of continuing to rebuild his career, uncharacteristically he did practically nothing and "just pottered." Finally, on the first Monday in February he checked himself in with high hopes that his troubles would soon be over. Alas, the next few days had nothing in store to justify faith in military medicine. The hospital gave him a room — then left him to his own devices, which meant chatting with another patient, Mike McKenzie of the 88th, though he was feeling 'pretty poorly inside'. He felt cold that night and there was snow on the ground in the morning. But there was still hope: word was that the new specialist, Captain Lanchester, was coming — and that Rufus was to see him. The good captain did indeed arrive, but then said he hadn't time to see him and went away again! Days went by and he did not return, nor was there word of him.

As it seemed silly to wait at Fairmont for things to happen, Rufus went off to look after Bee, in bed with a cold. While there he dug some papers out of his trunk and returned to the hospital with a scrapbook to begin creating his *War Book*. Later that week he saw a nerve specialist who declared his condition a nervous one that rest and a steady life would cure. Then — nothing for a week: Rufus slept at the hospital but continued to visit Bee, organized Derek's 6th birthday party, generally went about his business during the day — and thus ran into Nichol at the *Province* on the 14th. When that worthy heard that in eleven days at Fairmont he had been seen, briefly, by just one doctor — who had given a top-of-the-head diagnosis with no follow-up — he insisted on making an appointment for him with Dr B.D. Gillies, the reigning medical authority at Vancouver General Hospital. Thanks to Nichol's intervention, Gillies saw Rufus the same day, giving him what Rufus described as "a proper examination". He had to wait several days for lab work to be done, but on the 19th Gillies diagnosed an ulceration in Rufus's large bowel and prescribed bedrest for a month — in Vancouver General Hospital.

The next morning he saw the Fairmont administrator about his move to VGH. This seemed to pose no problem and he moved himself and his belongings across town, describing his new abode as "v. comfy". He was kept in bed, more or less, for fourteen days and attended to by Dr Brodie. During the first week he had several days of fasting; on one day he wrote: "no food at all, only whiskey",[81] though whether the doctor prescribed the last item he does not say.

Harry Lukin c. 1900, as Brig-Gen. in Cape Mounted Rifles. He later became Major General Sir Harry Lukin KCB, CMG, DSO, GOC British 9th Division

General Sir Arthur Currie, GOC Canadian Corps 1917–18 (courtesy City of Vancouver Archives)

First leave 1917, Rufus with Derek

Private J.H. Gould, Rufus's long-suffering batman

Rufus with 88th Battalion Insignia, 1916

Officers of 88th Battalion, Victoria Fusiliers, May 1916

Back Row, left to right: Lt H.B. Greaves (Training Officer), Lt Lukin Johnston, Lt T. Barclay, Lt R. Horton, Lt R.M. Finlayson, Lt J. Bridgman, Lt R.P.M. Baird, Lt V. Elliot, Capt H.D. Twigg, Lt H.G.E. Pocock, Lt R.W. Richards, Lt A. Morkill, Capt V. Low, Lt R. Day, Lt A.V. Macan, Lt D. James, Lt A.D. Crease, Lt G. Kilpatrick, Lt E.B. Hart.

Middle Row: Capt C.I. McKenzie, Capt R. Houghton (MO), Capt Horton (QM), Capt E.O.C. Martin, Major E.A.I. Pym, Major B.H. Harrison (2 i/c), Lt Col H.J.R. Cullin (CO), Capt R.H. Ley (Adjutant), Col G.H. Andrews (Chaplain), Capt H.B. Andrews, Capt T.B. Pemberton, Capt F.J. Marshall (Paymaster), Capt A. Gray.

Front Row: Lt J.M. McKenzie, Lt V. Taylor (Signals), Lt G. Benson, Lt V. Duke.

RFC air photo, showing Rufus's route (1.5 kms each way) from Waterloo to Bellevue, 26 October 1917, during the battle of Passchendaele. Note the shell-holes and the total obliteration of landscape features

2nd Brigade HQ staff at Etrun, France, June 1918
Gen. Loomis centre, Sandy McMillan behind him, Rufus to the General's left

Rufus, Bee and Derek during Rufus's six week staff-training course
at Cambridge University, England, August 1917

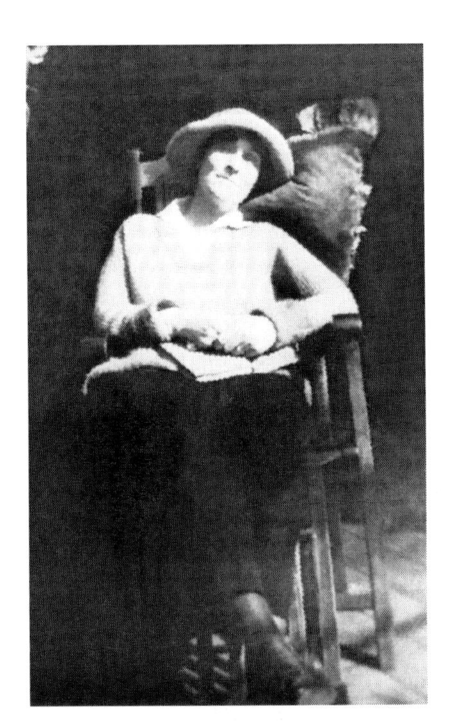

Bee and Rufus aboard *Empress of Asia*, returning to Canada
via the Panama Canal, January 1919

Bee, portrait, 1918

At Kitsilano beach, 1919. They used this picture for their 1919 Christmas Card

Rufus, Muriel Phelan, Bee, Maudie, Muriel's children flanking Derek
at West Bay beach, West Vancouver, 1921

Rufus, Bee in their 1920 Chevrolet, bought in July 1921

Major Matthews's 1343 Maple Street left, Major Johnston's 1337 right, Kits beach bandstand behind. (courtesy City of Vancouver Archives)

In the second week he started getting up for short periods, and in the third spent more time out of bed and left the hospital now and then for drives in the Hitchens' car. By the end of the prescribed month he was feeling quite well and able to handle a new restriction when Brodie told him to stop smoking. As a pipe-smoker, he loved the paraphernalia and little ceremonies that accompany that awful habit — so giving it up was hard indeed, but only for six days it seems, though it is not clear whether he started again with the doctor's blessing. By the last week in March he seemed as right as rain, though still living at the hospital and hammering out articles on the typewriter he had had delivered. These were Great War 'second thoughts' pieces: "Passchendaele 1917", "Canon Scott", "Heroes and Cowards", "Brass Hats" — all published in the *Province* during March, along with articles on the west coast scene for *The Times*. He and Bee had also started house-hunting and made several expeditions into Kitsilano, even into darkest Point Grey now that he seemed strong enough — usually in a borrowed vehicle.

It was wonderful — he seemed cured already but, inevitably, he overdid it. On April Fool's Day his old symptoms reared their ugly heads and, though he tried to will them away, within a week they had him back in bed on a starvation diet. This time things went more easily; maybe the nerve specialist had been right and all he had really needed was rest and a steady life. Compared to life as Loomis's Staff Captain 'Q', his life since entering VGH had been steady indeed — he had slept in the same bed every night, for instance, without hearing a single German shell exploding anywhere near — just the comforting bass vibrations, now and then, of the Point Atkinson foghorn. A week on a strict regime did the trick: he was up and about well before their anniversary on the 18th, which they celebrated by attending a protest-meeting of the Great War Veterans Association (GWVA), an organization he had joined just before being forced back to bed. Vancouver, like most Canadian cities, was in a political ferment because of the lack of jobs for the thousands of returning veterans. Rufus and Bee postponed their real celebration until the next night; then they went to the Orpheum to see Annette Kellerman, the sensational[82] Australian actress in the movie *Queen of the Sea* — in which she swam in a mermaid-suit of her own design.

Whether inspired by the mermaid or just by getting stronger, he had no further relapses. Though still living at the hospital, he plunged into civilian life and the last ten days of April became a bubbling mixture of house-hunting, journalism, and politics. After looking at many places, he and Bee rented a flat at 1521 Arbutus, close to Kitsilano Beach. When he was not house-hunting, his VGH neighbours had to put up with the clickety-clack of his typewriter as he produced "The State of the Nation" and "Soldiers and Politics" for the *BC Veterans Weekly*, a long article on shipbuilding for *The Times* and no doubt others for the *Province*. In the evenings, on his own or with Bee, he went to political meetings — Socialists at the old Empress Theatre one night, the Comrades of the Great War meeting with the Trades and Labour Council at the Avenue

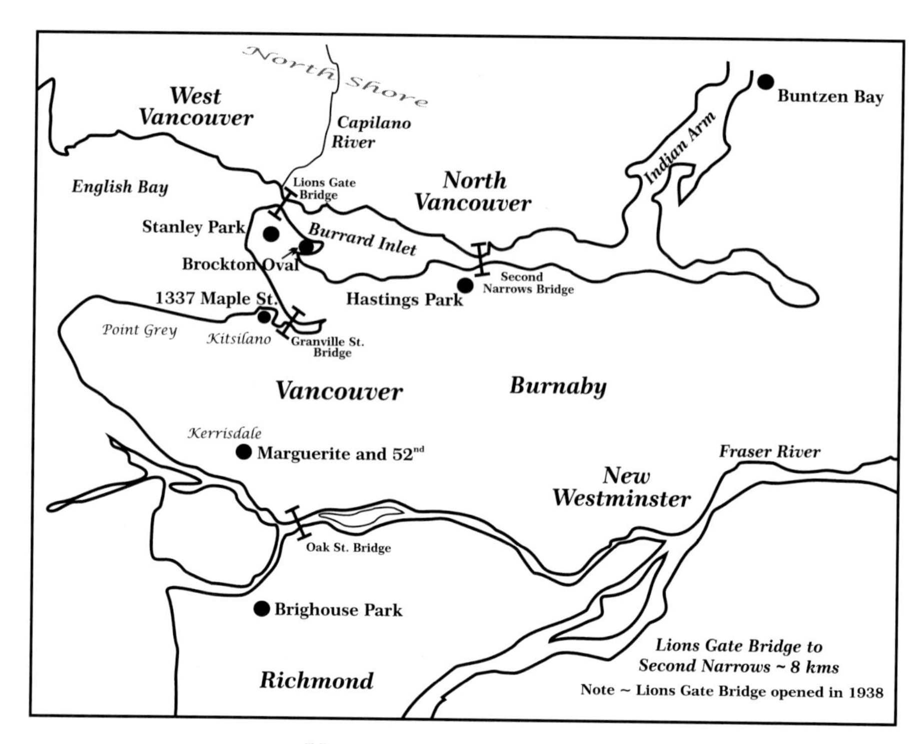

Vancouver and District

Theatre the next — both meetings under police surveillance, unbeknownst to him. At the latter meeting, he was greatly impressed by the speech made by "[W.A.] Pritchard, the labour leader." To be fair, he also went to hear the Tory leader of the opposition, W. J. Bowser, a man never likely to set False Creek on fire. When they had time, he and Bee, with Derek in tow, bought furniture for the flat and started hanging pictures and polishing brass. And to round off the month, 7th Battalion came home. Rufus went to the docks to see their ceremonial welcome by the Lieutenant Governor and to welcome old friends, men he had last seen in the drama of that August advance — Colonel Gilson, Major Philpot, and various others including Cowley, the runner with whom he had got lost looking for 2nd Brigade's new HQ on the night of 9 August — somewhere east of Amiens.

For Bee, the three months of his hospital treatment had been hard. She herself had had two spells of sickness, first with a cold and later with what Rufus called neuritis, on one occasion consulting Dr Brodie while she was visiting. They had done their best to look after each other and Derek had been packed off for days at a time, once to Mrs Mascall and then to Willum's, both in New Westminster. Bee had recovered quickly on both occasions, had done plenty of hospital visiting and most of the house-hunting. As she made friends easily, she was starting to have a social life, spending much time with Mrs Makovski, wife of Rufus's journalist friend, and being invited to tea by several other women. What was even better, for the time being she had no money worries.

At the end of April Rufus felt able to apply for his discharge. This happened on the 29th when, technically, he was discharged to the Department of Soldiers' Civil Re-establishment,[83] through which agency he would eventually receive a small disability pension. At the beginning of May he moved out of the hospital and into their new home. To mark that milestone, on May Day he visited the *Province* and arranged to start work in four days time, Monday, May 5. That evening he went to a GWVA meeting, called to decide whether to form the soldiers' political party about which there had been much talk. In a speech to the five hundred men present, Rufus comprehensively opposed the idea. He tells us, "My views were carried overwhelmingly and I got much applause although I got a bit tangled up in spots." It had been his first public speech and he discovered that he rather enjoyed it.

His last few days of postwar limbo were spent in their new apartment, cleaning windows, staining the sideboard, and hanging curtains. The *Province* phoned on Sunday 4 May — *SS Monteagle*, carrying Canadian troops back from Siberia, would dock in Victoria on Monday: would he please cover it? He packed a bag, took the night boat and was back in harness. All things considered, he could congratulate himself on having handled the hazards and delays of their return to Canada, and of his own 'civil re-establishment', with considerable dexterity.

Chapter 12
On the Beat
Vancouver, 1919–1921

"David, lad, you know very well you shouldn't ask me that. Don't spoil the spirit of these gatherings by trying to trip me up."

Warren Harding to journalist in the Oval Office, November 1921

It is a truism that war ruins lives. In Rufus's family the Great War ended his younger brother's; it may well have ruined his father's, as Rufus had suggested in "Make them Pay"; and it did few favours for his older brother, destroying the confidence of the self-reliant young fellow who had created a fruit farm from wild land beside Kootenay Lake in 1909. And Rufus? Well, the war certainly dulled his hearing, gave him intestinal problems with which he had to learn to live and increased his liking for alcohol and tobacco. But, crucially for his chosen profession, it also accustomed him to dealing comfortably with people in high places and provided him with networks of friends and strategic contacts in Canada and Britain. More important than either of these, it gave him answers to the questions about himself that every male asks: after Passchendaele and Amiens he knew what kind of man he was — few future tasks could ever seem too daunting. The young pup who had tried to rule the roost in Duncan, having been through the fire, had emerged at 31 with the potential to be one of Canada's most influential journalists.

Rufus was probably unaware of how great had been his personal development. He saw himself as the one-time editor of the *Cowichan Leader* and Night Editor of the *Colonist* and would have been satisfied with nothing less than editorial work. To his boss, Walter Nichol, the man who had headhunted him in France, his potential was obvious. How many journalists, after all, would have come back from the war as stringers for the prestigious London *Times*, and with arrangements to write for other papers too? But he also knew that Rufus's training as a journalist was sketchy, to say the least, and insisted he start as a beat journalist. Disappointed as he must have been, Rufus needed the job too badly to go looking elsewhere; he not only accepted Nichol's conditions, but, on that first day in Vancouver after three years away from BC and from newspapers, had actually seemed pleased with them.

It is no surprise, then, that his career as a journalist was slow to take off again. He had several preoccupations during 1919 which made it difficult for him to do much more than was asked of him. Uppermost in his mind, more pressing even than the need to sort out his own health, was the urgent need to restore Bee's. The symptoms for which she had consulted a gynecologist in London stayed with her and she had taken the opportunity, when visiting Rufus at VGH, to consult his doctor, Dr Brodie, who seems to have become her doctor too. Her condition reached a crisis in June when she was in bed for a week under Brodie's care; he decided, together with Dr Gillies from VGH, that she needed an operation, which she underwent on 3 September.

The next few days were tense ones for Rufus. Added to his worries about Bee, how was he to care for six-year-old Derek while his mother was in hospital? Roy and Marjory were still solving their own problems at the time, but fortunately Mrs Phelan, Bee's good friend whose two children Derek knew quite well, asked the boy to stay with her in North Vancouver until Bee could have him home again — a solution for which Rufus was most grateful.

For their friends' benefit he put an announcement in the paper on the 4th. "Mrs Lukin Johnston underwent a serious operation in the General Hospital on Wednesday. Her condition is as satisfactory as can be expected." She was quickly out of danger, however, and by the 7th he was allowed to take Derek to see her. Nevertheless, she was not home until the end of the month and even then Rufus, or Mrs Robertson who came to look after her, needed to trundle her about in a bath chair. The operation seemed to have been successful though she remained prone to ill-defined health problems from time to time. But by the end of the year they both felt able to stop worrying about her.

ALTHOUGH RUFUS WAS DISCHARGED from the army on 29 April 1919, in his mind it remained the central element of his life. The situation for returning soldiers was dire: the economy was flat, jobs few, veteran's benefits slow in coming and, as a veteran fortunate enough to have a job — and one in which he could actually *do* something about their predicament — his involvement with the GWVA was inevitable and he joined it as soon as he was on the mend. Its meetings were rowdy and there was much talk of forming an ex-soldiers' political party — something that would, thanks to Lenin, have introduced a counter-productive whiff of possible revolutionary intent. He had tried to calm things down with "Soldiers and Politics", an article in the 24 April *BC Veterans' Weekly*, but ultimately had been compelled to get up and speak at a GVWA meeting. His words made an impression and a week later he was chosen by acclamation as a delegate to the GWVA Dominion Convention, due to open in Vancouver on Dominion Day.

In his diary May and June reflected a crescendo of soldier politics as local battalions came home one after another, each adding five or six hundred voices to the disgruntled throng: the 7th Battalion was followed in May by the 16th, the Machine Gun Brigade and the 29th, and in June by the 47th and 72nd. Nevertheless, restless and aggrieved as some soldiers felt, their thunder was stolen by events in Winnipeg, where the General Strike was called on 15 May involving almost all the city's workers and grabbing the nation's attention. Winnipeg workers' grievances were rooted in an earlier strike — and thus not related directly to those of returning veterans — but most veterans naturally sympathized with them. Other general strikes followed in Calgary, Edmonton, Toronto, and, finally, on June 3 in Vancouver. Rufus was directly affected when the union to which the *Province*'s printers belonged not only joined the strike but insisted on using the presses to print strike journals.

By the 10th he may have decided where duty lay — or it may just have been all in the day's work. When that night's GWVA meeting was cancelled because of the streetcar strike, he went instead to a meeting of the "Law and Order League", a citizens' committee similar to Winnipeg's "Citizens' Committee of One Thousand". On another night, this time certainly in the line of duty, he attended a strikers' meeting in the Denman Arena. Vancouver streetcars were not running again until the 30th, but by then he seemed to have lost interest and, like everyone else, was focused on the tragic events of Bloody Saturday on 21 June and the ending of Winnipeg's strike five days later. At that time it was quite a shock to him to hear that W.A. Pritchard, whose speech had so impressed him in April, had been arrested and charged with 'seditious conspiracy' in Calgary. The federal government clearly had the wind up about Bolshevism, underlining the wisdom of his opposition to forming a soldiers' party.

The GWVA convention, which had seemed so important a few weeks earlier, opened in Vancouver against this background. Rufus attended its meetings as a delegate but the steam seemed to have gone from the soldiers' protests. Meetings were noisy, but also surprisingly orderly and . . . and . . . *boring*! Nevertheless he remained involved, not only for the rest of 1919 but he served on the executive right through 1920. The principal issue became the soldiers' demand for the reasonable and non-political idea of a war service gratuity, something dear to his own heart. This was essentially settled early in 1920: an unmarried private with three years service would receive $420, the amount to increase with rank and be reduced for less time served. Rufus, never one to let the grass grow, took his own case to the very top. In March 1920, at the GWVA convention in Montreal, he interviewed General Currie and took the opportunity of confirming his own gratuity and wired Bee two days later that all was arranged.

The military had entered his soul in a way he could never have imagined in Cowichan days. Then, he had hobnobbed with army types — men older than himself with exotic tales to tell of the army in India. He knew them as fathers, husbands, landowners, investors — but only by repute as soldiers. Now he was part of the unspoken fellowship of the thousands of officers and men who had been in France. They had lived the same hell — in many cases a worse one. He was well-known — his job had taken him to most of the messes and frontline trenches, OP's and listening posts, HQs and transport lines of every brigade in the corps — and he had their respect. Many had gone overseas with the 88th, as he had done, only to be split up among the BC battalions already at the front. In the case of the 16th (Canadian Scottish), to which he had been sent, many had come from the Seaforth Depot in Vancouver. Survivors of the original 88th came home with the 16th, the 72nd (Seaforths) and with other battalions. They remembered the same absent faces — amongst them Campbell, McGowan, Cornell, Rowan, and Johnson, all killed at Vimy; or Lyonel's friend Joe Mason, killed on the Drocourt–Quéant the day before Rufus left France. There was a bond between them all; while wives, families, colleagues — at least, those who hadn't been to war themselves — could never *really* understand what they had done or had been through, when veterans were together again, even if only briefly, they had no need to explain, no need even to speak. Just being together was better therapy than any hospital could provide and enabled them to begin their lives again.

So it was that Rufus could often be found at military events — fortunately, also part of his *Province* beat. He was there on the dock or the railway platform when each of the seven or eight battalions came home, and when *Monteagle* docked with Canadian troops from Siberia, amongst them General Elmsley whom he'd known at Vimy and Passchendaele, and Stayner, BM at 9th brigade. He was in the Vancouver Club, representing the 16th and 72nd, to discuss with General Odlum and others the perpetuation of the 7th Battalion,[84] and later, when General Currie opened the 7th Battalion rooms. When the 16th arrived, he went to its battalion dinner at the HBC with General Currie, Col. Godson-Godson and Charles Tupper (Jr), and later to the Seaforth Club to hear Col. Cy Peck speak. He knew and admired them all and could write about them with understanding.

In July he took a working field trip on a Union steamship to Rivers Inlet and back, gathering material for articles on the canneries, and everywhere chatted with returned men. He would drop in at the Seaforth Club occasionally and went to battalion reunion dinners in the fall, over which BC's short-lived prohibition was casting an unwelcoming pall. After a stolid, 'dry' event at the Hotel Vancouver, Rufus protested to his diary: "a reunion banquet without liquor is an impossible failure!" The 16th Battalion put that right at the Empress in Victoria a few night's later. "Generals Currie, Newburn, Leckie, etc., were there and about 150 all ranks. An excellent show with plenty of whiskey upstairs. To bed about 1 am."

Meanwhile he was doing his best to make his beat bearable. When he started work in May, he was shown round by another journalist — as if visiting the Stations of the Cross. That was not his style and his diaries mention the word 'beat' only once again — in 1920, when he was asked to cover hotels too. Judging by what he actually wrote about, his original assignment included the military, high-profile visitors, labour issues, and maybe the fishing industry — but not provincial politics, despite his Victoria contacts and knowledge. In the short term, of course, covering military topics was a full-time job and that suited him fine. He had made a good start before his official employment began, with articles on the war that Nichol nevertheless published. But for most of 1919 he had his hands full with soldier politics and the plight of returned men. Strikes, too, were within his territory, and 1919 gave him plenty of material.

On 28 July he had two columns on the first page with his own byline, celebrating "Currie of Canada" at a time when the general was being publicly accused of reckless disregard for the lives of his men by a bitter Sam Hughes and his son Garnett, by then an MP. Rufus loudly proclaimed Currie's greatness as a general and as a Canadian.

> Currie of Canada, a name known to half the people of the civilized world, a name which has rung round the world a dozen times these last four years. [He listed his triumphs] . . . Passchendaele, Amiens, Cambrai and finally Mons – which led to the complete rout of the German forces.

He then endorsed Currie's call for the recognition of Canadian nationhood in a recent London speech, reporting the great man's words.

> The war has brought about many drastic changes in the viewpoint of the Dominions concerning their relations with the Motherland. They now believe it urgent that a new basis be found which will recognize that certain parts of the Empire have earned the status of nations, and are anxious that every suggestion of political inferiority be removed.

Currie had a new tribune and their good relationship was henceforth important to them both.

His work for *The Times* not only brought extra income, it made it possible to choose what he would write about. In that first year he worked hard for them and was able to turn his recent local experiences to account. Long only asked him for specific news during the general strikes, otherwise he wrote about whatever he found interesting — impressions of England, Canadian trade, the One Big Union, BC's prospects, shipbuilding, Vancouver Island, the Rivers Inlet trip, and forest fires — quite a miscellany, making his work more enjoyable than it might otherwise have been. His material was picked up at various times by the *Sun* and the *Colonist*, even by the *Glasgow Herald*.

His first year included visits to BC of the Prince of Wales, and subsequently of Admiral Lord Jellicoe, the hero of Jutland and "the only man on either side who could have lost the war in an afternoon."[85] Though he interviewed the Prince, Rufus's interest seems not to have been much engaged. Not so when Jellicoe appeared off Esquimalt aboard *HMS New Zealand*. He had crossed to Victoria the night before and had gone straight to the Esquimalt dockyard. The admiral in charge permitted him to drive "as fast as possible" in a rented car[86] out to William Head — a restricted area. With the assistance of officers he must have known, he talked his way aboard the great dreadnought in a launch, met Jellicoe's private secretary, who arranged for him to have twenty minutes with the great man before the ship docked. After attending the dinner at the Empress that night, where General Currie was among the VIPs, he returned to Vancouver on the midnight boat. His story scooped every other newspaper, including the *Colonist* and the *Sun*, both of which ran his article, and it was distributed to a wider audience, free, by the *Province*. It would be his first scoop!

There was an entertaining sequel. Jellicoe, who had been asked by the Admiralty to report on harbours and naval facilities in the Pacific, asked Rufus many questions about the coast and also discussed with him, somewhat indiscreetly, a number of the Admiralty's strategic concepts — before requesting, belatedly, that these be kept off the record. Rufus, of course, agreed, and about a year later was delighted to receive a signed photograph from Jellicoe with a note on the back: "a memento of unbroken confidences".[87]

In spite of the obvious satisfaction that such encounters brought, Rufus continued to feel throughout 1919 that he should be able to find more rewarding employment than beat journalism with a bit of freelance work on the side. *What*, he asked himself, *if I was to open my own newspaper?* Surely, after his prewar work in Duncan and Victoria, he had the experience and the contacts — and while he was recovering in hospital the idea had preoccupied him. His friend Lionel Makovski had launched a newspaper during the war, which had failed. Rufus persuaded himself that Makovski was not a very practical fellow and that his paper would survive. The Johnstons and the Makovskis got along well and the two men discussed his idea. He consulted others too — his diary reads: "Leveson up to see me in the afternoon and we discussed possibilities for my paper. Tines, the printer, here in the morning." Maybe they convinced him it was a bad idea; more likely it was Bee who must have appreciated the security of Nichol's pay cheque when they were living on considerably less than a major's pay. Whatever the case, he abandoned the idea, as suddenly as he had taken it up, and was soon pounding out articles on his typewriter for other people's newspapers.

Still, the idea of there being 'something better' refused to go away. He kept his ear to the ground, and on 26 May heard that the BC government was inviting applications for an Industrial Commissioner at $3,000 a year. Sure that the sum of his experiences qualified him, Rufus shifted into top gear: he applied that same day, wired Generals Hill and Loomis for letters of support and wrote to others. Of the twenty applicants, nine, himself included, were invited to write an examination in the Parliament Buildings on 2 June. Alas, on the 14th he wrote in his diary: "Major Martyn, DSO, MC, appointed Industrial Commissioner. He is past president of the Liberal Association in John Oliver's [the premier's] riding! Enough said — but he may be very capable just the same." Such a charitable reaction does him credit.

After that disappointment he seemed to forget about non-journalistic ambitions, but the embers were alive — just waiting for the right breeze. Of all times this sprang up on Christmas Day, when he heard — maybe at early service at Christ Church or at the Phelans' in North Vancouver where they were eating Christmas dinner[88] — that E.O.S. Scholefield, provincial archivist and legislature librarian, had died that morning. At once he was determined to have his job.

On Boxing Day morning, unable to contain his eagerness, he rushed off to see Nichol about his new ambition. When that gentleman had presumably given him his blessing, plus a letter to William Sloan, Minister of Mines, he mailed his application to Victoria. The next day his editor Roy Brown gave him a letter to John Farris, Minister of Labour & Attorney General, and he contacted General Leckie for yet another. Thus equipped, at midnight on 28 December he left for Victoria on the *Princess May*.

The omens were not good. The *Princess* ran aground on a sandbar off Prospect Point, where she remained all night — but she floated off on the morning tide and arrived in Victoria just six hours late. That evening, after interviews with Dr McLean, the Provincial Secretary, and then the Minister of Mines, he felt "fairly hopeful." But the following day more probing interviews with Farris and then Hart, Minister of Finance — who probably pointed out his lack of obvious qualification beyond being a writer of good English — left him "not so hopeful." He seemed to accept this, went home on the afternoon boat and we hear no more about it. Having at least done something about his restlessness, he went back to trying to make a success out of journalism in 1920. The librarian's job eventually went to John Forsyth, a bookish gentleman who would hold it until 1934.

He and Bee had made a good decision about where to live. Life downtown had had merit for the bachelor set in former days, but railroad tracks, docks and factories on False Creek made it difficult to enjoy Vancouver as the seaside town it is. So, following the streetcar line across the trestle to Kitsilano, they found their flat at 1521 Arbutus Street an ideal location for summer. By mid-June, sometimes with Derek and occasionally Bee, Rufus was bathing daily in English Bay off nearby Kits beach — he could be in the water within ten minutes of getting home. When not on trips up the coast, he continued swimming until fall, though there were occasional no-swimming days even for him, when the water was covered in oil from a ship or in ash from Point Grey forest fires.[89] Their Arbutus location became a destination for good times on the beach for friends with families — the Phelans came several times and, when Roy and Marjory arrived in July, they brought Robin to play there.

Things turned out well for Roy. Rufus, through the GWVA, was familiar with the programs becoming available for returned men, was able to arrange interviews for his brother with strategic people and he had a job with the Land

Settlement Board within six weeks of their arrival. He and Marjory quickly became self-sufficient and went to live in North Vancouver.

There was soon another family refugee in town, fleeing hard times in England. This was Phil, Rufus's and Roy's much younger cousin and son of Uncle Jack. He arrived in early October and Rufus found him work in Duncan on Walter Paterson's farm. When he passed through Duncan some time later, Phil had moved to Hadwin's farm. That job did not last either and, just in time for Christmas, he was once more out of work and back in Vancouver. He was showing ominous 'black sheep' tendencies and Rufus lost no time arranging yet another job, at Cowichan Station, for which Phil left on Boxing Day.

As the flat on Arbutus offered no advantages in winter, they moved back into town. Reviving their Duncan custom, they took two rooms for the winter in the Abbotsford Hotel at 971 West Pender Street. Instead of being ten minutes from Kits Beach, they were now five minutes walk from Christ Church cathedral, ten from the Orpheum Theatre, and fifteen from Stanley Park. Christmas shopping had suddenly become easy; it was going to be a good winter. Living in a hotel also meant they often had free time in the evenings — Bee sometimes went to a movie with a friend, of which she had an increasing number, while Rufus went to a meeting or to his club. Thus, on 3 January Rufus's diary notes "Bee out to show at night — I to club till 10 pm". Derek, who turned seven in February, was both self-sufficient and trustworthy and seemed not to mind being put to bed or being left on his own with a book.

They must usually have eaten in the hotel dining room but when they went to a movie or a play, which they did often, they ate elsewhere — Barron's Café being a favourite. Rufus, one feels, hoped they would be regulars at Christ Church cathedral on Georgia and that they would go for walks in Stanley Park — in fact, in January they went twice to the cathedral and twice to the park, and not to walk but to feed the bears! After that, the only times he visited either was after they were back in Kitsilano — they were usually too busy or too tired.

Rufus was elected to the GWVA executive in January which involved a weekly executive meeting and a full membership meeting the following night; he was also on the committee that organized 'smokers', and was a GWVA delegate to the national convention in Montreal in March, involving an absence of more than three weeks. The gratuity issue was effectively settled by the spring though he kept pressing the powers that be, even bothering General Currie himself until the cheques came in May. This convention had been taken over by men of extreme views, in Rufus's opinion, who passed a resolution asking for a minimum cash bonus of $1000 etc, etc, ". . . with which I disagree entirely, and which means, in my opinion, that the GWVA forfeits all right to public confidence as a sane and reasonable body of men." As his opinion did not change, he submitted his resignation. This was not accepted and in September he wrote in his diary: "To GWVA executive meeting — since they refuse to let me resign." He served out the year for which he had been elected but allowed his membership to lapse in 1921.

Although the convention was frustrating, it gave him an opportunity, afforded to few in those days, to renew friendships across the country. He met numbers of men he knew from the war in France, including some good friends — among them Charlie Illseley, Leighton, Louis Younger, Canon Scott, General Loomis, General Currie, and Col Cy Peck, now an MP. In Montreal he looked up the Molsons, Bee's erstwhile employers, who entertained him royally; in Ottawa he bumped into Miall, his Govan partner from 1908, and they met several times — once going together to see a civil service commissioner, possibly on behalf of Roy;[90] in Toronto he visited Mrs Nash, his shipboard friend from 1905; and he stopped overnight in Humboldt, Saskatchewan, at the invitation of Judge and Mrs Dickson, friends from Qu'Appelle days. Of more professional benefit, he renewed a friendship with Stewart Lyon, now of the *Globe*, whom he had shown round the Somme battlefield in 1917, and made new contacts in the newspaper world, including Craig of the *Edmonton Journal*, and Parkinson at the *Toronto Star*.

Meanwhile, he continued to chafe at the restrictions of his job at the *Province*. 1920 had begun with a flurry of new jobs offered to him or new projects suggested. He had revived the idea of starting his own paper, perhaps by buying a small going concern, and had let his interest be known. Cryptic diary entries are the only sources for offers he received and what follows is a bit conjectural. On 5 February he had been approached by Robert Cromie, editor of the *Sun*, to take on the editorship of his *Farm and Home* supplement. In early March Frank Harris had talked to him about the *Citizen* — clearly not the one in Ottawa, maybe a small local paper but more likely the name for a proposed start-up; on 10 April, just back from Montreal, he saw Neel of the Employers Association about a job on *Balance*, Paton about the *Point Grey Gazette*, and also talked to Beveridge, a *Province* colleague, about the *Citizen*. He seems to have narrowed the field to the *Citizen* and to have negotiated a loan from General Odlum,[91] intended either to purchase a going concern or to fund a start-up. A week later he wrote in his diary: "I shall be under no obligation to him as regards the paper — the money will be purely a personal loan." The reader can be excused for hearing echoes of the Matson loan! However, after another talk with Harris on 28 April he "decided against the whole *Citizen* proposition!"

So it was probably no coincidence that in the previous two weeks he had been elected president of the just-formed Vancouver Branch of the BC Institute of Journalists and then, at its first meeting, provincial president — the members having scrapped the constitution in order to so vote! No other branch yet existed and they were seeking members among newspapermen across BC.[92] This supports the notion that he was realizing where his future lay — not so much in any particular journal that he might or might not control, but more rewardingly in the wider world of journalism where he was becoming known for astute reporting and memorable use of the language.

The latter was displayed in his progress report on the future Point Grey campus of UBC.[93] Few *Province* readers had yet seen the still-remote site when he described the view from the top of the unfinished Chemistry Centre, the first permanent building:

> Across the tops of the tall firs and pines to the north there is a clear view up the waters of Howe Sound, bounded by the snow-capped peaks of the Coast Range. To the west the mountains on Vancouver Island gleam in the setting sun, while to the south the waters at the mouth of the mighty Fraser are bathed in red and gold. Over all is the stillness of the forest; the giant blackened stumps of the great trees still stand erect in mute protest against the incursions of the white man . . . a few years ago Point Grey was primeval forest, its history hidden in the breasts of the Indians whose hunting ground it was.

It so happened, again probably not by coincidence, that the Imperial Press Conference — a pow-wow of journalism's big guns from across a still-formidable British Empire — was convening in Ottawa in August. As BCIJ president, Rufus was in a good position to ask Nichol to let him attend. He made his request in June and repeated it in early July. Feeling ambushed, no doubt, Nichol then agreed. At that point Sir Arthur Willett, *The Times* man in Washington, appeared in Vancouver and Rufus wrote an article on him, mentioning the imperial conference. Nichol suddenly took notice — he discovered that only members of the Empire Press Union might attend, which put a different complexion on things, so he summoned Rufus and announced that he, Nichol, would go instead! Rufus's trip east, however, was saved by the bell: as a man of many interests, Nichol ran out of time and, at the last possible moment, he told Rufus to start packing!

Bee may not have been overjoyed as this would be the second time he had deserted her that year. It had taken seven days to reach Montreal in March, much of it waiting for the track to be plowed. This time he reached Ottawa in four. Unfortunately, a Banff mosquito bite became infected and he arrived in great pain with a face like a pumpkin. Having the swelling lanced fixed the problem, but his unsightly and painful condition ruined the conference for him. Nevertheless he did meet the famous J.W. Dafoe of the *Winnipeg Free Press*, as well as Messrs Borden, Meighen, and Mackenzie King, prime ministers past, present and future, including a half-hour with Meighen. He also met Lord Burnham, owner of the *Daily Telegraph*, and Willison, *The Times* Canadian correspondent. It was all grist for his mill.

Feeling much better, on the way home he visited old haunts in Qu'Appelle. He spent a day with Creamer, the vet, and his family, while another friend drove him to visit "Old Henley", the surveyor whose judgment he had accepted on homesteading. The next day was Sports Day and, as a well-remembered and popular prodigal, he was pressed into judging the parade. Back in Regina, while waiting for his train west, he spent time with Sam Latta. They "had great talk of old times at Govan" — long ago Sam had been a printer in Govan or Strasbourg; now, at 55, he was "Minister of Railways in the Saskatchewan government and a great man."

At the end of April Rufus and Bee had moved back to 1521 Arbutus for another summer. It was not as hot as 1919 but father and son bathed just as often. Rufus played tennis when opportunity arose but his attitude to strenuous exercise was relaxed — he probably got plenty striding around town on the hotels beat. Derek had been agitating for a dog and as soon as they settled in 'Jerry' appeared. Unfortunately, the family dog jinx decreed a short tenure for this animal, about which we never discover much: they all took him for a walk on his very first day — then silence; six weeks later we are told: "Jerry bit young Dixon, the grocer's boy, rather badly — and had to be shut up." Finally, after a short incarceration, we learn: "Reg Harwood came and fetched Jerry away" — to what fate we never discover. But there was no (recorded) protest — and no immediate replacement.

In fact their lives were becoming less dog-friendly by the day. Rufus was often away or home late. Derek began school in January — half-days only at first — but he was certainly out all day after he started at Lockington's in September. And a new dog, which would need training and cleaning up after, would not easily have fitted into Bee's growing social life: she is recorded as having been out to tea two dozen times in 1920 and to have hosted plenty of her own 'tea-fights'. Of her friends at least twenty were named in the diary, of whom she had become close to six.[94] She had the makings of the kind of life that would have been no fun for Fido, one suspects.

In the first week of September Rufus and Bee packed Derek off to the Phelans and, after eight years of marriage, took their first-ever holiday together — such had been the restrictions imposed by war, journalism, and poverty! They took the ferry to Nanaimo, spent a couple of nights at the Tzouhalem Hotel in Duncan and the rest of the week at the Empress in Victoria. They made a loving, low-key progress through a mixed cast of friends in both places. They enjoyed every day, starting each with their favourite treat, breakfast in bed. In Duncan, they visited St Stephen's, their first house, and Somenos Church. Rufus, of course, could never leave journalism entirely behind — he had to take Bee to an election meeting of the Liberty League,[95] but they did meet old friends. They arrived in Victoria just in time for Rufus to canvass a meeting of newspapermen for the BCIJ; they later house-hopped among friends, visited Linden Cottage, Oak Bay, and Beacon Hill Park, and went to Matins in the cathedral, where Rufus, starved of theological discourse, relished Dean Quainton's polished sermon on the text "Why sentest thou me?" Then it was back to Vancouver where they had dinner at Barron's on the way home — "not good," Rufus commented in rare disapproval, adding sniffily, "and not a good class of people there in general!" Despite this judgment, by then uncharacteristic of them both, they had had a great holiday.

As 1920 wound down, they chose a different solution for winter quarters. This time they remained in Kitsilano but moved to a flat at 2456 Point Grey Road, rented from friends — the Orchardsons. Their reasoning is obscure as it was further from town and all were happy to move back again in April 1921. No sooner had they moved, however, than Rufus and Bee became completely involved in producing and performing the institute play. They chose *The Rest Cure*, a one-act play by Gertrude Jennings, for which Bee auditioned, netting the main female part. After a frenzied month of rehearsals in their flat, with Rufus responsible for scenery, props, venue, the programme and more, the play was a success in front of two hundred people at the Abbotsford Hotel. Apart from giving them both a sense of achievement, her role as Muriel launched Bee as an amateur actress in Vancouver and Rufus's success with his various tasks made him want to do it all again. Henceforth, amateur theatre would be central to their lives in Vancouver. The play also confirmed Rufus's leadership of the BCIJ, which would become his focus for the next few years.

Journalism was continuing to give Rufus opportunities to meet extraordinary people and his writing about them, among other things, was building his reputation. He had an arrangement with Kent, desk clerk at the Hotel Vancouver, to tip him off whenever a celebrity checked in — and there were many, most of them in transit to somewhere else. His scoop of the year was from his discovery that the Mrs T.B. Clarke, Jr. on the hotel guest-list was actually the red-hot silent screen star Elsie Ferguson on her way to California. Acclaimed by some as the most beautiful woman ever to tread the American stage, Elsie was at the peak of public adulation. She agreed to an interview and Rufus's article on her rang bells across the continent.

Less sensational, but probably more satisfying, were his encounters with the movers and shakers about whom he wrote. The most prominent of these were Paul Painlevé, a wartime prime minister of France; Samuel Gompers, boss of the American Federation of Labor, on his way to the Democratic Party convention, with whom Rufus walked from the train station to the San Francisco boat, firing questions and scribbling as he went; and W.H. Taft, ex-president of the USA and about to become Chief Justice of the Supreme Court. Painlevé, incidentally, had passed through New York a few days previously but no New York journalist interviewed him because none spoke French!

In the last couple of months of 1920 three events occurred which, in retrospect, were significant for Rufus's future. On 17 November he noted in his diary: "Interviewed a Hun — Kocher — on his way to Shanghai — the first Hun party here since the war." It may have surprised him that he could talk to the man; after two years, it seems, the emotions of his 1918 *Daily Mail* article had subsided and he would soon be able to contemplate visiting Germany itself. Then, he had a friendly chat at the Hotel Vancouver with F.I. Kerr, a Port Alice acquaintance who was returning to live in Montreal. Kerr invited him to look him up when next in the east, causing Rufus to observe that he was a nice fellow and, as the son-in-law of F. N. Southam, worth knowing.

The third event was the appointment of Walter Nichol as BC's Lieutenant Governor. With his departure to Victoria, and consequent withdrawal from daily contact with the *Province*, Rufus's relations with his immediate bosses — Cairns, News Editor, and Roy Brown, Editor-in-Chief — became more difficult. Rufus was a square peg in a round hole, a journalist whose interests knew no bounds having to limit his activities to a beat, to a particular area of news.

Both Nichol and Brown had started as office boys at Canadian newspapers and considered beat journalism a necessary apprenticeship for newspapermen whatever their talent. Nichol understood Rufus's frustration: before the war, when Rufus first wrote for the *Province*, Nichol had tolerated his undisciplined pursuit of stories on a more or less freelance basis — because his pieces, though often too confrontational for direct inclusion, helped sell the paper. Although he would not encourage his grander aspirations until he had done his time on the beat, he would cut him some slack because, in addition to writing ability, Rufus had life experience that few journalists could match, and consequently knowledge and understanding of the issues of the day.

Brown (known as R.B.) was much younger than Nichol, though still seven years older than Rufus. Brown's newspaper background and adult experience had been limited to Vancouver. Nichol had recruited him in 1901 for his accuracy and fine writing, and as time passed, his remarkable memory and deep knowledge of BC public affairs made him an excellent editor and resource. So it may have irked R.B. that his telegraph desk reporter was also special correspondent of *The Times*, not to mention founder and president-by-acclamation of the BC Institute of Journalists. The final straw would be Rufus's decision to go to the disarmament conference in Washington; one of his journalists was to be absent on assignment for 58 days without his having dispatched him!

1921 started badly for the western Johnstons. Marjory was expecting a baby in the last part of January and, when Johnstons and Squires gathered for the happy occasion, things took a desperately sad turn when the child was born dead. While Marjory remained in St Paul's Hospital, for ten days Rufus's and Bee's Point Grey Road flat became a temporary home for Roy, Robin, Marjory's sister Agnes Jardine, Agnes's five-year-old Marjorie — and Phil, at the time between jobs once more. Friends came in and out, some bearing food, all meaning well. The tragedy was hardest on Roy, Marjory, and Robin, of course, whose grief was hard to witness and to comfort, but the emotional stress, the constant coming and going, the passing off of children, the need to maintain good cheer, the chaos and the noise — all took an increasing toll on Bee. By the time Marjory was able to go home, Bee was, in Rufus's words, "fagged out and lying on the sofa all day." At this juncture, a Sunday, Cairns phoned — Rufus was off the hotel beat and Cairns wanted him on the telegraph desk next morning!

While deciding what to do about Bee, completely laid low, Rufus had a hard time digesting a job change — even such a welcome one. For a few days he arranged for friends to be with her while he was working. The pressure on him was compounded by approaching BCIJ events that demanded his time and he decided to put Bee in a nursing home. She had been there, recovering slowly, for a week, when a new specialist examined her and declared she needed another operation! The news hit Rufus hard. "All the good of the rest is undone now by this report," he groaned to his diary. However, when she came home she was feeling better, but still too low to go out for a week or two. Now and then during this period Rufus fed Derek at the fish-and-chip shop, about which he felt guilty though no doubt it pleased his son.

In the last week of February he may have felt his own health crisis approaching because he twice went for extremely long walks — something he had not been doing — as though trying to regain control. He put on a BCIJ dinner, at which he spoke, for the visiting actors Sir Martin Harvey, his actress wife, and about 75 members. Shortly afterwards the institute held a dance at the Stanley Park Pavilion. Bee felt too tired for either function but Rufus, of course, had to organize them. That weekend it all caught up with him — the worry over Roy and Marjory, Bee's uncertain state, his new job, the stress of being the institute's frontman and, to cap it all, feeling responsible for Phil who was still hanging around and unemployed. He tried to walk it off on Sunday but on Monday felt rotten and went home early. Next morning he felt even worse, was running a fever while all his wartime internal problems returned. After a couple of days hoping it would pass, on doctor's advice he checked himself back into military hospital. By doing so he put himself, as a handicapped veteran, back on the military payroll — important, because sick pay from an employer was still in the future.

He would be out of action from 3 March to 11 April. One suspects that the doctors had few ideas about what was really wrong and even fewer about useful treatments. Rufus was starved for ten days, consuming only milk or soup. He suffered daily internal douches administered by "a fool of an orderly" and once went over to Vancouver General "to have Dr Schinlien look at my interior — v unpleasant and somewhat painful — shows acute inflammation in the colon but he suspects more higher up." In fact, just being out of circulation for the whole of March was probably the best medicine. To keep him passive they taught him to make raffia mats and trays — better for him than hunting and pecking on a borrowed typewriter to make deadlines at *The Times*, although he did that too. By mid-March he was out of bed, able to take short walks and kind friends with cars took him, with other unfortunates, for drives around the new neighbourhoods. At the point where he was becoming obsessive about his mats and trays — actually hoping to give them to people — Bee started taking him out to shows in the evening, and in the daytime they both started moving their belongings, bit by bit, out of Point Grey Road and back into 1521 Arbutus.

While Rufus was in hospital there had been a curious incident. Vancouver received a visit from *HMCS Patriot*, one of the navy's two modern warships, and one of her officers, Lieutenant Smith — probably the ship's Number Two

— invited Bee and Rufus aboard. The fact that Rufus was in hospital did not deter Bee and she sounds to have had a great time. It turned out she had known young Smith in 1908 when she was working in Harrow, and that Rufus had also met him there. Had Rufus not arrived in Harrow when he did, might this encounter have provided an alternative ending to this story?

They moved back to 1521 Arbutus on April Fool's Day and his doctors arranged some home leave for him before he returned to work. He filled these days with gardening and Mr Fix-It tasks — his wilderness years having made him quite handy. It was all therapy and the more of it the better, because as soon as he did go back to work, he was immediately up to his neck, as neither he nor his employers understood the meaning of moderation. Fortunately, however, being Assistant Telegraph Editor, his official new title, prevented him from rushing about quite as much as he had. The job entailed selecting wire service copy from the teleprinter or telegraph and editing it for use by the paper — all of which could be done within the building. For the time being his excursions were limited to finding material for *Times* articles and doing unpaid work on the institute's behalf.

As a result, after their *saison horrible*, he and Bee began to enjoy living in Vancouver once more. Rufus was into the ocean before the end of May and bathed even more often than he had in previous years. He walked more often, to keep his health improving, and a favourite tramp was from Muriel Phelan's 6th Street house in North Vancouver up the trail beside Mosquito Creek. In addition, he started to play regular tennis on the Freemans' court in Kitsilano. He was chronically competitive, his style of play skillful and vigorous and he appreciated good opponents like the Freemans' daughter.

Although no longer able to find interesting people from the Hotel Vancouver guest list, the wire service was a good substitute and the institute gave him an excuse to create events by inviting exalted guests to institute dinners. So it was that he radioed Premier Massey of New Zealand, when his ship, *SS Niagara*, was still 1,300 miles away, to ask him to dine with the institute when he passed through Vancouver. A visit from a Commonwealth premier was big news in 1920's Vancouver, as was the Imperial Conference in London to which Massey was headed. Rufus scooped the story in style: this time he went out to *Niagara* off Esquimalt with a pilot (whose son had been with him in the 88th), and had a long talk with Massey during the eight-hour trip in to Vancouver. In fact 'Farmer Bill', as Massey was known, had no time for dinner with the BCIJ but did have time for lunch. Rufus tells us in his entry for the next day, "Lunched with Mr and Mrs and Miss Massey — v pleasant. To Capitol with Bee and Derek and supper at Leonards. Bee bought new hat." One could get used to such a life!

He did three other special articles that summer, only one of which he had to contrive. All his subjects held special appeal for ethnic Brits — a majority of *Province* readers at the time. The first, James Lowther, had been speaker in the

Westminster House of Commons since 1905. He accepted an invitation to dine with the institute, gave Rufus an interview and delighted a large BCIJ crowd with verbal sketches of British leaders.

The same day, Lord Byng was appointed Governor General. His last words to Rufus in 1917 had been "Goodbye my boy, the best of luck and be sure to come and look me up whenever you get a chance." Rufus, having once been the general's "sort of temporary ADC", knew Byng better than most of his contemporaries and was able to write an out-of-the-ordinary article for the *Province*, headlined "A Man among Men" — "my yarn" as he called it, a brief and glowing appreciation of the new Governor General, followed by a compendium of good stories. Among these was the occasion when soldiers had been warned to expect a visit from General Byng, affectionately known as 'Bungo'. "Unheard by a couple of sentries, the Corps commander came round a traverse with his ADC and other officers. 'When's old Bingo comin' along, Bill?' said one sentry to the other at the moment the party came round the corner. 'Not Bingo — *Bungo* they call me, my lad,' boomed the general and passed on smiling."

Only the third subject, Lord Northcliffe, caused Rufus to break routine. The owner of *The Times*, on a world tour, was arriving in Vancouver by train. *The Times* was admired and respected throughout the English-speaking world and Northcliffe was at least as prominent a figure as a prime minister. To achieve his scoop, Rufus had to leave town on an eastbound train and board Northcliffe's in Calgary. Next day, he recorded, delightedly, "At Revelstoke 7:15; had message from Lord N asking me to breakfast at 8:00. Lord N, Mr Steed[96] (Editor of *The Times*)], Proileau [N's principal private secretary] and W.F. Bullock (*Times* man in New York) there. Filed good interview with N to *Province* at Kamloops at noon. Lunch and dinner on Northcliffe's private car — champagne and a most delightful and interesting time. Vancouver at 10.30 pm."

Next morning he took the great man to the *Province* and introduced him to Frank Burd, the publisher of the paper, soon to be its managing director. To his diary he confided, "Confess I felt rather bucked as I drove downtown with N at my side." Bucked he may have been, but such grandstanding was not winning him admirers in all quarters, as events would prove.

Cairns and Brown, however, must have approved the ten-day trip that Rufus took to the Kootenays in early July. For someone who had supported himself for five years in rural Canada by his wits and the strength of his back, a trip through the Kootenay valleys was a homecoming. His was a schmoozing style — make friends with all comers and you'll soon know everything you want to find out, and more. He was the friendly newcomer in town who knew everybody's pals in the army and often ran across his own. The key was to latch onto the guy at the top of the food chain and in Invermere that meant Frank Stockdale. This worthy drove Rufus around the district — he spent afternoons watching sports in Windermere and Athalmer, evenings playing bridge or bowls, or just yarning with friends, or with old Williams, the hotel owner. Mornings were for walking and writing.

From Invermere he went to Creston by train — on which Guthrie, the conductor, had once been quartermaster of 10th Battalion — to stay a night in the soldier settlement at Camp Lister. Next day he left for Nelson on the stern-wheeler *SS Moyie*, a trip of fifty kms up Kootenay Lake, then thirty more down the West Arm. "Saw our old place by the lake at Harrop," he observed — a patch of cultivation wrested from the forest on the delta of Lasca Creek. He would have no time to visit it as he had allowed for just one day in Nelson. He spent the morning looking up old friends — Guy Smith at the *Daily News*, possibly the friend who had suggested journalism to him; Fred Starkey, the kindly grocer who had allowed Roy and himself credit and whom they had paid when they sold their crop. Rufus invited others to lunch at the Strathcona Hotel and spent the afternoon playing tennis at the club where Roy and he used to play. He left Nelson at 9 pm on the new Kettle Valley Railway. The train rumbled across Myra Canyon's spectacular trestles in darkness, but he enjoyed the "wonderful scenery along the route by way of Penticton" in broad daylight, though it was "very hot and dusty." The journey to Vancouver took twenty-six hours.

RUFUS HAD NOT BEEN HOME long before he made this diary entry: "Decided at supper we would buy a car!!!", implying that they both decided — unlikely, as Bee never showed the slightest interest in cars. In his customary spirit of *carpe diem*, directly after supper he went round to Dixon Motors, took the next afternoon off to look at nine other machines on his own, and later met Bee, with Dixon's Mr Corfield, to kick the tires of half a dozen more. By 6 pm that wily gentleman had convinced Rufus that a 1920 Chevrolet was just what he wanted. Thrilled to bits, the pair of them and Derek ate a quick supper before returning for their road trial at 7:30. They were in for a disappointment, the first of many — as Rufus put it, "the bally machine would not budge!! We came home in disgust."

Nevertheless, the next day they were back for the postponed road test, when the car, naturally, behaved impeccably. A delighted Rufus paid his deposit and arranged to pay the rest the following morning. As he then recorded, "I finally purchased the car for $700 and signed the necessary documents. I drove round Stanley Park with the salesman and later by myself — I got stuck once! I drove Bee and Derek round Marine Drive at night — OK, but I had trouble getting into the garage."

The next day was Sunday and he spent the morning receiving instruction at Corfield's garage. After that he felt competent to drive to the office next morning. The commute went well but trouble started at lunchtime when he got stuck three times on the way to his club. Unfazed by humiliations, Rufus gained confidence daily and within ten days, as mentioned earlier, was driving no less a person than Lord Northcliffe around town. He had had all the driver training he would ever have — now for the open road!

Their first road trip, four days up the Fraser Valley, followed in mid-August. The car went well and they travelled 80 miles in five hours, in spite of ten miles of terrible road before Langley Prairie. Their intended destination was the Vedder Crossing Hotel "or anywhere we care to stop" — his phrase catching the promise of freedom, the intoxicating appeal of early motoring to the Messrs Toad[97] of this world. At the farm hotel, city boys Derek and his pal Phil were thrilled by the rustic sounds and smells — up at six for milking, and fishing with worms in the river. On different days Rufus drove them to the hot springs at Harrison, picnicking *en route* in a hop-garden, to Cultus Lake, and to tramp through the woods near Bridal Falls. Life seemed to have gained a new dimension.

That is exactly what had happened, and the rest of his holiday was packed with activity. He and Bee developed a taste for horse-racing, as his diary attests. ". . . at Brighouse Park[98] with Bee. We lost about $20* until the last race. Then we backed Bill Sparks for a place and General Byng for a place and we picked up — so that we were $2.55 in on the day." One day the two of them packed Derek and five friends into the car and crossed to the North Shore by the ferry for a beach picnic; on another they took Muriel Phelan and her children to Cypress Park, where they swam in the icy creek; and on a third they took Muriel and children to the original Capilano River bridge. They accepted invitations to dine from far afield. "Out to Boyles at Kerrisdale to dinner . . . to Burnaby to fetch Derek from the Mortimer-Lambs . . . out to the Mortimer-Lambs to dinner . . . went to New Westminster fair. V jolly time."

It was not always jolly, of course — one day "the car broke down on Granville St Bridge. We got home eventually. Had mechanic out for car — $5.60." There were also more easily-fixed problems, such as "Out of gasoline and did not get home till 12:30 am." And the car had a mind of its own, of course. "Trouble with car," Rufus fumed, "out to Mills for tea and bridge. Car managed to get us home."

The social whirl that started with the car purchase continued well into fall and long after Rufus's holidays must have been and gone. The car proved most useful socially as they frequently drove other people home — from evening bridge parties, for instance — and no guest seemed to tire of being driven around Stanley Park or Marine Drive. Like others, he and Bee had been investing in the stock market — originally in dodgy gold stocks but by 1921, only in the tried and true — but there was one sharp reminder for Rufus of the financial tightrope that people were walking. He had just completed his car purchase in July, which must have stretched his finances, when he had bad news: Grant & Whyte, his stockbrokers, had gone bankrupt, as Rufus recorded indignantly, ". . . taking with them $651 we had paid them for CPR stock, which, apparently, had never been purchased at all." Rufus rushed off to see the Public Trustee, and then to beard G.P. Grant himself, "whom I told what I thought of him — said he was just a common criminal, etc." He had a point, though we never do hear the man's fate — only that Rufus discovered, at a later creditors' meeting, that something might be salvaged — eventually.

* Rufus was still earning $175 a month.

In October Rufus and Bee each became absorbed in their own ambitious plans. Bee was a talented actress, as the BCIJ had discovered the previous year, and her success in *The Rest Cure* had whetted her appetite. In October she started rehearsing for the part of the granddaughter in the one-act play *The Intruder* by Maurice Maeterlinck. Both she and Rufus were founding members that year of the Vancouver Little Theatre, and *The Intruder*, along with Harold Brighouse's *Lonesome-like* and Arnold Bennett's *The Stepmother* on the same program, were to be the VLT's very first performance.

Usually a stage groupie, Rufus, for once, was paying little attention. His own grand plan for breaking out of the 'provincial reporter' mold was to make a name for himself on a bigger stage, just as it had been in Duncan days. The world's first international naval conference would open in a month's time in Washington, DC[99] and, when he found that R.B. had no plans to send anybody, he decided to go himself, with or without his blessing. He would pay for the venture by persuading Canadian newspapers to take his dispatches. While Bee rehearsed, he was signing up newspapers — by the time of his departure he was accredited to the *Province*, the *Winnipeg Tribune*, the *Calgary Herald*, and the *Victoria Times*. When he reached Washington, by way of cities further east, he had added some, or all, of the *Ottawa Citizen*, the *Ottawa Journal*, *Maclean's*, and *Canadian Magazine*.

He left for Washington on 26 October and would be away until just before Christmas. During those two months he laid the foundation for his future in journalism. The journey there was all business and, for somebody without a secretary in the days before e-mail and mobile phones, he arranged an impressive schedule of appointments. In Calgary and Winnipeg respectively, he had meetings with Hayden of the *Herald* and Vernon Knowles of the *Tribune* to confirm arrangements and received an encouragingly warm reception. In Ottawa for a day and a half, he had to dig deeper: he called upon Martin Burrell, MP, whom he had known since 1910; on H.E.M. Chisholm, a prairie or army acquaintance who introduced him to the Parliamentary Press Gallery; and on the mysterious Col. H.H. Matthews whom he had known in France. Through one or more of these contacts he met D'Arcy Finn of the *Ottawa Citizen* and Grattan O'Leary of the *Ottawa Journal* to try to sell his Washington dispatches. He doesn't tell us with what success, but he saw O'Leary twice. Governor General Byng's ADC, his wartime staff colleague Col. Willis O'Connor, DSO, also came to see him but time did not allow for Rufus to interview his boss.

Next stop was Toronto for a couple of days. He called first on Sir John Willison, *The Times*' man in Canada whom he had met at the Imperial Press conference in 1920. That led to lunch with him the next day and to meetings with his pal Stewart Lyon, editor of the *Globe*, Newton McTavish of *Canadian Magazine*, and with *Maclean's*. He left for Washington that night, exhausted, but having drummed up enough business at least to break even on the trip — his real reward being a chance to start moving in journalism's big leagues.

Existing in Washington for six weeks presented him with problems. He was probably cut off from his usual *Province* salary, and his last *Times* dispatch in 1921 went out on November 7 as he was temporarily far from Vancouver. For this period his income depended upon irregular payments from eight or nine Canadian newspapers about whose payment schedules he knew little — he received nothing from them while away from home. Bee wired him on 1 December, presumably to tell him it was all right to draw money, which he did two days later.

The hotel where he slept his first night in Washington charged him $3 and he spent much of the following day combing the central area for something cheaper. He was about to give up when he happened upon the Oxford Hotel where they were asking only a buck-fifty. It was, he confessed, "a shabby old place" but it was cheap, central, and quiet. He was fortunate in other ways too: the Americans were going out of their way to welcome foreign correspondents, and the Brits were laying out the red carpet for dominion journalists. On his second day in Washington, he was swept off for a tour of the White House and the State Department by Robert Barry of the welcoming committee, who introduced him to Richard Bender of UP, Dick Oulahan of the *New York Times*, and other press luminaries. And he called on Sir Arthur Willert, *The Times* man in Washington, whom he had met in Vancouver.

Already he had filed his first dispatch. In Toronto he had arranged for the distribution of his dispatches with the CPR telegraph superintendent, so that he himself would have to send each one just once. Nevertheless, there was little time to smell the flowers, such as they were — he had five days to interview delegates before the conference opened and he started with Philip Tyan, Sun Yat-sen's ambassador from China. The same day he interviewed Sir Robert Borden, Canada's ex-prime minister and now its delegate.[100] Those interviews gave him material for his second dispatch. He wrote in the evenings and there were nights when he crept to bed at 1:30 am. The rest of the week was crammed with activity: an interview with Japan's naval attaché; the solemn ceremonial arrival from France of the body of America's "unknown soldier"; a reception for Empire journalists at the British Embassy at which he met Lord Lee, the British First Lord of the Admiralty; encounters with newspapermen with household names — H.G. Wells, temporarily of the *Westminster Gazette*, Maurice Low of the *Morning Post*, J.G. Hamilton of the *New York Times*, and Wickham Steed of *The Times*, whom he had met with Northcliffe.

And that was just the half of it. Before the week was out, he had seen the great Lord Balfour arrive, interviewed the delegates from New Zealand and Australia, attended a meeting of correspondents at the sumptuous (even then) National Press Club, and had driven, with four other "ink-stained wretches", to the Arlington National Cemetery for the unknown soldier's burial, following closely behind Vice President Coolidge's car, "as the 'secret service' [with whom they were supposed to go] never would have been there in time." Even so, the journey took nearly two hours and Rufus found it all very impressive.

The conference opened on November 12 in a building owned by the Daughters of the American Revolution. The principal delegates from the nine naval powers were arranged around a square horseshoe with their juniors massed behind. Above were two tiers of galleries, theatre-style, packed with mostly female onlookers. The press gallery, from which the few pictures that exist were taken and where Rufus sat, looked down upon the open end of the horseshoe. After President Harding's formal opening, "Secretary of State Hughes," he tells us, "in a splendid speech, proposed an amazing reduction of navies." Rufus was stunned: the American proposal was so radical that even cynical pressmen began to feel hopeful. At last they had something concrete to report.

However, the pace and stress of the first week had taken its toll. "Very much out of order internally," he noted on Sunday morning, though his problem seemed to pass as he became acclimatized. In the second week the British and Japanese accepted the American proposals for cuts, with reservations in the case of Japan, but there were few other developments. Rufus's days were filled by briefings and receptions — sometimes half a dozen in a day. Maybe that was why Rufus found it hard to keep his customers happy: he was not content with the amount of real news in his own dispatch one night and heard on Friday that the *Calgary Herald* was discontinuing. "A bad blow," he confided to his diary, but he wired Cairns[101] in Vancouver who managed to wring another week out of the *Herald*. It was all seeming very ho-hum when on Sunday he was swept up in the excitement of a grand barbecue laid on by the *Baltimore Sun*. Feeling he was experiencing life in the fast lane, he described how "fifty or more cars left in a procession for the sixty-mile drive — and went about 45 mph!" Once there, the press was treated to a wonderful show — "nigger[102] slave songs, a real barbecue, loads of refreshments, a wild west show, etc. — and charming people." He enjoyed it all very much, of course.

The third week was even slower, forcing him to rely on his wits to keep contributors happy. It had its high points: the legendary Marshall Foch came to the Press Club; he met Lord Balfour, whom he found charming; and the press was wined and dined at the palatial Racquet Club. But a reception at the Chinese embassy was desperately dull and he was reduced to writing about the writers themselves, by this time a band of brothers. Entitled "Journalistic Minstrels of the World",[103] he offered glimpses of twice-weekly press 'receptions' in the Oval office,[104] no less.

"There is no formality about them. No ticket is required for the newspapermen. Mr Harding stands behind his desk with his back to the big French window. The crowd gathers close around him and begins 'firing' questions at him. 'I have nothing to say on that matter,' he says decidedly when an indiscreet question is asked. Or he will mildly chide some too-eager correspondent. 'David', he will say — for he seems to know all the scores of Washington pressmen by name — 'David, lad, you know very well you shouldn't ask me that. Don't spoil the spirit of these gatherings by trying to trip me up'." In a postcard to Derek, Rufus mentioned that, outside the White House, he had seen the "turkey for the President's dinner being photographed with pink ribbon tied round his neck — the turkey's, not the President's."

The lack of news gave him another round of internal problems but his troubles were almost over. Newspapermen covering the conference were all in the same boat and by this time many of them had become friends. Some, like the *Manchester Guardian*'s H.W. Nevinson, were tempted to create their own news and one day he and Rufus took the train to the Edgewood Arsenal. There they saw "poison gas laboratories, bombs, shells, masks, relics, etc.," an unsuspected side of the United States that Rufus, and no doubt Canadian readers, found most interesting.

Ironically, just as the conference was winding down, he was beginning to feel comfortable: this most clubbable of men was able to use the Press Club as part of the job, had been entertained by friends at the smart Cosmos Club, and was now put up for a week's membership at the Racquet Club where he could play squash and swim. What was more, he had been approached by the *Baltimore Sun* to write a piece on Orientals — living on the west coast, apparently, made him an expert on such matters. Life was looking up. Consequently the fourth week slipped pleasantly by, only rating a diary entry on Saturday for the fourth plenary session on the all-important Four Power treaty.

That evening he attended the Gridiron Club banquet (akin to Ottawa's Parliamentary Press Gallery dinner). He enthused, ". . . the most wonderful function I have ever attended. The President, all the cabinet and the delegates were there, about four hundred in all. I sat next to Commander Courts, USN — very nice fellow, brother-in-law of Dick Oulahan." The evening's program names the accredited pressmen — 75 in all, including just three Canadians with Rufus the lone scribbler from west of Toronto.

His last week in Washington was spent destroying papers, packing, buying toys, wiring newspapers, worrying about their silence, entertaining friends and, as Japan was announcing its crucial acceptance of the ratio, leaving a final dispatch in the hands of Munro of the *Globe* before departing for Toronto and home. After calling on Judge and Mrs Dickson in Qu'Appelle and being met by the prodigal Phil in Swift Current — "looking fitter than I have seen him for a long time" — Rufus returned to the long-suffering Bee on 22 December where she met him off the train at 10 pm. Vancouver was slushy, slippery, and cold, and she and Derek had moved to winter quarters at the Abbotsford Hotel. Though they had written to each other often, Bee wanted to hear all about Washington and he to hear of her success in *The Intruder* and they talked into the wee hours. Next day they did some Christmas shopping, he dropped in at the *Province* where there was little to be done, and on the 24th they took the ferry to Muriel Phelan's in North Van, their usual Christmas haunt, and decorated her tree before she got home.

He did not return for his first day's work until the 27th. Only then did he discover that the universe had not unfolded entirely as it should have — Lane was at the telegraph desk and, according to him, Rufus had been assigned to some undefined "special advertising work." As Cairns and Brown were still away, it was not until the 29th that he could talk with Brown himself. "The idea is that I am to go to Victoria permanently for the *Province*. Brown says that my service is greatly valued, etc., etc., the usual talk. I am upset about this as no notice of any changes had been given to me."

If his reaction seems mild, he had probably anticipated something of the sort. By assigning himself to the naval conference, no matter how much prestige his articles, personally syndicated across Canada, might have brought the paper, he had sinned against the hierarchy. He would now have to face the music — so much for the return of the conquering hero. He had reached a crisis in his affairs.

Chapter 13
Telegraph Desk
Vancouver, 1922–1924

"I went to the President and appealed directly to him. Result was that he, Mrs H and all promised to be up at 9 am."

Rufus's diary entry on his 'management' of President Warren Harding, 24 July 1923

1922 began rather better than had seemed likely. There was no sign of action on Rufus's move to Victoria, and he continued working quietly on a series of follow-up articles on the conference, which was continuing until 6 February. They all moved to Mrs Cornish's in the interests of economy and three weeks into January Rufus would exclaim to his diary, "Back on the desk! Roy Brown is alleged to have had a row with Nichol and to have quit."

In fact the editor was said to have left for San Francisco but nobody knew for sure and the *Province* ticked along under temporary direction. Two days later the cause of the ruckus, apparently triumphant, was given a complimentary dinner by the BCIJ at the Citizen's Club, at which he spoke about the Washington Conference. We hear no more of the matter in his diary, but there was no change of editor at the *Province* that year and Roy Brown soon reappeared.[105] He may well have had a falling out with Nichol over his treatment of Rufus and have retreated to lick his wounds — if so, his apparent humiliation was skillfully finessed, probably by a compromise agreement with Nichol. There was some evidence of this when the sports editor died in December, and Brown promoted a more junior person, causing Rufus to complain mildly that "no official word was given to Lane or to me of our being passed over." Maybe the right to do just that had been Brown's *quid pro quo*. Whatever the case, honour was preserved and he and Rufus would enjoy a normal relationship for the rest of the latter's time at the *Province.*

It was to be a rather different year for both Rufus and Bee. Once back on his perch at the telegraph desk, his journalistic life remained relatively dull for the rest of 1922 — maybe deliberately so if he had made a no-grandstanding deal with the editor. It helped, perhaps, that he was rotated out of the institute's presidency and that his wanderlust was kept at bay by two week-long research trips, first to Prince Rupert and the Queen Charlottes and then to the Kootenays and the Okanagan. The only other time he was away was during General Byng's visit. He met the new Governor General in Revelstoke, attended the rally there, filed his story and was back in town — before anybody realized he'd been away — in time to witness a "remarkable demonstration of affection" for Byng from 3,000 veterans in the arena.

When Lord Northcliffe died in August, as the local *Times* man, Rufus was tagged with writing his obituary. Although not published over his byline, it is a monumental piece of work — four columns in which he takes readers through every twist of the man's innovative life. His admiration is in every line and anecdote.

> Lord Northcliffe once stopped for a few minutes' chat in the newsroom with a new employee. 'How do you like your work?' he asked. 'Very much, thank you,' was the reply. 'How much money are you getting?' 'Five pounds a week,' was the answer. 'Are you quite satisfied in every way?' 'Perfectly, thank you,' the unsuspecting one replied. 'Remember this, young man,' said the chief. 'I want no one on my staff who is satisfied with five pounds a week!'"

Nevertheless, he remained sufficiently objective to deplore Northcliffe's bitter attacks on Lloyd George. When he observed that the title was derived from the North Foreland, in the parish of St Peter's, Thanet, it reminds us that he had presented himself to Northcliffe in 1918 as "the red-haired choir boy" and son of his vicar! The long article was his acknowledgment of the service that Northcliffe had done him — the regular extra income as west coast stringer had made the difference between scraping by and the relative comfort that Bee and he were beginning to enjoy. Even after his benefactor's death it was a connection that would keep on giving, as events in the late twenties would demonstrate.[106]

During his west coast trip he visited Haida Gwaii, then called the Queen Charlotte Islands. There was no easy way to get there and he took the *SS Prince Rupert* to Prince Rupert, a chilly 36-hour trip, calling only at Ocean Falls where he toured the mill while cargo was unloaded. Prince Rupert could never please him and this time he grumbled that it seemed "just as god-forsaken as ever — can't see how it can ever be presentable." Nevertheless, after touring the cold store, he spent a fairly comfortable day there — holed up at the club where he dined with Pullen of the *Daily News*. He left, eventually, at 11 pm aboard *SS Prince John* and reached Masset in the morning.

If Prince Rupert was 'god-forsaken' one wonders how he found Masset. He was lucky enough to bump into friends at the windswept government wharf and "fed with them all day." In the afternoon he went down the inlet on the police boat to interview an English settler at Old Masset, the Haida village. Back at the wharf, he started playing bridge with other passengers waiting in the police house. The *John* was expected at 2 am. When she failed to appear some players dropped out but a hard core, including Rufus, blearily played on until she finally appeared — at six in the morning.

"Feeling like death," he and the card-players endured a rough passage to Skidegate. The 100 kms down Hecate Strait took all day; The *John* was desperately slow, standing on her end in the head-on breeze. "I was not ill," he tells us, "but nearly everyone else was." As they entered Skidegate Channel at dusk, he saw pretty Sandspit, but Skidegate itself, Charlotte City, and Aliford Bay, their other ports of call, were just lights and shouts in the darkness. After dropping passengers, the *John* headed back out to sea and he had a "splendid eight-hour sleep" while the little ship took another twelve hours to cover the 60 kms to Thurston Harbour on Moresby Island. There, the rest of the passengers, all loggers, went ashore.

After a chilly call at Jedway near the southern tip of the islands, the little ship headed southeast across Queen Charlotte Sound. This time the crossing was smooth and he and skipper Neddon enjoyed a long yarn until late. Next day, as they threaded their way in sunshine down Johnstone Strait, the islands were a windswept memory. They reached Vancouver at noon the following day.

While his journey to the islands was little different from such a journey today, the same could not be said for his trip to the Interior. He was covering British MPs on an official junket, starting at Revelstoke, where he arrived by train. The agenda involved speechy receptions and little substance, but the journey itself was remarkable. His diary casually notes: "Missed special train which left forty minutes early. Arrived Arrowhead 9 am — boat to Nelson — reception there etc — bed 2:30 am." The official party, in fact, had travelled there from Revelstoke by train, via Fort Steele and Cranbrook — at least 400 kms. To catch them up, Rufus caught the sternwheeler *Bonnington*, a coal-burning four-decker with a maximum speed of 25 kmh, down the Columbia River Valley and the Arrow Lakes,[107] eventually swinging east to Nelson up the Kootenay River — 250 kms of wilderness in a day, all to be in time for another dull reception, after which he must file a dispatch — no wonder he was late to bed!

Their KVR[108] 'special' left again at 9:00 next morning, this time with him aboard. They stopped briefly at Bonnington Falls, bought fruit in sweltering heat at Midway and Grand Forks, endured the long, smoky climb up the Kettle River Valley to over 4,000 feet, teetered around Myra Canyon on perilous-looking wooden trestles, then whistled down through the pines to journey's end at Penticton in the Okanagan Valley, 3,000 ft. below. Their reward was "a good hotel, dancing outside in the garden — bath! and so cool and quiet by the lake after a long journey. Bed at 2 am."

Remorselessly, the party left again at 7 am aboard the sternwheeler *Sicamous*, *Bonnington*'s sister ship, breakfasting in her upper-deck lounge as she travelled north. They landed at Kelowna about 10 am and piled into cars for a dusty drive, through orchards and pines and sweet-scented sagebrush, to lunch at Oyama beside Kalamalka Lake. After more speeches, they drove northwards past the improbably blue waters of Kalamalka to Coldstream and Vernon, where another 'special' took them north to Sicamous and the main line. It was a three-day marathon that few today would attempt.

Outside journalism that year, Rufus's energies were divided between politics and Vancouver Little Theatre. He was bothered by the apparent untouchability of John Oliver, the Liberal premier, and by the ineffectual opposition offered by W.J. Bowser, the Tory leader. Never content to grumble, he joined the so-called 'Young Conservatives', an informal group of younger party members, all devotees of the late Tory prime minister Sir Charles Tupper and led by his son, Charles Hibbert Tupper. Rufus had his own Tupper connections: ten years earlier he had considered starting a Tory newspaper to enable the same C.H. Tupper to oppose the 'corruption' of fellow-Tory premier Richard McBride. During the war, Tupper's son Gordon had served with him in the 16th and he had been shaken by his death at Vimy Ridge.

The March YC meeting had sent a delegation to persuade Bowser to resign. When that failed, the April meeting, which Rufus chaired, publicly demanded his resignation and was followed by articles in the *Province*, April 11 & 13 — in which he probably had a hand — that described Bowser's leadership as "a millstone around our necks." To no avail — Bowser ignored them and remained leader for another two years. Still pursuing alternatives, in early December Makovski persuaded Rufus to come to a 'confidential' gathering of the nucleus of the new 'Provincial Party' — though it seems a stretch to include journalists in such a 'hush-hush' project and by Christmas it was all over the newspapers.

Having recently shed the BCIJ presidency, Rufus had no appetite for new responsibilities but joined the executive of Little Theatre — "just as a convener of a committee affair," he optimistically claimed. In fact it involved a good deal more — occasionally chairing monthly meetings and all sorts of necessary jobs before any of the three productions, although it would be Bee who would make the most effort for the theatre that year. In addition, for the first half of the year he was BC's resident expert on the Naval Conference and invited to speak about it many times, most prestigiously by the University of British Columbia. He was becoming comfortable speaking to a crowd and did it well.

Bee remained in good health in 1922 and had a good year. She, too, had an active approach to life and was seldom idle. Twice she went to the races at Brighouse Park on her own or with a friend — the first time Rufus noted rather casually that she lost $20 and the second time, two months later, that she won it back. She had joined the Dufferin chapter of the IODE the year before but had done little with it. This year, however, she had allowed herself to be elected secretary and thus became extremely active, attending monthly meetings, organizing a bridge event, telling fortunes at their fête, and selling tickets for the visiting Scots Guards Band, in addition to carrying the IODE standard at the formal inauguration of a war memorial by the Lieutenant Governor. Her 'tea-fights' were consequently less frequent and seemed to be less formal.

In spite of all this, she put most of her energy into Little Theatre, now in its second year. They did five shows and she acted in three, each a one-act play in a triple bill. She took the role of Helena in *Helena's Husband* in April — a one-act historical comedy by Philip Moeller; in September she again played Muriel the maid in the Little Theatre version of *The Rest Cure*; and in late November she took the leading female role in *Everybody's Husband*, a comic drama by Gilbert Cannan. All involved up to a dozen long evening rehearsals, the last ending in a furious row with the producer about how she and the male lead were to play it — they won the argument and did it the actors' way. Although reviews were not as glowing as in 1921, her performances were obviously good and sold out the Templeton Hall.

She also decided to go to work for the Football Guide for 50¢ an hour — a mysterious part-time job connected to British football pools and the two periods when this kept her the busiest coincided with rehearsals — in fact in April she once worked and rehearsed on the same day and did so twice more in November, with the result that she became exhausted and had to spend days in bed recuperating. Rufus took a patronizing attitude to her working — he would write in his diary "Bee to work!" or "Bee insisted upon working", and his attitude probably made her want to do so all the more.

1922 had been the first year they had felt settled. The fact that not much happened was good — life had established a pattern and Rufus's insides settled down. Derek was going full-time to school — and showing signs of intelligence. He had also, for the first time, been sufficiently disobedient to have earned the "hiding of his life" from Rufus at least once. Rufus and Bee played an unconscionable amount of bridge with an increasing number of people — so much so that on 29 November Rufus was moved to write "evening at home for once."

After the war the *Province* was a good newspaper served by talented and loyal people. After Walter Nichol had made so much effort to hire him, Rufus might be excused for having expected some editorial responsibility. So, when Nichol saddled him with beat journalism — something he thought he had finally escaped — he was not pleased, but consoled himself with the freedom he enjoyed in his work for *The Times* and the hope that he could change things by hard work and enterprise.

However, there was little hope for promotion at the *Province* thanks to the exceptional calibre of those above him in the hierarchy. Roy Brown had the services of editorial writers of great ability in Snowdon Dunn Scott and D.A. McGregor. Scott, at 67, had been editor of newspapers in the Maritimes for twenty-five years before coming to Vancouver in 1910. He was an authority on constitutional matters for which Mount Allison College had made him an honourary doctor, and he wrote a column of casual comment, loosely on politics and the constitution, under the pen-name 'Lucian'. McGregor, an exceedingly modest man known as 'Mac', was thirty years younger but had worked for Nichol almost as long as Brown had; he was respected for his knowledge of

Canadian politics on which he "wielded a powerful and influential pen."[109] All three had been born in one of Canada's four original provinces, two had solid eastern educations and Brown, having come to BC as a child, had been the youngest pupil to enroll in Vancouver High School.

Also in the hierarchy was Frank J. Burd, aged 49, who had joined the *Province* in 1903 as Circulation Manager. He had begun as a reporter on the *Winnipeg Free Press*, then started the *Whitehorse Tribune* in a tent in 1889 before being hired as Circulation Manager of the *Vancouver News-Advertiser* in 1901. Burd had influence and power at the *Province* and was made managing director by the Southams when they bought the paper in 1923. When Walter Nichol, Rufus's sponsor, rode off into the sunset, Burd replaced him as the ultimate authority — higher in the pecking order than Brown himself. Rufus had been smart to have introduced him to Northcliffe in 1921 — two years later he realized that Burd's goodwill was something to be nurtured if he was to enjoy the occasional journalistic freedoms allowed him by Nichol.

It is possible, nevertheless, that in late 1923 Rufus started an end-run around both Brown and Burd. In the four months after the sale of the *Province* in August, although he seldom mentioned writing letters in his diary — except to his father — he recorded writing to Nichol several times. Why did he do so? Maybe because Nichol, having worked for William Southam at the *Hamilton Spectator*, knew the family well. And when he sold 'a controlling interest' to Fred Southam, he had retained a share, and thus a say in the *Province*'s affairs.

26 July 1923 was a special day in Vancouver: Warren Harding had arrived that morning — the first visit of a sitting US president — and Walter Nichol, as BC's Lieutenant Governor, resplendent in gold braid, had hosted a magnificent reception for the president at the Hotel Vancouver. After an official lunch Harding went off to speak to the crowds in Stanley Park — and Nichol, still at the hotel, sent for Rufus. They had a conversation that would probably explain a good deal if he had been less tight-lipped about it: he tells us only that they "talked for an hour about the trip, the office, my future and Brown's English proposals."

"The trip" referred to the past three weeks when he had been covering Harding's visit to Alaska. The significance of the rest of the conversation was that it took place two weeks before the sale of the *Province* was announced. The agreement was in the works and was the context for their talk about "the office" and Rufus's "future." Rufus would have made his feelings known about his desk job, and have asked for Nichol's help in improving his circumstances. For his part, Nichol would have pointed out the realities of seniority and the new ownership. But the seed had been replanted, along, maybe, with him promising to see what could be done and asking to be kept informed.

As for "Brown's . . . proposals", R.B. was on an English sabbatical, possibly at *The Times*. It had been arranged in the spring — negotiations in which Rufus had taken part, because of his position at *The Times*. R.B. had left for England in May and probably remained there for a year as Rufus would next mention him in September 1924. His 'proposals' seem to have been for Rufus also to take a temporary job there. It was tempting but he had been offered too little money: with a family to feed, he could not afford to get it wrong and some days later cabled: "unable accept unless guaranteed thirty five, minimum eight weeks."

The Alaska trip would also help Rufus establish his right to work of the sort he wanted. Soon after Brown had left, Rufus heard of Harding's upcoming trip — and decided to cover it. We must assume he talked to the acting editor, Dr Scott, about his plans. He wired his Washington Conference friend, F.W. Wile at the *New York Times*, received instructions from him on how to be accredited, then applied to Harding's secretary as instructed.

Nevertheless, on 5 July at the foot of the gangplank in Portland, Oregon, he was refused permission to board the president's ship. There were no instructions to admit a foreigner — period! As he pleaded his case, other journalists were arriving — including some he knew from 1921. There were greetings, handshakes, whispered instructions, laughter — and the problem solved itself. Accepting his rejection with apparent resignation, Rufus went on board "just to see friends to their cabins." Meanwhile another journalist quietly adopted his bag while dockside officialdom forgot about him. *USS Henderson* sailed and, once safely at sea, Rufus's presence was 'discovered'. When the stowaway was brought to Harding himself, the president remembered the red-haired guy with the limey accent — two years ago at the Naval Conference he'd seen him twice a week at Oval Office press conferences! "Welcome aboard, Mr Johnston," he said, probably feeling flattered that a Canadian would want to be.

The price Rufus had to pay for the subterfuge was to be billeted in crew quarters — which were "not comfy but not too bad." However, as the president's party numbered only 26, including the press, those not already acquainted, regardless of station, soon became so. It was a wonderfully unstuffy bit of American equality-in-action that Rufus reflected in his dispatches. The *Henderson* travelled north through the Inside Passage. BC weather, for once, was spectacular — "everyone delighted," Rufus noted, and their delight seemed to include the only Canadian in sight. Within a few days he found himself chatting at length with Florence Harding and Governor Scott Bone of Alaska. She was a real character, five years older than the president — she called him "Wurr'n" — while both she and Bone were newspaper people who had, at one time or another, each run their own newspaper. Rufus felt definitely included when he was asked to speak at a dinner on the fifth day out.

First landfall in Alaska had been Metlakatla at the southern tip of the panhandle. From there they took four days to Skagway, through ice in the Chilkoot Passage and past looming glaciers. It was Rufus's first Arctic experience and he loved it. They crossed open ocean *en route* to Anchorage. "Sea rough at night," he tells us — "some casualties! Chess with Col. Greeley" — one imagines him contentedly puffing on his pipe in the emptying saloon as he pondered a move. They made landfall again at Seward where a 'special' awaited. It was to be a stop-go journey northwards because the newly-built Alaska Railroad had no dining car, forcing the president and party to eat in construction workers' diners, and it was two days before they puffed their way into Fairbanks. Rufus filed a story headlined "President Roughing it in Alaska" and was thrilled to be included in a midnight sun Gridiron Club meeting in the Tanana Club, a rustic cabin full of elk, caribou, and bear trophies.

On the journey home life aboard ship became ever more convivial thanks to daily shuffleboard. On the first day he reported, "Major Baldinger [Harding's military aide] and I win, President and Roaf of Seattle also win." The next day the diary reads "Shuffleboard competition all day — I played with Baldinger and we were beaten. Am cross all day about pictures and at night, when anchored in Alert Bay, I went to the President and appealed directly to him. Result was that he, Mrs H and all promised to be up at 9 am tomorrow."

In fact, he had just persuaded the President of the United States, the first lady and therefore everybody else, to get up early for a group picture — planned originally for the following day! And why? Because at 10 am he, Rufus, planned to jump ship at Campbell River, hightail it to Nanaimo, catch the boat to Vancouver with the negative and scoop all his American chums with the picture, and the story of the president's visit to Vancouver!

In due course the president arrived and Rufus achieved a modicum of local celebrity. His dispatches had depicted a likable president and 50,000 citizens, thrilled that a US president had come to their city, turned out to hear him speak. Then he was gone, and a week later — at 7:20 pm — came the news he was dead! Vancouver was stunned, nobody more so than Rufus. "I went down to the office," he tells us, "and spent all night writing a three-column 'pen picture', etc." It ran in later editions the next day.

The article included an astonishingly intimate account of the president's last evening, the particulars of which he must have gleaned by phone from a member of the president's household with whom he was on friendly terms.

> The President passed with the sunset. The last rays of California's golden sunshine were pouring into his room, where Mrs Harding, the wife who has been by his side since he was stricken seriously last Saturday, sat reading to him from a magazine. The President was lying very still, listening to Mrs Harding read. He seemed to be resting quite comfortably. To the watchful eyes of his two nurses, Miss Ruth Powderly and Miss Sue Dausser, he seemed just as he had been all day – comfortable and in better physical condition than at any time since he became ill. There was no apprehension of impending tragedy in the minds of any there. Mrs Harding and the nurses had reason to feel easier about the condition of the distinguished patient than at any moment since illness overtook him. They were looking forward, without fear or anxiety, to the night – another night, they believed, when the restorative power of sleep would add a little more to the slowly growing strength of the President.

> It was a scene of peaceful quiet and contentment. Mrs Harding read on. She came to the end of a paragraph and paused. She turned to look at her husband. 'that sounds good; go ahead,' said Mr Harding. Mrs Harding turned again to the magazine and read. She had not finished a sentence when, as though someone had struck him a sudden and crushing blow, the President threw up one hand over his head convulsively. It was as though he sought to ward off the blow which death, in that peaceful, unguarded moment, had aimed with unerring directness at a vital point. Then, like a man struck by a bolt of lightning, the President stiffened and as suddenly dropped back limply. There was not time for a word of farewell to his wife; no struggle or fight or futile effort to cling to life. Mrs Harding sensed rather than saw that something was wrong. She turned quickly and with a gasp, half-rose from her chair, crying 'WARREN–,' but he could not hear. She knew it, too, but, stumbling and running, she went to the door, flung it open and cried into the corridor, 'send Dr Boone.' . . . But it was too late then for science or affection or any mortal help.

It was a wonderful piece. the *Province* sold a large number of copies and the following day, he received an unsolicited raise in salary. Probably this was Nichol's doing, if remotely; later that year F.J. Burd, the managing director, was 'unpleasant' to Rufus over payment for a special article, which probably eliminates him; it might even have been Dr Scott, the 72-year-old acting editor, but if so the influence of his benevolence would soon disappear — the editorship may have been too big a burden and he died on 9 December, to be succeeded by Burd.

The rest of 1923 was less dramatic. Rufus's nascent political stirrings had received a healthy cold shower in January when he covered the formation of the recently hush-hush Provincial Party. This was convening in Vernon with the politically-minded members of the United Farmers of BC. From the moment the train left Vancouver, he was in the thick of it — all his political friends, including both Makovski and General McRae, seemed to be there, talking endless politics into the night. He slept badly, and once in Vernon there was more of the same, all afternoon and evening — so that he only started writing at 11:30 and got to bed after 2 am. In the morning he had General Harmon in his bedroom before he was up, talking politics as he shaved, and a move across the street to the Vernon Club provided no relief — politics was the only talk in town. The convention started in the afternoon and elected McRae as leader; its sessions ran all evening and he had another late night.

The next day, Sunday, offered relief in those more traditional times: he went to church at All Saints, to hear with wry amusement his friend Bishop Doull urge the farmers, whose convention was about to start, to look for divine aid in solving their problems. After being invited to dine by Doull and having interviewed McRae, he spent the rest of the day writing. Provincial Party delegates went home but he decided to stay for the start of the United Farmers' convention — just in case there were fireworks over their mooted political action. It would be in vain: the farmers had heeded the bishop and Rufus endured a day and a half of bucolic tedium before going home. Even then there was no rest and he wrote, petulantly, "Terribly jerky train and squeak somewhere in car — no sleep at all." Arriving in Vancouver at 8:30 am, he went, briefly, to the office, and then home at 11:30, hoping to sleep. There he found Bee in a state of collapse, also very tired because "she went to the Morrisons' party last night." It would not be a happy day!

THE YEAR DID HAVE ITS SHARE of happy days, however. He had decided to exercise more and seldom did things by halves. The city had built new hard courts on 15th Avenue and Rufus immediately paid for a year's membership. He could play tennis whenever he wanted, and did so at least once a week and began teaching Derek. He was also walking further and more often — and continued to swim whenever he could through the summer.

Bee rarely joined him in the water or on the courts, although she enjoyed walking. Their joint entertainment continued to be bridge — at least once a week right through the year. It was a shared passion, remarkable because only Rufus was a competitor — he liked to compete at everything, meticulously noting in his diary how he had done, from shuffleboard to chess, to tennis, to speech-making. In fact they seldom had a social evening that did not involve bridge — which must have been awfully dull, something they would eventually come to realize. She had relaxed from her compulsions of 1922 — had resigned as secretary of the IODE chapter, we hear nothing of her continuing to work and she took no parts in plays. Little Theatre, in fact, became Rufus's thing for the time being. On the executive in 1922, in 1923 he allowed himself to be elected 'Mr Vice', "much against my will," he protested. However, once in harness he enjoyed it, partly because he greatly liked W.G. Murrin, the president — later to be president of BC Electric. Their major project was fundraising for a permanent home for the VLT; they canvassed together and, as Murrin must have been a hard man for businessmen to refuse, soon had the $4250 required to buy the Palace Theatre.[110]

Bee's lack of activity may have been partly because they had become house-owners. The previous year, they had rented 1337 Maple Street — the whole house — and had remained there in winter. In 1923 they decided to buy it. Once the decision was made, Rufus, certainly, and Bee, presumably, had few moments when they were not doing something for the house, though Rufus only speaks of his own twig-carrying — floor-staining, garden-digging, etc. Bee had also been ill and was in bed for two weeks in September. Whatever ailed her, it was serious enough for friends to be asked to look after her during the day. Once back on her feet, she went to Armstrong to recuperate with the Makovskis and was away until 7 October.

In the fall Derek, now ten, went to Mr Scrivens' Kingsley School as a boarder. This was in North Vancouver and Derek seemed delighted to be left there in the care of strangers, which only added to his parents' misery as they made their way home. He was soon home for an *exeat*, however, and everybody quickly adjusted. He was becoming increasingly good company for Rufus, who enjoyed walking and swimming with him. He had already beaten his father at chess but not yet at tennis. He was also doing well at Scrivens' but his parents worried about his thinness and, when he was sick in March 1924, they decided to bring him home. Doctors, who could find nothing much wrong, fell back on the panacea of prescribing tonsillectomy and, until his operation on 6 June at St Paul's, Derek stayed home. He was no longer in bed and enjoyed a pleasant, school-free time. After the operation he recovered quickly and within a week was well enough to go with Bee and Rufus to the Owens' farm at Mt Lehman, where he and Bee spent the rest of the month in hopes of fattening him up!

In their absence Rufus was busy. The Little Theatre AGM was so pleased with the Murrin/Johnston regime that they returned them by acclamation for another year. Then came the 1923 BC provincial election, in which McRae's new Provincial Party won only three seats and three party leaders lost their own seats: the distrusted Liberal premier Oliver, the despised Conservative opposition leader Bowser, and McRae himself — an interesting situation that Oliver, characteristically, finessed to remain in office. In other words, it was the election of the century and Rufus himself was in charge of getting out the Election Extra. This he managed, and even in time for him to catch the night boat to Victoria.

The next morning, he was watching the arrival in Royal Roads of a Royal Navy squadron from Beacon Hill. During the day he filed a story, interviewed Admiral Field on board *HMS Hood*, filed a second story, then attended Nichol's state dinner for the visitors. Both *The Times* and the *Province* required dispatches and each expected him to cater to their particular needs — not easily done before the word-processor. By the next day he was back in Vancouver and, despite it being Sunday, worked at the office for an hour or two before spending the evening writing at home. The squadron arrived in Burrard Inlet on Wednesday — *HMS Hood*, *HMS Repulse*, *HMAS Australia*, along with five light cruisers — a wonderful panorama of naval muscle against a backdrop of North Shore mountains. The big ships stayed a week, the weather was hot, and they had Vancouver's attention. Rufus, after a house-cleaning day for Bee's return, took Derek and her to the Hotel Vancouver's roof garden to see the searchlight show. Later in the week they went to a reception on *Hood*, while Derek and friends were entertained on *Repulse*.

The squadron sailed in July. For a while Rufus was able to get on with the business of summer — tennis in the Mainland League, tennis with Derek and friends, bathing at Kitsilano beach, taking the ferry to North Van to see Muriel and family, tea parties on the beach with them or with the Callaways when they came to visit — and all sorts of other social get-togethers.

Into this summer idyll, on 16 July another Imperial concern intruded: Major Stuart MacLaren, a celebrated British flier attempting to fly round the world in a seaplane, was missing — somewhere between the Asian mainland and BC. Immediately *The Times* wanted all the news Rufus could send, and sooner rather than later! But there was no news and MacLaren stayed missing through 17 July, only to turn up the next day, fogbound on Hokkaido, Japan. Rufus was on holiday for the next two weeks, during which MacLaren, fortunately, made no progress. However, the day he returned to work, the flier, after flying from Petropavlosk in Kamchatka to Nikolski in the Aleutians, damaged his machine so badly that he had to abandon the attempt. The next week was, in Rufus's words, "a week of worry on MacLaren — wireless and cabling, to him and to London, daily." The officer, now front-page news, was safe aboard *HMCS Thiepval*, a tiny Canadian armed trawler assigned as his support vessel which was heading for Vancouver. Rufus's goal, therefore, became to reach and interview him before the competition even knew he was near.

With that in mind, he left for Prince Rupert at midnight on 13 August aboard the *SS Prince George*, skippered by his old friend Neddon. By the afternoon of the 15th they were in Prince Rupert — about which, in his usual uncomplimentary way, he remarked: "Town somewhat grown — no more attractive than ever though." He spent the rest of the day quietly lining up a photographer and preparing the CN telegraph man — discovering in the process that his presence was "already much advertised by Waugh at CNR, which was the last thing I wanted." But fortune favours the brave: spies informed him early next morning that *Thiepval* had docked at 2:30 am while he himself had been asleep. According to his own article, "Mayor Newton with several members of his council, Peter Pyle, president of the GWVA, and a number of members of that organization, and prominent citizens, were on hand in the drizzling rain to welcome the gallant flier. Lashed to the deck of the *Thiepval* was the battered fuselage of the *Vickers–Vimy* amphibian plane in which the party nearly met their deaths on scores of thrilling occasions."[111]

Rufus himself only "went down to the ship at 7 am and had a long talk. I found him [MacLaren] a most attractive young man of 32. Worked hard from 9 am when I left him, to 12:30 when he and Col Broome met me for lunch at the hotel. Sent *Province* about 1,200 words — I hope without affecting *The Times*' rights. All pm working on story for *Times* which went off 3–5 pm, in takes." In this manner, both papers had the story in detail long before *Thiepval* returned MacLaren to civilization in Vancouver four days later. It was a textbook scoop. It seems that others may have been as pleased as he was — Fred Southam, the paper's new owner, for example, and even Roy Brown, his horizons expanded by his sabbatical. There had already been signs of change at the *Province* in the weeks following R.B.'s return from London, including the firing of two reporters. He took a week's holiday on 15 September to think things through, and on the 26th, as Rufus described it, ". . . sent for me and told me to take over features — I was in charge — and to 'get out an eight-page feature supplement next week!'" The following day he wrote, "I quit my desk job — after four years steady grind — thank heaven — and plunged into the features section. Hard at work — terrific day in the office." A reader might hear echoes of his first day at 3rd Brigade in January 1917.

Chapter 14
Magazine Editor
Vancouver, 1924–1928

"But with thoughtful estimation, we will make this observation that he also is a crack newspaperman."

from Bernard McEvoy's contribution to Rufus's stag party, 30 April 1928

From his first day as Features Editor, Rufus blossomed. Never a good fit in the roles he had been assigned at the *Province*, he had been a burr under R.B.'s saddle, capable of blindsiding him at any time by his own prominence — from his comfort with movers and shakers to his knowledge of the world or his local celebrity as speaker and performer. Now that he was off the treadmill, he could plan his time and escape from regularity for its own sake.

It was a good feeling that would soon feel even better. As Features Editor he moved into what had once been Nichol's private office. And when, on 4 October, his first features section rolled off the press to general acclaim, he made the pleasant discovery that, without fanfare, the paper was paying him more. Things were definitely looking up! Within days, Geoffrey Dawson, editor of *The Times*, rolled into town like visiting royalty. He and his wife joined Rufus and Bee for lunch at the Hotel Vancouver, for a drive around Stanley Park and then for tea at 1337 Maple Street. Amazingly, the two couples got along well[112] — a mutual liking that would one day prove useful.

The first features section was simply pages 21 to 28 of the *Province*, with little indication of a new departure. No doubt preoccupied with filling those pages, Rufus had not much concerned himself with dressing them up. That soon changed: the eight pages became the Magazine Section for the 11 October issue. Having established a formula for their content, eight pages expanded to twelve on 8 February 1925; and the twelve-page Magazine Section's anniversary edition, dated 31 January 1926, was celebrated with pictures and fanfare. The content was both eclectic and graphic. The first edition included many general interest articles, among them Alexander Mackenzie's journey to the coast, Britain's first female cabinet minister, the Prince of Wales as a romantic figure, and the USA as the world's most lawless nation. It contained book reviews — one on Buchan's latest novel — Bernard Shaw on films, pages of serious photography, cartoons, a local gossip column called 'Diogenes at Street Corners', poetry, and a folksy weather forecast. The Magazine Section soon developed regular columns: 'Diogenes' went international and became just 'Street Corners'; 'Books of the Moment' reviewed new books (*A Passage to India* on 8 February 1925), 'News Jottings from BC's Hinterland' was a page of reports from interior cities; and there was also 'Glimpses of Life in Britain and Distant Parts of the Empire'. In sum, it was a serious attempt to entertain and inform both men and women.

By early 1925 the Magazine Section was well-established and its editor able to devote more time to Little Theatre. Both he and Bee were happy to help with prompting, ticket-taking or other jobs at a moment's notice, and both acted in plays that spring. Rufus was cast as General Johnny Burgoyne in *The Devil's Disciple*, and Bee was persuaded to take a part in a play put on by Rotary for which the cast rehearsed in Vancouver but travelled to Portland to perform. Rufus tried out, unsuccessfully, for another part in the fall but the theatre kept him busy with executive meetings, socials or just going to shows with Bee.

Since June 1922 he had been Vice-President of Vancouver Little Theatre while W.G. 'Billy' Murrin[113] had been President. Over the next five years the two developed a comfortable friendship. Not only did they share a passion for theatre, but also a desire to serve the community, robust Anglican belief, and equally robust conservative politics. Murrin, assistant general manager of BC Electric — and president from 1929 — was a wealthy man. Rufus, for his part, was a dependable problem-solver, husband of one of VLT's better actresses and, from his perch at the *Province*, well-positioned to keep the VLT front and centre.

When Dawson appeared, Murrin had been able to assist by rounding up twenty leading citizens, including R.B., for a lunch to him at the Vancouver Club. A little later Sir Campbell Stuart appeared in town, the Canadian officer who had worked successfully to spread British propaganda into Germany and her allies during the war, and whose book about it[114] had given him status close to that of Lawrence of Arabia. Murrin encouraged Rufus to organize and host a high-profile dinner for Stuart, for which he would pick up the tab — be "fairy godmother" as Rufus put it — and the guests included the ultra-right-wing MP for Vancouver Centre, H.H. Stevens, the man who in 1926 would sniff out the customs scandal that brought down Mackenzie King.

Rufus got out of the city whenever he could — in order to be able to write about the variety of British Columbia for the paper. As soon as Derek returned to Kingsley School in April, his parents took an idyllic weekend on the *SS Chelosin* up the coast to Bute Inlet. They had a comfortable cabin, another couple for company, three days of spring sunshine and a courteous crew. While the little ship made calls at Sechelt, Savary Island, Powell River and Bowen Island, they basked in the sun and watched the action from their perch on the bridge.

Six weeks later Murrin provided them with a weekend at BCE expense. From the harbour, they were swished under the Second Narrows Bridge — still under construction — in the company launch, then up Indian Arm to Buntzen Bay. They were met by Elwell, a company official, and lodged in a cabin stocked with whatever they might need overlooking Indian Arm. In the morning Elwell escorted them around the hydro plants on which Rufus produced a spread in the *Province*. After two days of rural solitude the launch returned them to Vancouver, together with Elwell's daughter — who later came to stay for a few days.

After these happy times together, in late June Rufus set off for ten days in the Cariboo country of central BC. Whether or not the plan of writing a book had yet formed, he was researching a series of articles for the paper which, with very little effort, he would later turn into *Beyond the Rockies*,[115] to which the reader must refer for details of the trip.

To get there, he no longer had to labour up the old Cariboo Highway; instead, courtesy of a PGE[116] passenger train from Squamish, he was transported comfortably through a sparsely-settled hinterland to Quesnel. People there lived much as he himself had done in his prairie years — though in most cases contentedly and without his consuming search for a means of escape. Accepting rides as they were offered and everywhere trailing plumes of dust along unpaved roads, from Quesnel he travelled first to Barkerville, where he stayed at Kelly's Hotel while seeking out the fading tracks of the old prospectors. Thence to Williams Lake, whose three hundred citizens were holding their stampede in a brand new hall. It was a noisy celebration of their way of life by everybody from miles around, native and white. Amongst them he experienced two scorching days of cowboys and horses, a crescendo of sounds amid flies and drunks, before escaping to the deep silences and open skies of the Chilcotin Valley ranches. After nine days in this boundless landscape he re-entered his time machine, a PGE sleeping car at the Williams Lake station, and by the next afternoon was washing off the dust in tidewater at Kits Beach. It had been a good trip, one that had recharged his batteries as a writer. He understood better than most that the real British Columbia began where the city ended and it was his ability to convey this to readers that would build his reputation — and many townies discovered the kind of province they lived in through his columns.

Back in Vancouver, between hard-fought tennis matches — his ritual of summer — he and Bee welcomed Lord and Lady Byng to town, each in their own way — Bee at a ladies' tea and Rufus at the Military Institute dinner where Byng spoke. Such gatherings were becoming rarer as years passed but the emotions were no less intense for old warriors. He and Byng would have time to chat a few days later on a platform in Banff, where both were awaiting the arrival of Field Marshall Haig on a Canadian tour. Then he managed twenty minutes with Haig himself — all in all, a productive afternoon and evidence of his magic touch with the brass; without exception they gave him the time of day, maybe because they knew he'd been there, had seen the pressure they faced, and trusted him to give them their due.

Having sent dispatches on these old heroes from Kamloops, Rufus started a ten-day exploration of the southern interior. He had his contacts there, one a polo player whose pony he borrowed to ride around the SSB[117] settlements at Heffley Creek. Next, he went south to Vernon on "Armstrong's stage", a motor-bus despite its name. On the way he had little chance to enjoy the Okanagan parkland scenery because somebody's baby, whose chin he tickled, rewarded him by throwing up over him. In this condition he got a lift from Vernon to his old friends, the Makovskis, now at Armstrong, and these good people cleaned him up, fed him supper, and found him a ride back to Vernon. Next day Colonel Johnston of the SSB drove him round more soldier settlements near Lumby in the Coldstream Valley and then to his friend General Harmon's house outside Kelowna. That night he stayed at the Palace Hotel on Bernard Avenue — a stuffy, noisy place, back from the lake — and after a day watching fruit-packing and cheese-making, he met Bee and Derek at the Kelowna wharf. They had boarded the *Sicamous* in Vernon and together they continued south to Penticton.

They stayed first at the Incola Hotel next to the KVR station, then moved to the Penticton Hotel. They visited F. H. Keane's spread on the benchland, spent a day at the federal experimental farm in Summerland and another visiting more soldier settlers at Oliver near the US border. Okanagan summer heat ambushed the visitors and they swam wherever and whenever they could. It sounds like a holiday, and so it was for Bee and Derek, but Rufus filled every minute with appointments and invitations to dine — even dropping in at United Seed Growers an hour and a half before leaving for Vancouver.

The KVR train took twelve hours to cover the 400 kms. It hauled passengers across three mountain passes of over 1,000 metres; from the sagebrush of the Okanagan it wound along fertile valleys, past the bleak Coqihalla summit and into rainforest as it plunged downhill to Hope. Like the more easterly section of the railway, this section had its marvels, in some places running along rock and under rock on the wall of a precipice, and finally through the five Quintette tunnels — where the track ran straight while the Coquihalla River performed its furious slalom under the connecting bridges.

Rufus had left Bee and Derek enjoying the delights of Penticton to rush home and meet a new boss, John Jacob Astor V, owner of *The Times* after Northcliffe. He and R.B., with Cromie of the *Sun*, called on Astor and his wife while they waited in Vancouver for their ship to the Imperial Press Conference in Australia. Over a couple of days Rufus drove Astor round the park, talking shop the whole way, spent a Sunday working for *The Times* as a result, and went to Cromie's reception for the waiting delegates. These included A.P. Herbert of *Punch*, Sir Percival Phillipps of the *Daily Telegraph*, Sir Edward Iliffe, owner of the *Telegraph*, and Grattan O'Leary, editor of the *Ottawa Journal* — people whose influence could help him sell his writing, while the few hours spent with them trumped having to attend the conference.

August passed in a flurry of sedate beach parties, club tennis, tennis with Derek, seeing friends (*sometimes* without playing bridge) and bathing at every opportunity, even in forest-fire smoke. When Derek went back to school at Kingsley, Rufus could leave for ten days with his friend, Rev Alan Green, aboard the Columbia Coast Mission boat *Rendezvous*, an under-powered little tub that carried Green from service to service in settlements up and down the coast. From Lund, they sailed north to Refuge Cove on Redonda Island, across the sound to Squirrel Cove on Cortez Island, then up to a landing on Stuart Island and into Desolation Sound before turning south and back to Manson's Landing on Cortez — 200 kms in all. With his horror of idleness, he insisted on acting as crew whenever they were entering or leaving harbour. They basked in sunshine for nine days in towering fjords — unaware intruders into a world of orcas, bears and eagles of which he makes no mention.

In late September he had a pleasant Anglican interlude in Kamloops, where the first Bishop of Cariboo was to be consecrated. As he noted wryly, he spent three days in the company of "bishops, priests and deacons", though he did manage some golf with a more worldly member of the crowd. He had never met Walter Adams, the new bishop, though henceforth each would enjoy the other's company whenever they did, as was the case with Bishop Doull of Kootenay. From early days in Canada Rufus had found occasional immersion in clerical company sustaining and relaxing — and this despite his expected role of writing about them all for a public still engaged by church affairs.

He made yet another foray out of Vancouver in 1925: in November he took four days off to walk from Nanaimo to Victoria — three of them in the rain. The distance is about 140 kms and his main target was his waistline — a recent diary entry had read: ". . . round Stanley Park in the morning. Starving today, two apples only." But on the second day he could not resist calling on the "main guy" at the Chemainus mill *en route* to Duncan. The route had been carefully planned between friends' houses, including lunch at Milledge's — perpetrator of the "ghastly error" with their wedding photos — and ended at the Tzouhalem Hotel for an evening yarn with Duncan friends. The third day, still in the rain and eventually also in the dark, took him as far as Mill Bay to stay with friends. Only on the last day did the sun shine as he strode across the Malahat to the Empress Hotel in Victoria, arriving feeling "very tired" — and no wonder. Bee, who had also spent those days on the Island, found him there, chatting with R.B., who seemed at last to have become a friend.

In May Rufus heard from Uncle Harry. He wanted Rufus to use his connections to check the *bona fides* of an officer newly arrived in Cape Town, who claimed to have served with the CEF. "When a man poses as a Brig.

General," he harrumphed, "it is desirable to know whether he has any claim to that rank." Rufus asked his friend General Odlum[118] to check with the Adjutant General — which Odlum seems to have done though we never hear the answer. Harry formally congratulated Rufus on his promotion at the paper before letting slip that he was not at all well.

When he wrote again in November, his health was much worse but what was bothering him this time was that Field Marshall Haig in a recent letter had not mentioned meeting Rufus in Canada! It was perhaps a sign he was near the end and he died on 16 December. He had wanted to be a good uncle, as Rufus had wanted to be a good nephew, but for two men with much in common their relationship had been a frustration. This had been due largely to the older man's inability to express normal human feelings when they did meet, or to write in anything but formal language when they were apart. Nevertheless, he had admired his uncle and appreciated his role in smoothing his way in France. It had been Harry's words of consolation, coming from somebody of his rank, that had helped him put the disappointment about medals behind him — especially as only he, out of the whole extended family, could really appreciate how difficult, dangerous and extraordinary his nephew's contributions had been, at Passchendaele and Amiens in particular, and how much, therefore, he deserved recognition. In addition, Harry had been Bee's greatest fan and never lost an opportunity to praise or ask after her — a reinforcing contribution to their marriage.

In 1926 Rufus became further acclimatized to the role of Magazine Section editor and ever more part of the Vancouver establishment, thanks to two new claims on his energy, the Canadian Club and the St George's Society. As before, he made excursions into the hinterland, though these were fewer, and he continued playing competitive tennis. But in other ways the year was to be quite different: after June, their agenda would be all about Bee, and their improving bank balance allowed them to buy a lot and consider building on it.

Rufus had been VP of Little Theatre for five years. Now, at its AGM in January 1926, he became president of the St George's Society. At a superficial level the society was just a warm refuge for English ex-pats, but to him it appealed as a source of funds for helping English settlers — mostly ex-soldiers — succeed. In the Vancouver Branch's list of 'Objects' a new one stood out that year: ". . . to extend a helping, sympathetic hand to immigrants direct from England without attempting in any way to act as an employment bureau." Having just elected him president by acclamation, one can almost hear the members' consternation when he asked them to adopt this new object; they did adopt it, of course, but only after adding the disclaimer.

The society spent the next four months fundraising. Rufus's chum Murrin set the bar high with a donation of $100 and their efforts built towards 23 April, St George's Day, when they planned a banquet at the Hotel Vancouver. In the interim they ran a sale of work* and a concert. We are not told how much they raised but it must have been substantial: the concert in the Wesley Church was attended by 550 and the banquet by 225. As their contribution, Bee and Derek had a stall at The Bay selling tickets; and Rufus persuaded *Maclean's* editor Vernon McKenzie to run an article on the settlers. While researching this, he had involved himself in settler affairs: he had welcomed arriving families, seen they were housed and fed and had spent twenty-four hours with them at the Abbotsford training farm. Once the banquet was over and the money put to work, however, his diary makes no further mention of the society; its place was taken by the speakers' committee of the Canadian Club executive, of which he was also a member.

Bee had a bout of tonsillitis in January. Once she was out of bed, as the weather was "as warm as spring," Rufus took her to convalesce at the Grouse Mountain Tea Rooms which seem to have doubled as a resort hotel.[119] The patient enjoyed these surroundings so much — a magnificent view over the city when the clouds lifted, and close to Muriel's house and Derek's school — that she stayed a second week, coming home on 6 February in time for Derek's 13th birthday.

The North Shore's other attraction may have been its distance from Maple Street. Although it had suited them well, it was starting to feel less like home. In September Rufus had noted, gloomily, "Matthews' house next door let again." Sure enough, as he had feared, their new neighbours became increasingly inconsiderate over the winter. The blow-up occurred while Bee was away — "party next door till 1 am," he fumed one weekend. After she was home, the noise from next door became constant and Rufus summoned Matthews[120] to hear it for himself — but, of course, everything fell quiet when he arrived. When the noise resumed next day, Rufus was beside himself. "Row over noise next door," he wrote, "rang up Frederics and Matthews — Mrs Davis came in, etc." It was becoming a neighbourhood issue which seemed only to encourage the renters. A day or two later Rufus wrote "party next door woke Bee at 3:10 am," followed by "rang up Matthews re: next door *again*!" Matthews, it seems, couldn't or wouldn't evict his tenants, leaving Rufus and Bee with three options: take him to court, learn to live with it — or move.

It was the last option that most appealed. Many of their friends had built houses in the still-mostly-forested Point Grey district to the west and south of Kitsilano — though not all as grandly as the Murrins had on SW Marine Drive. Thanks to salary raises at the *Province* and to outside work, Rufus was making much more money by 1926. The ambitious journalist who had accepted Nichol's 1919 offer of $175 a month was now receiving $303 a month from the same paper. With outside payments from *The Times*, but also from the *Toronto Star*, the *Regina Leader*, *Tatler* and *Maclean's*, his income for the year would reach $4800. So they decided to buy a lot — with a view to building.

---

* A sale of goods and handicrafts made by the members.

As was their style, having made the decision they lost no time acting upon it. A few days after Rufus's last call to Matthews, they drove out to Third Shaughnessy to look at lots. There were three they liked and any one of them would do. Next morning, a Saturday, the CPR Land Agent accepted their offer along with Rufus's cheque for $190, 10% of the asking price. They had became proud owners of the wilderness lot at the northeast corner of Markham (now Marguerite) and 52nd but would go on living at 1337 Maple St for another eighteen months. Maybe the renters moved, making Maple St livable again, but it was really more pressing events that postponed building plans.

Bee took a part in the Little Theatre Spring 1926 production *Beware of Widows* and immersed herself in rehearsals until the performances towards the end of April. Rufus, as usual, was all over the map. A trip to Revelstoke to intercept Randolph Bruce, Walter Nichol's replacement, brought him two disappointments. After his interview with Bruce fell very flat, he dismissed him as "just a close-fisted old Scotsman in my opinion — no magnetism and little originality of thought."

He then tried for a scoop on the new rotary snowplows at work on a slide. He stowed away on one for that purpose but was discovered and "hauled off ignominiously." For a journalist, such humiliation brings the silver lining that he can write about it — and he did.

He had also made two trips to Victoria. On the first of these he lunched with Nichol at Government House. These were Nichol's last days in office and he drove Rufus out to Sidney to show him Miraloma, his enormous retirement pad — now a hotel. On a second trip to Victoria, he flew there and back in an open Curtiss HS 2L flying-boat from the flying-boat station at Jericho. Although the aircraft's maximum speed was 82.5 mph or 133 kph, the April air was chilly and before take-off he was provided with a long leather coat, leather helmet and goggles. Each flight lasted an hour, which gave him five hours in which to thaw himself out, interview Duff Patullo (then Minister of Lands) and drop in again on Walter Nichol. His diary noted blandly, "exhilarating experience — lovely day." In May he took the steamer to Nanaimo, then the stage to Qualicum, where Byng and his entourage were playing golf. Thanks to Willis O'Connor, the ADC, Rufus got his pictures of the vice-regal couple next morning and was back in Vancouver that afternoon. He would get his chance to bid the old soldier farewell later on.

In late May he left on the PGE[121] for the north and would be away sixteen days. He was exploring a region of the province beyond the ken of most British Columbians and his record of his travels and encounters not only appeared as articles in the Magazine Section, but also, eventually, as chapters 9 to12 in *Beyond the Rockies*, a literary project that was now part of his agenda. At this point in his career he was close to living his ideal of journalistic life — free to go where he wanted and to report on whatever engaged his interest. In those few days he visited most places between Prince George and Terrace — some, like Fort Saint James, being far from the rudimentary highway west — and often allowing his direction to be dictated by the lifts that kind locals offered him. Underlining the remoteness of this part of the province he could go no further west by road than Terrace, Prince Rupert being accessible only by train, ship or float plane. No wonder the little port had seemed to him "as god-forsaken as ever" in 1922.

To read about this expedition the reader must turn to Rufus's own account. In 2002 his granddaughter Val retraced some of his steps with this author, including his visit to the HBC trading post at Fort Saint James. The upper floor of the Chief Factor's house is usually off-limits to visitors but we were allowed up and found the "large upper room" described by Val's grandfather, with its "solid square chimney which passed up through the centre of it." There he had "pondered on the great figures of British Columbia's romantic past who had made history on that very ground,"[122] and we did much the same as we gazed at the little iron bed in which he had slept some seventy-six years before.

He arrived back in Vancouver on 8 June. Bee had not known precisely when to expect him — his wire had not been clear — so his appearance in the early afternoon surprised her. The next morning he received a call at his office from a neighbour: Bee had been hit by a Kitsilano-line streetcar at Maple Street, was badly injured and had been taken to St Paul's hospital. A *Province* article on the accident claimed she had been caught by the streetcar's fender and dragged nearly a city block before the motorman, his air-brakes having failed, could stop the car with the handbrake. She was carried into a house in the 1400 block of Walnut Street to wait for an ambulance — which suggests the paper was accurate about the distance she was dragged. Apart from heavy bruising, X-rays revealed a broken shoulder. Probably her humerus was also fractured as she would wear a cast and a splint until late July.

Five days after the accident Rufus contacted George Kidd, BCE's General Manager. Mr Kidd was most accommodating: accepting the company's responsibility, he proposed to pay Bee's hospital expenses, and as compensation for her ordeal, also to pay for a Hawaiian holiday for them both whenever she should be fit enough! The fact that the streetcar driver had dragged Bee so far because of failed brakes left the responsibility beyond doubt so it was perhaps just a coincidence that Kidd's number two at BCE was W.G. Murrin, Rufus's Little Theatre colleague and longtime friend.

The injury kept Bee in hospital until 31 August and, once home again, she needed months of rehabilitation before she could live normally, so they hired a temporary housekeeper who would also look after her and, at first, take her out in a wheelchair. While Bee had been in hospital, or recuperating at home, Rufus played more tennis than ever, most of it vigorous, competitive stuff. Although he and Derek still did many things together — tennis and swimming for example, or going to movies — the 13-year-old was increasingly independent and spent much of his summer holiday away from home — on the farm at Mt Lehman, as crew on *Rendezvous*, at camp on the Island, or staying with Muriel's family in North Vancouver — and was usually exhausted when he did come home.

Consequently Rufus was often free of ties which allowed him to work late when he wanted to, or to spend extra time on the courts.

In the fall he had two interesting excursions. The first was one of those velvety Anglican events that he secretly loved. In early September the foundation stone for the new cathedral in Victoria was to be laid with enormous ceremony — attended by no fewer than twelve bishops, including the cumbrously named Arthur Foley Winnington-Ingram, Bishop of London. Rufus went over on the night boat, whiling away the hours with a rubber or two of bridge with his new episcopal friend, Adams of Cariboo, and with the archbishop himself.

For the second excursion, later in the month, he was invited to inspect BC Electric's Bridge River hydro project. Having ridden a PGE freight to get there, he spent two comfortable nights at BCE's base camp at Shalalth; in the daytime he was driven over the hair-raising Mission Mountain road to the dam-site itself. It was the sort of trip that appealed to him, combining interest with immersion in back-country BC and a modicum of danger.

Rufus and Bee were fortunate: in 1926 a Hawaiian holiday was a rarity for middle-income Canadians, most being unable to take two extra weeks travel time on top of their holiday. They did not slip away unnoticed: on 17 November friends had filled their cabin on *SS Niagara* with flowers and more than twenty came aboard to see them off. Once under way, when the glow of the send-off had faded, they settled down to wait for warm weather as they steered a southwesterly course through heavy seas. After four dull days of bridge-playing, sunny skies and warm winds on the fifth day lifted spirits, and on their last day at sea Bee wore a cotton dress and Rufus his flannels.

They spent nine days from 24 November at the Halekulane Hotel at Waikiki. Theirs was a bungalow suite in a palm grove right at the water's edge — "a gorgeous spot" as Rufus enthused. He subsequently justified his absence by writing 'Hawaiian letters' from "Luke T. Johns" which he would turn into main features of consecutive editions of the *Province* Magazine, starting on 30 January. Their hotel was residential and quiet but, for more excitement, they had the Moana Hotel next door.

In the mornings they both found it hard to sleep — it was light too early and too warm for serious sleep. So they swam together before breakfast and, thus invigorated, Bee at first went with him to the shops or to a museum. But it was just too hot for that to be fun; instead, as she was not looking for excitement, she was happy to snooze or read in the sun or in the shade of their own patio. Rufus was no sun worshipper — the reverse in fact — but his restlessness and curiosity made him a bad tropical beach person and quite unable to settle down beside her with a book. So while she snoozed or read, he would be diving in and out of the waves or making long streetcar explorations of Honolulu. Fortunately, their network of friends, or the friends of friends, took them for drives — kind people, on different days, driving them all over Oahu — to Mount Tantalus at sunset or to Kailua Beach or to the Manoa Valley — and once right around the island. Meanwhile, the Hawaiian dancers shimmied and swayed most evenings in the Moana and they were so well entertained that they played bridge just once.

The voyage home on *RMS Aorangi* was shorter and more comfortable but Vancouver, when they docked on 9 December was wet and cold. "We don't like it," the traveller wrote of the weather in his diary, but neighbours had been in and had lit a roaring fire to heat the house. The end of the year passed quietly and they had Christmas at home for the first time since the war. But the best news of all, six months after Bee's accident, was that the trip to Hawaii had done the trick and she felt fine. She continued in good health through 1927 and was soon back to acting — in fact they would both strut their stuff at one time or another in the new year.

The year in which Rufus turned forty would be his last full year in British Columbia. It was memorable in several ways: first of all, this compulsive wanderer spent almost a quarter of it wandering — which was how he liked to live; it was also the year in which a friend re-introduced him to golf, henceforth a frequent pursuit, though there would be no retreat from tennis; it was the year when Derek could finally take him on, not only on the golf course, where both were tyros, but also on the courts — and was already a better swimmer; and finally, by year's end Rufus would have written enough about the wilder parts of the province to bundle the articles into a book, *Beyond the Rockies*, to be published by Dents, whose chairman, Hugh Dent, had been a fellow passenger to Hawaii.

On 23 April they sold 1337 Maple Street to a Miss Tyler — who was willing to let them keep possession until the fall, a very friendly arrangement. By April both were busy with their own preoccupations: Bee had been cast as the Abbess in the Little Theatre production of *Nursery Maid of Heaven* and was occupied with rehearsals; and, the day after selling the house, Rufus set off to explore the southern Gulf Islands on foot — killing two birds, once more, as his eight-day walkabout helped with his waistline while providing material for several articles and two chapters of his book.

Bee's play was the best in a programme of three one-act plays — "a rather dull bill but not a 'flop'" was how Rufus, the VLTA's longtime Mr Vice, assessed it. Her performance was "excellent," he thought, and a successful return to the stage after her misadventure. His own Gulf Island venture had relied heavily on people offering beds, meals, and boat rides. He had started on Mayne and ended up on Salt Spring, having travelled via Galiano and Pender. On each island he walked long distances and everywhere had friends to visit or to stay with, the last being Cy Peck, war hero and MLA for the Gulf Islands, whose re-election meeting he attended in Fulford Harbour.

Governor General Willingdon came to BC on his getting-to-know-you tour in April, along with Willis O'Connor, once Byng's ADC and now his own. O'Connor took 'His Ex' to Qualicum to play golf, a course that Byng had enjoyed, and invited his friend Rufus to come over for an interview and photo opportunity with his boss. In fact Rufus and Bee both went and Bee got on famously with Lady W. while Rufus was making his number with her husband. It would be a pleasant and useful relationship.

Given time, everybody seemed to come to Vancouver. So it was that, eighteen months after Uncle Harry's death, Rufus found himself welcoming his widow — his Aunt Lily — to Vancouver. Hers was no 'poor relation' visit — she travelled in style and had been three weeks in the country before coming to Vancouver. She was travelling with two companions, widows of South African officers like herself, and they stayed at the Hotel Vancouver. Once Lily Quinn, she had both Quinn and Johnston relatives to visit but came alone to lunch with Rufus and Bee at HBC the day after her arrival. She had seen her nephew for fleeting visits during the war but the Rufus she remembered was the red-haired six-year-old with the stunning singing voice she had known in 1893, while Harry had been taking courses. She might have been forgiven a smile or two as she equated her memories with this charming, dapper man, still red-haired and energetically seeing to her comfort, his unlit pipe forgotten in his hand as he did so.

Entertaining Lily was like dancing a minuet: three days later, this time with her companions, she came to tea; three days after that, Bee and Rufus held a bridge party for her, followed by a drive to the Grouse Mountain Tearooms. Then she went to Victoria for a while, before returning to stay, first with Rufus and Bee, and then with the Quinns. On her last day in Vancouver Rufus arranged a family lunch at the same restaurant. Everybody came: Aunt Lily, the Quinns, Roy and Marjorie, Rufus, Bee, and Derek — and Mrs Hartley, one of Lily's widows. Later, after a formal photograph, they all walked over to the CPR station where the two older ladies caught the train for England.

The rest of 1927, for Rufus, was full of memorable excess. He loved to play competitive tennis but did so rarely as regular commitments were hard to keep; he usually played 'friendlies', or with Derek and his pals. So when opportunity arose for serious competition, he played with almost manic energy and Lily's unexpected departure for Victoria gave him the opportunity. He had entered his club's handicap tournament, in which matches were forfeited if not completed within a certain time. On a Thursday evening he took on Wilmot, in spite of a drizzle, and beat him. The next day was lost to rain and Saturday became his last opportunity to avoid a forfeit. The courts were wet earlier but at 12:30 he played Lacey, his second-round opponent, and beat him too. After a short rest, he then agreed to play his semi-final opponent, Mitchell, at 3 pm. It was a hard contest but Rufus eventually won this match too. Soaked in sweat and feeling sore, his body told him it was time to go home; but Jack Braun, the other finalist, was at the club and hoping to play. Though they could also have played their final on Sunday, Rufus was unable to resist the challenge. So they played the final and, although he gave it his all, he had to settle for second prize. Ruefully he wrote in his diary: "I was foolish to play the third match today — terrible blisters on hands and feet." It is tempting to see the story as a metaphor for his life.

After that Rufus and Derek joined *Rendezvous* at Rock Bay, 50 kms north of Campbell River and spent a week among the islands that included many things near to Rufus's heart. Alan Green's parishioners were whomsoever they happened upon in the anchorages and settlements and Rufus was more than happy to yarn with them, or to read lessons while Green preached, his scribe's curiosity aligning happily with his host's pastoral purpose and his own liking for vicarious involvement in God's work. The sun shone on them and, when not tending men's souls, they took every chance to swim off sandy beaches in clear water — on some days, three and four times.

Still, Rufus would not have been satisfied had he not, now and then, done something a bit extreme. Feeling a need for vigorous exercise, he had Green drop him off with the dinghy at Cape Mudge. Despite blistered hands, he then rowed 6 kms to Quathiaski Cove, probably against the tide, arriving exhausted and after dark. Over the next two days he and Derek made two vain attempts to catch salmon at the mouth of the Campbell River. Though neither considered himself an angler, to have drawn a blank at that particular spot in 1927 takes a bit of believing — and ranks them, in spite of their other talents, among the world's worst fishermen. The next day, after *Rendezvous* had crossed to Savary Island in a full gale, it was perhaps the shame of fishlessness that made them attempt to bathe in the rollers crashing onto its north shore near the government dock. Battered and bruised, they thought better of it, walked the short distance through the trees to the south shore where the beach was sheltered from the gale and, in Rufus's terse words, it was "v. lovely — bathed again, etc."[123] In a timeless tip to swimmers he declared Mink Island in Desolation Sound the "best bathing of all".

Meanwhile, Bee had not been pining — far from it: she spent the week in Duncan with her friend Madge Barry and, on her way home, stayed with another friend, probably Muriel, on the North Shore. She made sure not to be back at 1337 until after the menfolk were home — let them make their own breakfast!

The rest of Rufus's summer was an athletic blur. While the weather held in August, he bathed most days while social life, as usual, centred on the beach. He played cricket once, making 22 — top score for his team, as he recorded with pride — and golf and tennis with Derek on several occasions. They all went to Cricket Week matches at Brockton Oval and to see the rodeo at the Hastings Park exhibition, forerunner of the PNE.

For most people the big event of the month was the second visit of the Prince of Wales, soon to be King Edward VIII, with his brother George, later Duke of Kent. Rufus took minimal interest in the prince's doings, although he himself actually met him. When the princes arrived, the Canadian Club hosted a lunch for them at the Hotel Vancouver and Rufus, as a member of the executive, was introduced to them. Bee was watching proceedings from the gallery and heard the prince speak, though Derek seems to have found something better to do — watching cricket in the park with his pal Smitty.

After lunch there was a group photograph in the roof garden — two federal ministers, mayor Taylor and officials, various movers and shakers, the Canadian Club executive and the princes, thirty-one men with not a single woman — an interesting memento.

FALL BROUGHT CHANGE TO THEIR LIVES. As they had agreed with the buyer, once Derek had returned to Shawnigan, Bee and Rufus began packing their possessions, sold furniture to Major Matthews, the next-door landlord, and prepared to vacate 1337 Maple Street. Before they had done so, however, on 12 September Rufus went off for a month-long walkabout in northern BC, leaving Bee to move to Glencoe Lodge on her own.

This northern trip was the subject of chapters 14–17 in *Beyond the Rockies* and needs no detailed description here. The expedition was the toughest and most adventurous of his British Columbia ventures — with the possible exception of his 1911 hike into the mountains behind Hope in search of the Steamboat mine. Having reached Quesnel by train from Squamish, he caught a ride to Prince George — not yet directly connected to the south by rail — then continued north, bound for the northeast corner of BC, a part of the Great Plains that looks and feels like Alberta. This area had neither road nor rail connection with Prince George and the only way to get there was as David Thompson would have gone. Rufus, therefore, teamed up with H.E.P. Robertson, a provincial court judge on circuit bound for Fort St John, who had experience in navigating northern rivers — though he had come to grief on his last trip, capsizing his boat and losing all his kit. With the judge's teenage son Seymour, they made a party of three.

From Summit Lake, 50 kms north of Prince George, they covered the 370 kms to Hudson's Hope in the judge's custom-built flat-bottomed boat that drew but 7 inches, was 28 feet bow to stern and beamy enough to take bedrolls and packs while leaving them room to move about. They poled their way down the shallow and aptly-named Crooked River or, where the river was deep enough, used the 'kicker', a primitive outboard. North of McLeod Lake they entered the Parsnip River which they followed to its junction with the Finlay, then swung east down the Peace as far as the little settlement of Hudson's Hope. On the larger rivers they ran with the current, steering with an oar, avoiding whitewater where possible and having to 'line'* the boat past rapids they could not avoid. Unwilling to risk another spill, before every 'lining' the judge had them unload the vessel and portage everything to a landing spot downstream. They lived rough — camping in the open under a tarp or sleeping inside the handful of cabins they came across. They observed the wilderness code, leaving something useful in lieu of payment and scrupulously respecting other men's property in a land where nobody locked a cabin door.

* Towing the boat with a line from the bank while those on board fended off rocks and the bank itself.

In 1927 the Parsnip and Peace river valleys were as remote as they had been in 1827 — possibly more so because the native population had been much reduced by disease. *Beyond the Rockies* records their few encounters — wonderful sketches of long-dead old-timers. But for almost all of their ten-day journey they were absolutely alone in a wild landscape — the only sounds being water slapping on rocks, the wind in the forest canopy, creaks and thumps from the boat echoed mockingly from the trees — and their own voices. Rufus saw many moose; there were bear, too, one of which he tried to shoot. The judge did bag a brace of teal one day, though some mallard and canvasback got away. Unmentioned are eagles and ospreys, patiently watching the river from a snag or flying slowly overhead as if people did not exist. Now and then the silence would have been broken by the nervous chatter of a disturbed kingfisher, or the *kraak!* of a heron objecting to their presence before flying slowly downstream. It being September, they may also have heard the eerie bugling of rutting bull elk.

At Hudson's Hope the judge sold the boat and they parted company. Rufus remained there two days, waiting for a boat to take him to Fort St John. Thereafter, his trip, which took him as far as the town of Peace River in Alberta, had more in common with his earlier trip to the Cariboo. Sadly, one can no longer follow his route down the Parsnip and the Peace — since 1968 both valleys have been submerged under the immense Williston Lake, created by the 600-foot W.A.C. Bennett dam west of Hudson's Hope.

He returned to Vancouver via Edmonton on 8 October. He found an unhappy Bee in a noisy and unpleasant Glencoe Lodge and they quickly moved to a flat at 745 Cardero Street. With slides made from his own photographs he delivered an hour-long lecture to the Canadian Club as if he had just returned from the Amazon — an indication of how remote northern BC still seemed to Vancouverites. He was already planning another trip, this time to the cities of eastern Canada. Before he left, they moved into the flat and he arranged with a contractor to start building their house in the new year. Strangely, back in August he had noted in his diary: "decided finally (?!) to sell lot at 52nd and Markham for $2,300" Presumably the (?!) indicated that he considered the decision to be far from final — as it seems to have been.

He left for Ottawa 2 November and was away five weeks, lost no time by calling on prairie friends, and was at work on Parliament Hill on the 7th , interviewing premiers gathered for their conference with Prime Minister King. This was his focus until the conference ended on the 10th but apart from BC's MacLean, he seems to have interviewed only Brownlee of Alberta, Ferguson of Ontario, and Taschereau of Quebec, likely the three whose policy had most interest for BC. He remained in Ottawa another couple of days, during which he was furiously networking, meeting and talking with a wide variety of out-of-the-ordinary people.[124] It was a remarkable two days, and the footnoted list omits several others who were more obscure.

He left for Montreal on 13 November and, to atone for good living in the capital, walked "several miles up the train and back." In Montreal his agenda was more personal. He dined twice with Bee's benefactors, the Molsons, tried but failed to see General Loomis, and spent an afternoon at the Ross Memorial Hospital with Sandy Urquhart, a friend permanently disabled in August 1918. He continued interviewing remarkable people: he lunched with J.M. Macdonnell, Manager of the Montreal Branch of National Trust Company, and Professor Carleton Stanley, Currie's assistant president at McGill — both well-known public intellectuals; he interviewed Izaak W. Killam, a financier and philanthropist, by reputation Canada's richest man; Dr W.J. Black, chairman of the Soldiers' Settlement Board; J.M. Gibbon, the CPR's General Publicity Agent; and Harry Smith, manager of the CPR press bureau. If railway officials sound prosaic, recall that there was not yet a serious long-distance alternative to train travel. He also spent a morning at the *Montreal Star* and *La Presse*, observing the new technique of Colorgravure in action.

On the 18th he left for St John, New Brunswick, where Sandy McMillan, his staff 'learner' from 1918, "took him in charge" and with whom he stayed for the four days he was there. Sandy had been his best-loved wartime buddy but he had not seen him since 1918. The McMillans were a large, influential family and for four days he existed in an old-worldly cocoon; they ate meals at the houses of sisters, nephews or cousins, met Sandy's friends and on only two occasions took the opportunity to slip away to a movie or a club where they might, if they chose, revisit the past.

Eventually he set off for Sydney, first by boat across the Bay of Fundy to Digby, thence by rail to Halifax where he had dinner, and finally catching the overnight train to Sydney — a "very trying" 24-hour journey of some 700 kms. This latter part of his trip was all hard work and he spent the whole of the following day, a cold and windy one, visiting gritty coal mines and steel mills — at that time among the engines of Canada's economy. The same night he caught the train back to Montreal, a 36-hour marathon over what he called "Canada's worst section of railroad."

After a horrible journey he arrived in Montreal on a Saturday morning but moved immediately into his agenda: he phoned Fred Southam, head of the family and his ultimate boss, found him at work and went round to see him. They talked all morning and, before they parted at lunchtime, Southam had invited him to dinner to meet his wife, daughter, and son-in-law Philip Fisher, and then to go to a hockey game. He also rang the Molsons but as May was ill, agreed to join John Molson in the family pew at Christ Church cathedral for Sunday morning service — a rather feudal idea that appealed to him, especially as the Bishop of Niagara was preaching. Later he visited Urquhart again.

On Monday morning he toured the printing works at Southam's *Montreal Gazette* and was then included in a lunch at the St James Club that Southam was giving for various notables. These included General Currie (as Principal of

McGill), General McRae (sometime leader of the BC Provincial Party, now a Tory MP), Smeaton White (MP for Mount Royal and sometime editor of the *Gazette*), and I.W. Killam. Later he had tea with Killam and, after dining with the Fishers, caught the train for Toronto.

After a night on the train, he once more hit the ground running and his agenda was endless. During two days he found time to talk shop with Napier Moore at *Maclean's*, with McMillan at the *Toronto Star* Weekly, whose plant he visited, and with Fred Kerr at the *Hamilton Spectator*. He dined one night with the Very Reverend F. H. Cosgrave,[125] provost of Trinity College, and the other night with the Nashes, visited his publisher, went to a play, saw Carroll Aikins, one of the originators of Little Theatre, and had another long talk with I.W. Killam who hoped to inveigle him into working at, or possibly editing, the *Mail & Empire*, his new acquisition.

As he lay in his bunk on a westbound train, he must have gone over in his mind his many conversations with the Southams. As successful editor of the *Province* Magazine and with Nichol's recommendation, he was an obvious choice to head up any new venture. He would surely have told Fred Southam of his interest in such things and have felt that the chief appreciated his talents. For his part, Southam would have wanted him to perceive the special treatment he received as recognition and thanks for the fine job he was currently doing at the *Province* Magazine, hoping thereby to prevent him being poached by Killam or any other marauder. It is most unlikely he was encouraged to expect a new offer from them soon — why, in that case, would he and Bee start building a house in Vancouver?

He got home on 6 December and had been so anxious to get there that he hardly made diary entries along the way. But he had to for the last night of the journey because he and his fellow passengers were lucky to survive it. Even so, all that his entry said was: "At 2:30 last night, bad crash — engine turned completely over on edge of precipice. No-one seriously hurt."

Assuming that he used words judiciously, the engine, still coupled to carriages full of passengers, might just as easily have fallen from that precipice with drastic consequences. But for someone who had survived much worse on a regular basis, consequences that did not happen were neither alarming nor even worth explaining — for him, such learned fatalism was one of the few benefits of the war.

Once again he found Bee troubled by noisy neighbours and he soon joined the chorus. But it was too close to Christmas, the weather too wet or slushy, to think about moving and they decided to grin and bear it. He actually convinced himself they were "quite cozy in the flat — breakfast in front of fire, etc." They had Christmas with Muriel's family and the year ended in a round of parties, both adult and teenage — Derek now being old enough for his first dance and able to worry his parents by coming home late. In spite of the season, a time when modern people would only have less serious gatherings in mind, Rufus cheerfully arranged to talk to the Board of Trade six days before Christmas and to the Women's Canadian Club five days after, on the topic "Canada Today" with reference to his trip.

1928 arrived with an unexpected and unwelcome bang: on 3 January Rufus received a cable at the office from Kent, England — either from Bee's father or from friends of her family. It seemed that Bee's mother was in a poor way, having been knocked down by a car outside their Canterbury cottage. He cabled for more news and meanwhile decided to keep what he knew to himself. Finally on 16 January he reported: "Letters from Mr Robins and Mrs Dadds telling us of poor Mum." As there is no other mention of 'Mum' or of her dying, presumably the letters, which have not survived, brought that news. It was left to Bee's granddaughter, much later, to fill in the details from the records: the old lady had survived the accident but died soon afterwards from septicemia.

Considering that she loved her mother, Bee seems to have taken her death very calmly, though Rufus seldom if ever mentioned emotions — his own or other peoples'. He was certainly sympathetic but makes no mention of her staying in bed or cancelling her activities. However, he did provide two immediate distractions: on the 17th he began putting together the manuscript of *Beyond the Rockies*, which he asked Bee to help him proofread; and that weekend they both walked out to inspect progress on their house, on which the contractor, Cromie, had just started work. The only signs that Bee may have been in mourning for her mother was that she spent $62 for a dress that week and was not involved in the first VLTA productions of 1928. Otherwise life went on and there is no further mention of her mother in the diary. As a footnote to her feelings, when her second granddaughter was born in 1948, Bee asked for her to be called Frances after her mother and she was duly christened Hilary Frances Lukin Johnston.

In contrast to Bee, Rufus twice found himself involved in acting in the first three months of 1928. As VP of VLTA, he continued to have general responsibility for the success of productions, and on 11 February, when an actor became ill at the dress rehearsal, he took over the part. Opening night was three days hence and he would be washing greasepaint out of his hair until one in the morning for the next week — until even he admitted to being very tired of the play. By that time, however, he had started readings as Crichton, the butler in *The Admirable Crichton*. This was no minor part and it monopolized his time until the curtain finally fell on 31 March. It was during this time of maximum stress that his world would change forever.

On 7 March R.B. told him that Southam wanted him to go to Washington as their representative. That afternoon Nichols of Southam called to offer him $5,000 a year and an annual living allowance of $1,800 — $2,000. He must have been excited at the prospect but couldn't consult Bee as she was in Victoria. Nichols had given him time to think about the offer, so he discussed it with Murrin and Muriel among others, reporting to his diary, "All advise me that I *cannot* turn down Washington offer."

After arranging a weekend free from *Crichton*, he took the night boat to Victoria, went "for a long, windy walk" with Bee and, after visiting Derek at Shawnigan, accepted the job — on conditions. Then he plunged back into *Crichton* rehearsals and it was not until the 21st that he had their next word. "R.B. had a telegram from Nichols who finally decided the Washington job." In other words, it had gone to somebody else. Probably he had had reservations about the offer as there is no mention of how he felt — he had no time for feelings anyway as he was at full stretch rehearsing or performing nightly, at the same time as producing the weekly magazine section. So his diary entry for 29 March comes as a complete surprise: "Show — v. tired. Final agreement with Herb Woods re job in London!" And a week later: "Long talk with Fred Southam re London job — he willing to relieve me of house, etc." In retrospect, Southam's decision to send him to London rather than Washington seems so obvious that one wonders how it could have been a 'second thought'.

Exactly a month remained of his life in Vancouver and the last two weeks of that became a non-stop goodbye party for them both — they had certainly made their mark in these eight and a half years. This started with a family gathering at Roy's house, when photos were taken of solemn adults and grinning children, for whom the reality of parting had not yet sunk in. They had to undergo three official goodbyes including speeches and poetic tributes — from the Little Theatre, from the Canadian Club executive, and from the gang at the *Province*. They themselves gave a tea party at the Georgia Hotel for 130 friends, a dinner there for the oldest and dearest of these, and Rufus had a drinks party at the office. And as if that were not enough, on 3 May twenty people came to see Rufus off — Bee and Derek would follow later when school was out.

There were three poetic tributes, each showing Rufus through colleagues' eyes. Bernie McEvoy, a retired scribe, wrote a nonsense song to be chanted at their stag party for Rufus — for which the refrain went:

"He's an actor, he's a hiker, he's a Major, he's a man!
But with thoughtful estimation
we can make this observation,
that he also is a crack newspaper man."

Another colleague, Kenvyn, wrote "Bye Bye Lukin", to be sung to the tune of "Bye Bye Blackbird":

"Let us sing a song of woe, not too slow, 'fore you go,
Bye bye Lukin.
When you're far across the sea, think of me, in BC,
Bye bye Lukin.
We will miss your red top in the morning,
and that rank cigar smoke in the dawning.

When they say 'Here comes a duke', we'll shout 'NO, its just Luke'.
Lukin, goodbye."

The third was a poem by Herbert Beeman of Little Theatre, in which each of three verses — all about their future, glamorous life in London — ends with the lighthearted refrain, itself a line from *Crichton*, Act 1:

"There is no doubt that it will add
To the Young Person's chances."

McEvoy's whole refrain would have pleased Rufus, especially the 'crack newspaper man', though that also sounds like something he might often have said about those he admired. Beeman, too, refers to his ability and it may have been obvious to those he worked with that he was a journalist of rare quality. Kenvyn's "rank cigar smoke in the dawning" — another office joke — is the first revelation of this habitual pipe-smoker's additional bad habit. Beeman's refrain about "the young person's chances", surely kindly intended, suggests that his driving ambition was no secret to his friends who no doubt joked about it — it would certainly have got a good laugh from Roy Brown.

On the train that night Rufus was alone with his thoughts. A life in British Columbia he had come to relish had just ended — in fact, he had ended it. Now, after the next few weeks of travel and meetings, a sort of intermission between acts, he would start to piece together a life in London. He had few worries about his new job, or about his ability to provide readers with interesting dispatches — he brimmed with professional confidence and was headed, after all, for the world's most interesting city. It was the rest of it that troubled him: they were leaving those wonderful summers by English Bay, his tennis and golf, Bee's acting and the Little Theatre, their friends, Derek's school and his pals, the North Shore mountains, trips through the Gulf Islands, even the moan of the Point Atkinson foghorn on winter nights. Everybody in Vancouver knew Lukin Johnston, even if only through his articles. And he knew everybody, was welcome everywhere — was a big fish in a small pond. How would this big fish fare in a much bigger pond? *Maybe*, he thought, *I've thrown away everything we love and depend upon. And all for my wretched ambition — and a few measly bucks!*

If he ever had such doubts they would have been three-in-the-morning blues. Faced with his irrepressible optimism, they would have given way to other, more positive, thoughts as morning sunlight flooded his compartment. He remembered Derek's excitement upon hearing he would be going to school in England, and how excited his father had sounded at the prospect of seeing them all again. And Bee? Well, Bee was being a good soldier, he couldn't deny it; she had little reason to want to see England again, God knows — with its suffocating class-consciousness ever ready to punish the unwary Eliza for her slightest misstep. But even she was looking forward to visiting places she remembered from wartime leaves — the Troc in Piccadilly, the Old Ship at Brighton, the river in Cambridge, the Rose in Canterbury, and so many others.

He had time to take stock of what he had accomplished. From its beginnings the Magazine Section had showcased his inventiveness and judgment as an editor. At its first anniversary it had celebrated its own survival — but that had never been in doubt. Rufus's concept of the magazine, like the motorcar, was an idea whose time had come. He reasoned that readers not only wanted information but entertainment too, and because most Vancouverites of the day had British roots, even periodic immersion in their British past. And he had delivered: his columns were filled by the best of a new generation of journalists, writers, and academics, to many of whom he gave a start. Amongst them were Bruce Hutchison, an increasingly respected young political journalist; Bruce Alistair 'Pinkie' McKelvie, a longtime *Province* colleague and the first writer of popular BC history[126]; Don Munday, mountaineer and explorer of BC's Waddington range; George Godwin, one-time Fraser Valley homesteader and author of *The Eternal Forest*; Frederick Soward, the young head of UBC's new Department of International Affairs; Dorothy Livesay, whose first poem he published when she was a teenager; Dorothy Bell, a 'women's issues' journalist controversial enough to have been fired by three Vancouver newspapers — and not forgetting Maple Street neighbour, Major James Skitt Matthews, self-appointed city archivist and contributor of quirky items on Vancouver history, or Annie Harvie Foster, widow of the editor of the *Nelson Daily News* and a friend from 1910[127] days, whose early work he had been happy to publish. The Magazine Section also serialized works of well-known popular authors like Mary Roberts Rhinehart, L.G. Baum, P.G. Wodehouse, and Arnold Bennett.

It was because such innovations had improved the *Province*'s bottom line that Fred Southam had rolled out the red carpet for him in November, and was now taking the gamble of establishing him in London — on the sound military principle of reinforcing success. And if Rufus reasoned this far he had probably begun to feel quite pleased with himself.

Chapter 15
In England Today
London, 1928–1930

"Siegfried then came home at sixteen to one."

Rufus's diary, 19 June 1929,
on a winning trip to Ascot

Rufus woke up in Edmonton on 5 May. His little family's busy life in Vancouver was definitely over, he may have reflected, but it would still be a long time until they could start piecing together their new one. He was not booked to sail until the end of May, which left him more than three weeks to fill; not only that, but for the first time in years, he was under no obligation to file a single word until he reached journey's end. Most people would have accepted those weeks as a time to do very little. Rufus, however, remained busy, preparing for the task ahead though managing to enjoy himself in the process, of course. For him, as for any journalist, just the break from having to file dispatches was the most Heaven-sent relaxation he could think of.

For the first ten days he soldiered his way across the country, visiting editors who would be receiving his dispatches. In Edmonton the editor of the *Journal* and his daughter gave him a grand tour and he invited the editor of the *Telegraph* to dine with him. In Calgary he met Charlie Smith, Southam's pick for Washington, and together with Hayden of the *Herald* and the ex-mayor they played golf — his first foursome. He and Hayden lost, but consoled themselves by going for a spin in an aircraft. In Regina, Leighton of the *Post* drove him around his old haunts and later, with his wife, joined him for dinner. Rufus knew too many Regina old-timers to be able to pass through unremarked and his diary included the intriguing line: "Frances Smith and Mrs Hay Nichols (late Ella Carol) of Qu'Appelle spoke to me!" A hint of some unreported youthful flirtation?

At the *Winnipeg Tribune* he met the editor 'Biff' McTavish, and M.E. Nichols, the official who had offered him his job. That led to lunch at the

Manitoba Club, more meetings and then dinner with the Nichols and the Cromies — R. J. Cromie of the *Vancouver Sun* and his wife. It was all very pleasant and inclusive and made him almost sorry to be leaving. But the next morning he continued eastwards and reached Ottawa eleven days after leaving home.

The capital must always be a magnet for Canadian journalists and Rufus found it compelling. He had business, of course, with Wilson Southam of the *Citizen*, and spent an evening at Harry Southam's house where he met his wife and children. Otherwise his time revolved around the Parliamentary Press Gallery. He soon had meetings arranged with Prime Minister Mackenzie King and the new Leader of the Opposition, R. B. Bennett — the latter inviting him to lunch at the Rideau Club and, on another day, seeking him out in the press gallery. He also met with two leading Vancouver Tories — King's nemesis H.H. Stevens, and General Clark — and with Dr Simon Fraser Tolmie, MP for Victoria and soon to be premier of BC.

After a night in a sleeper, Rufus reached Toronto on the 17th. Here he visited *Maclean's*, the *Mail and Empire*, the *Globe* and the *Hamilton Spectator*, at each of which he knew the editor or owner; also Dick Southam with his wife and children, in their box at the Woodbine Racetrack. He also visited Dent's, his publisher, discussed the distribution of his London dispatches at the CP telegraph office and found time for friends — Colonel and Mrs Foster and the Nash family — visiting the Nashes twice and buying presents for their children.

He arrived at his Montreal hotel on a Sunday morning to find an invitation to spend the day with the Molsons at Beaurepaire. Margaret and her husband drove him there and they had a "very happy time." After an afternoon drive — with Rufus and John Molson dodging the rain from the rumble seat — all went to the cathedral, where he much enjoyed the music but found the sermon "awful". The next day the red carpet was rolled out for him at Southam's head office; after "arranging financial details", he was entertained royally by the patriarch, Fred Southam, and then by his daughter and son-in-law Philip Fisher. On his third day there Rufus left for New York, but not before buying and sending off Bee's birthday present, together with money for flowers.

His two days in New York seem to have been all fun — and the fact that his companions were journalists was, for him, also fun. His main contact was W.F. Bullock, the *Daily Mail* man in New York whom he had last seen on Salt Spring Island. They had an evening with Bullock's inkstained friends and Rufus was mildly disconcerted that they included a newspaper*woman*. Then he went "rubbernecking": he went up the Woolworth Building, then still the world's tallest, rode in an open-top bus, took the subway and the el train and, of course, made a pilgrimage to the overshadowed Cathedral of Saint John the Divine. He lunched with a friend at the spectacular Bankers' Club on the 32nd floor of the Equitable Building and treated a Naval Conference colleague to dinner at "Doval's on 47th St E — in great comfort and at my great expense!"

On the way back north he started a day in Boston by meeting the foreign editor of the *Christian Science Monitor*, spent the rest of the day as a tourist and caught a night train to Quebec City. Writing from "a lovely room at the Château Frontenac overlooking the harbour," at Quebec, his vicarage conscience bothered him and he added: "$6 a day with bath, not too bad for such a luxurious hotel" — which was probably covered by the 'financial details'! He had three days to fill before sailing and, for the first time since leaving home, found himself impatiently cooling his heels. He filled the days with long walks and historical sightseeing — roaming the Plains of Abraham and visiting Kent House at Montmorency Falls — where the Duke of Kent, Queen Victoria's father, had once lived with his sweet Canadian mistress, Madame de Saint-Laurent.

He sailed on 30 May aboard *Empress of France*. The voyage was long and forgettable, being foggy and cold "with no-one aboard of very great interest." He even read a couple of books, something he only admitted to during wars or ocean voyages, and only then when he wanted to escape people. He was probably anxious about the task ahead — essentially, elbowing his way into the clubby worlds of British journalism and politics, quite a stretch for a scribe from the bush leagues though he was as well equipped for it as any Canadian newspaperman.

Peter and Mary, the brother and sister he had last seen as children of 16 and 13, met him off the boat train. Now adults in their twenties, he had much to discover about them, and they of him. They took a taxi to the Charing Cross Hotel — across the Strand from the Golden Cross where he had spent his last night in 1919 — and while they ate lunch, he heard the family news and was no doubt grilled about his own assignment. Eventually, when Mary had to get back to the hospital where she was training, Peter took Rufus to see his Boys' Club in the east end, so it was not until the following morning that Rufus showed his face at Printing House Square.

Southam was a reasonable employer and nobody was demanding news before he was ready to deliver. It was not that he had nothing to write about — far from it — but the contrast between London and Vancouver was so great, the speed and busyness of the metropolis so unexpected, that at first it took his breath away. Normally the most punctual of men, he found himself arriving late for appointments because of 'traffic jams' — still rare events in Vancouver. So it was a good thing that he took the time to create some fixtures in his new life. He visited his bank and the BC Agent General; he made the rounds at *The Times*, calling on Geoffrey Dawson and Lord Astor — and on Lints Smith, the office manager — formidable people all, though he had met them before. He visited a tailor, and later had himself signed in as a member of the House of Commons Press Gallery. He began creating a comfort zone: wrote his dispatches at BC House, got to know the people at CP cable, and started using the British Empire Club to meet and entertain. His first temporary home was the austere Thackeray Hotel but he soon moved to the Kenilworth in Great Russell Street. This offered bed, bath and breakfast, with hot and cold running water in his room, for ten shillings a day — luxury indeed, or, as he put it, "comfy and obliging."

He found he had friends in London and George Godwin, a prolific writer of fiction whose work he had published in the *Province* Magazine, became an early crony. Before the war Godwin had homesteaded at Whonnock in the Fraser Valley, had written a book about it[128] and would soon publish another about his war experiences in the Canadian Corps.[129] His anti-establishment tone and mockery of the brass were so far from Rufus's conservatism that their friendship may reflect a side of Rufus not obvious from his writing. As the years passed, the unconventional Godwin would challenge him to question his assumptions as they witnessed the Versailles settlement — achieved with such suffering — gradually start to unravel. Certainly Rufus would develop an increasing need to explain the world around him, something that gave his reporting a growing urgency. Furthermore, Godwin's emphasis on the psychological and physical horror of the war may have begun to make sense to Rufus, who had previously swept all such considerations under the rug.

At BC House he ran across several other old acquaintances: W.H. Hayward, friend from Duncan days; Sir Campbell Stuart, author of *Secrets of Crewe House*, whom he had met more recently in Vancouver; and General McRae, now a Tory MP and follower of R.B. Bennett, whom he'd known since Provincial Party days.

He spent his first weekend with his father and Florie at Marden. He wrote in his diary: "Lovely quiet evening with Dad — and F." It had taken him twenty-five years, but he had finally accepted Florie as essential to his father's happiness even if she would never be much more than 'F' to him. The weekend provided needed decompression: a long walk with Mary (who had come specially to see him) through countryside "gorgeously beautiful and so peaceful"; long, interesting talks with his father, whose mind was as sharp as ever; a Saturday with him, watching Kent play cricket; and the unchanging routines of Sunday — early service, reading lessons and singing in the choir.

It was not until Monday 18 June — appropriately, Waterloo Day — that he moved into room 233 in *The Times* building. This not only gave him an office, but also access to *The Times* wire service, a valuable asset. This arrangement, set up by Southam on his behalf, was made possible by his nine years as an energetic *Times* representative in Vancouver and by the excellent copy he had provided. It had been easier to make because Geoffrey Dawson knew and liked him, and because he had had a good relationship with Northcliffe, and now with Astor, the current owner. Although new, he was certainly not unknown.

He had filed his first story a few days earlier. He had arranged to meet Turner, of the Empire Press Union, at the corner of Downing Street and they walked down Whitehall together to the House of Commons. The occasion was

Bee in costume for Little Theatre role, c. 1922

Rufus (kneeling far right) with President Harding and company on board *USS Henderson*, 25 July 1923

President Harding in Vancouver, 26 July 1923; left to right: General Odlum, President Harding, Major T.V. Scudamore (courtesy City of Vancouver Archives)

Rufus with Bishop Adams of the Cariboo, 1927

Walter Miller, Rufus at the Williams Lake rodeo, 1925

W.G.(Billy) Murrin, from 1929
President of B.C. Electric
(courtesy City of Vancouver Archives)

Col Cy Peck, VC, DSO
CO 16th Battalion, later MLA and MP

Roy Waldo Brown (R.B.), 1930 (behind), Editor of the *Province*,
with the Vancouver retail magnates Chris Spencer, left, and W.C Woodward
(courtesy City of Vancouver Archives)

Rufus, T.V. Scudamore, 1926 — at Jericho air station, about to fly to Victoria

Running Finlay Rapids, 1927 (from *Beyond the Rockies*)

Rufus (top row, 4th from the right), as member of Canadian Club executive, with T.R.H. the Prince of Wales and Prince George, 1927

The house that Rufus and Bee built in 1928 but never inhabited, at Marguerite and 52nd, Vancouver. Picture taken in 1930

Bee and Rufus, off to the races at Ascot, England, 1929

Rufus with his boss Fred Southam at Ripon, England, 1928

A bookie at the Derby, 1931

the debate on the revised Church of England prayer book, an arcane subject of intense interest to Rufus and his father, that may have had significance for some older Canadians but was unlikely to quicken the pulse of Southam newspapers' average reader. In spite of this he filed the story, then turned immediately to others that he knew would appeal to readers. In the last days of June he covered the spectacle of top-hatted riders in Rotten Row, fashions at Ascot, electing Mister Speaker, and 'Tea in the Air' at Hendon — an expensive cuppa while joyriding over the capital. And for a change of scene on a nice day, he took a train to Oxford, rented a bicycle and rode it to Abingdon. It all made good copy in Canada.

His diary dried up until the end of July when he and his father went to Poperinghe, Belgium, and stayed at Skindles, where Rufus had eaten several times when the brigade was out of the line during Passchendaele. Next day, after they had visited Lyonel's grave together, R.E. went home and Rufus remained in the area for another week. He had to be in Ypres the following weekend for the British Legion pilgrimage ceremony but until then would have been on his own. It was an opportunity to attend to his personal memorial agenda; so many men he knew had been killed nearby — Talbot Papineau, for example, among a hundred others.

Once back at the Kenilworth, he had just two weeks to wait until Bee and Derek arrived from Vancouver aboard the merchantman *Pacific Reliance*. The family was delighted to be together again; but far from approving of their temporary digs, the newcomers denounced the 'comfy and obliging' Kenilworth as uncomfortable — even morgue-like, in fact.

The search for a replacement home was abruptly interrupted: on their third day in London, Derek and Bee left it again for Paris, but this time with Rufus. The occasion was the signing of the Kellogg-Briand Pact, whose signatories would renounce war "as an instrument of national policy" towards each other. As they included Germany, there was the desperate hope that the Great War really might have put an end to war, and thus much excitement. Rufus witnessed the signing at 3 pm on 27 August in the Salon d'Horloge at the Quai D'Orsay and his dispatch about it would be his first on international events. They spent two days in Paris at the Hôtel Buckingham, 43 Rue des Mathurins, and while Rufus attended to treaty matters, Bee and Derek went shopping and sightseeing. They all met for dinner at L'Auberge du Père Louis in Montmartre.[130]

Then they left for Geneva, where they stayed a fortnight at the Hôtel Pension Regina on the Quai du Mont Blanc overlooking the Jet d'Eau. To Vancouverites homesick for water and mountains, the view across the lake to Le Salève, Geneva's mountain, was comforting, and their verdict glowing. "All of us in love with Geneva," Rufus wrote. So, while he attended the annual opening of the League of Nations Assembly, some of its subsequent sessions, and those of the League Council, Bee and Derek were happy to be left to their own devices.

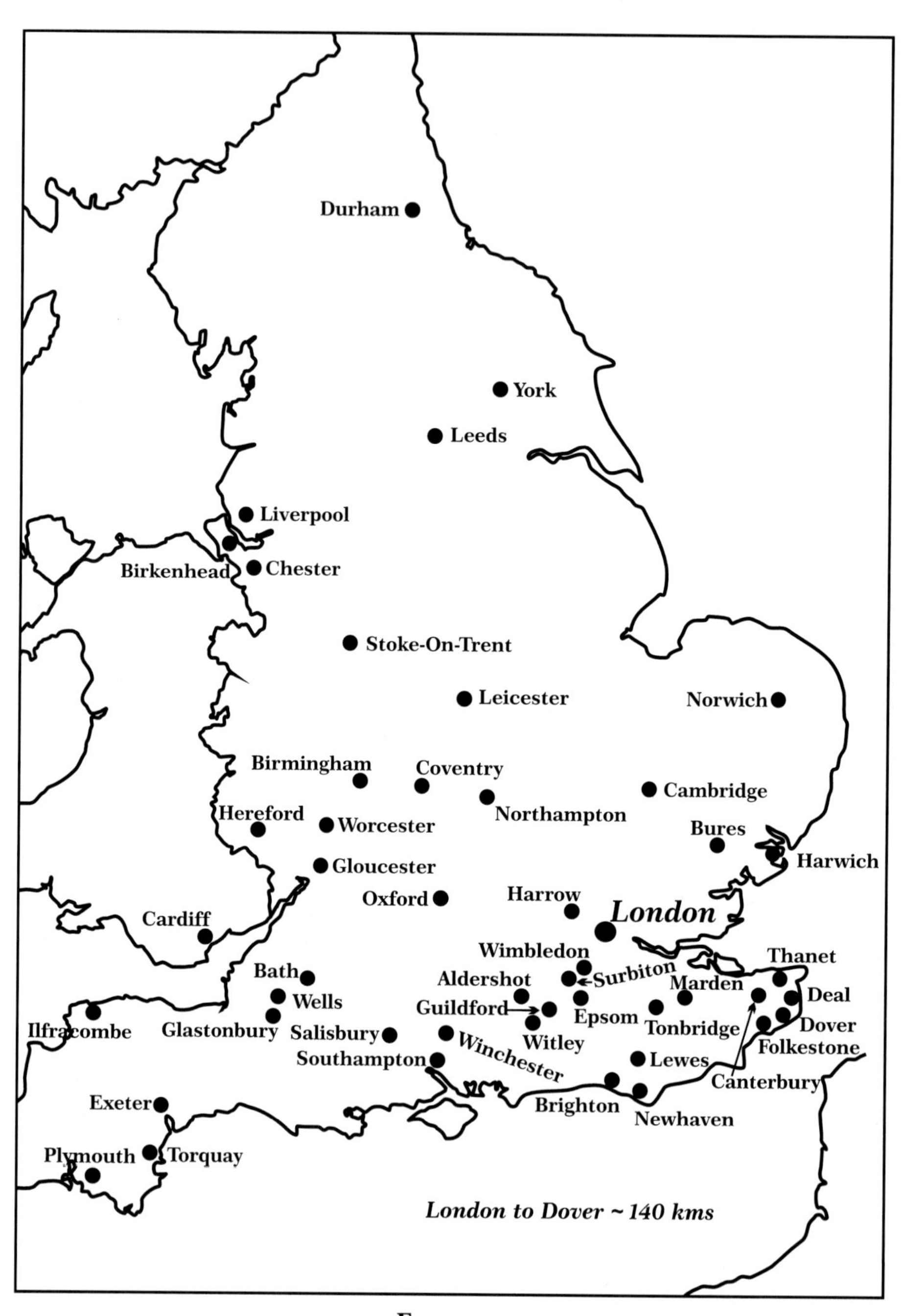
Durham
York
Leeds
Liverpool
Birkenhead
Chester
Stoke-On-Trent
Leicester
Norwich
Birmingham
Coventry
Cambridge
Northampton
Hereford
Worcester
Bures
Harwich
Gloucester
Oxford
Harrow
London
Cardiff
Wimbledon
Surbiton
Thanet
Bath
Aldershot
Marden
Wells
Deal
Guildford
Epsom
Dover
Tonbridge
Ilfracombe
Glastonbury
Salisbury
Witley
Folkestone
Southampton
Winchester
Lewes
Canterbury
Exeter
Brighton
Newhaven
Plymouth
Torquay
London to Dover ~ 140 kms

ENGLAND

He quickly found attending League sessions an ordeal — there was none of a parliament's cut and thrust and he had little tolerance for tedium, even of the best-intentioned sort. One could hope that a delegate would say something sensational, as Dr Worm-Müller of Norway apparently did one day, but from early days the League, crippled by caution and indecision, had been depressing to witness. The social events and receptions were another matter — there was always a chance somebody interesting or famous would be there, though the Canadian reception for Mackenzie King, to which both Bee and Derek came, was unfortunately an exception.

For two weeks Rufus stuck to his task, doing what he had to do and filing stories in occasionally sweltering heat. At weekends, however, they explored their surroundings energetically. One Saturday they took a lunchtime boat the length of the lake to see the Château de Chillon at Montreux but were too late to see much of the castle — something that Bee and Derek remedied during the week. The next Saturday they all took a train to Lausanne, explored the town and the cathedral, visited a school they may have been considering for Derek, and returned by boat. On Sunday they took a train into the mountains, hiked for a while, bought themselves the makings of a picnic, and were back in time for dinner.

On 10 September Aristide Briand spoke in the assembly, a marvellous speech that lifted Rufus's gloom. Bee and Derek watched the assembly in the afternoon, and that night Rufus and Bee went to a dinner given by Mackenzie King at the Hôtel des Bergnes. "All the toffs of all the nations were there," he wrote. "Bee was 'taken in' [to dinner] by Buler and I took in Mrs Clark and next to me sat Sir Edward Chamier (of India)," while a German diplomat sat next to Bee.

10 September was also Rufus's last diary entry for 1928, and probably their last day in Geneva. Tonbridge School, where Derek was about to start boarding, would be starting soon and both parents wanted to take him to the school for the first time, as they had done at Shawnigan. They then had to decide where to live. From another hotel, chosen by Bee, they started house-hunting near London and, before winter, were established at Barton's Mead, 3 St Martin's Avenue, Epsom. It was a three-storey brick house with four bedrooms on the second floor, two on the third, and a large back garden. Heat in winter came from coal fireplaces in the rooms and the architect anticipated that the owner would employ a cook and a maid — without modern appliances it would have been hard to run without them. By January 1929 it was also home to a Jack Russell called Totem and the energetic little beast would finally allow them to beat their dog-owning jinx.

Rufus may not have kept up his diary for the last quarter of 1928 because he was too busy: he seems rapidly to have expanded his journalistic work and the filing of news stories to the point that he needed not only a secretary but

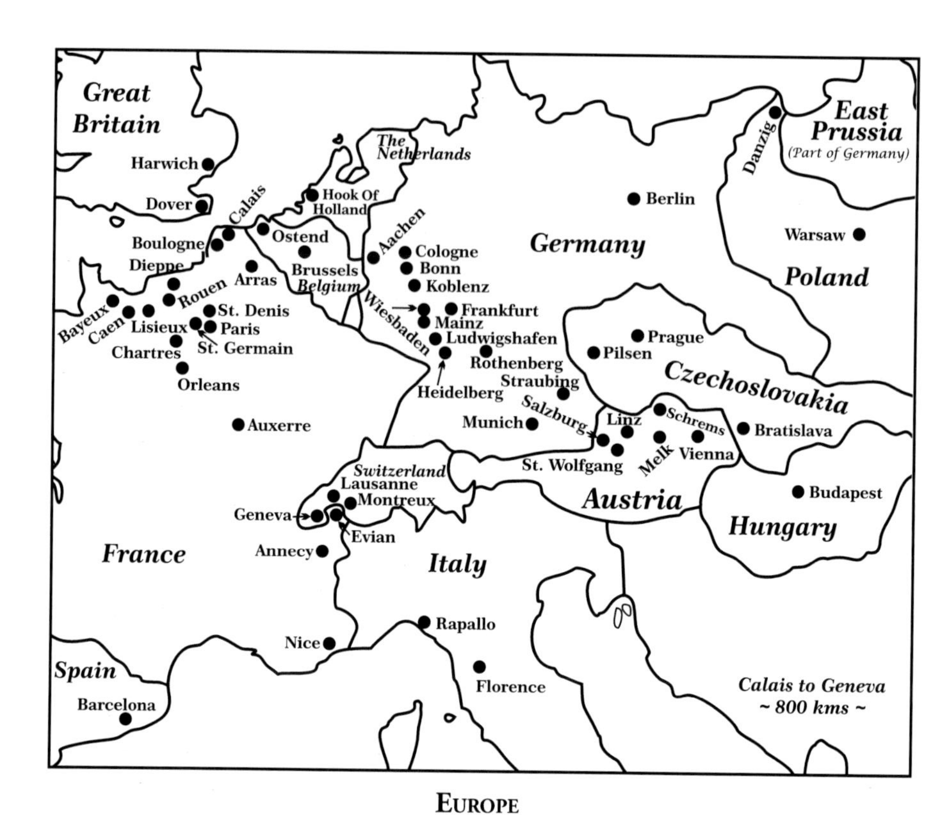

Europe

also another journalist to act as assistant and office manager. These problems were looked after in early January. On New Year's Day 1929 he moved into more spacious accommodation at *The Times* — his was now Room 239. That same day, A.C. Cummings reported for work as his assistant, a man with whom he would never be close but who ran an efficient office. A week later, Miss Grace Knowles started as his secretary. She was the classic executive secretary who very soon, and in a completely non-threatening way for Bee, became his 'office wife'. Although no doubt suffering silently from 'Prossie's complaint', Miss Knowles was as useful to Bee as she was to Rufus and generally helped with simplifying his life.[131] To underline the amount of news being generated, Southam newspapers and *The Times* between them instituted a new cable service, specifically for his use. Evidently, the experimental London bureau was proving its value.

A final improvement took a little longer to happen: although he now lived just a short walk from a main line railway station, Rufus could no longer imagine living without a car and, with the arrival of spring, came an inevitable diary entry:

> May 10
> "Car driving lesson. Completed purchase of 1928 Standard car from J. Armitage. (£330)."

Although the year 1929 sounds ominous to the reader, it passed without Rufus mentioning an economic crisis in his diary. From his point of view the earth-shaking event of the year was the hung parliament produced by the British election of 30 May. This resulted in the replacement of Baldwin's Tories by Ramsay Macdonald's Labour — an event he must have viewed with at least suspicion. But although he had covered Baldwin campaigning in both Durham and Cardiff, and had even canvassed with Nancy Astor in her own riding, the election itself rated not a mention and his subsequent interviews with Labour ministers Philip Snowden and J.H. Thomas were entered without comment. He also made no mention of the Crash, in spite of the fact that he was in the House of Commons Press Gallery on 28 and 29 October to cover other matters. The fact that his father stayed with them for a week from 28 October is perhaps more significant — he may have owned shares and have wanted advice on what he should do. Rufus and Bee, however, having wisely sold their own shares before leaving Canada — making a capital gain of $238.50 — may not have been sufficiently in the know to have been able to help.

Instead of the anticipated worries, the year is more notable for the Johnston family's readiness to enjoy themselves; because their London posting was only for two years, *carpe diem* became their ruling principle. Thus, the day after Derek's return from Tonbridge for the Easter holidays, they left for ten days in Normandy, staying in Caen, Lisieux, and Rouen, and returning from Dieppe. As their only pre-car holiday it was probably what Rufus needed: inside the towns they walked everywhere, with Derek he cycled the 27 kms from Caen to Bayeux to see the famous tapestry, and he took several 'long walks' in Rouen on his own. He indulged his love of mediaeval cathedrals, visiting five and as many churches; he and Derek went to the Good Friday service in the Abbaye-aux-Hommes in Caen, Easter High Mass at Lisieux, and a wedding in Rouen, activities that Bee begged off with a possibly diplomatic 'bad throat', although she was well enough to have a flutter at the casino in Dieppe.

In May Rufus bought his car and thereafter he and Bee were often on the road. Their first drive was to Hove for a weekend with "the girls", friends from wartime. Then they were off to Birmingham for Rufus to cover election meetings and a couple of days cathedral-crawling through Worcester, Hereford and Gloucester on the way home.

On 13 June Bee received a wire that her father had died and, some days later — on the morning of the event itself — was told about the funeral. Taking that in stride, they drove to Canterbury for the service, returning almost immediately afterwards. Rufus did not report her having been upset, either on hearing the news or at the funeral. In fact, she appears to have been unmoved by the whole thing; she had not considered dashing off to Canterbury when they heard of his death and may not have been to see him since coming back to England. For her, it was just a matter of turning the page and the feeling seems to have been mutual: William Court's estate totaled £85 and he left it to a friend.

The rest of summer seemed a hedonistic blur. They spent two days watching the tennis at Wimbledon — just ten miles from home. They went to Ascot, Bee in her beige costume and Rufus in topper and tails among the flapper generation's *fashionistas*. It was a hot day, he perspired profusely, lost on every race until the fourth, but after "Siegfried came home at sixteen to one" they could dine in style on their winnings at the Compleat Angler in Marlow. Days later they were at Aldershot for the military Tattoo dress rehearsal at night, creeping home at 1 am. In July they went to Hever Castle in Kent for *Times* Day; they went to Lady Astor's Rhodes Scholars garden party at Cliveden; they were at Lord's cricket ground for the Tonbridge and Clifton match, social highlight of the Tonbridge year; and a few days earlier had been at the Royal Garden Party at Buckingham Palace. The summer of 1929 seems to have been one long party — so much so that Rufus remarked on 21 July: "first Sunday alone, and slacking, for weeks."

It had also convinced Bee that motor touring was not really her style. So when he invited her to accompany him to the World Scout Jamboree at Hoylake, near Birkenhead, involving a day's drive through congested industrial towns to get there and another one to get back, the alternative — staying home alone, with her cat[132] and her dog and a garden to care for — suddenly seemed more enticing. Rufus set off regardless, spent parts of three days in the jamboree camp, much of it with Canadian scouts, got soaked twice by west coast rain, schmoozed with journalists and with the Prince of Wales — to whom he must, by then, have been a familiar face — visited Chester cathedral, walked for miles along Hoylake sands and, four days later, greasy from the cheap sausage rolls that sustained him when his money ran out, came home broke but happy.

Derek had been at school while these excitements were happening. When he came home, the family left for their summer holiday. This was a motor tour of the west country, visiting popular spots, optimistically hoping to find hotels wherever they stopped. After surviving car trouble near Winchester and having visited both that city's cathedral and the one in Salisbury, they spent their first night, comfortably, at the Old George in Salisbury. The next day, Sunday, they greatly enjoyed the cathedral service and lunched at the George. After a visit to Stonehenge they drove on to Exeter, where they visited the castle and bishop's palace but had difficulty finding a hotel. It was getting late when they settled for the Bude Inn, about which Rufus commented: "very poor." Slightly better things awaited however: after spending the following day coast-crawling from Torquay to Torcross and being rebuffed at every hotel, they found one at last in Kingsbridge — inland, but where at least there was a putting green. They decided to stay two nights and to visit Torcross Beach next day, hoping it would be warm. Instead, the water was cold, the breeze brisk, and they didn't linger. After lunch at a beachside restaurant, they returned to Kingsbridge to warm up on the putting green.

After that they gave up on the English Channel and motored in a northwesterly direction to Westward Ho on the Bristol Channel. Maybe, they hoped, the water would be warmer and they coast-crawled to an eventual welcome at the Imperial Hotel in Ilfracombe, which was "good but crowded." It was the middle of August, the beach looked tempting but once again it was windy and cold. This time, instead of swimming, they amused themselves at the Skidway and the shooting gallery on the pier. In the morning, they gave up on beaches, played a few holes on the "gorgeously beautiful Ilfracombe links," and headed east. After visiting Glastonbury Abbey and Wells Cathedral, they spent the night comfortably at the Pump Room Hotel in Bath. Maybe Brighton Beach had seemed so enjoyable in 1917 because the alternative for Rufus had been living in a hole while being shot at!

Two weeks after their holiday, Rufus was off to the League Assembly again, this time alone; he arrived in Geneva on Sunday 1 September having sat up all night on a train from Paris. Once again he took a room at the Hôtel Regina, swam with Mack Eastman,[133] saw his friend Burrows[134] at the press office, and interviewed Senator Dandurand, Prime Minister King's 'Man in Geneva'. All told, a profitable day on no sleep, made possible by his networking ability.

This time he remained in Geneva just four days, bombarding Cummings with daily dispatches phoned from Burrows' house. He interviewed Briand, heard him speak, also Dandurand and Ramsay Macdonald, and haunted the assembly and its committees. Once again it was extremely hot and he bathed in Lac Léman when he could, twice with Hugh Spender, a British friend working for the *Christian Science Monitor*. The League impressed him no more than before and on Friday he left by train for Wiesbaden in Germany's Rhineland, where there were still British occupation troops.

Rufus realized that the Rhineland was more likely than Geneva to hold the key to European peace and needed to see things for himself. Once there, he called for advice at the *Cologne Post and Wiesbaden Times*, the unofficial British army newspaper, where he met G.W. LeCrevar, a reporter whose assistance would prove invaluable. With his entrée he was able to visit British barracks, meet troops in the NAAFI, meet a senior staff officer and be shown around by Sergeant Castley of the Secret Service. Castley took him across the Rhine into French-occupied Mainz and to a Republican (Weimar loyalist) torchlight meeting in a valley north of Wiesbaden. There he heard Philip Scheidemann speak, a Social Democrat in the Reichstag who had made public the army's opposition to the republic.[135] Rufus felt uncomfortable at the meeting and his diary comment about it was "a weird time." Next day LeCrevar and he travelled by steamer downriver to Coblenz, then by train to Bonn. It was a fine Sunday and after visiting Beethoven's birthplace, they dined beside the Rhine. As they ate, they witnessed boatloads of excursionists coming home on the river, exuberantly singing, in a troubling roar of male voices, "*Deutschland über Alles*." He parted from LeCrevar in the morning, travelled on to Cologne, visited its cathedral, then went home by ferry from Ostend. He had been right about the Rhineland: these two incidents, straws in the wind perhaps, had given him a glimpse, a hint, of the strength of the political undertow that might one day sweep away the whole Weimar constitution in an irresistible nationalist riptide.

For the first time that year he came back to Epsom "tired out and very unwell inside." The Rhineland experience had been unsettling and he decided to take a break. He spent two days alone at home, writing and playing golf, then joined Bee and Derek in Brighton where they were staying with 'the girls' for a three-day weekend. Though it was mid-September, the Channel was warm — Bee even bathing before breakfast — and when he returned to work on Monday, he felt restored. At the beginning of October, maybe inspired by his pal George Godwin who had just published *Why Stay We Here?*, he treated himself to a five-day walkabout. He hoped to counteract the side effects of a scribbler's life by tramping for miles through the chalk and flint landscapes of the South Downs. Along the way he would spin his encounters with locals into articles for Canadian readers, to be later collected into his own second book, *In England Today*.[136] The characters he met that week live again in his book's Chapter IX, the Very Fat Boy among them.

He based himself at several villages — South Harting, Storrington, and Midhurst — from which he made day-long tramps. And, as he had the car, he broke his tramping mid-week and drove into Brighton to hear Phillip Snowden, Chancellor of the Exchequer, speak at the Labour Party Conference. In the process he bumped into Selden of the *New York Times* whom he knew. They left Brighton together for the Spreadeagle Hotel at Midhurst, though the American did not join Rufus for his tramp the following day.

1929 wound down quietly for Rufus and Bee, events on Wall Street seeming to have slipped by below their radar. Rufus spent several days in and around Parliament and in the process had a minor car accident near Grosvenor Place when he smashed the rear window of his Standard by backing into the shaft of a cart. He was showing signs of driving 'competitively', twice sounding pleased with journey times in his diary: from Epsom to Southampton in two hours, and to Tonbridge in one! He was starting to be in demand as a speaker as he had been in BC, and three times that fall lectured about the Peace River district. He and W.H. Hayward went to the Canadian Corps ten-year memorial dinner, attended by 600 veterans and 16 surviving Canadian VCs who had travelled from Canada to be there — amongst them Cy Peck, whom he met off his ship in Southampton.

He and Bee were beginning to be accepted in Epsom: he joined a choral group performing a Christmas oratorio — we never hear what it was — and emceed a sale of work in the parish hall. And although so recently the heart and soul of the experimental Vancouver Little Theatre, he revealed his inner Victorian when Mary took him to Lenormand's 1922 play, *The Eater of Dreams*, in trendy Notting Hill. The plot, which involves an amoral love triangle, and includes hints of incest, a suicide, and a large dose of Freud, was far too 'modern' for Rufus. In his diary, while applauding the "fine acting", he dismissed it as "an 'interesting' and unwholesome play."

He sang his oratorio on Christmas Eve. We don't know whether they had Christmas at home or with his father, but the day after Boxing Day the family was on the 7:47 from Epsom to London and caught the boat train to Paris from Victoria at 9:00. From Paris they would take another train to Barcelona and eventually an overnight ferry to Palma de Mallorca. It had all been too much of a rush and on the train to Dover Rufus made a dreadful discovery — he had left his wallet, with all their money, on his dressing table! There was a moment's panic — did he have their passports? Yes. And the tickets? Yes. How much money had Bee and Derek brought? Just £5 between them, not enough to pay for incidentals and their meals on trains and ferries. It looked as if they would have stay in Dover while Rufus went home to fetch his wallet. But then a complete stranger in their compartment, for whom Rufus had spoken up when the conductor had tried to move him to a third-class carriage, offered to lend them £5. With the other £5 it would be enough — it was gratefully accepted. 'Wasted' years in the military came to the rescue and the Staff Captain 'Q' produced his Plan B. From Dover he wired Miss Knowles, the most efficient person he knew, to go to Epsom, pick up the wallet from their maid, and airmail it to him at their hotel in Palma; he then telephoned Mary, his most efficient relative, giving her the details so that, if required, she could help Miss Knowles. The plan worked smoothly, of course: Miss Knowles found the wallet, airmailed[137] it as instructed and it was waiting for them when they arrived in Mallorca — 48 hours after leaving home.[138]

Warm midwinter days by the Mediterranean would be their reward for a year among the chilly cobwebs of old England and they made the most of every day. None of them had seen lemons and oranges growing on trees before, nor olive groves; and the fierce heat of the sun on their backs — when it shone — reminded them of passages through the Panama. It was January and nobody was swimming, but it was fine tennis weather and ideal for walking, especially in the morning. On two occasions they drove through the mountains — to the Manacor stalactite caves, and to the monastery where Chopin and George Sand had lived — on perilous roads and in vehicles with primitive brakes, risks considered acceptable by Rufus but which made Bee grateful for their "very intelligent and careful driver as our way back was a series of hairpin curves." Their hotel catered to the English and their ways, so that Bee, though happy with nightly bridge, rejoiced on the one occasion they escaped having to dress for dinner. And when a *thé dansant* was sprung upon them, led by Rufus they fled through muddy streets — it had rained — to spend their evening listening to the cathedral organ. They liked the cathedral and attended two services there, though once left early as they "couldn't stand the impassioned oration of the Spanish priest."

All three, for different reasons, had had a memorable holiday — Rufus for churches and walks, Bee for her letter writing and souvenir shopping, and Derek for the girls and the sunshine. They left the island on a rough sea at dusk and arrived next morning in Barcelona, dead tired and with a day to kill. Nothing daunted, they not only took in the Barcelona World Fair, then in its final week, but would have stayed longer had railway schedules allowed. Instead, they spent another sleepless night on a crowded train to Paris, having to admit an unknown youth to their compartment, a lad nevertheless pronounced "quite decent" by a surprised Bee.

It was Friday morning when they arrived in Paris so they could spend two days there before Rufus must leave and, although Bee was at first exhausted and lying low, they dived into whatever Paris had to offer — ate at the Auberge Père Louis and the Auberge Chanteclair, visited the Louvre, watched a German movie subtitled in French and, before catching their train on Sunday morning, spent an hour at the service in the Madeleine where the singing rivalled that of Canterbury. Having crossed the channel in the "storm of the century" without any of them becoming sick, they returned to Epsom to make their peace with two overjoyed animals, Totem the dog and Kiki the cat.

It was clear that his dispatches were appreciated at the highest level in Canada: he had received a Christmas letter from R.B. Bennett, Leader of the Opposition, who said, "I think you are doing good work. I read your dispatches with interest. The service is excellent and productive of much good, of that I am sure." After predicting Mackenzie King's imminent defeat, he ended with, "Drop me a line sometime when you are free to do so. I will be glad always to answer any inquiry you may have to make."

Nevertheless, Rufus seems not to have anticipated pressure from his employers to stay longer. This must have been beginning when his diary of 23 May noted: "Met Nichols and Col.Woods with Kerr at Euston" — all Southam names. Two days later he and Bee dined at Grosvenor House with a Mr and Mrs Nichols, probably the M.E. Nichols who had offered him his current job. After the waiter had swept away the crumbs, Nichols was probably working on them both to agree to at least another two years in London, offering an expenses-paid trip to BC that summer as an inducement. It would have been hard to refuse, even for Bee.

The crowd of Canadian scribblers gathering in London in late May were delegates to the fourth Imperial Press Conference, due to begin on 2 June. It was the second international conference of the year, Rufus having been swept up in the first one as soon as they got back from Mallorca in January. This had been the London Naval Conference, a much more important affair and, as one of the few 'survivors' of the 1921 Naval Conference press corps, he enjoyed some celebrity among those covering it. Out of a press corps numbering in the hundreds, only forty had been in Washington — and he and Bee were guests at a dinner in their honour at the Savoy.

The Naval Conference dominated the London scene for the first part of the year and because of it both Rufus and Bee received many invitations and were exposed to the pomp and circumstance that the Brits love to put on and which outsiders find so compelling. Rufus witnessed George V opening the conference, with trumpets and razzmatazz, in the Royal Gallery of the House of

Lords — a gilded, neo-gothic barn of a place dominated by gigantic paintings of a dying Nelson and a triumphant Wellington — a surprising choice for a conference with the French, one would think. He was also a guest at the City of London's Guildhall dinner to the delegates which he considered "a very wonderful affair," though maybe its most wonderful part was the thunderous cheer for Aristide Briand, the French delegate. Since his pact with Kellogg, Briand had been 'man of the hour' — or maybe just the straw to be clutched at in a time of ebbing hope. Bee was often included in invitations connected to the conference, the finest one being Lady Londonderry's reception for conference delegates at Londonderry House on Park Lane, which even Rufus thought magnificent. But he alone went to tea at Chequers, the British PM's equivalent of Camp David, whither Prime Minister Ramsay Macdonald and Miss Ishbel, his daughter and hostess, had invited about twenty journalists — an event he much enjoyed.

Meanwhile, Bee was at last managing to break the ice in Epsom. The foreword and first few chapters of *In England Today* hint at the isolation that she and Rufus experienced in their early days there — had they but known, Epsom was considered uniquely stuffy even by the English. But in February 1930, for the first time, she went to a meeting of the Epsom Little Theatre.[139] This led to monthly visits so she may have been on a committee of some sort — and the second time she went, she did so with two other women who came back to tea, one of whom Rufus later drove home. Whether or not this was a tipping point, it is notable that in the following weeks Bee held a tea party for nine women and thereafter invitations for her came thick and fast and they both went out to several bridge evenings. Among other things, Bee had taken to going to church on her own when Rufus was out for his long walks, which she would only have done if it felt comfortable.

At this time she made a friend of Katie Lukin, the 75-year-old cousin of Rufus's mother Nellie. Katie had never married, loved to keep in touch with the family, and was living on very little at St Leonard's-on-Sea. A caricature of impoverished gentility herself, she knew all about, and hugely enjoyed, the 'joke' of Bee's successful Eliza Doolittle role. The two would meet for lunch in London, sometimes Katie would come to stay, or Bee and Rufus would drive to her house. She liked to tell stories, and when she occasionally muddled family relationships, would exclaim, "Oh *dear*! It's all due to that *wretched* Reverend John and his four marriages!" Once Bee admired her hat — completely covered with different-coloured flowers. "Yes my *dear*," she replied, "I've had it for *years*! I never buy a new one — just buy a new flower when it needs brightening up!" and let out a peal of laughter.

Bee had taken to joining Rufus in his activities much more than she had in Vancouver, where she had usually been too busy. Her doing so is only partly explained by having little to do at home — like their neighbours, they employed domestic servants. She assumed, as he did, that time was short and so seized opportunities to go to spectacular events that she might never have another chance to see. Thus they were often away from Epsom, which interrupted the tricky process of winning local hearts and minds.

In late March she joined Rufus for a four-day road trip to the Grand National at Aintree, near Liverpool. They had two days of race-going on the Aintree course, examined the notorious Becher's Brook, and Rufus backed both the winner and the runner-up, winning £6. When the race was over, both entered 'the enclosure' — where an otherwise entirely male crowd of eager men in cloth caps were jostling each other around the horses. Predictably, Bee "had a rough time," according to Rufus, but she was not hurt and they went home in easy stages, staying the night in Warwick, going to church there in the morning and again, later in the day, at Christ Church Cathedral in Oxford.

April brought more excitements. They both went to the Parliamentary Press Gallery dinner at which Lloyd George was the principal guest, accompanied by his long-suffering wife Margaret and their youngest daughter Megan; and a few days after that, at a Beaconsfield movie studio that Rufus had been invited to visit, they met George Bernard Shaw[140] who was supervising the filming of one of his plays.

May brought another grand affair to which they both went — the Archbishop of Canterbury's funeral. Archbishop Davidson had resigned two years earlier when the Commons rejected his prayer book revisions after the debate that Rufus witnessed. The funeral and grand procession of bishops was a two-day event and, as usual when in Canterbury, they stayed at the Rose. In June, among other events, Rufus wangled tickets for them both to see the Trooping of the Colour on Horse Guards Parade. At the last minute, however, Ramsay Macdonald decided to speak to the Imperial Press Conference that morning, a speech that Rufus must not miss; so, through "the kindness of Commander Hynes" — a certain 'somebody he knew' — it was arranged for Bee to take an Epsom friend instead.

Meanwhile R.E., who had turned 71 in May 1929, retired as vicar of Marden, a living he had held for more than twenty years. The church offered him a house at Bures in Suffolk where he would be required occasionally to perform services in the adjacent and ancient thatched church of St Stephen's.[141] It was a long way from Kent and the people he knew well, but the offer was gratefully accepted. Rufus first visited him there in February 1930 and the old man was now able to come and visit them for a week or more — something not possible while he had been in harness.

The first two years in England had been intense for them both. Helped enormously by his association with *The Times* and his King's School background, Rufus had quickly been accepted by the London press community and moved easily in political circles. His willingness to plunge into Europe at any opportunity, always expecting to enjoy himself, and his engaging with Europeans and others in an unprejudiced way, made him a shrewd observer of international events. And although he moved easily among the public-school educated political class, and even talked like them, his adult experience, much of it brutally hard, had all been Canadian. This served him as a 'get out of jail' card, freeing him from whatever English conventions he chose to ignore and allowing him to write objectively about the country.

These were much harder years for Bee. In BC, where there was general acceptance of newcomers whatever their background, she had been a recognized amateur actress at the centre of an admiring circle of friends. And, in Muriel Phelan, she had had a friend with whom she could share everything. Any town in England would have been second-best to that, and making a go of things in Epsom had been a real test of her loyalty to Rufus and of her own adaptability. She had been, at first, an invisible woman, with neither callers nor the casual neighbourly interaction she was used to. And although, in self defence, they soon hired domestics, the worry and hard work of keeping or replacing them fell upon her. However, by the time they left for their Canadian vacation, her social life in Epsom had picked up considerably.

Bee's main difficulty was that she was an Eliza Doolittle. Middle-class English people set store by who your mother and father were and where you had gone to school, so Bee could never admit the truth about her own family to Epsom neighbours and expect them to accept her as an equal. So she had to finesse, all the while dreading the (eventually inevitable) encounter with someone from her former life who might reveal all. Her education, ironically, may actually have been an asset: to have been to a school run by French Catholic sisters, just as being a Canadian was for Rufus, was off the social-class scale and therefore not constantly judged!

We must wonder whether the pair of them, in some quiet moment of their upcoming trip, discussed their hopes and fears for the future. For while he was enjoying his work in England and was so appreciated by his employers that they had paid for this trip to persuade him to stay, Bee must have been silently hoping for a miracle to save them from having to come back: England would never let her feel at home while British Columbia most certainly did.

Chapter 16
In Germany Today
London, 1930 – August, 1932

"Busy-looking young men skipped about with a look of terrifying earnestness on their faces. As they passed each other they raised the right hand and said 'Heil Hitler . . .' the whole atmosphere of the place seemed to me like that just before the curtain goes up on an amateur theatrical show."

Rufus, the *Province*, February 1932, on the Nazi Brown House in Munich,

A vacation to British Columbia was a rare experience in 1930, beyond the reach of most English people. Unfortunately, travel and business stopovers ate up most of the two months Rufus was away, leaving him just 18 days in BC for a 'holiday'! Bee and Derek could be there much longer, only needing to return in time for Derek to enroll in language courses in late October.

Bee and Derek enjoyed travelling with Rufus on the outward trip as they could be tourists in their own country. In Montreal she at last got to see Margaret Molson again, visiting her at home and meeting her "two dear kiddies," while they all went to tea at the senior Molsons' place at Beaurepaire. She loved every minute, writing in her own diary, "There were 22 people to tea. Lovely hot day — I wore my white dress!" And when Rufus had finished his business with Paul Reading, a Southam director, Reading drove them all up Mount Royal and then out to St Hubert airfield[142] to see the visiting British dirigible, the R100.

In Ottawa, thanks to Willis O'Connor, Derek and Bee were invited to tea at Rideau Hall. Bee wrote rather breathlessly in her diary: "Lord and Lady Willingdon were very charming to all of us. A great experience for Derek." And while Rufus was with Vincent Massey, Canada's first ambassador to Washington, Derek and Bee toured the Parliament buildings which Bee thought "very fine and the Memorial Hall is lovely. Went up the Peace Tower, and saw the carillon bells."

In Toronto they stayed at the new Royal York. Rufus needed to see Fred Kerr at the *Spectator* so they took the train to Hamilton where Kerr met them "in his cool car and drove us to Niagara Falls," Bee enthused. "Then we went on the *Maid of the Mist*, a great thrill." The next day Rufus had a list of people to see in Toronto, mostly friends but including his boss, Fred Southam, and

General Currie. Then they took a bus back to Hamilton for the opening of the first-ever British Empire Games by Lord Willingdon.

They spent the next week either on trains or in Winnipeg, Calgary, or Edmonton and only arrived in Vancouver at 9 am on 23 August. Their rooms at the Georgia were full of flowers from friends and immediately the city felt like home. They spent much of the morning answering calls. Later, Rufus went to the *Province* and, later still, they went out for a Saturday night supper and a show with the A.H. Johnstones. On Sunday morning, while his mother slept and his father worked on speeches, Derek took the streetcar to the service at St Mark's in Kitsilano. To complete the illusion of never having been away, after lunch they took the ferry to North Vancouver and, as so often before, went to tea with "Roy and M", and then over to Muriel's for a drive and supper. It was just like old times.

However, the illusion of being in control of their lives was shattered on Monday. While talking to friends on the phone, they had accepted many invitations, but actually going to them all gave them ten days of dashing hither and yon, always the focus of attention and everywhere facing the same questions about their life in England. Bee and Derek handled it better than Rufus did — Derek by disappearing to do things with friends, and Bee by briefly going to earth, first with Muriel and then with another friend. For Rufus, unfortunately, instead of being part of an enjoyable holiday, these became days of stress and tension. His diary entries were jotted names and times, in different pencils, at odd angles and with much crossing out. He met with many large groups — starting that Monday by lunching with Billy Murrin at the Vancouver Club to meet the downtown business crowd. On other days he and Bee were guests at a BCIJ dinner in their honour at the Vancouver Hotel; one lunchtime Rufus spoke to 250 at the Canadian Club and to as many at the Women's Canadian Club the following day; and finally he spoke to a thousand people at evensong in Christ Church cathedral on the Sunday before Labour Day, an address that was also broadcast.[143]

It was more sermon than address. Asked to speak to the theme of the day — "The Cause and Ideals of Labour" — he finished his remarks by calling on the Church to lead a crusade to "stem the forces of selfish materialism which underlie the troubles of the present day." He arrived at this climax after offering his listeners word pictures of the history of the machine age, of the situation of unemployed men in England which, though vastly more severe than that of Canada's unemployed, was nevertheless better than the situation facing those in most European countries. He told the congregation, "In the Midlands and North of England, where unemployment and poverty are at their worst, I have talked with scores of unemployed, and have seen deep down into the souls of splendid men and women, humiliated and worn down by the ghastly tragedy of the utter impossibility of finding work."

The cause of labour, the right to a decent living, he declared, "is the paramount challenge of the World to Christianity." Times had changed, largely thanks to the efforts of English unionists; for mostly thanks to them was " the astonishing change in the Public Conscience which has come about in the last twenty-five years. No-one today denies the right of man or woman to a living wage — or to the right to exist."

So what was to be done? He put his listeners on the spot — The scourge of unemployment was the business of humanity itself, and if they claimed to be Christians, he left them with the feeling that it was *their* moral problem.

It was powerful stuff. He had been seen in Vancouver as a visiting pundit on things English and European. Those who invited him to the cathedral no doubt expected something like his speeches to Canadian Clubs, perhaps with a choirboy's twist. What they got was worthy of a bishop, and a window into the soul of the speaker. Who knew, from his diaries and letters, that he felt so strongly about the moral issue of unemployment? It must have been clear to friends that there were depths to the man — this pipe-smoking, genial fellow with red hair — that few had suspected. Not just a guy who wins tennis matches, then!

Had these been their only engagements, they might still have enjoyed a relaxing holiday together in Vancouver. But they had also accepted twenty-two invitations to lunch, tea, dinner or tennis. These were all with friends they really wanted to see, of course, but the cumulative effect was less than pleasant. Rufus did play tennis once and went for a walk but he never found time to bathe at Kits Beach — his favourite summer activity in Vancouver. By Thursday in their second week he was fit to be tied — his record of their final engagement, a pleasant tea party at the Chapmans to which Roy and the Calloways had been invited, was followed by one word: "*Free!!!!!*" When they stepped onto the Victoria boat that night it felt like an escape from prison. It was certainly not how he had wanted it to feel.

Four days together on Vancouver Island, by contrast, were a real holiday. They rented a car, picked up Derek in Nanaimo, and stayed at the Maple Inn[144] on the shores of Maple Bay, a "lovely restful spot." Next day, they sniffed around old haunts in Duncan, including St Mary's, Somenos, where they had been married, and even went to see old Father Christmas who had married them. Then, by way of Shawnigan Lake School, they drove back to Victoria and to dine at Government House with Lieutenant Governor Bruce, the "close-fisted old Scotsman," to whom, on better acquaintance, Rufus seems to have warmed.

They stayed at the Empress and in the morning, went to the Sunday service in the new cathedral. Rufus had been present at the laying of the foundation stone in 1926 and the half-finished building had been consecrated in their absence. So attending this service was a thrill, one he looked forward to relaying to his father. Afterwards they lunched with the Hodgins, in whose Duncan house Bee had slept the night before her wedding, and spent the rest of the day with different sets of friends. On Rufus's last day in Victoria he and Derek played tennis at the hotel, went for a long rambly drive up the Saanich peninsula, lunched with friends, played clock golf somewhere and swam at the Crystal Pool. After dinner it was time for Rufus to leave. "A lovely quiet, family day," he wrote in his diary. "I left on the boat at night — alas!" Ruefully he added: "Bee and Derek stayed on."

He arrived in Vancouver early on 9 September, facing a day of renewed goodbyes that would be hard to take. Murrin had again put on a lunch at the Vancouver Club for him and twenty-five others, an occasion probably protracted, jocular and wreathed in cigar smoke.

Afterwards he went round to the *Province* where there were things he could usefully do, but this visit, too, inevitably led to further goodbyes. He dined at the Georgia with Roy, they were later joined by Bob Harrington and the two of them saw Rufus off for Edmonton. Though sad to be leaving, and in spite of his stressful time in Vancouver, he must have been reasonably satisfied: he and Bee had certainly not been forgotten — quite the reverse, in fact; and the response to his speeches had been encouraging for an ambitious newspaperman, planning more books and looking forward to coming home for good in a couple of years.

His cross-country return was speedier, though it too was extended by stopovers. He met with fewer newsmen though these included a day and a half with Fred Southam. His boss wanted to impress on him the importance of his dispatches and urged him to agree to spend longer overseas. Such blandishments Rufus resisted, mostly for Bee's sake, and the conversation would have gone nowhere.

Otherwise his journey was an extended speaking tour at Canadian Clubs with his thoroughly road-tested speech. He spoke first in Edmonton — "very good comically rural[145] throng and it went over very well"; then in Winnipeg — "about 250–300 there and women, very good show"; and finally in Ottawa — "very good turnout — 200 or so — and speech seemed to make very big success." From his own account his name seemed a draw for CC members across the country — more evidence that his columns were appreciated. He had no speaking engagement in Toronto, but Button of Dent's did accept the manuscript of *In England Today* for publication.

In Montreal he also saw John Molson, briefly, but there was little else to keep him from going straight on board *Laurentic*. Once again he pronounced his fellow passengers "very unexciting" but the next day discovered among them Dr H.M. Tory, ex-president of the University of Alberta, and the current president of the new National Research Council. As Tory had also run the Khaki College for Canadian veterans stuck in England in 1918 and 1919, they had plenty to talk about, and he introduced himself. Nevertheless he soon went back to his book, this time Compton Mackenzie's *Sinister Street*, and when the second day out was cold and miserable, he continued to read, but in between naps. By the third day, however, the compulsive competitor within forced him out for a few games of ping-pong and on the fourth day he won the golf competition. His demon temporarily appeased, the prospect of a fancy dress dance on the fifth day was enough to drive him back to his book. About the dance, he told his diary: "very pretty — did not dress up and went to bed at 9 pm!"

He landed in England on 27 September just as Bee and Derek were leaving Vancouver. In spite of her longer stay, Bee hated leaving. "Feel utterly miserable," she wrote; "went to bed on train about 5 pm." She had made few diary entries but enough to give a hint of a carefree social whirl in Vancouver — for much of the time without Derek who had been somewhere up the coast — and a real contrast to the constraints of Epsom that awaited her. But she was always enthusiastic about new experiences and places: the very next day, misery forgotten, she was writing, "Arrived Jasper 8:35 am. We had a lovely walk — gorgeous scenery and very comfy rooms. In the afternoon we walked around the lake, then up to see the bears come down to feed. Quite thrilling. I wrote letters to Helen and Renee, Mrs Fyfe-Smith, Pennykins, Mrs Tait, Mary Murrin and Mrs Douglas, sent pc's [postcards] to "girls", Mrs Wilcock, Mrs Hooper and Miss Coulter. Went to bed early — frightfully tired." After all that, no wonder!

DEREK AND BEE ARRIVED HOME 12 October. At the time Rufus had his hands full. At the Imperial Conference, Canada was pushing to make Governors General responsible to the dominions and no longer to Westminster, while the R101 had just exploded in a fireball north of Paris. Both were emotionally charged issues for Brits and he could not possibly go to Geneva with Derek. Imperturbably, Bee took over. She and Derek left Epsom on the 22nd. Derek settled in at Geneva — *en pension* with the Mirimanoffs at 11*bis* Rue Toopfer — to begin language courses, and Bee, after a brief hover, took the scenic route home, developing a taste for solo travel as she went. Rufus met her at Newhaven on 2 November.

The Imperial Conference of 1930 failed because of the delegates' radically opposite points of view. Rufus was daily faced by Englishmen feeling betrayed: *When the dominions had fought so bravely at her side, why*, they insisted on knowing, *did they now want to cut every tie to Britain?* So he published a long piece in *Fortnightly Review*[146] to explain dominion nationalism to English readers: far from being anti-British, he claimed, dominion policy was motivated largely by other threats to their independent survival — in Canada's case, the gravitational pull of the United States which she could only resist by having absolute control of her own foreign policy. At the same time, he claimed, Canadian sentiment in favour of the crown and the British connection was as strong as ever. As he wrote, he was rationalizing his own contradictions: for not only was he a Tory to the core, emotionally attached to the crown, the empire, the church, and the public school network, someone who enjoyed hobnobbing with the great and the good — including a few with extreme right-wing views such as Odlum or Murrin — but he was also a Canadian nationalist with a love for the wilder edges of Canadian life, a respecter of the Common Man, a hater of injustice and violence, and a believer in the power of understanding and knowledge to solve problems. Moreover, he was itching to get back to Canada, with all its new world equality and lack of pomposity.

Remarkably for Epsom, their social life did rekindle after their various absences, albeit slowly. In November and December they gave a dinner party, then a bridge party, and were themselves invited to dinner and to tea. It was not much, but if these embers were carefully nourished, who knew whither they might lead. Rufus had his annual outing with Mary to the Gate Theatre, this time to a more acceptable play, *The River*, and just before Christmas Derek came home from Geneva. They had a quiet Christmas at home and on New Year's Eve, with Mary and Peter, joined R.E. for lunch at his London club. The genial and gregarious Derek provided light relief to this subdued year-end: his Tonbridge friend Julius Griffith joined them for three days over Christmas and he invited six friends, boys and girls, to a party before New Year — they "played Court Whist, etc." One hopes that his middle-aged father's diary entry concealed a party at which the young folk had fun.

Until the fall, 1931 may have seemed an anomaly amongst those years of momentous happenings. Life bumbled along for most of it, the newspapers preoccupied by unemployment and the decline of industries and trade. While many people were more concerned with the constant rain — the weekend of 25 July being the 25th wet weekend out of the 29 so far — the far-sighted understood that in some parts of Europe these very things were leading towards another war as inexorably as the military adventures of nationalist governments with which we associate the thirties. Meanwhile, Rufus and Bee had hit their stride socially and exchanged invitations during the year with many families in and around Epsom, of whom maybe the Ellermans, the Parsons, and the Renjers had become friends. They had been accepted and to the locals must just have seemed *those funny people from Canada, always dashing about and never at home.*

This certainly described Rufus in 1931 though he spent much less time abroad than formerly. Southam newspapers were running his popular column about the byways and characters of Olde England under the title 'In England Today', also the title he chose for his second book. So he continued exploring England, sometimes combining factory visits in the cities with walkabouts among the hills and villages between.

In early February he made a Cotswold trip by way of Thame. On entering the Spread Eagle Hotel there, he encountered a tall man dressed in black, with a black-and-white floppy tie and big Cromwellian buckles on his shoes, "who asked rather brusquely if there was anything I wanted." To his inquiry as to whether he might have a room, the man replied: "Yes — I suppose you can if you want to." This was the eccentric landlord, John Fothergill, with whom he passed happy hours and to whom he devoted pages of his book.[147] Though at first disconcerted that Fothergill should regard his request for Worcester sauce as an insult to the cooking, Rufus concluded that "for the food alone, this inn was worth going many miles to enjoy." And because he never willingly passed by a friend, he went to considerable trouble to find the village of Radnage to visit Ralph Marshall, an OKS and his employer in Saskatchewan in the winter of 1906–7. In the book he puts a rosy gloss on their meeting, though Marshall still owed him a winter's wages! On other days of this trip he managed long walks between villages, over frozen lanes and fields, and returned to Epsom well-pleased with his fund of bar parlour stories.

It was the first trip of many that year, including one nine-day tour accompanying Ramsay MacDonald electioneering — he was away from home and driving round the countryside on six other occasions before year's end. In March he took a solo trip to Aintree and the Grand National; in April he and the family took a short Welsh holiday, staying in Hereford and Monmouth and indulging two of their passions in those places — respectively, a cathedral service and horse racing. In the first week of June he went visiting factories in Birmingham and Cardiff. Friday and Monday were his city days, while from Thursday through the weekend he tramped every morning and after lunch explored by car.

He had one other solo trip for the column, a two-day jaunt to the Kent hopfields that became a bit of a pantomime. Having accidentally dropped his shirt into his morning bath, he had perforce to wear his pyjama top all day, earning himself some funny looks in the hopfields. As he later admitted, "unfortunately I wear pyjamas of particularly lurid colours — brilliant blue and pink — but flatter myself that most people I encountered rather admired my taste in ultra-modern shirts!" However, when someone hesitated before accepting a lift with him, he remarked, "I didn't blame him — with my battered hat I suppose I looked more like an escaped lunatic than usual."[148]

In December he and Bee took a week's holiday in Cornwall, where it was still warm enough to be enjoyable, though too cool to swim. They stayed in grand hotels at St Ives and St Austell, Rufus took long walks daily, and both enjoyed chatting with the other guests. Although most of these were there for the golf, Rufus limited himself to nine holes during the week. By week's end they were so much into the swing of things that they joined new friends at the golf club dance. Driving through Plymouth on their way home, they spotted an auction in progress. They stopped, joined the bidding and, much later, arrived at their Dorchester hotel with a trunkload of pictures. After a final day visiting Beaulieu and Buckler's Hard in Hampshire, they limped home nursing a car with a broken spring, but having had a real holiday nevertheless.

There were other solo trips. In June he left England for a few days in France and Belgium. His official goal was to inspect progress on the Canadian memorial at Vimy but he stayed first at Poperinghe in Belgium and, with a friend, went round the Ypres Salient and dined at Skindles once again. Next day he went to Vimy, then to Lionel's grave and Béthune, before driving down to the Somme battlefield and finishing the day in Arras. In the morning he drove to Calais and "home on 3 pm boat."

He was back in France in July for a one-day visit to the Colonial Exposition at Vincennes. No doubt to the amazement of Epsom neighbours, he flew. His itinerary read:

7:15	*depart*	*London,*
8:15	*depart*	*Croydon,*
10:15	*arrive*	*Le Bourget,*
11:00	*arrive*	*Place de l'Opéra,*
	to	*Colonial Exposition.*
3:45	*depart*	*Paris,*
4:30	*depart*	*Le Bourget,*
6:30	*arrive*	*London.*

He flew Imperial Airways in a Handley Page HP45 biplane. Its 38 passengers entered the enclosed cabin amidships and had to walk up or down to their seats. Rufus, an old hand, accepted this as business as usual and was more impressed by being met in London by Derek, who later drove him home.

His last 'shop' trip of the year was to follow electioneering politicians in the North-East, as previously mentioned. He started in Birmingham, dining with Peter before hearing Baldwin speak. The next day he reached York, and on the third, after morning service at the Minster, pressed on to Durham where Ramsay MacDonald arrived by train. In pouring rain he followed the PM to Seaham Harbour, where he heard both MacDonald and his Labour opponent speak, before attending a Labour meeting at a coal mine. It was wet, gritty business with feelings running high, and he and four fellow newshounds later discussed it over dinner at the Mason's Arms in Durham. Along the way he visited interesting pubs, met all manner of people — most with vigorous views — but none appeared in his books. Maybe the hurt and anger of the North-East was meat too strong for the lighthearted tone that readers of 'In England Today' had come to expect.

Bee, meanwhile, had returned to her independent ways and was included less often in his activities. When Wimbledon was on, she sat through three or four days of tennis on her own, probably with a local friend though that was mentioned only once. On another occasion she chose a day at the tennis in preference to accompanying her menfolk to the thrills of the Hendon Air Show. And when Rufus decided to go to Canterbury one Saturday to see Kent play cricket, even romantic memories of Cricket Week could not persuade her to go with him. They did go together to Ascot, the Derby, and Kempton Park, though nobody won any money, and to the Royal Garden party, to which they seem to have had an annual invitation. But Bee, with her slowly expanding social life, was busier than before — and often involved in the search for domestics. They had started hiring girls fresh off the boat from Europe, an expedient that was seldom successful for long.

There was another reason for her inactivity. Derek had returned from Geneva in March and, after their short holiday, had started work as an articled clerk with a London accountant. He continued living at home, commuted daily by train, and she wanted to be home for him as much as she could. All went well until 8 August, Rufus's 44th birthday, when Derek came down with pneumonia. In those days there were no antibiotics, nor any other remedy: the patient's fever continued to rise until either the fever 'broke' — or the patient died; a doctor could do little, except make the patient comfortable — and wait. So there followed a worrying week, Derek's temperature hovered around 103° for four or five days and his father's terse diary entries touched upon nothing else. Not until the eighth day, when his temperature was down to 96°, could everybody relax and Rufus write, "the crisis seems past." That was 15 August and, although Derek continued to improve, he was so weak that it was not until the 27th that he ventured outside the house.

Whatever plans the family may have had, their priority then became to get Derek strong enough to return to work. Rufus's diary for 3 September reads: "Dr Heckels[149] to see Derek and says he can travel tomorrow — gave me prescription for sleeplessness." Sunshine and warmth, the doctor had recommended, and father and son set off for the south of France and the Italian Riviera — without Bee. They stayed briefly at Nice, for nearly a week at Rapallo and ended their trip with a two-day cultural immersion in Florence. The weather did not disappoint and Rufus made no mention of bad nights until their very last day — unsurprisingly, on the train to Paris. They had their share of minor disasters: Derek left his walking stick on an Italian train and had to employ all his new language skills and a great deal of time in its retrieval; days later, at the station in Geneva, they discovered there was no train to Paris at the time shown in the timetable, requiring a hectic dash to Lausanne — in the dark and in a rented car with flickering lights. Not to be outdone, Rufus then left their camera in a Paris taxi and never saw it again. Nevertheless, the verdict on their holiday was "a wonderful trip, but we both wanted more time in Florence." They might have stayed longer but Ramsay MacDonald was about to call an election and Rufus wanted to be in England when that happened. Bee did not go with them because she was exhausted from looking after Derek and had decided, in her modern way, that it was Rufus's turn.

The prime minister did call his election, but after they were home, and for a while Rufus was busy. But the day after they got back, an event occurred in distant Manchuria that was to change his attitude to his job. This was the Mukden Incident, a bogus act of terrorism against Japan that that country used to justify the invasion and conquest of the Chinese province of Manchuria — and eventually of China itself. After his return from the North-East, Rufus's diary entries had stopped, restarting only when he and Bee left for Cornwall in December. During this interval China appealed to the League, the League told Japan to withdraw, and Japan — while slyly keeping the League talking —

continued its advance into Manchuria. By Christmas, those who believed, or even hoped, that the League could stop aggressors were being forced to admit they were wrong.

Rufus and Bee decided to spend Christmas 1931 at home, instead of at Ye Olde Hop Pole at Tewksbury as previously planned, mainly because Joyce was bringing Felicity to a London specialist and would need Rufus's help. However he was also anxious about the international situation — about Manchuria and about developments in Germany and central Europe. As he wanted to see things for himself, he left for Europe on 19 January 1932. His ultimate destination was Geneva, where the League Council was convening that day and was expected to make decisions about Japan's aggression within weeks. He saw no need to rush there, however, as League processes were glacial. Instead he headed to Berlin where Robert W. Keyserlingk, a young friend in charge of UPI's Berlin office, had agreed to help him meet Adolf Hitler, the wild card of German politics.

That July, Keyserlingk himself had been one of the first journalists to have interviewed Hitler. When Rufus reached Berlin, Keyserlingk and he met daily to plan his own access to the Nazi leader.[150] Because Göring had forbidden press access to Hitler, he would have to be circumvented and, to help achieve this, Keyserlingk had recruited the help of Björnsen, "a vulgar little Bauherr [contractor] friend of Hitler's." And as Rufus wanted to meet as many German movers and shakers as time allowed, Björnsen took him to interview Prince Victor von Isenburg, with Keyserlingk as interpreter.

Isenburg was a Hitler supporter. Under the Austrian Empire he had been director of the Skoda works in Pilsen — one of Europe's great arms producers — and he scoffed at the prospects for the approaching Disarmament Conference. The fix was in, he claimed: the French ambassador, Poncet, a member of the French arms manufacturers' group, was currently negotiating with the Nazis "for a Franco-German bloc as a bulwark against Russian influence, and for this purpose Germany must be armed again with the aid of French finance. All else was of secondary importance to Herr Hitler." All would be revealed, he predicted, "when Herr Hitler's party came into power within the next few months." He also claimed that arms firms were making huge profits selling obsolete weapons to all comers. "Incidentally," he added, "the 'little' war in Manchuria has brought millions in profits to many European countries — to Germany among them, for rubber goods, beds, bandages and what not."

It was a shocking glimpse of the cynical forces arrayed against the League and its hopes for general disarmament. In his article in the *Daily Province* on 28 January, Rufus called these views ". . . astounding and disturbing — expressed to me by a man whose position makes it impossible to regard them as irresponsible chatter."

He forbore to name Isenburg, perhaps hoping not to stir the pot, but he claimed to have checked, as far as possible, the detail supporting the Prince's more cynical claims and was pessimistic about the League's chances.

Interestingly, after interviewing Isenburg, Rufus went next to see von Neurath, Chancellor Brüning's ambassador to Britain,[151] and was met with denials, one imagines — Isenburg had said Brüning knew nothing about the arrangements.

Rufus was also shaken by what he saw in a Berlin movie theatre. Before its main feature it was running a current affairs 'short', similar to a future television newscast, in which he witnessed a speech by Dr Groener, Brüning's defence minister, evidently trying to steal Nazi thunder.

> "Germany will not stand much longer to be kept in a position of inferiority to other nations," he calmly declared. "Germany must be free to maintain armed forces on an equality with the nations who claim they were victors in the war. The unjust Treaty of Versailles was responsible for Germany's inferior world position today and the Reich will only regain her place in world trade and affairs when either the other nations reduce their armed forces or when Germany has regained an equality with them."

Rufus's article continued:

> "Every reference to Germany's new spirit was loudly applauded. There flashed on the screen a map with Germany shown in white ringed by glistening bayonets. Figures of the armed forces of surrounding nations appeared – France 4 million, Czechoslovakia 1.5 million, Poland 1.8 million. Then Germany – one hundred thousand. Then were shown fleets of airplanes heading towards Germany: from France nearly 3,000, from other neighbouring nations hundreds more. Germany – under the Versailles Treaty – has none. There followed a brilliant patriotic film based on the story of the German General Yorck in the Napoleonic War of 1812. Its theme – the glorifying of feats of German arms a century ago. The theatre rang with applause time and again as drums beat and victorious troops eventually marched by."

He concluded the piece:

> "Indeed the stoutest optimist would have a hard time to keep his spirits up in Berlin today. Oppressed on every hand by evidence of economic distress, his ears filled with the gloomy foreboding of worse distress to come, he turns for relief to the movies. There's not much relief for nerves on edge in shows like that noted above."[152]

Realizing the seriousness of the situation, he had begun a series of articles that Southam newspapers would publish under the title 'In Germany Today'. These would appear at intervals of a few days between early February and the middle of March, by which time no newspaper-reading Canadian had an excuse for ignorance about the true situation in Germany, nor of its implications for disarmament and peace.

He described Germany's economic situation, its unemployment numbers, the frail grip on power of 86-year-old President Hindenburg and Chancellor Brüning — whose centrists held the balance between murderously opposed Communists and Nazis, and who could only hope to remain chancellor if reparations were cancelled and the economy recovered. He described the parties in the Reichstag and the shrinking number of members who still valued their democratic constitution.

In another article he explained the credit binge of the late twenties when American and British loans had poured into Germany — used to rebuild export industries, to make Berlin shine with modern apartment buildings and infrastructure and to create a brief prosperity — and then the crash in 1929 when America called in its loans, banks failed, industry disintegrated, new buildings stood empty, and Berlin alone had 700,000 unemployed. By 1932 the gulf between rich and poor yawned wide: while theatres, restaurants, and clubs were still packed with well-dressed people, "in its streets there were more beggars than in any city in Europe . . . . In the two weeks I was in Berlin, at least six people were killed, twenty wounded and fifty arrested in street clashes between 'Nazis', Communists and police."

He had witnessed a brutal assault on a man who had heckled passing soldiers, the same day that a youth selling Nazi newspapers had been swarmed and killed by Communists. The Nazis, who claimed that 300 of their street fighters had been killed and 9,000 wounded fighting Communists in the last three years, even paid pensions to the widows and gave financial aid to the wounded. With millions in the private armies of these and other political parties, German friends told him that Berliners were living on top of a powder magazine which a spark might set off at any moment.[153] He described a visit he and a companion made to Communist strongholds in a poor area of Berlin:

> . . . walking many miles through a labyrinth of drab streets; seeing tenements where whole families live in one room; passing from Communist 'district headquarters' to the rival Nazi headquarters, nearly always just round the corner from each other; being addressed now as 'Comrade' and now greeted with the Nazi slogan of 'Heil Hitler' with right hand upraised; all the time feeling that suspicious eyes were watching us.

Nothing in his experience had prepared him for the people he came across that day, and their behaviour. His article read:

> Here we are in a low dive, not far from the corner of Kosliner Strasse . . . where Red Flags hang from half the windows of the tenements . . . It is a Communist nest . . . in a far corner three or four young girls,

> dirty, bedraggled and slovenly in appearance . . . in the midst of them is a lad of 18 or so wearing a black Russian blouse, his greasy, tousled hair brushed over his forehead in Cossack style – he is repulsive to look at and leers and gossips with the girls . . . .[154] We enter another beer hall. It is crowded to suffocation and the stench is appalling. Men and women, clad in rags, are seated about at rough tables . . . some eating sausages made of horsemeat, one or two drinking beer. A barber sells us copies of a banned Red newspaper. We pass into another room where men and girls sit around in attitudes which would hardly be considered conventional in polite society . . . some girls and men are dancing. It is a place of squalour, vice and filth. In the furthest room men and women are sleeping with their heads resting on their hands before them on the tables.

Their communist guide described these young people as beggars, but they were also, as Rufus told readers, "the raw material of one of the 'armies' which threaten the stability of the German Reich."[155]

But it was a different revolution — that of gender equality — that had horrified him. A striking feature of Lenin's Bolshevik Party, it had become enshrined in the German party thanks to their veneration of former leader Rosa Luxemburg, murdered in the 1919 Spartakist uprising. In these beer halls the Communist party, of course, was looking after its own just as the Nazis were — their young people being a good deal poorer, grubbier, and less conventional than young Nazis. Compounding Rufus's personal horror of Marxism, these youths shocked him deeply with their free and easy ways. In his description of what he saw, his habitual objectivity was abandoned for more judgmental language — a reflection of his own inhibitions and Victorian views on gender relations in which he was far from alone.

On 27 January he left Berlin for Munich where he had been encouraged to expect that Hitler would see him. He had been sleeping well, thanks to his new prescription, though with some bad nights after the Isenburg meeting. He stayed at Munich's smart Bayerischer Hof and was immediately visited by Simson of *The Times* — who seems temporarily to have filled Keyserlingk's role — and they saw much of each other in the next four days. In preparation for his meeting with Hitler, they visited the Brown House — Nazi party headquarters — which was in sharp contrast to his visit among Communists.

> We found ourselves in a large, lofty hall. The walls were of yellow-brown marble . . . the carpet was soft and thick in shades of brown. Swastika signs seemed to be everywhere and they were the chief decoration of the ceiling . . . busy-looking young men skipped about with a look of terrifying earnestness on their faces. As they passed each other they raised the right hand and said 'Heil Hitler' . . . the whole atmosphere of the place seemed to me like that just before the curtain goes up on an amateur theatrical show.

He was ushered into the office of Ernst Hanfstaengl, at the time Hitler's Foreign Press Bureau chief and friend. Hanfstaengl was a wealthy Harvard-educated German American, called 'Putzi' by Hitler, who loved his piano-playing. As his mother was American, he spoke excellent English and Rufus found him courteous and kind, if a bit patronizing. At first they chatted about Canada which he had visited. His theatrical gestures, however, fitted right into Rufus's earlier impression and when talking about Hitler "he became positively lyrical," so much so that Rufus had a hard time keeping a straight face. Getting down to business, Hanfstaengl wanted to know everything about his visitor — where he'd been born, his age, his education and career, whether he had a list of questions to submit — all of which Rufus found mystifying and unusual.

> At length, when this high – and talkative – personage had had his say – we proceeded on a tour of the building. We were shown the memorial plaques to the twenty-three adherents of Herr Hitler who lost their lives in the 'outbreak' of 1923.[156] We went into Herr Hitler's private office – about twenty feet square, furnished sparsely, richly and simply. Across one corner stood his desk – of mahogany, inlaid with brass. On the floor was a rich, red-toned rug with the everlasting Swastika woven into it. There were one or two chairs and a table with papers on it. On the walls were at least three portraits of Frederick the Great. Behind Herr Hitler's desk on the wall hung a plaster mask of the great emperor's features. In another corner stood a fine bronze of the head of Mussolini. Another wall was decorated with a painting of a scene in the Great War – it showed German infantry stepping out from their trenches to storm the British lines. Herr Hitler, by the way, served for four years with the German army on the Western Front, had a fine fighting record and was awarded the Iron Cross for gallantry in the field. I asked my guide whether he had ever run against the Canadians in the war. "the Canadians? Ach – you just ask him when you see him what he thinks of Canadian soldiers," he said. "He'll make your ears burn."

When Rufus asked about Frederick the Great, Hanfstaengl claimed Hitler was his great admirer, that the Nazi movement, and Hitler personally, were inspired by his principles and by his maxim that 'though he was emperor, he was the greatest servant of the state.'

Thereafter, while waiting for a summons, Rufus worked on his 'In Germany Today' columns and visited tourist spots — the Bierhalle, the Deutsches Museum, the Old Masters gallery and, on Sunday, the cathedral. It was after the service there that he heard from Putzi that "the Hitler interview was off." He must have been disappointed, but makes no mention of that in his diary and left at once for Geneva.

He arrived, exhausted, at 5:45 am — after seventeen hours in a train. It speaks volumes for his professionalism that he nevertheless spent the morning at the League Council meeting on the Manchuria crisis, phoned in a story at noon and spent the afternoon visiting friends who could update him on League affairs — Burrows at the League press office and Willert, head of the British Foreign Office news service — both friends since 1920. Next morning, 2 February, Rufus was at the opening of the Disarmament Conference for which diplomats from the western powers, the victors of 1918, had spent ten years preparing. It was accepted among them that only by its success could peace be assured, and as an indicator of how important it seemed to other countries, the conference was also attended by the USA, the USSR and Turkey, all important non-members.

In spite of this, from the start Rufus found the atmosphere pessimistic, reflecting his own feelings. He summed up the situation for readers:

> What happens here within the next few days may decide the future of the League of Nations. One more false step, or lack of decision with regards to China's crisis, may wreck whatever chance remains to the Disarmament Conference. If that conference proves a fiasco, the League may suffer a blow from which recovery will be impossible. No one can gainsay that an air of depression hangs over Geneva just as the long-awaited conference is meeting. While the League battles for its life with its back to the wall, hourly reports come of further fighting and of tales of disaster and horror in Shanghai where two of its members are at each others' throats . . . Watching tensely every move in the League's handling of the situation are France and Germany, both ready, if for different reasons, to abandon all faith in the League in case of Far East failure . . . The only optimists are those who say that the world situation is so serious that the League's failure at this time cannot be contemplated. They refuse to allow hope to be extinguished but believe that some measure of success must come.[157]

It soon became clear that neither France nor Britain, the prime movers, planned to reduce their own armaments. After hearing Sir John Simon, Britain's foreign secretary, Rufus summarized Britain's attitude as "a good-natured stand-pat one — clear, benevolent and willing to be helpful, but no more."[158] The French foreign minister, Tardieu, to great applause, proposed a League army to be available at short notice to help victims of aggression. But neither Britain nor France had a plan for general disarmament and, without one, the emperor had no clothes — though the conference was in its ninth day before any delegate dared to point this out. To general surprise it was Maxim Litvinoff, the Soviet foreign minister, who finally did so. In Rufus's opinion:

> . . . he packed more home truths into his half-hour speech than the Disarmament Conference has yet heard. Moderate in tone, expressing Russian willingness to co-operate in reduction – if total abolition of armaments is considered impossible – he was listened to with rapt

> attention." Russia was offering "a progressive, proportionate method as the most equitable and impartial for reducing armaments, allowing exceptions in favour of weaker countries in danger of aggression." He skewered the French proposal at some length "and in a satirical jest, added: "After all this, the League army could hardly bombard both sides simultaneously so as to make sure of hitting the aggressor." Unless disarmament is achieved, he forecast the approach of another world war, which, he predicted, would be more terrible than the last.[159]

In his writing one can sense Rufus's relief — finally the cards were on the table and somebody at Geneva had been forthright and honest — though such was the fear of Communism that few delegates wished to hear it from the likes of Litvinoff. Nor was it popular in Canada, where the *Province* printed his article on page 14. At any rate, after hearing the Russian, Rufus went home to Epsom. During his time in Geneva he had heard all the principals speak: after Simon and Tardieu he had soldiered through the contributions of Gibson, the American ambassador, Grandi, the Italian foreign minister and Dr Brüning, Chancellor of Germany. He had attended their receptions, some in dreadfully overheated rooms, and had made time at the weekend for a long solitary walk on Saturday and a joint assault — with the Burrows and the Eastmans — on Le Salève on Sunday, not surprisingly finding himself "very weary at the end of the day."

Back in England, Rufus found it hard to muster enthusiasm for wandering through peaceful villages. The League's lack of the will and determination to deter an aggressor, plus the failure of the democracies to show a united front at the Disarmament Conference, had shattered his optimistic assumption that "the universe was unfolding as it should." Peace was threatened because it was not protected. However many unemployed there might be in Britain or France or America, he now realized peace was more at risk from the cauldron of extremism that hard times had spawned in the old Austrian Empire and before the year was out he would return to explore it.

He was in two minds about Germany. The Brown House had been reassuring if anything. Its ludicrous theatricality tempted him to write off the whole party — with its 'Heil Hitlers' and swastikas — as lunatic fringe. How could the slightly ridiculous Putzi — a classic court jester — be the front man for anything sinister? Misguided, perhaps, but nothing to worry about, surely? As for Hitler, his reported thoughts on Canadian soldiers and his personal courage predisposed Rufus to think well of him. And those evil-smelling Communists, weren't they just the result of huge unemployment? If the Great Powers would abandon reparations might not Germany's economy recover and steal their thunder? But then he remembered the street battles, the thousands of dead, the failure of democracy, the antisemitism, the thuggery on all sides, the rich who fiddled while Rome burned, the insistence that Germany had not lost the war — these were sinister indeed.

Their life in Epsom had reached a new normal of which part was their tendency to be away. Rufus had been out of the country for nearly a month in January and February, was to be away again, touring Midlands industrial towns, for a week in May, and would be back in Europe in June — at the Lausanne Conference. Meanwhile, Bee had held the fort at home, with Derek for company in the evenings, and Rufus now tried hard to make it up to her. Apart from including her in an intriguing invitation to take tea with Sir George and Lady Younghusband[160] at the Tower of London — where, as Keeper of the Crown Jewels, one hopes the gallant knight offered Bee a peek at the hardware — he tried to make their 20th anniversary in April enjoyable.

According to his diary their celebrations began on Friday the 15th with dinner at the Troc and a theatre in town. But, as it was raining cats and dogs with more on the way, they cancelled their planned weekend in Margate. Instead, after a Saturday matinée with Derek, Rufus and Bee took in a George Arliss film and then went to the Troc for dinner and the cabaret. But the rain was relentless, so on Sunday, after leaving Bee in peace while he and Derek went for a soggy tramp, Rufus took everybody to dine at the RAC Country Club just south of Epsom. Monday the 18th was their big day and, with no mention of rain, Rufus, clutching a dozen red roses, left the office to catch the noon train home. It was only as he reached the front door that he realized *he had left the darned roses on the train!* Robbed, suddenly, of this most acceptable of all tokens, he was forced to express his feelings on the doorstep — something he was not good at doing. After lunch he took Bee to the racecourse, hoping to make up for it all with some minimal success on the horses. But it was just not to be: between them they lost £2 10s. and their celebration ended with a whimper — tea for two, back at the RAC Country Club.

As significant anniversaries go, this one was passable but he still felt a need to make things up to her, a feeling redoubled by a solo trip to the Midlands in early May. So on Saturday 21 May they both drove down to Folkestone where he installed her in solitary splendour at the Lyndhurst Hotel. There she stayed for a fortnight — she had not been ill, there was no talk of convalescence, it seems just to have been a treat, a respite from navigating the social minefield in Epsom, from dealing with a maid and a cook only one of whom spoke English, from spending her days waiting for 'the men' to come home to supper. The following Saturday he drove down for the day and stayed the night. Derek arrived on Sunday morning and, after spending the day with Bee, both men drove back to Epsom.

During the next week he went to his fourth Derby, alone but with Bee's wager-money in his pocket. As was often the case, her instincts were better: she had picked the winner, April the Fifth, and he collected £4.12.6d on her behalf; meanwhile, he backed losers in several races and lost £3. The next Sunday, 5 June, he and Derek drove back to Folkestone, lunched there with Bee, and then they all drove home. One hopes Bee had really enjoyed her view of the Channel.

As Rufus was mentally preparing for his next trip into Europe, other things seemed less important and his diary fell silent until 21 June when he left for Geneva and the Lausanne Conference. This meeting, between Germany and the four main recipients, recognized the impossibility of Germany making further reparations payments and — in effect — cancelled them. It was too little, too late: too little to bring about German economic recovery and too late to prevent the collapse of the democratic Weimar republic, as Rufus may have begun to suspect. He stayed in Lausanne until the major decision had been taken on 29 June. When he arrived there,* the buzz from Geneva had been all about the attractive but ultimately futile Hoover disarmament plan; he managed to interview Robert Boothby and Neville Chamberlain and to attend the final six-power meeting, yet his comment to his diary when turning for home was: "an unsatisfactory expedition in all." The fate of Europe, he felt, did not hang on the matter of reparations. He had a hunch that decisions on war and peace would come as a result of other blunders made by the peacemakers, affecting countries far from Geneva, and he planned to inspect the results of some of them on his next trip.

He arrived at Victoria Station, feeling jaded, at 3:30 pm on 1 July. There was nobody to meet him — Bee was at Wimbledon, Derek at work — so he took himself to a Turkish bath. From this he emerged, revived and in evening dress, to meet Derek at the Savoy for the annual Dominion Day[161] dinner, a major social event for Canadians in London. The following day the family casually attended events to which most Londoners would have loved to accompany them: Bee went to Wimbledon for the men's final, to witness the American Ellsworth Vines defeat the British champion Bunny Austin, while Rufus and Derek[162] went to Hanworth in south London to see the arrival of the German airship *Graf Zeppelin*, accompanied by the enormous *Junkers 2500*, the all-wing aircraft, both machines on the cutting edge of 1930s aviation technology. Although neither of these outings rated further description, the fact that his diary fell silent for the next two weeks is an indication that they seemed pretty special, even to him. And apart from a pair of personal events — a visit to his father at Bures and, later, his own 45th birthday — Rufus made no further entries until the eve of the family's great trip to central Europe in late August.

It is surprising that momentous events were happening during his silent period. It may be that European politics were so depressing that he could not bring himself to write about them in his diary — that he had had a bellyfull when filing his reports for Southam. But in light of his later preoccupation with Hitler it is surprising that the German election results on 1 August did not compel him to reach for his pencil. He had been at home on 10 April and would certainly have known that Hindenburg defeated Hitler that day in the German presidential election, but that Hitler had won 40% of the votes. He had made no diary entry then, nor did he for the next four days. Now he was silent again when the Nazis won 230 of the Reichstag's 608 seats (up from 107) to become the largest single party. And in the succeeding days and weeks it became obvious that only the desperate manoeuvres of anti-Nazi politicians were keeping Hitler from the Chancellor's office.

---

* Lausanne is 70 km from Geneva.

Chapter 17

Touring with Mr Toad

London, September – December, 1932

"How empty now seems all the loud hurrah-ing of those far-off days!"

Rufus, dispatch to Southam, September 1932, on Canadian troops crossing the Rhine in 1918

As was their habit, Rufus and Bee's departure coincided with the start of Derek's holiday. They set off in their car, lovingly referred to by Rufus as 'PK', after much preparatory palaver. Rufus, a 'king of the road' in his own mind, began his diary entry for 28 August: "Mileage 45150, 8¼ gals gas; quart oil Epsom, quart oil Canterbury." But, as they had only left Epsom in mid-afternoon, they got no further than Dover by nightfall. It was an inauspicious start, compounded by their choice of the Lord Warden hotel. "Never again!" he harrumphed. "A dreadful place," chimed Bee, who was also keeping a diary for the duration.

If their first day had been bad, the second was a disaster. Rufus seemed obsessed and his diary entry all car stuff: "Mileage 45242, Bought 5 gals petrol. Arrived Calais 1pm. [After waiting for PK to be unloaded by crane] Left for Ostende, Bruges, etc., 2pm. 2 gals petrol (from can), 1 litre oil. Dinner at Ghent (Les 3 Suisses), arrived Brussels 10pm." It was all so much about the motorcar that it might have been penned by Mr Toad himself — "Poop! Poop!" he might have added.

Bee's entry, by contrast, reflected his passengers' plaintive view. "Very unpleasant day. The roads were ghastly and I feel bruised from top to toe. Should have so much liked a bathe at Ostend but Rufus wouldn't stop! No sleep all night — man with squeaky shoes over my head, and a running tank."

The outcome was a passenger mutiny: next morning she and Derek refused to be driven over any more "ghastly Belgian pavé", so Rufus dropped the mutineers at the railway station and in due course picked them up 140 kms further east at Aachen, just inside Germany.

While eating a lonely lunch, he had time to reflect and it was no longer Mr Toad who picked up the train travellers. He even sounded as if he was beginning to have fun. "Arrived Cologne about 5:45, piloted by German boy and bike. To cathedral — immensely impressive — and thence, again piloted part way by the boy, to Bonn, which we reached at 7:15. Goldener Stern Hotel — quiet, comfy hotel — down to Rhein after."

From that point on, perhaps soothed by the better German roads, Bee soon regained her sense of adventure and Rufus his sense of proportion. She still boycotted PK for part of the next day, taking the steamer up the Rhine from Koblenz to Bingen. This was nice to do anyway and Rufus had had his fun earlier. While she was still in bed, he and Derek had driven to Cologne and back along the "marvellous new road", the first of the famous Autobahnen,[163] opened just three weeks earlier. No doubt he had discovered how fast PK would go and had blown Mr Toad well and truly out of his system! That afternoon he drove slowly and alone up the west bank of the Rhine and they all spent the night at Wiesbaden. Their diary entries read: "[Rufus] . . . to casino after dinner"; "[Bee] . . . where we had a very nice time — casino is a glorious building"; "[Rufus] . . . and we lost 17 marks."

In his dispatch for Southam, Rufus recalled for readers the historic scene of General Currie taking the salute as Canadian troops marched across the Rhine bridge at Bonn ". . . in the first full flush of victory. How empty now," he lamented, "seems all the loud hurrah-ing of those far-off days!"

But if his gloom was caused by apprehension about Germany, his family's experiences at Ludwigshafen on 1 September dispelled it. With Derek driving, they broke down there on the way to Heidelberg. "Had to be towed by a motor-cycle to the garage, in the midst of an admiring crowd of small boys and natives!" The work, which cost them 15.60 marks, took four hours and was done by Christian Brandt and Ernest Schoubusch, the latter having recently returned from 2½ years as a gardener in Victoria, BC, and as chauffeur to the Catholic bishop there. But it had been mainly muscle power that got them to the garage as the motorcycle was assisted by a Communist and a 'Hitlerite',* both cheerfully pushing the heavy car from behind. Thanks to a joint effort, they reached Heidelberg that night as planned.

They enjoyed Heidelberg and meandered thence slowly southwards, through friendly tourist villages and towns, to Munich. They became camera-toting consumers of folk-dancing, band concerts and farmers' markets. They visited churches and castles where Bee and Derek (though not Rufus) were keen climbers of towers and steeples — up 342 steps on one occasion. They spent two nights in the quaintness of Rothenberg. As Bee put it, "the moment we drove through its massive gateway, we were transported back to medieval days."

Rufus enjoyed the Bavarian farm country with its "slow oxen teams, men and women at work in the fields until dark, and villages that look as though a high explosive shell had just fallen into a manure pile!" Mr Toad limited himself

---

* A member of the Nazi party. The use of the term 'Nazi' only became general in 1933.

to cleaning the sparkplugs one morning and he and Derek even took off the engine head, or so he claimed. When their run into Munich went smoothly the next day, he could claim "PK behaved better after Derek and I had spent an hour at the sparkplugs."

Rufus took them to his Bayerischer Hof in Munich, which Bee considered "a topping hotel and the manager, Herr Damert, charming." They slept well and next day were busy at the Deutsches Museum, lunching near the Glockenspiel to watch its figures do their thing and later going to a spectacular operetta, *Die Liebe Augusti*, at the Deutsches Theater. PK had been guzzling oil, which quickly fouled the plugs and must also have been smoky and smelly, so Rufus took it to a big-city garage. There could be no quick fix, declared the mechanic, unhelpfully — only 'new pistons' would solve their problem.

Next morning Rufus, whose real goal was Vienna and the countries of the Austrian Empire, found it hard to get Bee to leave Munich, with which she had fallen in love. The charming Herr Damert had offered them a tour of his hotel and Bee enthused over ". . . the enormous wine cellar, which has over 300,000 bottles of red and white wine, barrels as well. Two bottles were opened for our benefit — we left Munich reluctantly!" Well, she would go, but not before the afternoon fashion show. This gave them time for the Alte Pinakothek before lunch and not until 4:30pm could Rufus leave for Salzburg in Austria.

PK was running smoothly, for once, and their drive that evening, always in sight of mountains and forests, reminded Rufus of BC — ironically, as they were about to have a series of only-in-Europe experiences. At their Salzburg hotel neither Rufus nor Bee slept a wink. "An awful night," Bee exclaimed. "36 church clocks struck all night and I'm sure that mass was celebrated in every one of them at different times starting at 5 am!" Despite this, in the morning they were ready for anything: after 'doing' Salzburg, they set off in a newly-ailing PK for what Rufus called "some hectic hill drives", eventually reaching St Wolfgang on the Wolfgangsee. There they spent two restful nights at a lakeshore hotel in an Okanagan-like environment. They bathed and rowed boats, took the mountain railway up to the Schafbergspitze at 9,000 feet, wrote letters and went for walks — and Rufus sent letters of introduction from their London friends to his Vienna contacts.

The time came to pile back into PK for the drive to Vienna. Austria was a poor country, its roads much worse than Germany's, and they took their toll on the vehicle. PK was misbehaving again and they decided, over lemonade in a riverside café at Linz,[164] to take the road along the Danube as it would be flat. With increasing complaints, the car wheezed its way to Melk, almost expiring as they pulled up at the Melkerhof Hotel. Seeming unworried, Rufus wrote in his diary, "Melk Abbey in the moonlight almost compensated for the roads." In her own diary, Bee wrote, "Rufus and I went to a café for a liqueur and listened to some men singing. We bought them a drink and they sang for us." Neither seemed to anticipate the disaster that awaited.

The next morning, 10 kms down the road, PK finally quit in Armsdorf, fortunately right outside a *gasthof*. The garage mechanic came to have a look and Derek, as family linguist, was spokesman. "Car engines were quite beyond my limited German," he admitted, but the Pichler family strolled by and Uncle Clement "spoke good English and kindly translated." Armed with whatever Derek had told him, the lad, according to Rufus, "fiddled with the car for hour after hour," or, as Bee put it, "pulled all the inside to pieces and we despaired of it ever starting again." Twice he disappeared — once to the next village for sparkplugs and later, and more ominously, to distant Vienna with the magneto.

Meanwhile, the Pichlers had invited Derek for the night at the gasthof where they were staying. The bearded Herr Pichler was an artist and the family party included Marie and Drecl, his glamorous daughters of about Derek's age, and their Uncle Clement with his daughter. Rufus and Bee found a bed for themselves with Frau Ehrlich, the village grocer, and next morning they called at the *gasthof* to see Herr Pichler's paintings. Rufus paid seventy schillings for a watercolour of Melk Abbey, which he and Bee had visited. The two families were getting on famously when the mechanic, an enterprising and competent lad in spite of their fears, arrived back from Vienna with a functioning magneto. When he had fitted it, PK was ready to roll again and, after taking a photograph of the whole group,[165] the Johnston family, whose youngest member had "had a happy time," reluctantly took its leave.

As it had after the last repair, PK ran smoothly as they drove into Vienna and when Rufus and Derek cruised the Ringstrasse early next morning. As usual, their hotel, the Osterreichischer Hof, was noisy. As this would be Derek's last day, they made the most of it, visiting the Stephansdom, the Deutsches Museum, Schonbrunn Palace, Karl Marx Hof to see the new workers' flats, an opera in the evening and a nightcap at Sacher's Café. Rufus, of course, could drive to all these places and park outside, it being 1932 and Austria very poor.

When Derek left for home on 13 September, Bee's and Rufus's holiday came to an end; henceforth he left her to her own devices while he went about his business and, as the day wore on, became increasingly distracted by sharp pains in his right foot which he took to be gout though he had never had it. He had meetings all day — with Dr Otto Rosenberg, an Austrian economist[166] who contributed to the *Financial Times,* Hugo Neumann of *The Times*, and Herr Gentilomo, a Wickham Steed contact. He and Bee dined together and later went to meet Best of UPI[167] "and many other interesting and amusing newspapermen," at the Café Louvre, a group described by Bee as "Fodor and his wife,[168] with lots of queer folk." She enjoyed the encounter hugely but by then Rufus's foot was so sore he could hardly walk.

The next morning, hardly able to walk or drive, he consulted an orthopedic specialist who diagnosed not gout, but arthritis, for which he prescribed medication. Assuming he had seen the worst, Rufus tried to ignore the problem. He and Bee, guided by Herr Gentilomo and his friend Frau Gelber, visited the Sandleiten in New Vienna, described by Bee as "a huge community flat place for poor people, where they live for very small rents — and there are nurseries for the children, baths, washing and ironing rooms, etc."

Afterwards, as Rufus was leaving for Budapest, they moved Bee's things to Frau Gelber's house as she had kindly offered Bee a bed in his absence. That night, however, Rufus's pain worsened. In the morning he cancelled his travel plans and spent two days in bed at the hotel, being ministered to by Bee — in the intervals of her new social life, as she was being introduced, progressively, to Frau Gelber's many sisters, each more chatty than the last. They discovered the cold compresses recommended by the hotel's head waiter to be more effective than Dr. Strauss's remedy — so much so that by the morning of 17 September Rufus felt well enough to be on his way.

It was to be more difficult than he had hoped: Thomas Cook's had overbooked the aircraft, there was no seat for him, so he spent his afternoon on a train to Budapest[169] and his evening walking, gingerly, on the promenade by the Danube and telephoning contacts to invite them to his hotel. As a result, the following day, Sunday, he was able to hold court there and was visited successively by Wernher of AP, Ottlih, brother of *The Times* man, and Dr Rustern Vanling, with all of whom he had long chats. On Sunday afternoon he explored the city by taxi — "they are not cheap," he told his diary, "but I can't avoid them under present circs."

Things really fell into place on Monday: at 9:30am, ". . . Paul de Lipovniczky of [the Hungarian] Foreign Office came to call — prepared to be at my disposal, a charming man who made himself my guide, consultant and friend." Apparently it was considered in Hungary's interests to help this persistent Canadian get his story, and perhaps influence his message in the process. Whatever the reasoning, Lipovniczky's mission was most helpful and Rufus was soon affectionately calling him 'Uncle Paul'. Together they went to the Foreign Office to request an interview with Prime Minister Károlyi, to the British legation, to the Church of the Coronation, and to the Parliament. Later, Dr Vanling, his visitor from the day before, returned, and he and Rufus spent the afternoon driving "miles and miles" in another taxi "to see the hovels of the poor — terrible conditions." That evening he interviewed the British ambassador, Lord Chilston, and ended the day entertaining Uncle Paul to dinner at the luxurious St Gellert hotel.

In the morning, after Rufus had waited several hours to hear whether Károlyi would see him, Uncle Paul arrived to say that an interview was impossible owing to a cabinet meeting. This was no white lie — unknown to Rufus, and probably also to Uncle Paul, Károlyi was being pressured to resign at that very moment and would do so the following morning, 21 September. Meanwhile, Rufus wasted no more time. After he had lunched alone with Chilston, Uncle Paul picked him up and took him on an appallingly dusty drive to see Slovak, Hungarian, and German villages where conditions were desperately primitive. No sooner was he back at his hotel than his other guardian angel, Dr Vanling, arrived with the leader of the Progressive Agrarian Party, Tibor Eckhardt, with whom he had a long talk. The day ended with dinner with both Dr V and Uncle

Paul at the Magyar Athletic Club. It had been a successful whirlwind visit and next morning he flew back to Vienna.[170]

Having no car in Budapest had probably helped his foot but once back in Vienna he wasted no time getting behind the wheel. After a quick re-pack, he picked up PK from the Osterreichischerhof garage, consulted Dr. Harris at the British consulate about his foot and set off for Bratislava in Slovakia. He would have expected to cover the 80 kms in an hour and a half. At the border, however, the "customs people were very curious about me, my passport and car, and a letter [of introduction] to senator Stodola. So I rang up the British consul which finally did the trick." He stayed at the Carlton Hotel in Bratislava, slept well and by 8:30 am was ready for the voluble Stodola, who doubled as president of the chamber of commerce. After another interview at the hotel, Arthur Dowden,[171] the British consul, came to see him. Rufus spent a couple of hours with Dowden, chatting and driving round Bratislava, before returning to Vienna.

It is is hard to say at this point whether he was more tested by the pain in his foot or by the unreliability of his beloved PK. Once back in Vienna both returned to haunt him and he had a miserable afternoon. After checking out of the Osterreichischerhof, he set off for Prague, hoping to visit the new residential complex at the Friedrich-Engels-Platz in northern Vienna on the way. Alas, the car died on him just across the Danube bridge: he had to spend time and money getting it towed into the city, stayed there another night and never managed to see those new houses. That evening he telephoned Dr. Harris about his foot and this gentleman probably encouraged him to be stoic — the pain would eventually go away and there was nothing he could do about it anyway. Not satisfied, Rufus called on him in the morning and, perhaps in desperation, Harris told him to go and buy some slippers! This Rufus did but it was not until halfway through the afternoon that he paid 93 schillings to get his car back and left once more for Prague.

He soon realized that the pricey repair had been botched; PK started behaving badly again and gave up the ghost 80 kms away — on a hill, just as it was getting dark. It was towed ignominiously into Schrems, a small forest and mining town near the Czech border, initially creating a sensation when nobody could be found who spoke English — forcing Rufus to speak German. He lodged at the Gasthof Gruber, and though Gruber himself spoke no English, his nephew Arnold understood a little. He and Rufus managed to communicate and, unasked, Arnold procured a 'ray-treatment' machine which seemed to do little good. However, in the morning Rufus was impressed when PK was ready to go at 9:30; and more so when it performed well for the 200 kms into Prague.

He spent as much time in Prague as he had in Budapest but it was a less productive visit on the whole, partly because of his foot and partly because Dr. Hani of the Czech foreign office, his Uncle Paul equivalent, would not play the same role. As he had done in Budapest, Rufus relied heavily on *The Times* man and on British Embassy officials for briefings on the national scene. On his first night he dined with Kadich of *The Times* and his wife, and would see them and their family frequently. At the British embassy he saw Taylor, the consul, and Gurney, chargé d'affaires — and was later entertained by them at their homes. But although he lunched with Hani on his first day, the official was neither prepared nor authorized to be as open with him as Lipovniczky had been. Nevertheless, his visit was worthwhile and its highlight an interview at the foreign office, conducted in French, with Dr. Kamil Krofta, foreign minister Beneš's[172] right-hand man. In addition Hani did take him to hear Rennie Smith,[173] a well-respected British ex-MP, talking on the state of Europe. As he had his own vehicle, Rufus managed to visit the main points of interest in the capital and did his own entertaining at Marie's restaurant near the Karl bridge.

He left Prague, after lunching with Kadich at Marie's, on 28 September, and drove the 90 kms to Pilsen. There he met Colonel Denis Daly, British military attaché, and dined with him and his wife. In the morning a Czech foreign office official escorted him to the Skoda works — where, for 2½ hours, he was shown the arms manufacturing plant that had long ago been directed by von Isenburg. To witness peacetime arms production on such a scale was horrifying and he was happy to move on to the Pilsen brewery — "much more interesting," he decided, "malt houses, cellars, etc., and *hors d'oeuvres*."

He left Pilsen after lunch, crossed the frontier into Germany and, after a night in the small town of Straubing, reached Munich, where Bee was waiting at the Bayerischer Hof, by lunchtime next day. It was 30 September and he hadn't mentioned his foot in two days — in fact, though he never admitted it to his diary, he had recovered. The attack had coincided exactly with his investigative tour and once they were back in holiday mode, the pain went away.

Bee had fared well in his absence. After two more days with Frau Gelber, she returned to Munich where she knew Herr Damert would have a welcome for her. He did indeed, sending his porter to meet her train and welcoming her in the lobby. A woman alone had limited options and Bee spent parts of most days either in the English Gardens, in a museum, or window shopping. She enjoyed the gardens and was happy to walk there for hours — museums fascinated her and she found many exhibits so interesting that she would tell her diary about them — and she window-shopped because she had very little money. Towards the end of the two weeks, wearying of her own company, she went to tea with the Simsons. "He is *Times* correspondent here," she wrote, "and has a German wife who is quite clever, I think. I don't care for him, although he is very harmless." She later added, "She is really very nice, and, I think, the brains of that family."

The two women clicked and the next day took a train out of the city to walk in the countryside. They went to the zoo the day after that but Mrs S was busy for the following two and lent Bee a book, *The English: Are They Human?* by R.G. Renier. This gave her a chuckle and they all got together for tea when Rufus came back.

They took a week to drive home and mixed business with pleasure as they went. "We left Munich, to our great regret, at 11:30," Rufus wrote, "with Herr Damert and the rest bowing us off." They had been good customers in hard times. PK suffered its fifth breakdown in Augsburg, 80 kms away, another in Paris and the final one in Arras. They had passed through Rheims solely to see the cathedral — "very tragic to see the war scars but the outside lovely still," Rufus wrote — and through Paris to go to the *Folies Bergères* — "an excellent show," they thought. For a whole day they revisited scenes of Rufus's war north-east of Amiens — Bee's introduction to the horrors he had endured. No doubt she enjoyed visiting the château at Warvillers, 2nd Brigade HQ after the battle of Amiens, which Rufus photographed and where they met the countess who now lived there.

That evening PK just managed to crawl into Arras where Rufus had arranged to meet Major Unwin Simson, the Canadian engineer in charge of the construction of the Vimy Ridge memorial.[174] Simson's driver took charge of PK while Rufus and Bee went to the major's house for coffee and liqueurs. The next morning Simson spent a couple of hours with them at the memorial. It was a work-in-progress and they met the Italian sculptor Luigi Rigamonti, creator of the towering marble figures. As their car was now running smoothly again, thanks to the soldier-driver, they slept that night at Boulogne, had PK hoisted aboard a steamer in the morning, spent their last few shillings on lunch at the Rose in Canterbury and then drove home without breaking down again, though the engine was 'missing' badly. On their six-week trip they had covered 4,608 kms, 6.8 kms for each litre of gas, 80 kms for each quart of oil and had broken down completely every 650 kms. With this appalling record Mr Toad seemed content — he had done it! It was, after all, 1932 — not 2012.

He had achieved his main objective — to see the problems created by the treaties of 1919 for himself. In an article that appeared in the *Edmonton Journal* under the title *Central Europe Today*, he wrote:

> Had I suffered from the delusion, like so many people who live at a comfortable distance from the heart of Europe, that the documents signed at Versailles, Trianon and St Germain in the summer of 1919 had brought peace to this continent, that delusion must surely have been shattered by the time I had absorbed the viewpoints of Vienna, Budapest and Prague. The further I travelled the more definite became the feeling that, far from being at peace, the war was still in progress in these countries; not, perhaps, a war of shells and bayonets (though the shadow of Central Europe's vast armies is never far away) but bitter, unceasing economic warfare, with an accompanying background of intrigue and suspicion, little dreamed of in placid England, much less in far-away Canada.

During the past six weeks he had filed stories whenever he had had a chance. Now he decided to rest his foot at home for as long as it took him to digest his impressions and put together a longer summary piece. The result, 5,000 words under the title "The Harvest of War and Peace", illustrated with his own photographs, was published in the November issue of the *Review of Reviews*. The editor had prefaced the article with this introduction to readers:

> The London editor of an important group of Canadian newspapers spent a month this autumn in Austria, Hungary and Czechoslovakia. He has written for the Review of Reviews a most vivid article describing conditions in Central Europe, which may come as a surprise to people who do not understand how widespread is the political and economic confusion that has followed the war.

It was well-stated and deftly summarized Rufus's purpose — to alert British people who did not understand. After exposing the naïveté of the peacemakers' doctrine of self-determination, which had resulted in the shattering of the defeated Austrian Empire's customs union, he portrayed its consequences in general terms for the successor states, Austria, Hungary and Czechoslovakia:

> Boxed in behind fantastic tariff walls, these little nations have tried for thirteen years to battle against the economic laws of nature. Common sense in international relations has been swamped beneath the wave of unreasoning desire to be free, at whatever material cost, of partnership with, or dependence on, any neighbour whose ambitions might conceivably run counter to their own.

Autarkic economic policies have had dreadful consequences:

> Trade is being brought virtually to a standstill. Hundreds of thousands of workless are on the verge of starvation, kept alive in some cases, by a beggarly dole from the state; in others, dependent for the barest existence on Charity.

The ethnic nationalism encouraged by self-determination had been made more dangerous by the large ethnic minorities within each of the three states:

> 2½ million Hungarians have been wrenched from their fatherland and handed over to neighbouring states . . . within Czechoslovakia, 6½ million Czechs live beside 3¼ million Slovaks who for centuries have followed the fortunes of the Magyars . . . 750,000 Magyars by no means content with their lot . . . 500,000 Ruthenians, whose ultimate ambitions lie with Russia . . . 3½ million Germans who may be presumed to be more interested in the Grosse Deutschland movement.

He continued:

> . . . Fear of their neighbours force the Czechs to maintain a huge army . . . As I drove through the country, I passed huge guns, columns of transport and khaki-clad troops on the march. I asked a prominent Slovak politician what chance there was of Czechoslovakia reducing their armaments. His reply was what I expected. "How can we reduce our armaments," he said, "while Germany is in a state of turmoil, while Hitler's followers breathe fire and slaughter and the *Grosse Deutschland* movement gains momentum every day? How can we disarm while Hungary maintains her present attitude?" [not to accept the terms of the peace treaty until Hungary is reunited]

The article was a testament to the wisdom and understanding of this self-educated scribe. Only near the end does he mention Hitler, and even then in the words of the voluble Stodola — the Nazi leader had not yet forced his way into his worry space. For the time being the alarm bells in his head were stilled by memories of the comically theatrical inhabitants of the Brown House, the co-operative group of helpers after PK's breakdown in Ludwigshafen and, maybe, of the uniformed Hitlerites peacefully eating lunch in one of his 'snapshots.'

That would change in 1933.

Chapter 18
Hitler, Game-changer
London, January – October, 1933

"What is going to happen at Geneva? And in Germany? It looks as if that terrible 'next war' is beginning to show over the horizon."

R.E. to Rufus, 5 March 1933

By 1933 Rufus's diary had become hit and miss. In the four months from April 26 to August 20 he made just one entry, while during the rest of the time before mid-November he made entries only when away from home. Significant foreign events seldom made it into his pages and although 1933 was full of such events — starting with Hitler's appointment as chancellor on 30 January — few rated an entry.

Nevertheless, he had few illusions about the state of the peace, something he made clear in his article for *Review of Reviews*. He was not alone in his pessimism — on 5 March his father, a student of foreign affairs, concluded a letter to him with "What is going to happen at Geneva? And in Germany? It looks as if that terrible "next war" is beginning to show over the horizon. Have you read *The Collapse of the Austro-Hungarian Empire* by von Glaise-Horstenau?"[175]

What is the world coming to? he must have wondered, if even his most-Christian father was sounding resigned to the inevitability of another war. He himself, by personality and profession, was compelled to seek answers and like other journalists had read the writing on the wall before the politicians — although Churchill was already trumpeting Ramsay Macdonald's lack of a disarmament policy and the implications of Hitler. Rufus was an early Churchill fan and on 23 March had winkled Derek away from his auditing to hear his speech in the House. A month later he and Bee heard him again at the Society of St George banquet. Winston had not yet rung the alarm about German rearmament — that would come in August — but it is hard to imagine him speaking approvingly of the Hitler government's record to date. Derek's lifetime preoccupation with Churchill started at this time — with a little help from his dad.

1933 began pleasantly enough. As 2 January was a Canadian bank holiday, Rufus declared one at 162A Great Victoria Sreet: he and Bee spent the morning playing golf — something they could have done in Canada only in Victoria, perhaps — and then went to visit "the girls", their wartime friends in Brighton. Derek was much in demand and was invited to four dances in the first week of the year. But by the second week it was back to the grind for both father and son and on the 22nd Rufus left for a two-week trip to the industrial Midlands.

He managed to turn a winter visit to Northampton, Birmingham, Leeds, Stoke on Trent, Newcastle under Lyme, Coventry and Leicester into a trove of stories for his third book, *Down English Lanes*, to be published later that year. On his first weekend away he stayed at the famous Izaak Walton Hotel in Dovedale. It was bitterly cold, roads were icy and PK needed chains to navigate the scenic road across the Pennines — although a safer alternative existed. On the second weekend he drove and tramped through the vale of Evesham, visiting villages and homing in on the churches. Hoping to hear the sermon at Bredon on Sunday, he sat expectantly in the pews although dressed for hiking. When the vicar announced there would be no sermon, he tried to sneak out unobserved — an impossibility, alas, in hob-nailed boots. Already embarrassed, he compounded his confusion at the church door by colliding noisily with a lady in brown tweeds who was entering late.

Once outside, the charms of the village restored his composure and so delayed his intended walk that, while still exploring the place, he unexpectedly met the vicar on his way home. Of course they talked — the sort of parish prattle that Rufus loved — and the vicar, delighted with a new acquaintance who enjoyed his stories, invited him to lunch. Imagine Rufus's momentary discomfiture when the daughter of the house, late for lunch and coming to sit beside him, turned out to be the tweedy lady in brown!

He returned to Epsom on 2 February. Although he played a round of golf with Bee the following day, by the 14th she was in hospital undergoing what seems to have been a hysterectomy. His diary read, "Dr Rawlins of Elizabeth Garrett Anderson hospital, Drs Heckels and Kendal. Ten times more severe than we expected as they found all kinds of complications — notably intestinal. Bee in operating room 2¾ hrs — doctors came to me after an eternal wait of 2½ hrs. Bee not conscious and condition very grave." In a letter to his boss, he wrote, "For many months she had been unwell, and occasionally in severe pain from some undiscovered cause. Fortunately, the surgeon we had from London (a woman) was one of the ablest of her kind."[176]

For days her condition remained grave and not until the 18th could he write: "Bee definitely somewhat better." She came home a month later and took her first outing on 25 March. For those six weeks Rufus's wings were clipped; he saw Bee every day and his diary contained little but bulletins on the patient. He did, however, record two foreign events — Japan's withdrawal from the League on 25 February, and FDR's inauguration on 4 March. But after Bee was home, his diary entries became spotty once more, and from 26 April ceased entirely.

In the first week of April, however, he had filled blank diary pages with conversations with himself about Hitler — who had definitely now entered his worry space. Since his appointment as chancellor, the German scene was becoming increasingly sinister and Rufus must have wondered how he could ever have found those busy young men and their salutes amusing. Within a month the Reichstag caught fire — for which the Nazis blamed, then outlawed, the Communist party, their most serious opposition. A week later, new Reichstag elections gave the Nazis a majority and, before March was out, they had used it to pass an Enabling Act giving Hitler the power to rule by decree. Hitler had what he sought and Rufus and many others saw it as a Nazi *coup d'état*.

His 1 April entry started, "Italy's Fascist revolt is hardly comparable to Germany's." He compared the two regimes' attitudes to capitalism and industry, then made observations on four separate topics: "Italian masses neutral and Germany's masses certainly not. Between 30 and 40% of all adult Germans employed in industry. Communist Youth established Nov 1919 — answered by "Hitler Youth" and by 1932 bulk of children belonged in one or the other. 64 million Nordics felt themselves threatened by 600,000 Jews."

His entry for 2 April was a collection of quotations: from Hitler's *Mein Kampf* (which he calls the 'Big Book'), from Goebbels' speeches, and from Rosenberg's book *The Myth of the 20th Century*. Together they gave a picture of duplicity as policy, complete ruthlessness, and the glorification of war — all motivated by evil racial myths. If this was Rufus's initial understanding of the Nazis, it is remarkable that it was essentially the same as the judgment of history, after genocide, an aggressive war, and other murderous horrors — events he could hardly have imagined.

In the space for 3 April Rufus summarized the big questions he had about Hitler's policy, many of which he would later put to the chancellor when they met: "Hitler desires association with other powers — yet he pulls out of Geneva, his best chance. Will Germany go back to Geneva after Nov 12 [a referendum on Germany's withdrawal from the League and the Nazis' own performance]? and on what terms? Are the leaders in earnest in the cause of peace? Did Germany's withdrawal [from the Disarmament Conference] mean she intended to rearm, defy the world, etc.? — or was it really a demand for equal treatment? Are there dark and dangerous designs on Europe — or only a domestic crisis for Hitler? What does Germany think of Britain? And Canada?"

These things were top of mind for him and would continue so through the year. Under 5 April he summarized the difficulty of reporting on German public opinion: "Changes day to day — to generalize unsafe — best to record views of selected types." He goes on to offer ideas from Lord Noel-Buxton,[177] an apologist for the apparent excesses of the German government. "One feels that Germans are ignorant of much that has gone on in the persecution [of Jews]. In England we have heard only the seamy side; in Germany one sees nothing of the ugly aspect. Do not try to judge Germany by our standards — see Noel-Buxton." In contrast to his partisan reaction to German communists, he was making serious efforts to be objective.

Clearly the news out of Germany — the boycott of the Jews on top of the Enabling Act — demanded to be sorted out and digested; once he had done that, normal life could resume and from the 7th until the end of April the diary reverted to normal. From the 10th, he took a week off, spending four days driving and hiking in the New Forest area of Hampshire in search of material for his column and book. He called on his Uncle Will[178] and Aunt Sis at their rectory in Michelmersh and joined them for a frugal lunch of bread and cheese. Then he returned to Epsom and took a much-recovered Bee to the local Passion Play. For a while the seductive normality of middle-class life blotted out Hitler and his works: he played tennis with Ernest Parsons, now a good friend (he had rushed round with champagne when Bee came home from hospital); people came to tea now and then, and everybody played croquet in the garden; he planted his sweet peas as he had done every peacetime year since they were married; and he and Bee celebrated their anniversary quietly before going to the vicar's wedding soon after.

However, like rising flood water, news of the German leader and his government could not long be ignored. When Rufus dined with Wickham Steed at the Reform Club near the end of April, they talked of little else. Steed had been editor of *The Times*, was well-informed and respected, and his had been one of the first voices expressing alarm about the new chancellor. Rufus valued his insights — like himself, he had once been a foreign correspondent in Europe. The interest of the evening increased when they were unexpectedly joined by Paul Scheffer, foreign correspondent for *Berliner Tageblatt*,* though Steed later claimed this had 'cramped' their conversation.[179] Nevertheless, Scheffer had conceded in the course of conversation that the Nazis' ultimate aim was to retake the Polish Corridor by force, and that Goebbels' constant accusation that France was contemplating 'preventive' war against Germany was just propaganda.

The last diary entry on 28 April concerned Neville Chamberlain's budget — he declared it "the dullest speech and the most unimaginative budget" he had ever heard. With that, diary entries ceased for four months with this note to self: "Is there any real improvement in Germany's trade and employment?" — improvements that Goebbels had recently been trumpeting.

Whatever Rufus was doing in May, it caused his father to be sufficiently worried about him to insist he take a break. On the 29th, R.E. wrote, "I want you to take a real holiday, you need one. After the trouble with your foot and then your hand and wrist, it is evident that physically you need a thorough toning up and you cannot possibly get it whilst you are in the midst of the whirl of work. Don't say it is impossible — you let Cummings go and did his work; he can do yours for a few weeks. Surely it is wiser to take a precaution in time rather than to delay till a breakdown compels you to take a longer rest."

---

* *Berliner Tageblatt*, in order to support Goebbels' claim that the German press was free to print what it liked, was not required to reprint his propaganda but was the only German newspaper allowed such freedom.

He suggested a cruise, three weeks at somewhere like St Austell, or at Bures with himself and Florie. And, for any of them, "*no work* — long quiet nights and the healing countryside."

Rufus probably continued working, fending off these suggestions with token improvements to his regime. And Bee, who would have seen how stressed he was, had probably asked R.E. to write the letter. If so, while she was worrying about him, Rufus seems to have relaxed about her. In early July, to signal her health crisis over, he wrote to thank Dr Heckels for his part in her treatment — which, he informed the doctor, had been completely successful. Heckels, loath to accept praise, replied quickly. "It was a great pleasure to look after your wife. I know what she went through and how ill she was and, in spite of our numerous jokes, she was a splendid patient. We have to thank Miss Rawlins, and the nursing she received, for the good recovery she made." Is it possible that Bee had been the butt of male jokes about malingerers? Heckels was as straight an arrow as Rufus, and if so, she must really have given them cause.

But, apart from a diary entry for July 20, when they took Aunt Lily to the Royal Garden party, the only sources for what he was doing in most of the spring and summer of 1933 are his articles in Southam newspapers. On the other hand, everybody knew what Hitler and the Nazis had been up to: by mid-July they had established the Gestapo, banned trade unions, then strikes and lockouts, and finally political parties, one by one, until only the Nazi party remained. Jews were increasingly persecuted and driven from business and professions, labour and concentration camps were opened and the Brownshirts were busy burning books. It was not a happy time for German democrats.

Against this background the Johnston family left for a continental holiday on 20 August. They had gone but thirty miles when — *bang!* — PK ground to a halt at Wrotham. Something was wrong with the drive shaft, repairs took a day and a half, cost Rufus a small fortune and some to-ing and fro-ing to the Lyndhurst Hotel, Folkestone — whither Bee and Derek had repaired. So it was lunchtime on the third day before they reached France but thereafter problems faded away. Two days of trouble-free driving took them to the village of Talloires on Lake Annecy where they spent a week at the lakeshore Hôtel l'Alberge. Rufus relished his 8½ hours of undisturbed sleep on that first night. The next day, they all bathed several times, Rufus walked 5 or 6 miles and Derek took Bee for the short drive to Annecy at the head of the lake. In the evening Derek played ping-pong with Dumins, a French guest, while Rufus and Bee went to the Annecy casino. It had been a gorgeous day. The weather held, and similar days followed — they swam, walked, rowed on the lake, went for drives, and enjoyed losing money at the casino.

One day, however, was much more strenuous. According to Rufus, he and Derek left the hotel at 7:30 am to climb "to the Col between La Tournette and La Fretti (5,000 ft). But owing to losing the way and heat, we stopped short at 4,300 ft and lunched. Home at 3 pm, very exhausted." Derek remembered the day rather differently in his *Personal Memoir*. "We went up a road which, though not paved . . . led to two or three villages on the slopes above Talloires and . . . was not especially steep. We did not attempt a rapid pace and I remember feeling a bit surprised that twice during the hike of some 2½ to 3 hours, my father apologetically called a halt and said he must rest for a while. If I were to take that walk now [he was then 65], I should be even more surprised that a "young man of 46" should have to stop and rest from such a relatively easy pace. We concluded the climb rather earlier than expected and turned back to Talloires. My father adjured me not to say anything about our halts to my mother and this did not strike me as particularly important — at 20 one thinks little of potential health problems."[180]

The oddest thing about this tale is that it seems not to have been a cautionary one for Rufus. At the end of their week at Talloires the family divided: while Derek and Bee drove to Geneva to await his arrival, Rufus set off for three strenuous days of hiking. The first day he really threw caution to the wind and tramped 22 kms in scorching heat, confessing to being "about all in" when he reached the comfortable Hôtel Savoie at Thorens-Glières. After a night disturbed by roosters, he covered a similar distance the following day, although in easy stages and including a short trip on a train. He ended up at Boëge and again slept badly, this time blaming the thin walls between rooms. On the third day, although much of his route was trending downhill towards Lac Léman, he must have walked about the same distance again, for the latter part of which he was nursing "a very blistered left foot." Because of this at Douvaine he paid a mechanic to drive him to Tougues on the lakeshore, where he bathed and slept, presumably in a hotel — he doesn't say. Though exhausted, he was obviously happy, rhapsodizing, "A full moon over the lake, lovely colours at sunset behind the Juras (Nyon) and the distant lights of Geneva and the French Douane." In the morning he took the steamer into Geneva to rejoin Derek and Bee. If he undertook this three-day jaunt to prove to himself there was nothing wrong with him — then he had probably succeeded.

He and Bee stayed two days in Geneva — visiting friends, having a flutter at the casino in Evian, and swimming off the beach. After Rufus had made a short radio broadcast with Burrows — we are not told about what — they picked up Derek from the Kalirs' house, where he and Derrick Parsons had been staying, and left for home. They reached Boulogne in two and a half days, by way of Orleans, Chartres, and central Paris — a distance of 978 kms. They stayed the first night at Auxerre and the second at St-German-en-Laye outside Paris. They visited five cathedrals, taking time to climb the tower at Notre Dame, visit the tombs of the kings at Saint-Denis and linger over the windows at Chartres — "the most marvellously lovely glass we had ever seen." Their only time-economy was eating roadside picnics. When you consider that PK, while behaving much better than in 1932, might have reached 80 kph on the flat and was much slower on hills — once having to be left to cool for half an hour before they could continue — it was remarkable to have travelled so far and done so much in the time. They reached home on 8 September after "an *excellent* holiday."

Back at work, Rufus returned to irregular diary entries — consequently the diary gives little indication of what he was up to. While at Talloires he had heard from Mary that their father had angina and had been ordered to bed for a month. So, as soon as possible he visited him at Bures, finding him not too bad but "by no means well."

That fall they received several invitations to play tennis at the Parsons'. Bee and Rufus had a large tea-party in their garden and they went to see a number of movies and West End plays — amongst which Rufus really enjoyed Somerset Maugham's new play *Sheppey*, just opened at Wyndham's. On 5 October he and Bee met Harry Southam and his wife off the boat train. Harry was Fred's younger brother and a director of Southam Publishing. He was Managing Director of the *Ottawa Citizen*, had visited London nearly every year that Rufus and Bee had been there, and seems to have been Rufus's immediate boss. He had told Rufus in 1932, "I have been so impressed with your cables and mailed stories from Germany — I am tempted each time I read one to cable you my appreciation and thanks. Since you have been our London editor you have never sent us anything more effective or more interesting than the Germany series. If the times were better, personally I should like to have you cover France, Spain and perhaps Italy and Russia, but that will have to wait. At our last meeting of directors in Montreal, everybody was most enthusiastic about our London correspondence."[181]

Rufus met him four or five times before leaving for Germany, including two lunches alone when they would certainly have discussed his plan to land an interview with Hitler. As part of his preparation he and Derek went to hear Wickham Steed speak on "Europe" at Chatham House and were invited to lunch with the great man two days later. Derek remembered only that "he spoke scornfully of Hitler but also apprehensively of his powers for evil and aggression." Although considered an oracle in some quarters, Steed seems not to have convinced Rufus; as they walked away afterwards, he remarked to Derek, "He's an interesting old fellow, but rather an extinct volcano."

For another point of view, Rufus had twice taken Derek to lunch with Vernon Bartlett, a journalist who had just published *Nazi Germany Explained*. As a contemporary review summarized his thesis: "What if Hitlerism is the effect of despair, and if that despair was created by the French and by ourselves through our stupid unwillingness to let bygones be bygones, and our dishonourable refusal to fulfill our written undertakings? That Mr. Vernon Bartlett believes this to be an explanation of Nazi Germany will surprise nobody who listens to his BBC talks." In other words, the divergent views of Bartlett and Steed were useful boundaries for an investigative journalist whose own views lay somewhere in between.

At the same time Robert Keyserlingk visited England and came to lunch at Epsom, after which he and Rufus went for a walk; they had much to discuss as he would be in Berlin in ten days' time. Rufus's last recorded preparation for this trip was to take his father a copy of *Down English Lanes*, hot off the press and dedicated to "the wisest counsellor and most true friend man ever had — *my father*." In his diary he wrote, "Dad seems much better — but was back in bed when I arrived at 6:30." Later he remarked sadly to Bee: "You know, I don't think I'll see the old chap again; he seems so fragile and he looks so old!" A premonition, perhaps, but the old man would live another ten years.

Chapter 19
The Garden of Beasts
Berlin, October – November, 1933

"Let's hope the lights will keep on twinkling — and that the lads in Germany will stop playing soldiers!"

Rufus in "Nach Berlin",
***Ottawa Evening Citizen*, 4 November 1933**

In his years as a journalist, few goals had monopolized Rufus's agenda so completely as this desire to interview Hitler. The seed of the idea had been planted when he discovered that his friend Keyserlingk had interviewed the Nazi leader in 1931. In February 1932, with Keyserlingk helping him, he had waited two weeks, first in Berlin and then in Munich, for an appointment with Hitler — only to be rebuffed without explanation. Since then the stakes had risen greatly: no longer just the leader of one of many opposition parties — albeit the most vocal and violent — Chancellor Hitler had transformed Germany in a few months from an ungovernable debtor nation into an orderly and assertive one. He had also withdrawn Germany from the Disarmament Conference and the League. The resulting uncertainty about his real intentions and press speculation about his rearmament plans — first voiced by Churchill in August — had started alarm bells ringing that no Disarmament Conference could silence. Reasonable people, including Rufus's own father, were beginning to accept the possibility of another war.

For Rufus, who had endured two years of horror in the trenches, had had a brother killed and another wounded, whose father had been prematurely aged by worry, and whose own small family had had to abandon its house in Victoria, BC, sell its belongings and live for years in temporary digs in England, the very idea of accepting the possibility of another war was intolerable. Surely, he insisted to himself, there must be another way. It was no good waiting for the Disarmament Conference to work a miracle; since Germany's withdrawal it had been dead in the water — indeed, had seemed so to him from the beginning. Nevertheless, there *must* be a way to repair the damage done at Versailles — there just had to be! And the only way to find it was to go back to Germany and Europe, look at what the Nazis were doing, ask questions wherever he went and talk to this man Hitler — whose intransigence seemed increasingly likely to make war happen. It became his overarching project — to find the reasonable and the good within Hitlerism, in spite of indications that there was none.

So it is not surprising that when he and Bee travelled to London on Tuesday, 24 October, he was in a gloomy mood. She saw him off from Victoria on the train for the Dover—Ostend ferry and very soon wartime memories had him scribbling away. What he wrote that afternoon became his first dispatch from Frankfurt and was printed by the *Ottawa Citizen* on 4 November under the headline "Nach Berlin . . . 1933!":

> I'm going to Berlin. I ought to be pleased at the prospect – of course I ought! 'How interesting – how lucky you are,' said my suburban train-companions when they saw my grips piled on the rack. But there's something 'queer' about this expedition. I am not as enthusiastic about it as I am usually at the prospect of travel. The atmosphere of Europe oppresses me. For weeks everyone has been talking of the possibilities for war. And I'm going to Germany where the new youth are drilling again; where, apparently, the schoolchildren are being taught that war is glorious and desirable and inevitable; where the women are being told that their most noble destiny is to bear 'warrior sons'!
>
> I hope I shall find things in Germany better than one has been led to expect. For I like Germany and the German people. It is a hateful thought that in quiet Bavarian villages and towns, where one has had happy times, the young men are parading again with dummy rifles, playing at war and being crammed with ideas that can only lead again to the shambles.*
>
> Perhaps the memories evoked by the journey from London to Dover have something to do with my mood. Perhaps this date – October 26[182] – is the cause of depression, for on this day 16 years ago the Canadian Corps attacked Bellevue Spur at the foot of the Passchendaele Ridge – and victory was plucked from the very edge of disaster – as anyone who was there in the C.E.F. will tell you.
>
> We have just passed Westenhanger, a tiny station ten miles from Folkestone. Eighteen years ago with my battalion we detrained there on a wet night in May. We had been cramped up in a train for many hours on the journey from Liverpool. In our 'carriage' there were Caren Martin, our company commander; Arthur Crease, young Dick Day, Rupert Howard and Bob Horton. Howard – most loveable of men – and cheery Bob Horton were killed within a few months, and of the others one at least is crippled for life. The platform of the siding is overgrown with weeds now – that platform where Marcus Pott, the

* Rufus intends the original meaning of 'shambles' — a meat market.

APM, met us and gave us our orders to go to Otterpool Camp. I hope the weeds remain undisturbed. Oh, the misery of that first night at Otterpool — the long soaking-wet grass inside the newly pitched tents. We were all soft then. A few months later perhaps we should have thought Otterpool luxury!

Now the train is rushing through Shorncliffe station. How many of the old Hamilton Machine Gun Battalion are alive to remember that pouring night we entrained for Crowborough? (Our battalion, the 88th, had been broken up for drafts and I had been attached to this M.G. unit.) Mayne was our adjutant, Colonel Stewart our CO — to be killed a few months later at Vimy — and there was Clifton, also killed at Vimy, and Armstrong and Sarginson and a score of other good fellows. How the rain lashed down that night while we waited on this Shorncliffe platform for the troop trains!

And so we come to Dover — to the harbour station where those of us who were lucky used to climb aboard the leave trains going to London and think we were in heaven; to leave again ten days later knowing we were going back to hell!

Now we have pulled out from Dover harbour. The grim old castle crowning the heights is becoming a dim shadowy silhouette in the murky twilight; the white outline of the cliffs is fading and lights are beginning to twinkle in the town. Except for the lights it looks much as it did all those years ago.

Let's hope the lights will keep on twinkling — and that the lads in Germany will stop playing soldiers!

If he was seeking to restore his optimism about Germany, he found no justification in the next twenty-four hours. When the train reached the German frontier at Aachen, an unpleasant surprise awaited: "*Very* thorough search of all baggage," his diary noted, "12:30 am — every paper and book examined and money checked." He reached Frankfurt at 5:40 am feeling tired, having slept little in an overheated sleeper. His hotel there, the Kölner Hof, he told Bee later, "was extremely depressing. I found it was the Headquarters of "The Leader" when he is there and it had an enormous swastika in red lights on the roof. Whether for this reason or mere pilfering, I found a chambermaid in my room after dinner, much flustered and pretending she had lost something, and thereafter found my pocket-books and papers had been thoroughly pawed! That put me off the place and I have no keys to my bags."[183] It had not been a great welcome to Nazi Germany.

There were other reasons why his stopover in Frankfurt was unsatisfactory: *The Times* man there, "was not, I thought, a very good judge of things and only an amateur journalist." Nor could the British consulate be relied upon for advice — as he told Bee, Consul Smallbones[184] and Vice-Consul Butler "take exactly opposite views on everything, so cancel out!"

But by the time he wrote to Bee he had had two encounters that lifted his mood. The first was with "a German student who 'picked us up' in old Frankfurt and showed us most fascinating old houses. That is a story and interested me more than all the rest."

Even more encouraging was a chance encounter on the train to Berlin. "I had a perfectly fascinating time with an elderly doctor — a Stahlhelm.* He must be a very big shot for he told me he had been to England seven times since the war for consultations on heart cases — once with Lord Dawson [the king's doctor]. His conversation was most interesting. One of his sons in the war was in the next bed to a Canadian (prisoner) when both had typhoid — and the old boy's son and the Canadian still write to each other." Rufus strongly empathized with his new acquaintance and was thus willing to reserve judgment on Hitler, of whom this doctor had said, "He is a clean man, a reasonable man. He has given back to Germany her pride and reunited the nation 95% as no other man could have done."

In foreign policy, from the premise that Germany's present disarmament was a humiliation no longer to be borne, he argued for equality and believed Hitler would be hostile to no one and would not pick a fight with France over the Saar or Alsace-Lorraine provided Germany was honourably treated; and although he insisted the Polish corridor must be altered, it was a matter for negotiation between reasonable peoples. "This was an honest, able man," Rufus wrote in his notes. "I was not hoodwinked by a clever propagandist. It was heart to heart." Consequently, his letter continued, "You and Derek must not be surprised if I come home prepared to shout 'Heil Hitler!' My views are certainly being modified, to some extent at least! Well - "I have arrived in Berlin" and tomorrow I shall be on the job. No time now to tell you about Consul-General Smallbones and his very handsome Swedish wife and piano-playing daughter."

It sounded like the old ebullient Rufus. The elderly doctor had offered him the *possibility*, at least, that the horrors reported about the Nazis — the persecution of Jews, the internment and brutal treatment of communists in concentration camps, the militarization of young and old, the absolute censorship of the media, etc. — were expedients justified by the political and economic crisis the Nazis inherited, and would be relaxed once it was over. Rufus was prepared to wait and see.

He penned another article as from Frankfurt, dated October 28 in the *Ottawa Citizen* under the headline "German People Gravely Apprehensive of Future" right across the front page. By then he was in Berlin and the article reflects his new willingness to give the Nazis the benefit of the doubt. He started by describing reactions to their economic measures:

* The Stahlhelm, or Bund der Frontsoldaten, was equivalent to the GWVA of which Rufus had been a member in Vancouver — but the Stalhelm had also acted as an anti-communist paramilitary in the twenties. It supported Hitler.

> In this important financial and industrial centre of the Southern Rhineland, despite ruthless suppression of free speech and a free press, discontent and anxiety are furtively expressed on all sides by bankers and employers no less than by the workers.

But he gave Hitler his due:

> In the minds of the majority there is no doubt of the sincerity of Hitler's desire to solve the appalling economic problems of Germany, but faith in his methods weakens as the months pass without genuine improvement. Employers who are forced to hire more and more unwanted hands and who are not allowed to raise prices or lower wages regard the future with dismay. Workers, whose incomes remain stationary while prices rise and their meagre margin of earnings over expenses is wiped out by continually increasing new taxes and 'voluntary contributions' for innumerable relief measures, are growling ominously.

And he offers a graphic example:

> Last night on a streetcar, for instance, a conductor and passenger exchanged views in my hearing. The passenger had been 26 years employed by the city of Frankfurt. Two years ago his wage was $70 a month at par. Now, he said, reduced by the enormous income tax deducted at the source, a 'voluntary' contribution to the winter relief fund, the church tax, and payments for unwanted Nazi literature, his monthly wage is reduced to $42.50. The streetcar conductor reckoned his wage left for keeping his family was less than $4.50 per week.
>
> Thus far the population have borne the burdens while worked up to an ecstatic fervor of patriotism. They have supported Hitler's amazing expedients for dragging money from the people's pockets and thus reducing the general standard of living in the interests of the state as a whole. The government can boast rightly that beggars have disappeared from the streets, ordinary crime has decreased and the country has been saved from a social upheaval by such expedients as labour camps and huge public works, that the people who might otherwise have created disorders are kept busy marching and parading and labouring, that corruption in public affairs which was rife under former regimes has been checked.
>
> But there are signs that the people are getting fed up with the privations to which they see no end, with giving up every weekend to sport, to marching, parading and listening to interminable Nazi

speeches. Hitler knows well that his real test is coming, not on political ballyhoo lines, but on his ability to put the nation back on productive work.

Rufus moved into the Kaiserhof in Berlin on Friday, 27 October, and would remain there, except for a three-day trip to Danzig and Warsaw, until the morning of 16 November. He told Bee, "This hotel is a totally different kettle of fish, and I shall do good work here. Keyserlinck has arranged a 7 marks a day rate which is very reasonable." However, as in Frankfurt he had unwittingly picked Hitler's favourite hotel, though minus the rooftop swastika. A grand building with a cavernous lobby and arched entrance portico, it had been Hitler's Berlin home until he became chancellor and he still often had lunch or tea there, surrounded by his 'chauffeureska'.* He would enter the dining room informally with his group, whereupon chairs scraped as diners scrambled to their feet to salute the dictator with a loud "Heil Hitler," but when he had sat down, conversation just resumed. It was over tea in the Kaiserhof dining room just before Rufus arrived that Hanfstaengl had introduced Hitler to Martha Dodd,[185] the US ambassador's daughter.

Over the weekend Rufus's Berlin support system fell into place. His first call on Saturday, 28 October, was to Keyserlingk's office and while he was there, Charlie Woodsworth,[186] a young Canadian journalist friend, walked in. He spoke German and offered to come to the Kaiserhof every morning to read him the newspaper headlines — an offer he gladly accepted, although, as he told Bee, "there is practically no news; it is all official 'dope'." The third pole of his support system, Norman Ebbutt of *The Times*, he knew from his 1932 visit.

He saw much of the Keyserlingks that Sunday, 29 October. In the morning he came across Sigrid Keyserlingk, who asked him to lunch, where he also met their six-month-old son — "really a topping kiddie" — and he and Keyserlingk talked politics all afternoon. In the evening he went to see Ebbutt[187] again and, later still, they collected Keyserlingk and the three of them went to Die Taverne, a well-known Italian restaurant with a regulars' *stammtisch* — a large round table — reserved for a group of foreign correspondents, mainly Americans and Brits, who would begin arriving around ten and might linger as late as 4 am.[188] Rufus, one imagines, spent his time listening to their talk of the Nazi reality, of which he had already experienced a sample: while breakfasting on *Unter den Linden* he had seen "much marching of Brown Shirts and girls,"[189] a Nazi Sunday ritual.

That Friday, while he had been en route to Berlin, a *Daily Telegraph* reporter, Noel Panter, had been arrested in Munich and charged with espionage, and then high treason. At issue was his attempt, with the aid of a German citizen, to

* Putzi Hanfstaengl's choice term for the low-brow group (which did in fact include his chauffeur) with whom Hitler liked to move about.

obtain information about military bases near Munich. The British government protested strongly and Panter was eventually released and expelled. Although Rufus had no plans to do anything similar, the incident was a reminder of the nature of the regime and of the thin line to be trodden by those wishing to remain *persona grata*.

It certainly did not help him relax and that night he slept badly — had nightmares in fact. Monday, 30 October, would be his first working day in Berlin and, after Charlie had read him the headlines, he called Hanfstaengl, whom he had last seen at the Brown House. They made an appointment to meet the following day, though, as Rufus ruefully told Bee, "I fear he does not like me much for what I wrote previously." He lunched with Edwards from the British Consul's office and spent the rest of a wet afternoon writing.

Although he had known what to expect, the reality of Nazi Germany, when compared to the friendly, somewhat disorganized country he had known, had taken some getting used to. The aggressive border guards, the possible searching of his room, censored newspapers, constant propaganda, all the uniforms marching in the street, and now the arrest of Panter — it seems to have taken his breath away. It also made him obsessively careful about communications — his letters contained such lines as "one does not know how much it is wise to write down under present conditions" or "this is not the time or place to discuss it!" So, after testing the regular mail for evidence of interference, he was using it for dispatches in preference to the much faster cable service for which he possessed an *ausweiskarte*, or to the telephone, now made ruinously expensive and justifiable only for a scoop or in emergency.

Once again he had a disturbed night, as he told Bee. "I have been sleeping shockingly badly — worrying over work I suppose, and nightmares wake me up in a perfect bath of perspiration. Can't you tell HSS that I must have a month without looking at a newspaper?! I shall get some allonal* this afternoon." His reference to Harry Southam is in jest, and he sounds more annoyed than alarmed by his own frailties. Nevertheless he concluded: "PPS: Do not say anything, of course, to Dad about my feeling groggy."

Tuesday, 31 October, was nevertheless a busy day — as he told Bee "I have half a dozen appointments, one of them with Hanfstaengl," though he made no subsequent mention of what transpired. Putzi Hanfstaengl was no typical Nazi and was more likely to have chuckled than have been angry over his 1932 article. He almost certainly did arrange Rufus's eventual meeting with Hitler, who still considered him a friend. Putzi had been a party member since before 1923, had sheltered the injured Nazi leader in his house after the failed Munich *putsch*, and Helene, his American wife, is said to have persuaded Hitler not to shoot himself when police came to arrest him. Rufus would not be kept waiting to punish him; rather, the delay was a result of Hitler's preoccupation with the 12 November referendum.

---

* A sedative.

Other appointments were with various government officials: Herr Hartman to obtain a seat at the Reichstag Fire Trial, Herr Voigt to arrange a visit to a Labour Camp; and Dr Borner at the Nazi foreign bureau and Dr Winter at the Agriculture Ministry for less obvious reasons. The last named turned out to be a "charming fellow — a civil servant who was at St Paul's [school, in London] and whom you could not possibly distinguish from an Englishman — almost the only such case I know." Intriguingly, his diary also contained a note to self: "Call up Bismarck's introduction," referring to the eldest grandson of the Iron Chancellor — another Prince Otto, a diplomat in the London embassy with whom he had had dealings. Bismarck had given Rufus an introduction to Baron Marschall von Bieberstein, German Consul in Danzig, who, with his wife, would help look after him when he went there.

On Wednesday, 1 November, he had planned to go to Leipzig with Charlie to see Hitler perform at an election rally. However when the day's destination was switched to Weimar, he decided to stay put — Weimar was too far, and he would have an opportunity to see the Fuhrer in action in Berlin in a week's time. Instead, he spent the day in meetings with another list of officials, revisited the foreign office and dined with Edwards.

His meeting with Herr Voigt bore fruit the next day, Thursday, 2 November, when he visited a Labour Camp at Velten,[190] 24 kms northwest of Berlin. Unfortunately his dispatch on this — if one was ever sent — seems not to have been published by Southam. A Labour Camp, of course, was not a strange idea to Canadians, nor the reasons for its existence: the previous year R.B. Bennett's government had opened so-called Relief Camps, run by the military in remote areas of Canada, where the hundred thousand or so single unemployed men, under military discipline, were set to work on infrastructure projects such as the Hope-Princeton highway in BC. Bennett hoped thereby to safeguard public order in the cities while protecting the men from being recruited by the communists. So it was hardly newsworthy for Goebbels to be touting Labour Camps as part of the Nazis' solution to the same problems — provided they were run humanely, they might even seem improvements on their Canadian equivalents.

Rufus returned to Berlin at five but still had arrangements to make — at the Nazi Foreign Office and with Armsrat Puifhé at the Prussian Ministry of the Interior — before dining at Keyserlingk's house, whose birthday it was. Only when he finally returned to the Kaiserhof did he have time to write, and then send, a dispatch concerning the November 12 election and referendum. It is clear he had no illusions about Nazi methods of manipulating voters, which he described in detail. Nevertheless he found himself almost admiring the grand scale of the manipulation and only towards the end did his attitude darken as he pointed out the unmistakable trend towards militarism and war.

The article, with the dateline "Berlin Nov 2," appeared in the *Calgary Herald* and the *Province* under the headline "Foregone Conclusion":

In ten days 30 million Germans will go to the polls in the most amazing 'election' of modern times. Never in history has propaganda been mobilized on such a vast scale or with such crushing efficiency to bend the will of a whole nation to a single political doctrine.

It is a foregone conclusion that for the plebiscite approving Germany's defiant exit from the League of Nations there will be a vast favourable vote and none against.

That is one issue, at least, on which every German thinks alike since the opposition parties have ceased to exist, and the watchful eyes of the storm troopers will check voters in thousands of small electoral districts. There will also be a thumping vote for Nazi Reichstag candidates which the government will take as a vote of confidence and a willingness of the nation blindly to follow their Hitler in whatever further sacrifices he may demand for the sake of the state.

How blind will be this vote may be judged from the fact that so far only a handful of candidates has been announced. Yet, fantastic though the campaign and issues involved may seem to a foreigner, the German people take it desperately seriously. Under the conditions existing there is nothing comparable to election-time excitement in Canada. In a series of mammoth meetings a handful of Nazi leaders are blanketing every corner of the land with their doctrine, the central part of which, at the moment, is the 'persecution' of Germany and her reiterated demand for equality.

Speeches delivered originally to great gatherings from 15,000 to 100,000 people are relayed to as many as 60 packed halls. At meetings there are brass bands galore, marching brown shirts, waving swastika banners and much genuine enthusiasm. Faithful Nazi supporters are asked to stay out of the halls so that room may be found for doubters who may be converted.

Berlin's streets are strung with streamers bearing such legends as "With Hitler against the Madness of World Armaments", "With Hitler for Peace with Honour and Equality", "Hitler's Fight is a Fight for the Real Peace of the World".

Vacant store windows are plastered with diagrams showing Germany defenceless and surrounded by oppressors armed to the teeth with aircraft, bayonets and cannon. Three or four 'War Exhibitions' are drawing crowds in different parts of the city. A 'colonial exhibition' showing lands overseas taken from Germany by the Versailles treaty and products they used to furnish the 'Fatherland' is a feature of another main thoroughfare.

Every bookstore window is filled with literature glorifying the martial deeds of Germany on historic battlefields, extolling the virtues of the German race, and with the lives of former dictators, Cromwell, Julius Caesar, Mussolini and Frederick the Great.

> Accompanying all this, every weekend sees tens of thousands of men, boys and girls marching to martial airs behind bands and banners, lustily singing patriotic songs, some of which sound crudely brutal to foreigners.
>
> Out in the woods and fields is endless drilling and manoeuvres – and if you care to you can buy in the stores a nice looking storm trooper's knife with the legend 'Blood and Honour' inscribed thereon, or a full-size dummy hand grenade of the type the German soldiers carry attached to their belts.
>
> But the Germans, in a stereotyped answer to every comment on these apparent militaristic tendencies, stoutly reiterate that all idea of war is abhorrent to them and would be national suicide for Germany. It is their leader's way of bringing back to proper discipline and unity a nation which, until nine months ago, was in danger of splitting violently asunder.
>
> One may believe in the sincerity of these utterances. One may feel strongly it is intolerable for Germany to remain defenceless in the midst of neighbours armed to the teeth – but no unbiased observer can be blind to the menace in the future of the whole youth of the nation of 70 millions being trained on such lines.
>
> Meanwhile Germany, in defiant mood, is utterly indifferent to foreign opinion. She has set her course and, while professing readiness for peace and understanding, seeks the sympathy of none.

The next day was Friday, 3 November. "I cannot write more than a line," he told Bee in a letter before going to bed. "I am dead beat at 12:30 after an exhausting day." He had spent twelve hours travelling to Lichtenberg and back by car, touring the concentration camp there and stopping for lunch and tea, a round trip of 350 kms. "It was a rather trying journey," he told Bee, "but an interesting experience with plenty of good copy in it." There had been eight of them, a mixed bunch: a German General, a Swedish journalist, a German YMCA missionary, a young Norwegian on a European tour, a German preacher from Brazil, a man from the Red Cross, councillor Puifhé from the ministry — and himself. Although tired, he had written an article on the day's events in the UPI office after dinner. It appeared in the *Ottawa Evening Citizen* on 6 November under the dramatic headline "Lukin Johnston rejects German censorship":

> Before visiting the concentration camp at Lichtenburg, near Leipzig, where sixteen hundred 'politically dangerous' persons are confined, it was suggested to me whatever I wrote must be submitted to the authorities for the correction of any 'misunderstandings'. I could only refuse the suggestion point-blank. No more was said on the subject and I duly visited Lichtenburg castle.

Nothing in the Nazi regime has been the subject of more criticism abroad than the administration of these camps, and foreign newspapermen frequently have been accused of untrue or misleading reports. Being fully warned, such visitors as myself are shown only the best side of such places and can only report that. If small evidence was observable of brutality there was ample evidence of discipline of the harshest kind in regulating these people whom one is repeatedly told are not regarded as 'criminals'. Indeed, it is understood arrangements are to be made for them to vote in the forthcoming election which one can only regard as one more fantastic feature of the amazing campaign.

Among other prisoners with whom I talked was Herr Ebert, son of the first president of the German republic, formerly a leading Social Democratic member of the Reichstag whose only offences appear to be his father's career and his own of differing from the Nazi party. Great indignation was aroused recently in the British press because it was reported he had been brutally treated at another camp, beaten unconscious and forced to declare before prisoners and guards 'My father was a traitor.' This, it was stated, occurred in September.

Ebert was asked as to the truth of this report by a member of my party and replied he had been ordered to make this statement by a storm trooper and had refused, following which the storm trooper, he said, had been disciplined. When asked why he was imprisoned he replied in the stereotyped phrase, 'because I was considered a danger to the state.' While it is true Ebert now appeared in good health and showed no signs of ill treatment, it is strange that this was the first occasion any journalist was allowed to see him since the reported outrage.

One incident which savoured to Anglo-Saxon eyes of barbarous bullying of the kind alleged above was when a miserable undersized prisoner was forced to state before the assembled party and a score of his fellows ranged along the dingy passageway, 'I was a murderer. I stabbed a Nazi leader in the back.' The commandant immediately behind him thundered, 'say it again louder!' and the wretched individual complied, the performance being repeated a third time. It was stated he had been sentenced to only four months imprisonment for the crime by the former German authorities, but on the other hand it is certain many Nazis are given the lightest sentences for similar crimes.

For the rest the prisoners' health seemed good, the administration highly efficient, but one thinks Hitler will get few genuine votes from such camps as this.

The next day was Saturday, 4 November, and, in spite of it being a weekend, a frantically busy one for Rufus. His diary began with a to-do list: "To Polish embassy re visa, to bank, to [Thomas] Cook's, to see Colonel Thelwall, British Commercial Attaché (Noon), to Reichstag Fire trial."

He had chosen to attend the only session in the whole tedious trial when drama was guaranteed — Hermann Göring, the star witness, was due at 9:15 to give his evidence and everybody had wanted tickets. So it was lucky for Rufus that Göring was predictably late — an hour and a quarter late, in fact, while he was still scurrying around organizing his trip to Danzig and Warsaw. Even so, once on the stand the big man spoke for nearly three hours and must have been in full flow when Rufus — having had his papers and pockets checked by armed police ringing the building — eventually took his place among the 81 foreign correspondents cramming the press gallery. In spite of himself, he was impressed: "This morning I heard Göring give part of his evidence in the Reichstag trial. He is a handsome man — and a spellbinder second to few. A very impressive scene with the judges all in crimson robes and funny crimson velvet berets."

Unfortunately, he was too busy to spend the rest of the day in the courtroom. Had he done so, he would have witnessed his 'spellbinder' being tauntingly cross-examined by one of the defendants. "Göring, unaccustomed to challenge from anyone he deemed an inferior, grew angrier by the moment," causing him to shout at his tormentor: "You will be afraid when I catch you. You wait till I get you out of the power of the court, you crook!"[191] Which would have answered the questions that had been so bothering fair-minded people like Rufus — about the regime's integrity and believability.

That evening, after dining with Reed,[192] Ebbutt's number two, and writing to Bee, he caught the midnight train to Danzig, where he arrived at 7:30 am on Sunday, 5 November. After a sleepless night, Rufus was descending wearily onto the platform with his 'grip' when the cries of newspaper carriers caused him to prick up his ears. It seemed that the Nazi vice-president of the Danzig[193] senate had ordered the firing of all non-Nazi Danzig policemen and the arrest of non-Nazi newspaper editors. Danzig had been a Free City under League protection since 1920 and this order defied the League and ratcheted up international tension. It was hold-on-to-your-seats stuff that he'd walked into and during the day it became more tense when a protest to League High Commissioner Rosting, and to President Rauching of the Free City senate, was met with Rauching's contemptuous retort: "Who is governing this city, the League or I?"

There is nothing like a potential scoop for concentrating a journalist's attention. Wartime staff habits kicked in and Rufus was suddenly wide awake. In fact he would function well all day and even confessed to having thoroughly enjoyed himself. In spite of the early hour on a Sunday, he immediately phoned Keyserlink's cousin Countess Paula Keyserlingk, who was most welcoming and invited him to lunch. Then he phoned Barton, *The Times*' man in Danzig, who kindly offered to be his guide and opener of doors for the day. They arranged to meet right away and together set up interviews for the afternoon. Then Barton drove him the 25 kms to Gdynia to see the port Poland had built since the war to avoid being held hostage by the German dockers of Danzig, now Gdansk.

When Barton and he arrived for lunch, "the Count and Countess Keyserlingk proved really charming — young and good English speakers. They had asked Rosting and his Swedish wife also to lunch and all spoke English." As Rosting was a player in the day's events, lunchtime conversation — no doubt totally concerned with breaking news — must have been fairly tense, but at least Rufus, who was still pursuing a scoop, understood what was being said.[194]

After lunch he and Barton spent an hour and a half with the Polish Commissioner to Danzig before going to tea with Baron Marschall von Bieberstein and his wife — Bismarck's friend, von Bieberstein, was the German Consul, a Rhodes scholar, and an apologist for the Nazis. Rufus told Bee, "To dinner, I had the local secretary of state, Dr Blume, who talked history and politics for three solid hours — very interesting too. I think I now know something about Danzig and the Corridor!"

However, he had been so busy and communications so difficult that he had let the scoop slip through his fingers. As he explained to Bee, "it being Sunday, there being no possible way of reaching Cummings by night when [international] phone costs are lower, I had only the satisfaction of giving it away to Barton — wrote it for him and also phoned it to Berlin — by Monday every paper had it in any case." After all, Barton "had been very kind, if very slow," and giving him the story seemed a fair exchange. Barton would perform one more service by driving him to catch the midnight train for Warsaw. It had been more than a busy day and he was *tired!*

After a second consecutive night on a train, he arrived in Warsaw at eight on Monday morning, 6 November. "Near dead-beat now!" he told his diary, as he surely must have been. So it was a good thing that his day was a little more relaxed. He told Bee, "I spent the morning in the company of the local Lizzie Montizambert,[195] — actually Fraulein Czarnowsky of *The Times* — who insisted (very kindly) on taking me to see all Warsaw and took me all over the old town and to see the Royal Palace and the Belvedere — in a taxi for which I paid, of course! Very lovely and interesting. Warsaw is a huge city of 1.2 million — fine parks and a marvellous history of which I know almost nothing. The streets are stiff with soldiers and every school-child has to learn how to put on his gas-mask! To lunch I had Jerzy Szapiro, a friend of Vernon Bartlett. From 4:00 to 5:00 I spent with James Savery, the British Consul. Now I've had supper and am off to catch the 7:25 for Berlin — dead-beat but with a lot of good copy. Tonight will be my third consecutive night in the train and I have not had two consecutive hours' sleep in that time! However, I am OK, if tired." And after two days spent amongst them, he had this to say about the Poles and the challenges with which the Treaty of Versailles had landed them: "my humble opinion is that there is no solution aside from war, which every Pole looks forward to quite calmly."[196]

He arrived back in Berlin at 8 am on Tuesday, 7 November, and returned to the Kaiserhof. After working all morning, by 12:30 he was ready to send a dispatch to Cummings in London, which for once he did by phone. As he later told Bee, "the cost is simply ruinous and it can't be done again — which severely limits one's opportunities for sending cable matters." In fact the call had cost him 71 marks — the equivalent of ten nights at one of the city's most prestigious hotels! There were no credit cards; he was expected to pay cash while overseas, probably from his own account, and claim expenses once back in England. Exorbitant international phone charges were just another method Dr Goebbels employed to isolate Germans from foreign opinions.

The 500-word dispatch, datelined "Berlin Nov 7", appeared in the *Winnipeg Tribune* under the headline "Poland and Czechoslovakia Expect and Prepare for Warfare with Germany". After paragraphs explaining recent events in Danzig, he continued:

> In Warsaw there is no response to Hitler's repeated protestations of a desire for peace. They fall on deaf ears. Poland calmly expects, and is prepared for, war. Nothing which German leaders can say in the present circumstances will change the Polish belief that Germany intends to choose her own time to recover, whether by force or subtle diplomacy, what she lost by the Treaty of Versailles.
>
> Poland's great army is at the highest point of efficiency and she will endeavour to maintain its standard against 'the day' – be it soon or late. Just as in Berlin, Warsaw school children and citizens are taught protective measures against bomb attacks and shop keepers are learning measures to minimize dangers of shattering glass. All citizens are familiar with the use of gas masks and in fact a state of preparedness exists in all departments.
>
> In Czechoslovakia defence against any possible German action is just as thorough and there is the added consciousness of danger in the present German regime, by reason of the 10,000 refugees who have poured across the frontier. Neither of these countries will yield one soldier or one gun in response to any specific appeal of the German nation, whose preached doctrines are contradicted by every other evidence observable.

After more reference to the Nazi coup in Danzig he went on:

> Action of this sort by Nazi hotheads, flushed with the anticipated triumph of next Sunday's vote, may easily lead to stirring up trouble, with disastrous consequences. The German people are kept in ignorance of foreign opinion, and therefore are deluded into thinking they are impressing the world with their unanimity, are meanwhile promised a grand finale, on an unexampled scale, to the referendum campaign calculated to arouse enthusiasm to the highest pitch.

> All Germany will be silent one minute Friday next at one o'clock as a prelude to a nation-wide broadcast by Hitler. Dr Goebbels, Hitler's propaganda minister, has ordered that for this moment all movement must cease throughout Germany. Sirens of the factories will give the signal for work to cease. All traffic will stop and even school children will be silent. At the end of an hour's speech the *Horst Wessel* song will be sung.

In the evening he went with Keyserlingk to what, in his letter to Bee, he called "a big political meeting in the Sportsplatz." One wonders why he did not tell her he had witnessed Dr Goebbels himself whipping up the support of Berliners for the referendum on the 12th. It was, as he told her, "a rather amazing show — with scores of banners, hundreds of brown shirts, bands and bally-hoo!" Apparently, like Göring, Dr Goebbels did not yet seem to him a sinister figure.

Rufus with his father at Epsom, England, 1931

Panorama of the Vancouver skyline, taken by Derek from the Georgia Hotel during the family's 1930 BC holiday — the Marine Building was still king

Bee with friends, cruising on Vancouver's English Bay in September 1930 aboard the Harbours Board yacht *Fispa* — from left: Mrs Renison, Mrs Shallcross, Mrs A. Johnstone, Robert Norman, Bee, host T.V. Scudamore

PK bcing loaded aboard ship at Dover, England, August 1932, at the start of their 6-week working holiday in Central Europe

Fokker FX 1 aircraft in which Rufus flew from Budapest to Vienna, 1932

PK broken down at Ludwigshafen, Germany, 1932

The Pichler family helped out when PK broke down at Armsdorf, Austria, 1932 — from left: Maria & Drecl Pichler, their father, Bee, Uncle Clement, his daughter, Derek

Dr Vanling, Rufus's local guide, with children living in squalor, near Budapest, 1932

RMS *Prague,* the ship he disappeared from (postcard)

Rufus tramping in Switzerland, September, 1933

Hitlerites having lunch near Baden Baden, Germany, August 1932;
Nazi Brownshirts were temporarily banned from displaying Nazi insignia

Left to right, Putzi, Hitler and the 'chauffeureska'
(commonly available on internet sites)

Chapter 20
Talking to a Tyrant
Berlin, 8–17 November, 1933

"You're damned lucky to get out."

Herman Göring to Rufus,
at the door of Hitler's office

Wednesday, 8 November was a frustrating day. As Rufus confessed to Bee, "All day I sat at a typewriter in my little room. Not successful yet — but I have hopes still. It is the beginning that is so hard." With all that good copy, he was temporarily unable to begin the articles he had in his head. Tense and unable to relax, Rufus, that most prolific of wordsmiths, was suffering from writer's block! He took two breaks: in the first he walked round to *The Times* office to see Ebbutt and Reed, perhaps hoping for inspiration, then to the UPI office to see Keyserlingk; in the second break he went to the foreign press reception at the Deutsche Club. Later, he had supper with Keyserlingk at his flat and they were joined by Paul Scheffer of *Berliner Tageblatt* whom he had met with Wickham Steed, plus another German journalist, "and there was much talk."

Thursday the 9th was another day of hoping for a call from Hitler's office. He had decided to wait until the weekend. "I expect to leave for home on Sunday night, possibly Monday," he told Bee in a letter, "but please do not let the office know for I want a quiet day with you before I go back. Also I want to have half a dozen more articles ready for Miss Knowles — as it has been physically (and mentally!) impossible to do more than two or three so far." That afternoon the weather was pleasant and he and Charlie walked and shopped. "Tonight," he wrote, "I go to dinner with a charming German named Winter," about whom he had told her before. Dinner was at the Winters' house near Potsdam and the company included his secretary and Keyserlingk as well as Frau Winter and their son and daughter who spoke no English. With both Winter and Keyserlingk able to translate, it was an amusing evening and the conversation "frank and interesting."

On Friday the 10th he made no diary entry, nor did he write to Bee. But he did go to Hitler's final election rally, held in Berlin. Cured of his earlier funk, he dispatched an article the same day. It appeared in the *Calgary Herald*, among other Southam papers, with the dateline "Berlin Nov 10" and the headline "Hitler Closes Whirlwind Reichstag Vote Campaign Defying Foreign Powers".

> All Germany must have heard through the nation-wide radio hook-up a thunderous shout of '*Heil*' from 5,000 workers in Siemens' great factory on the outskirts of Berlin today, when in a whirlwind finish to Sunday's referendum vote Chancellor Hitler made his final appeal to the nation for a united front.
>
> Never in German history has an event of this kind been staged on such a grandiose scale. Just before Hitler spoke, a silence of one minute throughout Germany was proclaimed by the shrieking of sirens. In factories in which he spoke, every wheel in the country stopped to indicate the nation's undivided support of Hitler. As a preliminary there was a brief commentary by Dr Goebbels, minister of propaganda, and then to heighten the desired effect of the union between Hitler's government and the common workers, sounds of machinery were broadcast.
>
> Time and again cheers broke out during his three quarters of an hour speech. Workers, both men and women, were perched on every point of vantage on huge pieces of machinery or scaffolding. Cheers were particularly vociferous every time Hitler hurled bitter taunts at foreign nations.
>
> "They have persecuted and tried to keep the German nation down," he thundered. At the same time he reiterated Germany was ready at any time to return to Geneva or join other international councils provided always they went back on terms of equality. For five miles the chancellor drove from his palace through the streets lined with thousands of citizens and gay with bunting. Many school children were on parade with thousands of brown shirts, storm troops and steel helmets lining the route.
>
> The approach to the factory was heralded by a growing roar of cheers, and finally when he appeared, bareheaded, wearing a light raincoat with his big guard of black-coated storm troops, he was met by shouts of '*Heil, Heil!*' that could not be quieted for several minutes.
>
> Throwing off his raincoat he then mounted the tribune, disclosing his plain black coat, black tie, brown shirt and breeches and high field boots. The same wild scenes of enthusiasm were repeated at the end when he had to push his way out of the factory.
>
> Hitler hurled defiance at foreign nations in the pre-election campaign speech. The German populace gathered throughout the

nation to hear their leader, through loudspeakers erected at vantage points everywhere, before they go to the polls Sunday to elect a straight Nazi ticket.

After the chancellor had spoken 12 minutes to the entire nation today, the radio hook-up which carried his voice to every part of the Reich, suddenly ceased to function. The radios resumed, however, after 4 minutes.

"If anyone has the right to address you, my workers," Hitler declared in beginning his address, "it is I, for I came through your ranks and always considered myself one of you. Through industry and study, yes, through hunger, I worked myself up," he continued, speaking directly to a great throng of labourers. "In this historical hour, I address you . . ."

Hitler then resumed his strictures of the Versailles treaty, saying it tried to perpetuate the victors and the vanquished, and rested on the wrong assumption – one nation's ill fate is another's gain. "We will not have Germany ruined for the sake of the existence of some organization or other – the workers' solidarity is a sham because the international clique is setting one people against another. I was inspired to undertake my fight for Germany's liberation because I had boundless faith in the quality of the German people. My program combined Nationalism with Socialism, because such a combination alone could save Germany."

Amid thunderous applause, he continued, "it was not the intellectuals upon whom I depended, but upon the two classes I knew best – the workers and the farmers. I am not so crazy as to want war. I know war. Many other statesmen do not. Germany's calumniators never saw a bullet."

Derisive boos from the hearers answered the speaker when he said: "you are represented abroad as bloodthirsty beasts." Hitler reiterated his desire to stretch out the nation's hands to all former enemies, and said Germany's security alone is endangered, not that of others.

Saturday, 11 November, seems to have been a hold-your-breath sort of day — while Rufus was waiting for a last-minute call from the chancellery, the country was keyed up for the following day's referendum and election. Whether he heard from the chancellery, he did not say, but he went to the British Embassy to see Birne, the press officer, and when he asked to stay over until the following week in case Hitler still might like to see him, Birne asked him to call Hitler's private secretary on Monday morning.

THE BIG ELECTION DAY, Sunday 12 November, finally arrived. In his diary Rufus wrote: "Met the journalistic crowd at Ebbutt's flat at 11 am and made a tour by car of the districts — Wedding, etc. I in Reed's car with Brenda [Reed] and a Miss Clyman — Canadian — and definitely BAD."[197]

As for the great event of the day, in the following article, written on Sunday and dispatched on Monday, he captured the pride and the fear, the exultation and the chagrin, the excitement and the despair, experienced by different groups of Germans in the divided city. With the dateline "Berlin Nov 13", the *Ottawa Evening Citizen* ran it under the bland headline "Election Day in Berlin".

> There was less excitement in this city yesterday – the great day when the poll was taken on issues which may have worldwide repercussions – than I have seen many a time in small Canadian towns over the election of a mayor and council. Berlin has known no election like it since the war. There were no broken heads; no communists bands clashing with Nazis; no party headquarters wrecked; no soldiers armed to the teeth, complete with stink bombs, as in the old days before the Nazis came to power.
>
> There was plenty of noise, of course, for in any case Sunday is the big day in Germany when tens of thousands of men and maidens don their uniforms and go marching, marching, marching interminably behind their bands and banners. Fat middle-aged citizens who during the week are normal sober businessmen, deck themselves out in heroic attire every Sunday at the orders of their storm-troop leader and join the marching armies.
>
> But perhaps on this particular Sunday there was more marching and more bands than usual. There were innumerable columns of schoolchildren parading through the streets singing lustily their songs; there were the Nazi 'speaking choirs' rushing about in lorries; there were processions of cars bearing huge signs with the one words 'Ja!' atop them – a rather superfluous indication to the voter as to the way he should vote. Then there were processions of soldiers crippled in the war, and ambulances and stretchers were provided for invalids who could not otherwise reach the polling places.
>
> Over it all there seemed to be a noticeable spirit of comradeship which has been one of the chief aims of the highly efficient propaganda that has been flooding all Germany for weeks. The German people have had it hammered into them that all the world was watching this demonstration of national unity. Every German man or woman, whatever their domestic differences, must stand shoulder to shoulder, they were told, to show the foreigners that the German nation had found its soul again. That was the basis of all the election propaganda – and it worked.
>
> For the rest, it was an extremely orderly day in Berlin. Long queues were lined up before the cafés where polling took place before the doors opened, showing the enthusiasm of the people to do their

duty. Driving about the city, visiting polling booths in districts that were once centres of Communist activity and others in better-class districts, one saw no incident of disorder – and I marvelled as I compared this air of peace with what I had witnessed in Berlin little more than a year ago. At that time there were daily street shootings and murders; innocent citizens were constantly involved in fracas and it was unsafe to walk in some districts of the city. Whatever their shortcomings in other directions, the Nazis are entitled to high marks for transforming Berlin into one of the most peaceable cities in Europe.

For me the interest of the day began when, shortly before 9 o'clock in the morning, I came upon a small crowd gathering outside a small café on Jager Strasse not far from the president's palace. I learned that President von Hindenburg was to cast his vote there at 9 o'clock. Before the old marshal's arrival the crowd had grown to considerable proportions; press photographers were lined up and police had difficulty in keeping back the people.

Great shouts of "Heil, Heil!" greeted the old warrior-president when he stepped from his car. For two years I had not seen him and had thought to find him failing with old age. Instead he walked as erect as ever, leaning slightly on his heavy cane, and doffed his Derby hat to the crowd, who cheered. To meet him at the door of the café were an aged countryman and his wife – the man dressed in the blue smock of a farmer – and the old president stopped and chatted with them before he went inside.

Later I visited a polling booth in the Wedding district – the poorest working-class district in Berlin and, until the present government came into a power, a hot-bed of Communism. To this café I had come with a friend just 18 months ago to learn about the activities of communists. At that time Kosliner Strasse, most notorious of 'Red' districts, had been been a sea of 'Red' and republican flags. The café itself had been frequented by Communists, with a number of whom we talked. But the 'Red' flags have all vanished today. Kosliner Strasse – except for a few intransigent houses – was a mass of bunting, but the swastika flag and the old national red, black and white had replaced the revolutionary flags of 18 months ago. The proprietor was reaping a rich harvest selling beer to thirsty voters and the room once used for revolutionary meetings now did duty as a polling booth.

If you ask whether the proprietor and his customers are genuine converts to National Socialism, one can only say that they gave the Hitler sign of greeting with the best of 'em and, if they retained awkward communist convictions, they managed to conceal them successfully. The Nazis claim that probably two thirds of the 14 million who voted Socialist and Communist one year ago have been converted to their way of thinking. But the fact is that in Germany

> today any demonstration of independent political thought is apt to find its reward in the concentration camp or, at least, may cost the demonstrator his job. So the wise Communist keeps a still tongue in his head, hangs out a nice big swastika and votes 'ja' when Hitler tells him to!
>
> The polling booths were conducted with every evidence of scrupulous secrecy. At the door of the polling room was stationed the inevitable man or woman with the collecting box for the 'Winter Relief.' In exchange for 5 pfennigs dropped in the box the voter was given a tin badge having on it the one word "Ja" Thereafter the voter passed on to enter the booth itself and to mark his ballot "ja" or "nein" as he chose. His badge marked '*Ja!*' became more precious to him than gold – as I discovered when, unthinkingly, I offered to buy one from a man who confessed to me he was still a communist at heart. The badge, he said, was his only protection on a day when streamers in the street branded everyone a traitor who did not vote.
>
> In Kosliner Strasse, where 'the barricades were up' in 1929, one saw the only evidence of still-existing independence, or hostility to the Nazi government, in the green posters torn down and trampled in the mud. But for the most part Germany went to vote as though the task was a sacred one in which pilgrimage and crusade were blended. In their millions they voted "ja" in support of the government's withdrawal from the Disarmament Conference and the League. As for the Reichstag vote, through which the Hitler regime has been given a blank check for the next four years, no-one will ever know how many voted "ja" from sheer indifference although, had political freedom existed in Germany, they would have voted "nein."

Sounding rather middle-aged, that evening, as he told Bee, "I took the Keyserlingks out for their promised 'bust' by way of return for very much help and kindness. We had dinner at the Winter Garden where we could watch the acts from our table. Later we went to the Haus Vaterland — a queer and extremely interesting place where you get beer or coffee and can sit and look at a lighted view of Vienna in one section, at Constantinople in another; at Egypt in another and then go and hear a genuine Bavarian band blaring away in another. It was good fun but I thought they would never get tired and go home. We did not leave Vaterland until 1 o'clock!"

By Monday, 13 November, Rufus had been waiting for an interview with Hitler for sixteen days, including his Polish side-trip. Because he had not really considered how much Hitler might have been focused on his referendum, or had perhaps not been seeing any foreigners, journalists included, during this time, he was feeling thoroughly grumpy.

Consequently, when he called Dr Hans Thomsen at the chancellery at ten that morning, he was not delighted to be asked to call again at five — as if his request was 'new business' to be added to the chancellery agenda. Nor did he lighten up when young Thomsen talked to him politely and straightforwardly with none of the "Heil Hitler" claptrap that so impaired the ability of outsiders to communicate with most party members.

Thus, when he called back at five as requested, he felt indignant when Thomsen still had no answer for him, asked him to call again at noon on Tuesday and then wanted to know whether, if necessary, he could wait until the end of the week! He was so indignant, in fact, that he did something not normally recommended when dealing with dictators — he delivered an ultimatum! "No," he told Thomsen firmly — he had already waited sixteen days and, unless Hitler could see him on Tuesday or Wednesday, he had to leave!

Had he been dealing with another party functionary, that would probably have been that — and he would have gone home disappointed. But Thomsen was unlike other Nazi functionaries; diplomats liked him because he talked normally with them — in non-ideological language — and could be trusted to tell Hitler what they wanted him to hear. US ambassador Bill Dodd encouraged Thomsen, who spoke English and was comfortable with North Americans, to visit him often; they would have frank and quite 'undiplomatic' conversations and both Dodd and his daughter Martha referred to him as 'Tommy'. In Rufus's case, it is likely that 'Tommy' had already decided to persuade Hitler that talking to this persistent Canadian would be a good idea. His problem, like that of anybody who serves the powerful, was that of finding an opportunity — and it might take him a while.

If Thomsen had hoped to seem encouraging, Rufus interpreted their conversation as an attempt to keep him happy. After the second phone call he grumbled to Charlie Woodsworth that the Nazis were wasting his time. In his diary he wrote: "So Charlie went on ahead to Hanover — I fed up." In his letter to Bee that evening he fumed, "It is maddening to be kept hanging on — just as it was in Munich two years ago. If at noon tomorrow I am told that nothing can be done until Friday or Saturday, I shall take the 1 pm train and be in London Wednesday morning as already arranged. Otherwise I may have to stay a day or two longer."

However, when Rufus called on Tuesday, 14 November, Thomsen asked him to come and see him. He had good news: his interview with the Fuhrer was arranged for 6 pm the following day! The dictator had met his deadline! For Rufus it was wonderful news — the culmination of seventeen days of exhausting work. And it was after Thomsen had given him a quick primer on conversations with his boss that Rufus realized, suddenly, that the man was actually rooting for him and they parted with a handshake.

He went to see Keyserlingk with the news. As the latter remembered, "we had had lunch together and, both feeling rather overworked and the lack of fresh air and exercise, I suggested going out of town for the afternoon and taking a stiff two hour run [meaning 'walk'] through the Grunewald. He thought it would do him a lot of good too and so we had a very refreshing run till after dark."

It was probably the best thing Rufus could have done and he felt all the better for it. In the evening he scribbled a quick note to Bee. "This must get off in a hurry if it is to catch the night air mail. I am to see the Chancellor at 6 pm tomorrow and shall leave here 1 pm Thursday — home by about 10 am Friday [17 November], I hope. I hope the interview will be a success. He has never before talked to a Dominion newspaperman and it is the first thing of the kind, of course, since the election." The last sentence, one imagines, was something Thomsen had impressed upon him.

That night he slept better, he told Keyserlingk, and the headaches that had been bothering him had gone. He spent Wednesday morning, 15 November, preparing carefully for his interview. At some point during the afternoon he went to Keyserlingk's office and in his words, "we still discussed his interview before he went to see Hitler." When it was time, Rufus walked over to the Kanzlei, where, after a short wait, either Thomsen or Hanfstaengl showed him in to Hitler's office.

> . . . a room panelled in mahogany without pictures, without ornamentation. As I entered, he rose from his desk and came forward, clicking his heels together as the introduction was made and we shook hands. He wore a light fawn tunic of military pattern, black trousers, with an Iron Cross on the left breast and under his left arm a band bearing the swastika sign. More than half an hour our conversation lasted, during which the chancellor submitted to a barrage of questions. The conversation ranged over many topics, the international situation, reminiscences of many occasions when he came face to face with Canadians across barbed wire in No-man's Land, and took in the question of the alleged militaristic training given the youth of Germany as well as the matter of the concentration camps. There was a complete absence of formality about our meeting; as we talked we sat in arm chairs on either side of a small table.

As Rufus's German was poor and Hitler spoke no English, there was also an interpreter. In spite of Hitler several times becoming characteristically 'animated', their long conversation was polite and at times cordial. Rufus's article based upon it appeared 17 November in the Vancouver *Daily Province*, as in other Southam papers, under the headline "Germany Ready To Reduce Arms, Claims Hitler".

> "Germany stands ready to consider favourably any invitation from the other great powers to recommence negotiations for disarmament or limitation of armaments. She does not care whether the negotiations take place within or without the framework of the League of Nations. Her only condition is that she will enter only on terms of absolute equality. She awaits the call to Geneva or elsewhere. She believes

the time has come when there is a general feeling that some new instrument should take the place of the Versailles Treaty."

Such were the unequivocal statements made to your correspondent by Chancellor Hitler in an exclusive interview here. This is the first statement of Germany's future policy since Sunday's monster referendum constituted Hitler the absolute ruler of Germany. Incidentally, it is the first interview he has ever granted to a Canadian newspaperman.

Answering my questions, Hitler stated that last Sunday's great vote did not alter by one iota Germany's claims regarding disarmament. "Our position is just as it was before," he declared. "We demand absolute equality in the negotiations that we undertake with other powers – no more, no less. Given these conditions we are prepared to resume negotiations at any time." When I asked whether he considered it was up to Germany to make the next move, or to other powers, he replied: "It is difficult to answer at this moment. But my opinion is that the initiative should come from those states which have not disarmed. Germany after all cannot disarm because she has disarmed already."

My next question was whether, in view of last Sunday's vote and recent developments, some other instrument might not be devised to replace the Versailles Treaty. "The Versailles Treaty," he said, "is the only existing document which gives a legal basis to the present state of affairs. In itself it provides for revision and there is growing a general opinion that as a treaty it has been a danger to both victors and vanquished alike, and that it ought to be replaced by something better."

At this point, when I had interpolated that Canada was vitally interested in European affairs, I asked the chancellor if he had ever met any Canadians during the war. He at once forgot he was the chancellor of Germany and became a war veteran, talking reminiscently. He smiled and gesticulated as he reeled off dates and places where he had been opposite Canadians. In fact he said: "You bet I met Canadians during the war – at Armentières in 1915, Bapaume on the Somme in 1916 and in France later." To my suggestion that he should know Canadians as a virile people, he laughed and thoroughly agreed. These reminiscences brought a flood of words to his lips.

"As a Canadian who was in France and Flanders you ought easily to understand," he said, "the attitude of Germany after the revolution. The soldiers who actually faced each other across No-man's Land must surely have a clearer view of each other than the politicians who never fought. From what I know of Canadians and the British as soldiers I cannot imagine that if they had been defeated in the war they would have submitted tamely to the treatment handed out to Germany."

I told the chancellor that Canadian opinion was much exercised by statements that children and storm troops were given military training which went far beyond what could reasonably be considered as defensive training; also that a grave danger to world peace was seen in the new doctrine of racial supremacy being taught in Germany. It was considered retrograde and even savage by other nations. With much vehemence of gesture he declared that the training he was trying to give young Germany was not militaristic or aggressive but merely educative. It took the form of strict discipline.

"When in opposition," he said, "I had to work with a great mass of men and fight communism in the most violent form. Do you think I could have done that with a crowd of street preachers?" Striking the table with his fist, he said: "Now with the success of the revolution I want to keep up that spirit of discipline but I insist again that it is not militaristic. You can not have a huge following without some form of organization, and that organization naturally takes on a military appearance.'

He declared utterly untrue the statements made recently that the storm troops have been told secretly that the leaders of the nation were making pacifist speeches for foreign consumption and that they were to be disregarded.

"I should like to have before me the man who made that statement," he said. "It should be clear that if we have succeeded in uniting forty million people on a platform of peace and equality, it would be impossible to give out secret instructions to the contrary." Again he flatly denied the assertion that army magazines have been instructed to suppress anything promoting peace. No such instructions were issued, he declared.

My next question was, in view of the known desire of Germany to have colonies, which overseas possessions he might wish to have returned. He replied that certainly Germany would be happy to regain the possibility of colonial activity because it would help world trade. Germany would gladly cooperate in exploiting undeveloped territories. All industrialized nations were more or less congested and must seek new outlets.

In reply to a question on the religious controversy now raging in Germany, the chancellor said that, as in Canada, so in Germany, there are two great religious bodies, Roman Catholic and Protestant. This was in itself a safeguard against any attempts by the state to impose any undue measure of control or limitation on the liberty of the conscience or the preaching of the gospel. The state could not tolerate, however, that the churches should return to the old conditions of affairs in which they were actually the basis for political parties. Beyond that no interference was contemplated.

> Finally I asked the chancellor whether he could indicate when he thought the concentration camps, which had aroused so much criticism abroad, would be abandoned. Here again he became voluble. "People abroad have not realized the seriousness of this question to us," he said. "In no other country has the government no power to fight against six million organized communists. Other countries can deport undesirable citizens, but Germany has had no such opportunity, such as France, for instance. We should be most happy to get rid of our troublesome people, and would gladly pay their fare to Canada if Canada would take them. But Canadians would be rather astonished at the kind of people they would have to welcome. Canada has always had strict immigration laws and Germany has admitted too many people who have abused the privilege of citizenship." According to the chancellor there are now only 17,000 people in the concentration camps.

When Hitler rose to signal the interview over, he handed Rufus a signed photograph as a memento. In spite of the critical implications of some of the questions, the atmosphere between them had remained good and their final handshake was as courteous as their introduction.

Nowhere in his reporting of the event did Rufus mention that, in addition to an interpreter, Hermann Göring had been in the room, or at least the anteroom, during the interview. But this was the case, it seems,[198] and as he was leaving, Rufus turned to shake his hand as well. Göring, however, would have none of it; with his hands firmly behind his back, he growled at him in English:

"You're damned lucky to get out."[199]

Reeling from this parting shot, Rufus left the Kanzlei and walked round to Keyserlingk's office. He finished his article and both of them went over the text. As Keyserlingk had to work late, they arranged to meet at Die Taverne and Rufus left for Ebbutt's office. *The Times* had a private telephone line to London which Ebbutt was allowing Rufus to use for the occasion and he read the article to Cummings over the phone. It was quite a moment — the biggest scoop of his career, and one that would raise his prestige and give him bargaining power with Southam.

Keyserlingk told Bee in a letter that he "joined Rufus later at night at a little café where a number of colleagues join after work to discuss the events of the day." Rufus was possibly the centre of attention — after two weeks working in the city he would have known most of the journalist crowd. In a later conversation with *The Times*, Putzi Hanfstaengl also claimed to have met him that evening and to have discussed with him his impressions of Germany. This could have been at the Kanzlei while he was waiting — but was more likely at Die Taverne, where "various Nazi press officials" would often go to meet newsmen informally.[200] As Keyserlingk recounted the evening for Bee, "we were joined by Mr and Mrs Reed from *The Times* and Bodker of Reuters and spent a very jolly evening which lasted till fairly late." Rufus was said to have been in good spirits but, not surprisingly, concerned by the hostile attitude of Göring.

Next morning, Thursday 16 November — probably not very early — he went to the UPI office to pick up copies of his dispatch that Keyserlingk had had made. They went to the Kanzlei to leave a courtesy copy and for Rufus to say goodbye and to thank Hans Thomsen, and maybe Hanfstaengl, for their efforts — no doubt with an eye to the future. By that time it was 11:30 and they hurried to the Kaiserhof where Rufus packed his bags and they had a light lunch. Then they went to Charlottenburg station and Keyserlingk remembered him frantically searching for an amber necklace he had bought for Bee, and finding it eventually in his overcoat pocket. His train for the Hook of Holland left at 1:25 pm. According to his sister Mary, "he was alone in the compartment until just as the train was about to leave when two men got in with him."

His first-class ticket to London included a seat on a train at either end and a cabin on the LNER steamer *Prague*. It is over 700 kms from Berlin to the Hook; the train had to cross the Dutch border and it would not have arrived until about 10:30. Along with the other passengers "he boarded the ferry," Mary reported, "with two men — presumably the two who left Berlin in his compartment — and they were all three seen later in the bar on board." The cabin steward collected his ticket and, as the ship was not full, assigned him two single cabins. He left his bags in one of them and went to the dining room for supper. The ship sailed at 11:00 while he was eating and he went back to his cabin after his meal. Some time after that the steward popped in to ask about his wake-up call. He found Rufus "rummaging in his suitcase, rather upset because, he said, he had lost the signed photograph that Hitler had given him at the conclusion of their interview." The steward saw him again at 12:50 when, in spite of the hour, he was going on deck. That he was doing so instead of getting into his bunk seems odd, but was actually quite rational. He suffered from insomnia and found it especially hard to sleep on trains and ships. Going to bed, therefore, did not guarantee sleep and this was an alternative.

It was by then Friday, 17 November. All accounts agree the weather was bad and the sea rough — though none mention it being particularly cold. The *Prague*'s promenade deck occupied the forward two-thirds of the ship. The bow section of the deck was open to the sky, the stern section covered, though open on the side above the rail, and between them was an enclosed section with windows where there were lounge chairs, each with a pillow and blanket. Rufus was wearing a hat and scarf and probably an overcoat. No doubt he took a few turns round the deck, passing through the enclosed section on each circuit, but the *Prague* was a small ship and soon a lounge chair would have seemed more appealing. He lay down on one — it was late and he was tired, and apparently he nodded off. Several reports agree that a seaman saw him fast asleep in a chair — according to one report at 2:20 am, an hour and a half after he had gone on deck. If he had looked miserably cold, the sailor would surely have woken him and suggested going below, but he did not. Later — an hour later according to another report, and so maybe at 3:20 — another sailor passed by, saw a hat and scarf on a chair and took them to the purser's office to be reclaimed. But he saw nobody in a chair or on the deck.

When the steward knocked on Rufus's door in the morning, he found both cabins empty and the bunks not slept in. Of him there was no sign, though the steward looked on the deck and in the dining room, and he reported this to the bridge. For the captain it was an emergency: in June another passenger had gone missing from his ship and, a month later, the body had washed up on a Dutch beach. This time, therefore, he had the ship searched from bow to stern. Before he would allow anyone ashore at Harwich, all passengers were lined up and questioned — according to one source, everybody on board. In spite of this, nothing or nobody suspicious was detected, nor had any passenger or crew member seen or heard anything that might help throw light on the mystery.

Rufus had vanished without a trace!

Chapter 21
Exploring the Mystery

"Oh, foul play of course!"

Wickham Steed, 17 November 1933

From what he had told her in his last letter, Bee expected Rufus to be home from Berlin on Friday 17 November, possibly as early as 10 am. When he did not arrive, she was not concerned, thinking he had been delayed by weather or had missed connections and that she would soon hear from him. If he had missed the boat train on Thursday, he would have had to wait another day and might not have phoned because of the high cost of international calls. Neither she nor Derek were particularly concerned that night and he left for work on Saturday as usual.

Only at 11 am on Saturday — a full day after police had known about Rufus's disappearance — did they start to hear what had happened, and in the most upsetting manner imaginable. Bee received a call from Cummings, who had been contacted by police, but he managed only to blurt out that there had been "an accident" before having to put down the phone, too upset to continue. Suddenly dreadfully worried, Bee called Derek at work and asked him to go and see Cummings at the Southam office. By the time he arrived there, the man was calmer and able to repeat, more or less, what the police had told him — that Rufus was missing and presumed drowned, having fallen from the *Prague* during the night. What made the situation worse was that the police had known this on the 17th but chose not to tell Rufus's employer — they never did tell Bee — until they had completed their inquiries. Compounding that piece of heartlessness, they had released the same information to the press when they contacted Cummings, which gave Bee and Derek no time to break the news to family members before they might hear it or read it for themselves.

The police had confirmed that Rufus definitely boarded the *Prague* on the 16th. During the previous 24 hours they had investigated the circumstances and could offer no hope that he might still be alive. As he listened to Cummings's grief-laden voice, 20-year-old Derek's happy and relatively carefree world "suddenly seemed to go very black indeed." He went to Epsom to break the news to his distraught mother — who, not having heard the police report herself, insisted for a day or two on maintaining a faint hope that it was all a mistake and that Rufus would come walking up the path. However she was realistic enough to see that a number of things had to be done quickly — first, to inform Rufus's father and siblings before somebody else did, then to go to Harwich to talk to whoever might help them understand exactly what had happened. So she did the best thing she could have done — telephoned their closest English friends, Ernest and Muz Parsons, to ask for help.

Those kind people came over right away with comfort, advice, and practical help, and, while Muz stayed with Bee, Ernest drove Derek to Harwich. They interviewed the Inspector of Harbour Police who showed them notes of the interviews the police and the ship's captain had carried out. Meanwhile Rufus's half-sister Mary went to Bures to break the news to R.E. It would be a terrible shock for everybody, but for his old father, who had so pressed Rufus to care for his health, it must have been worst of all.

There was no inquest and no inquiry into Rufus's disappearance. Maybe there would have been an inquiry had he not been Canadian, if he had been working for *The Times*, or if he had had a British MP to write to. There could be no inquest because his body was never found — and as neither police nor the *Prague*'s captain had found evidence of foul play, there were no suspects. In fact, there were no witnesses at all — apart from the crew members already mentioned.

Rufus's disappearance remains officially a mystery. Though his body was never found, available reports[201] suggest he went overboard in the early hours of 17 November, probably at about 3 am. Why and how did he fall? Possibilities can be reduced to three: either he jumped, he fell accidentally, or he was pushed.

Neither Bee nor Derek ever accepted suicide as a possibility. In his monograph on his father, Derek, in fact, summarized the reasons why his father would never have considered it: his happy home and family, his increasing professional success, and his transparent enjoyment of life. But, in spite of this, Rufus did have a motive for suicide, even if only "while the balance of his mind was disturbed."

No human could avoid being affected by the trauma of that terrible war and the things he had seen. Underneath his habitual busy cheerfulness, what effect on his subconscious had his war experiences had? More imminently, what are we to make of the change in his behaviour since the Nazis appeared on his horizon — his despair over the feebleness of the League, his preoccupation with Nazi militarism, and his dawning acceptance that the democracies would probably have to fight Germany again? One remembers his dark mood three weeks earlier on a train through Kent, reflected in his gloomy "Nach Berlin . . . 1933". He had sought to reassure himself about Hitler's intentions and at first had partially succeeded. But now he had spent three weeks in the country, he could no longer accept the regime's assurances in the face of transparent preparations for war. That night he may have felt horror at his own behaviour earlier — sharing comradely 'old soldier' talk with the only man in Europe who could bring back the bloody shambles of a general war — and thereby cause his own, and Canada's, and Britain's sacrifices to have been in vain? It is a long shot, but it is a case for suicide.

Vernon Bartlett, whom he had consulted before leaving for Germany that year, believed it. He told Mary[202] many years later. "I assumed that, like me, he was very depressed about the way the Allies were behaving towards Germany and, in a moment of despair, had taken his own life. Certainly many of us who saw the way things were going in Central Europe felt desperate, and had a feeling of failure because we could not persuade our respective governments to stand up for principles."

People have suggested that seasickness or heart problems caused him to fall from the ship accidentally, but neither was possible unless he had been standing at the one place on either side where it was possible to fall — a three-foot gap between the end of the promenade deck rail and the port or starboard lifeboats, a gap fenced with a chain and marked with warning signs.

Seasickness is hardly a possibility: he was an excellent sailor, had made a dozen multiple-day voyages and literally hundreds of shorter ones. Even in the roughest seas there is no mention, in diaries or letters, of him even feeling sick, and he experienced rough seas many times — one thinks of the 'storm of the century' on the English Channel, Hecate Strait on the *Prince John*, and the first few days aboard *Empress of Asia* in 1919. It is just possible that he ate something that made him ill that night, but if so, as he dined on board, why was he the only sufferer? And why would the steward, who had talked to him and had later seen him go on deck, not have noticed he was feeling unwell?

He had, however, recently acknowledged heart problems. Two months earlier, on 'a very mild climb' with Derek in France, he had twice had to stop and rest and eventually abandon the walk. Then, in the weeks before he left for Berlin, Grace Knowles had twice found him looking very white in his office, breathing hard and leaning back in his chair. Both Derek and Miss Knowles had been asked to accept fatigue as the cause of such 'funny turns' and had been sworn to silence. Recently, however, when he had an attack of giddiness at the Kaiserhof, he told Bob Keyserlingk about it, said he thought he had a 'strain on his heart' from overwork, and would have to take a rest to get back into shape when he got home.

That night, under the blanket of his lounger chair, had he felt another 'turn' coming on? Feeling desperately in need of fresh air, it is tempting to believe he got up, staggered through the aft doors of the enclosed section, crossed to the ship's rail and continued aft until he reached the gap mentioned above. The wind blowing through it was what he was after and, bracing himself between the rail and the lifeboat, he breathed it in deeply. Whatever happened next

— a roll of the ship perhaps, an attack of giddiness, maybe a fiercer gust — made him lose his grip and fall outwards into the darkness. If he shouted as he fell nobody would have heard — over the sea and the wind — as the *Prague* steamed into the night.

His sister Mary* however, scornfully dismissed such a scenario, writing, "It is not in my view credible that anyone suffering from a heart attack would have left his cabin and 'gone up on deck to get a breath of night fresh air'[203] while travelling on a rough sea at night. A person having a heart attack does not behave like that; he may be breathless and/or have pain but these very facts preclude the possibility of any such activity; the person so affected would sit or lie still and hope the attack would pass."[204] In other words, exactly what Grace Knowles saw Rufus doing during his 'funny turns'.

Finally, there is a strong possibility that Rufus was murdered by the Nazis. This was first mooted by Wickham Steed, who was treated with respect by the foreign policy community in Britain. Having briefed Rufus before he left, his first reaction upon hearing of his disappearance was: "Oh, foul play of course!" This was not by any means fanciful, despite the immediate elimination as suspects of the passengers and crew by the captain and the harbour police. When R.E. realized that little more would be done to unravel the mystery, he launched his own investigation with the help of his lawyer Francis Steed, coincidentally the brother of Wickham. They corresponded with anybody known to have had contact with Rufus in his final days and their findings were the source of Mary Johnston's statements in her 1991 letter.

The Nazis certainly had a motive. Their foreign policy goal while they remained militarily weak was to have the world believe their declarations of peaceful intentions. It was plain from Rufus's writing that he no longer did so, he was a writer with Canada-wide readership, his connection with *The Times* gave the impression that his influence was wider still, and he had enough material, after three weeks in Germany, for a series of articles — maybe a book. It was not that he had made enemies — Hitler himself seems to have liked him — but from the point of view of such psychopaths as Goebbels and Göring it would have seemed sensible to stop him writing such a book while it could easily be done. This was, after all, the Garden of Beasts.

Fair-minded readers may object that Putzi, on behalf of both Hitler and himself, contacted Ebbutt at *The Times* office in Berlin as soon as he heard of Rufus's death. As reported by Cummings in the *Ottawa Citizen* of 20 November,

> Dr Hanfstaengl expressed his sincerest regrets at the tragic fate of Mr Lukin Johnston. He had met him, he said, the evening before he left for London, and discussed with him his impressions of Germany. Both

* Mary Johnston spent a lifetime in nursing, was on a hospital ship in World War II and finished her career as an Inspector of nursing in the London area.

> this time and two years ago, when he met Mr Johnston for the first time, he was struck by the fair and loyal character of this Canadian journalist who so frankly pointed out those things which he found worthy of criticism and those features which he found praiseworthy. Dr Hanfstaengl said he was authorized to speak in the name of Herr Hitler when he pointed out that the chancellor was deeply moved by the news of this tragic loss, not only to Canada but to world journalism, because anybody who had come in contact with Lukin Johnston could not help but realize that he was dealing with a man who had fully lived up to the high responsibility of his profession.

The clumsy sincerity of Putzi's words speaks for the man — and perhaps for Hitler who may actually have been moved by Rufus's death. Any decision to get rid of him was probably made by Göring. As minister responsible for the Gestapo, he also had the means to carry it out. There was no attempt by Scotland Yard or the LNER to perform more than a superficial check of the passengers and crew, any one of whom could have been a Gestapo agent; the *Prague* was not full, making it easy to book a passage at short notice; and thanks to Rufus's explanations to Thomsen, not to mention his penchant for staying at Hitler's favourite hotels, his travel plans were easily ascertained.

As for how it might have been done, at around 3 am one, maybe two men could have entered the promenade deck through an internal door. As their quarry was asleep, it would have taken just a single blow from something heavy — an innocent-looking hammer perhaps — to ensure that he made no noise. Then it would have been the work of seconds to carry his limp body from the enclosed section, heave it over the rail and watch it disappear into the foam of the wake.

Regarding the credibility of Mary's assertions, she speaks with authority on the heart attack issue but is less credible in the matter of foul play. The Göring story — improbably melodramatic, but believable because of the known out-of-bounds character of the man — was not included in Rufus's dispatch to Cummings for obvious reasons. Its source must have been one or more of the four people known to have talked with him that evening at Die Taverne — Robert Keyserlingk, Douglas Reed of *The Times*, his wife Brenda Reed and V. Bodker of Reuters[205] — all, presumably, later contacted by R.E. and Francis Steed.[206] The story of the two mystery men entering Rufus's train compartment may have reached R.E. in the same way but, as Keyserlingk was the only one at the station, he must have been the source. So far so good.

Sources for later sightings of the two men, however, had to have been passengers or crew; but no article in Bee's clippings file on Rufus's disappearance mentioned them — and they would have been more than mentioned had dockside newshounds heard even a whisper about them. Rufus's last-minute companions were probably tardy travellers whose later appearances with him in the ship's bar occurred only in Mary's memory. In 1991, after all, she was 85, writing without notes and with a case to make. She did well under the circumstances.

Another tragedy five months earlier lends credibility to murder as an explanation for both incidents. Cecil Brooks had gone missing from the *Prague* on 16 June. He was a P&O Commodore who had just retired to become adviser to the Egyptian government on the purchase of merchant ships. His body washed up on Terschelling Island, 230 kms to the northeast on 17 July, and was buried locally. Mrs Brooks realized that her husband, a healthy teetotaler of 58 with 40 years at sea, would hardly have fallen overboard accidentally. Suspecting foul play, she went to Holland, had the body exhumed and brought it home to Paddington for an autopsy and inquest in London.[207]

The autopsy was carried out on 17 August, by which time decomposition was so advanced that the process was, in the coroner's words, "a very terrible ordeal for all concerned." The forensic surgeon, although he reported on the state of the limbs, joints, heart and lungs, declaring the first three sound and undamaged and the lungs so shrunken as to make it impossible to tell whether the victim had drowned, does not seem to have examined the head — beyond saying that the four parts mentioned above were "much better preserved than the other parts." Mrs Brooks had asked to give evidence but the coroner refused her request and delivered an open verdict — a conclusion he had pre-judged when he admitted to having thought the inquest futile from the start. Neither his inquest nor the autopsy were thorough.

That would seem to be the end of the matter, but the widow had her say. She took her husband's body for permanent burial to her family plot at Greenock, and the McInnes family stone in the graveyard carries this inscription:

> "Commander Cecil Brooks, DSO, RD, RNR. Born Stowerburn 14 Jan 1875. Foully murdered in Holland June 1933. He had a bullet through his head."[208]

Mrs Brooks had not seen the body before its burial at Terschelling and had identified her husband by his monocle and cufflinks. But she did go to Terschelling to arrange the exhumation and may have seen it then; she may also have been told of a bullet-wound by somebody who had seen the body when it was recovered. She is unlikely knowingly to have had a false statement inscribed on her family stone and thus, for whatever reason, clearly believed it to be true.

In fact Brooks — excited by his new career, in better health than Rufus and a professional sailor — was even less likely to have ended up in the sea for any reason other than having been dumped there. Nazis had as good a motive to kill him as they had to kill Rufus: as a wartime naval skipper, he would have been a prime recruit for British military intelligence seeking evidence of illegal German naval rearmament; and his new 'job' — advising on the purchase of merchant-ships — would have given him reason to request access to foreign shipyards and thus cover for snooping. While the disappearance of neither man is clearly a murder, the disappearance of both within five months, in a year when the Nazis were desperately trying to conceal their warlike purpose, makes it more likely that both were murders.

Göring's part in this story rings true. As a World War I flying ace with 22 victories he was a national hero. Like Hitler he had been wounded in the Munich *putsch*, was a member of Hitler's inner circle and had for years tried to prevent him granting press interviews. For that reason alone he might have been there — at least in the anteroom. But as minister in charge of the Gestapo he may also have been aware of the tenor of Rufus's reporting. His reported snarl at him suggests that to be the case, and is in line with his reckless outburst at a defendant in the Reichstag fire trial: "You wait till I get you out of the power of the court, you crook!", mentioned in a previous chapter. What was more, given their emotional or professional involvement in seeking the truth, no participant in the story's transmission would have been likely to have invented it.

As to why the story first saw the light of day in a 1991 letter from Mary to her great-niece Val, the answer is family politics. Whatever R.E. learned from his inquiries, there was nothing to be gained by contacting press or police about their suspicions — if they were right, the villains would have been well protected and no amount of painful publicity could have brought Rufus back. And although R.E. and his daughters Mary and Joyce may have found it comforting to discuss it among themselves, it could have given no comfort to Derek or Bee.

In the end, we must ask two questions: why would a man who loved his family so dearly and who lived by the written word commit suicide without leaving a note; and why would a man who took no unnecessary risks have stood in so dangerous a place on a heaving deck in the dark? If answers refuse to come, we may reasonably conclude that his death was neither suicide nor accidental. Melodramatic as it sounds, murder remains the only reasonable explanation.

Epilogue

*"My father, your **grandfather** . . ."*

Derek's customary preamble to any story about Rufus that he told his children

In spite of Rufus's absence, he remained the centre of family life for many months and there were few things going on that did not concern him. It must have provided consolation for Bee and Derek to discover the extent of the impact he had had on the lives of strangers, many of whom were sufficiently moved by his death to write a letter of condolence. There were also many letters from friends and colleagues in Canada and in England, and Bee insisted that any letter — be it from friend, colleague or reader — be personally acknowledged. This she and Derek did, and there were 500 from Rufus's readers alone, quite apart from the many others.

Rufus, like most people in their forties, believed he was indestructible and had not yet made a will — except for a signed sheet of paper, discovered in his desk, that declared: "I leave everything to my wife." As it turned out this was good enough to move legal wheels. Equally important for Bee's peace of mind, Fred Southam cabled her — in sparse telegraphic language — that Rufus's salary would be paid for the next two months, and asked her, once she had determined her financial situation, to ". . . please accept renewed assurances sympathetic consideration your own and Derek's personal and financial problems," which was nice to be told about so soon and later translated into a regular pension. Bee found herself left with little else, apart from the house and the twice-yearly publishers' royalty cheques for Rufus's books. These did not provide a sufficient income by any means — in the second half of 1935, for instance, Dents had sold 270 copies of *Beyond the Rockies* and 618 copies of *In England Today* for a total of £13.2.9d, though Heath Cranton probably managed more from the more recent *Down English Lanes*.[209]

Apart from letters, every newspaper with which Rufus had ever been associated published its own obituary, and a reader detects real emotion and sense of loss in them all. On 29 November a memorial service was held in the journalists' church, St Bride's in Fleet Street. Members of Rufus's extended family were there including Uncle Jack Johnston and Aunt Aimée (LeBrooy) but not Rufus's father who was probably not well enough. There was a sizable contingent from Epsom, from *The Times* and from other members of London's fourth estate including the BBC. Otherwise it must have been quite a surprise for English friends and family to find themselves outnumbered by Canadians — every Canadian institution in London was represented, from the Chamber of Commerce to the CPR to the Bank of Montreal and including the High Commissioner and the Canadian government — in the person of H. H. Stevens, MP for Vancouver Centre and Bennett's minister of Trade and Commerce, whom Rufus knew well from his days at the *Province*.

When the dust had settled and the letters had been answered, Bee sold Barton's Mead — it was bigger than they needed and awash in memories — and took a smaller place on Squirrel's Way. She named it Linden Cottage after the house they had had to give up in Victoria when Rufus went to war. She and Derek tried to pick up their lives again, and of the two of them it was Derek who had the least problem: he just continued with the familiar daily grind of an articled clerk's life in a London CA's office. His romantic life was more exciting and he soon fell for a young relative of Muz's whom he met at a Parsons family dance. This was Diana Myers and their courtship had its ups and downs, on one occasion causing Derek to fail his exams. When he finally qualified in 1937, he had a marketable qualification and a fiancée but before he and Diana could marry, he needed to return to BC and find a good job. He was ready to leave whenever Bee said the word and was surprised to find her somewhat reluctant.

She had had the harder job adjusting to life without Rufus — in fact, she must have felt completely bereft as her life had been more centred around him since they had lived in England. As a woman without a past that she could talk about to new English friends, it had always been a challenge for her to create a successful and independent social life in Epsom. After Rufus died, married friends were kind and kept her included. But things felt different — and not much fun — without him. By November 1936, whether or not they still had Linden Cottage, she and Derek, who was still finishing his articles at McClintock's, were living in rooms in London. Feeling desperate about winter in London and its constant fog, she made a sudden decision. At a friend's suggestion — that she could live in Munich for half of what it would cost in London — she booked into the Pension Bayer in that city and, within three days, had moved to Germany.

She started giving English lessons, enrolled for *ausländerkurse*[210] soon had a circle of German and international friends, friends she had made herself as a single woman, including Herr Doktor and Frau Bayer who ran the pension.

The Germans amongst them, naturally, were enthusiastic Hitler supporters, and Bee, who loved the colour, drama and razzmatazz of Nazi parades, soon picked up their attitudes. Derek, by contrast, was a fan of Churchill's — at the time still a gadfly MP constantly warning the House about Hitler's rearmament — and was dismayed by his mother's naïve enthusiasm. He came to visit when he could — in December 1936 for a holiday with her in the Bavarian mountains, and for Christmas 1937 in Munich itself — and no doubt tried, gently, to disabuse her of it. But the signal for urgent action only came when he received a letter from her dated 13 March 1938, bubbling over about the Anschluss[211] parades of the previous day and including this astonishing observation: "Everybody here seems to think it a wonderful triumph for Hitler, and I agree. I really think he will go down in history as the greatest man of his age, and the sooner England and America recognize this, the better it will be for the peace of the world."

Derek was practiced at giving her "Mother dear" advice and on this occasion needed all his skill. He went to Munich, told her he had a job offer in Vancouver from Price Waterhouse and persuaded her, against her own inclinations, that war might come at any time and that they should go home while they still could. They sailed soon after that and Diana followed them in 1939 — repeating Bee's own romantic odyssey of 1912. She and Derek were married in Vancouver within weeks and the birth of their first child, Val, in April 1940 made Rufus the founder of a three-generation Canadian family which, by the time of this writing, has been extended to five.

As the quotation at the start of this chapter makes clear, Rufus's descendants felt they knew him because of Derek's frequent stories. But no bereaved twenty-year-old — even one as sharp as Derek — is likely to have analyzed his late father's attributes; and the stories he chose to tell, even in later years, tended to cherry-pick among his father's virtues and mention only those vices that would get a laugh. Not surprisingly, Rufus was a much more complicated character than the one his descendents knew only from stories.

He was a product of a cash-strapped nineteenth century vicarage with all that that implied. His father the vicar spent much time talking while others listened; he did good works often — it was part of the job; he had a large household of all sorts of people, high and low; so he got along with them — all of them, almost all the time — he had to and it was also part of the job. The vicar, and his wife, and any of their children old enough and available, worked for the parish, and visited parishioners all round the town — not now and again but every day, most of the day and all year — that too was part of the job. And you enjoyed doing it because it was all you knew. And because you had very little actual playtime, you became good at having a good time, anywhere and everywhere, with whatever was available. And that included going to church, the fixed point on your activity calendar. Somebody had to, and you were able to, so you sang; and you decorated for saints' days and for harvest festival and for Easter and for Christmas. You read lessons, you taught Sunday school, you counted the collection, you helped the old guy mowing between the gravestones. And it was all fun because you made it fun.

When Rufus went away to school, he just took it all with him. Why would he not sing in the cathedral if he sang in the church at home? And why, also, would he not get along with all the boys at King's School, or in 2nd Brigade mess, or in the *Province* newsroom, or at Die Taverne in Berlin, if he got along with the lodgers in the vicarage and the people his mother used to visit? And if he could talk in a friendly way to the smart-looking strangers who would call at the vicarage for tea why would he find it difficult to talk to the Archbishop of Canterbury — or to Field Marshall Haig at the front — or even to Adolf Hitler for that matter? Furthermore, if he was comfortable reciting a poem at the concert in the parish hall, why would he be less comfortable singing a solo in the cathedral, or writing his first editorial in Duncan, BC, or talking to the Canadian Club or even to a thousand-strong congregation in Christ Church, Vancouver?

But one suspects that a good deal of Rufus's mature personality had its roots in the five years he spent between landing in Canada in 1905 and landing a job with Walter Nichol at the Vancouver *Province* in 1910. If you had survived the winter of 1906 on Ralph Marshall's farm at Qu'Appelle, Saskatchewan, when only a fur coat could keep a man alive on a horse-drawn sleigh, or those three months alone in a shack at Kipp, Alberta in the winter of 1909, maybe you weren't too fussed by the sleet at Vimy or the mud at Passchendaele or the drenching rain on his strange wanderings on Vancouver Island or the icy roads in the Pennine chain when most people found a fireside to sit by. And if you had lived by your wits through five years of hope and disappointment in the Last Best West, well, maybe the idea of always trying to improve your lot once you did have a job, always pushing for something better, something more challenging, that thing people call ambition — maybe it had all become second nature back in those hardscrabble prairie days.

Rufus was what he was, and most people he met found him agreeable company. He mellowed as the years passed and the 'fiery old stick' of early days had nearly disappeared. But he turned out to be a very good journalist — he preferred the old-fashioned word 'newspaperman' — and the reasons for that were various.

Journalists communicate and Rufus had mastered the basics of this by the time he left school: a deep grasp of English grammar — so much second nature to him that he seldom, if ever, made an error — and an ability to write legibly under all conditions. These assets put him ahead of the pack for any white-collar work, but especially for journalism. He developed an unpretentious and efficient style in which nouns were employed precisely, lessening the need for cluttering adjectives, and his message was delivered through vivid word-portraits of situations and events, studded with transparently believable encounters with real people.

A good journalist, however, needs constantly to make judgments, not only about facts, but about values too — what is right or wrong, desirable or undesirable, timely or belated, moral or crooked, expensive or cheap, and so forth. How is a young fellow to do this in Canada, if he's spent his early life in an English vicarage? Well, in Rufus's case, by spending five years in two dozen jobs in four Canadian provinces, and by already possessing a good knowledge of the way the world works, especially Britain and its empire. After he died, his Vancouver friend A.J.T. Taylor, future builder of Lion's Gate Bridge, observed, "he wrote with a complete knowledge of his readers, having had a remarkably wide personal experience in nearly every phase of Canadian life." By the time he died, that included his military experience of course, to which he had added two extraordinary American interludes and a European immersion.

Along with his experience came several other reasons for his success. As his old friend Hugh Savage observed in his obituary, Rufus "let nothing and nobody stand in his way of getting a story," something that had always been his style, from Steamboat Mountain to his siege of the German chancellor. He was popular with the business crowd because, from experience of his columns, they knew they could trust his information while "his ability to select and outline the news in crisp and clear sentences" appealed to those needing to understand a political situation quickly. On top of that, he told it as it was or, as the *Province* put it,

> . . . he knew the obligation of the honest reporter not to write anything either too much up or down, but to pitch his note to the tone that was appropriate.

From the time he was first let loose on the features scene — his appointment as editor of the new *Province* Magazine Section — he demonstrated what for many was the most compelling part of his writing — his ability to describe distant, sometimes unfamiliar, communities and scenes so well that his readers were transported into them. This wonderful ability, employed first on the remoter parts of British Columbia and subsequently on old world communities in England and Europe, made a large impact on readers, especially natives of those places. These articles were the stuff of his three books and there can be little doubt that a fourth, *In Germany Today*, was on the drawing board when he died.

There are still further strands in why Rufus was so successful. First, as his friend J. Butterfield of the *Province* put it in his column 'The Common Round':

> He was a very forceful person. He got things done. It was his strong point to get things done. That is how one gets on in this world. By getting other people to make your ideas concrete. Lukin did it. He won by hard work and responsibility.

It was the hard side of Rufus and it really did exist. But, paradoxically, his soft side was equally responsible. His talent for making friends meant he was "a popular figure everywhere he went" (*Victoria Times*) and "among his colleagues he was cordially liked and his conscientiousness much admired" (Charles Swayne). The workings of both were on display in Berlin during those final few weeks, and the reader might contemplate the number of fellow scribes who willingly put their lives on hold to help him achieve his goal.

In the five years he had been working in London, Lukin Johnston became a household name in Canada — at least in the households that subscribed to any of the major dailies owned by the Southams.[212] These dailies covered Canada's large cities, except for Toronto, Regina and Halifax. Had he lived, there is reason to suppose he would have become a household name in countries other than his own, and partly through his popular books. Nevertheless, his brief career as a foreign correspondent — now forgotten by public memory, even by institutional memory — had notable achievements in the opinion of his contemporaries.

The first of these was that his articles educated Canada. As the *Edmonton Journal* put it:

> Lukin Johnston performed a really great service in giving Canadians a clear understanding of what was happening in Britain and on the European continent. We constantly learned for the first time of developments of the utmost importance from his dispatches.

The *Hamilton Spectator* went further, claiming that

> . . . he has contributed greatly to the creation of an informed public opinion in this Dominion in matters of primary importance to the Empire and the world.

MacTavish of the *Winnipeg Tribune* agreed and explained how hard Rufus had had to work in order to do it:

> He was the greatest correspondent ever to represent a Canadian newspaper, or group of newspapers, in London. He was greatest because he observed accurately, studied closely and interpreted most ably the currents and trends of thought and action in the UK and in Europe.

Dr Wallace, President of the University of Alberta, considered

> ". . . his death a serious loss to all who wish to obtain a clear knowledge of international problems."

That was quite an epitaph for a journalist, but there were more. Others declared he had done great things for Anglo-Canadian relations. Thanks to his rambles down English lanes, his frequent features on English life, both political and social, the *Winnipeg Tribune* wrote:

> He has helped in no small degree to keep Canada in close and sympathetic touch with the Old Country and to keep both in unison of purpose during the past several trying years.

Along the same lines, if more empathetic, the *Victoria Colonist*, for which Rufus had worked before the war, claimed:

> No Canadian correspondent ever sent to England interpreted more truly the attitude of that country towards the Dominion.

Many readers had developed real affection for his columns about England. At his death, they poured out their sadness in letters to the editors of Southam newspapers across the country and amongst them was this poem from A.M. to the editor of the *Daily Province*:

Lukin Johnston

He brought us news of home,
quaint tales of old world village scenes;
'tis hard to think that he no more will roam
In stately mansions fair, or under cottage beams.
Much joy to exiled hearts he brought
with views of English hearth and lanes,
Queer wayside inns, and London when it rains.

The twinkling city lights, the duke or statesman passing by,
were not alone the things he knew in life's great race
A wee thatched house and children by the sea;
A ragged urchin small, or country folk at tea;
His spirit fares now forth upon the higher quest,
A soul set free to find a greater happiness.

Sadly, Rufus has no grave, no memorial and, after eighty years, his place in memory is dim. If this book can go some way towards recalling his life and the prominence he achieved by his own efforts, it will have restored to him some small part of the recognition he deserves. His path was never easy and along the way he overcame many of the hardest challenges confronting Canadians of the time. He is a worthy ancestor for his descendants.

Like Dick Whittington, he set out to seek his fortune, and like him, by hard work he found it.

Endnotes

1. Nellie's *Rough Diary*, 1893, published annually by Letts' of London.
2. Maj.-Gen. Sir Henry Timson Lukin, KCB, CMG, DSO. In *Military History Journal*, Vol 7, No. 3 (June 1987).
3. Letter from R.E. to Bee, 2 Jan 1942.
4. This must have been Mrs (Emmeline) Pankhurst because none of her three daughters would have been old enough.
5. Letter from R.E. to Bee, 2 Jan 1942.
6. Derek's memories in a 2006 questionnaire thrust under his nose by Val! The streaking story came from Aunt Mary and she could not possibly have witnessed it herself.
7. Derek confirmed in 2006 that math had been his father's least favourite subject.
8. Johnston, Derek, *Edwin Harry Lukin Johnston, 1887–1933 — A Personal Memoir.*
9. Cosgrave, Joyce, *The Way it Was.* Handwritten childhood recollections by Rufus's sister, written in 1997.
10. Rufus letter to R.E. Aug 11 1906 — he asks for Roy to get him a photo of the KS Army class of 1905.
11. See the Lukin family tree — there are two possible candidates for this lady. When she wrote to Rufus, May 2 1919, her name was Lucy Allan Davies, Hotel Mont Fleuri, Lausanne.
12. Rufus to Aunt Lily, 12 Sept 1933.
13. Sifton was Laurier's Minister of the Interior who wanted 'stalwart peasants' as immigrants — in preference to 'gentlemen' like Rufus & company.
14. Johnston, Lukin, *In England Today*, p. 96.
15. This prescription is not as odd as it sounds: All the known species of gentian are remarkable for the intensely bitter properties residing in the root and every part of the herbage, hence they are valuable tonic medicines. (Botanical.com). Maybe the beer was just to take the taste away.
16. Beaver Lumber was formed in 1906, by a complicated series of amalgamations, and boasted about 70 outlets in Rufus's day, by far the biggest operator of lumber yards. It was a community-based business which focused on building relationships with its customers. It seems that this was what Rufus was doing — he was a natural! It became a Western Canadian institution until it fell prey to Home Hardware.

17. Rufus to R.E., Nov 6, 1910.
18. Encyclopedia of Saskatchewan — http://esask.uregina.ca/entry/milling.html. No such mill appears among the 37 built in Saskatchewan by 1915.
19. As recorded by Val many years later after a conversation with Bee.
20. As told to Val in the 1950s.
21. Rufus to Uncle Harry, Aug 9, 1912.
22. There is no indication who Hudson was. Judging by his subsequent delay in reminding them about repayment and interest requirements, he was not a businessman. He may have been a well-off family friend — in a letter to his father dated 16 Jan 1911, Rufus claimed a travelling clock which he had left in England, saying "The Hudsons gave it to me years ago." The poor man probably never saw his money again, unfortunately; he had not collected it before both men married and after those events and the outbreak of war, it was hopeless. (see Rufus to Bee 1916 June 2, on board SS *Olympic*, but sent Nov 22, as he sailed for France.)
23. Kipp, actually 12.6 km NW of Lethbridge (Google Maps), is just a name on the map today — no sign of buildings.
24. The evidence for this assertion is that R.E. had sent him the best book available on fruit tree pruning.
25. Rufus to R.E., Nov 23, 1911. Rufus thinks there is a chance of getting a few hundred from the sale of his Govan property — $500 being the most he could expect. This probably means that, because of the fire-sale nature of the transaction, he invested considerably more than that. As far as one can tell, he never actually received any money from it.
26. Martin Burrell's appreciation of Rufus (*Ottawa Citizen* Nov 1933) acknowledged that he knew him in the Kootenays in 1910.
27. The only pick-your-own strawberry operation in the Kootenays in 2011 puts harvest time from the end of May to October. (http://www.pickyourown.org/canadabc.htm) It thus seems unlikely that Roy and Rufus could have harvested and sold their crop much before the middle of June and possibly it was even later.
28. Roy eventually managed to sell his Harrop property in 1911. Unfortunately, the proceeds went straight to pay his medical bills — he had nearly died from typhoid.
29. Johnston, Derek, *A Personal Memoir*.
30. *Dictionary of Canadian Biography* Online. Entry for W.C. Nichol.
31. Rufus to R.E., 24 Feb 1914.
32. They might have been Folkestone people of that name mentioned in Nellie's diary for 1893. October 3 — "May Sharp, husband and baby came to lunch" — good friends, of course, because she used Mrs Sharp's Christian name. Rufus later mentions that they were interested in fruit farming, which fits with their coming from Kent, the "garden of England."
33. Difficult to pinpoint but the following extract and website help. The trail described in the second part of the extract could well have been Rufus's

access route to the Steamboat mine: "Allison Pass is named for John and Susan Allison, who used the Dewdney Trail in the 1860s and 1870s to reach their homestead near Princeton. Curiously, my oldest map, a 1914 provincial government Lands Department map at a scale of 4 miles to the inch, shows no established trail through Allison Pass. But it does show (as well as the Dewdney Trail) an established trail running along the Similkameen River all the way to Princeton from the area that today is the Manning Park headquarters. Interestingly, this trail continues due west from Cambie Creek through the Gibson's Pass (today's cross-country and downhill skiing area in Manning Park), then descends Nepopekum Creek on the south side of Steamboat Mountain (past an intriguing dot on the map called Jarvis) before swinging to the northwest along the Skagit River, then heading upstream along the Klesilkwa River to its headwaters, crossing yet another divide before picking up Silver Creek, which descends through the mountains and drains into the Fraser River just west of Hope." http://www.michaellucnkner.com/bciw2hopeprinceton.html.

34. He had already turned down one offer. Rufus to R.E., June 4, 1911.:"Watts, the Inspector of the Royal Life Insurance Co is just back from England. His 2nd in command is leaving to be Provincial Manager in Manitoba. He has tentatively offered me the job as his 2nd in command. This would be certain — if I was satisfactory — to lead to a Provincial Manager's job in a few months. He is keen that I should get Alberta. However, we shall see."
35. Rufus to R.E., 14 Dec 1911.
36. Bee's charge chez Molson was daughter Margaret. The 1911 Census shows only one, Margaret D. Molson, born 1905, aged 5, daughter of J.D. Molson and his wife Mrs M.C. Molson, both born 1867, aged 44. They had three young unrelated females in the house, none being Bee, who presumably only started to work for them later in the year. Molson was manager of the Market and Harbours branch of Molson Bank in Montreal.
37. For background information on Duncan I am indebted to Tom Henry's *Small City on a Big Valley*. (Harbour Publishing, 1999).
38. Rufus to R.E., 29 Sept 1911. I have no idea what his source might have been (not the 1911 census — too soon).
39. The last sentence is borrowed from Rufus's letter to R.E. of 11 August — but it fits much better here!
40. *Here shall the Press the People's right maintain, unawed by influence and unbribed by gain: here patriot truth her precious precepts draw, pledged to religion, liberty and law.* Joseph Story, 1779 (US Supreme Court judge 1811-45).
41. The *Colonist* insisted that Bee was "handsomely attired" in white.
42. Rufus to 'My dear Father Christmas', May 7 1929.
43. Guy Sutton Rothwell, the same age as Rufus, who lived alone with a Mr Sing, a Chinese servant.
44. Henry, *Small City*, pp 65-66.
45. Census1911.

46. *London Gazette*, 1 Jan, 1906.
47. Valerie Green and Lynn Gordon-Finlay, *If These Walls Could Talk.*
48. Roy, *White Man's Province*, p. 248.
49. "History of *Times Colonist*," Victoria *Times Colonist*, Jan 2, 2008.
50. Johnston, Derek, *A Personal Memoir*, p. 10.
51. A survivor's memoir of Delville Wood among Derek's papers.
52. Bairnsfather's humorous cartoons in the English magazine *Punch* captured the predicament of soldiers in the trenches.
53. Currie, a Victoria businessman, as a reader of the *Colonist*, would have been familiar with his name. He may have known his face from the Union Club.
54. Donald S. Montgomery with whom Rufus, briefly, went to school at KSC, together with his brother Bernard, the World War II Field Marshall. Donald was a Vancouver barrister.
55. T. Stewart Lyon, 1966-1946, had been appointed Managing Editor of the Toronto *Globe* in 1915, and in 1917 became the first Canadian newspaperman to file from the trenches. He and Rufus became friends after this encounter.
56. *Province*, June 3, 1921.
57. Val has a late 1940s memory of this bizarre object hanging beside her grandmother's front door in Victoria — for bashing burglars. She worried that a burglar might get to it first.
58. Arthur Currie had achieved some fame as the CO of the Dandy Fifth, the 5th Canadian Garrison Artillery Regiment. This was a Victoria militia regiment whose gunnery skills under his command became proverbial — in 1912 and 1913 leading the Garrison Artillery of Canada in both general efficiency and target practice — at that time a big deal and well publicized.
59. They were 22 twin-engined Gothas flying at 15,000 feet, above the ceiling of RFC fighters. One Gotha could carry a maximum bomb-load of 500 kgs. On this raid only one was destroyed and three others damaged.
60. Canadian official war photography, including life-size images of soldiers in the battle for Vimy Ridge.
61. William Wasbrough Foster became a good friend of Rufus in Vancouver during the twenties. When not fighting the war, he was a mountaineer, businessman, and policeman. As Vancouver's chief constable in 1935 he led the VPD in the Battle of Ballantyne Pier against striking longshoremen. His politics were notoriously right-wing and after WWII, as head of BC Hydro, he led the fight against unions.
62. Princess Patricia's Canadian Light Infantry, formed in 1914. Princess Patricia of Connaught was Prince Arthur's younger sister, and their father, the Duke of Connaught, was Governor-General of Canada, 1911-1916.
63. Lt. Col. Dan Ormond, DSO & Bar, was a legendary survivor in the Corps, having played heroic roles at all 1st Division battles since 1915. He was popular with his men who had christened him Dangerous Dan.
64. His early recall put paid to any chance of seeing Beaverbrook on this leave. Possibly, however, Bee had already talked him out of it.

65. O'Keefe, *Great War Commands*, p. 89.
66. See Loomis's 1917 portrait by war artist Edgar Bundy.
67. Harcourt Sunderland, aged 19, youngest son of David and Mabel Sunderland.
68. One wonders how this gentleman justified his expenses!
69. Presumably the re-supply effort for which Gen. Loomis recommended him for an MC though Loomis dated it "on the night of August 9th."
70. The Siegfried Line in World War I was just a section of the Hindenburg Line, from Arras to Saint Quentin.
71. Dancocks, *Sir Arthur Currie*, p.163.
72. A Google search for a list of duties for a DAAG came up almost dry — but a Pakistani officer holding that title describes his job as "looking after legal and discipline matters, administration, recruitment and selection, promotions, retirement" among other things more specific. Rufus would have admitted to the first three, one suspects. Pakistan and Canada both adopted British army organization.
73. Either Rufus was not permitted to use his name while still in uniform, or he didn't want to.
74. This was the prototype corner house, a huge restaurant on four or five levels employing something like 400 staff. Each floor had its own style and orchestras played to the diners almost continuously throughout the day and evening.
75. Lord Northcliffe had been one of R.E.'s parishioners at St Peter's in Thanet and would remember Rufus as the red-haired chorister.
76. Derek estimated that his father and mother were better off in the fall of 1918 than they would be for the next 10 years.
77. Woodrow Wilson was in Europe for the Peace Conference.
78. *The London Gazette* was, and still is, the official organ of the British government — the authoritative source for government announcements, including military promotions and medals. In World War I it announced Canadian medals.
79. The 16th Battalion, in which he served as a platoon subaltern in 1917, although formed in 1914 at Valcartier, Quebec, was in 1917 officially re-designated a Manitoba battalion as reinforcements increasingly came from the Manitoba Reserve and Depot Battalions.
80. According to a picture-postcard of the ship's arrival in Rufus's *War Book*.
81. This must have been the bottle they won on the Asia — alcohol was prohibited in BC 1917–1921, so he was breaking the law!
82. Annette Kellerman was the first major actress to do a nude scene — in *Daughter of the Gods*, 1916; unfortunately for Rufus, she kept her mermaid suit on in *The Queen of the Sea* though there was underwater photography to compensate.
83. Canada was the first allied country to recognize that rehabilitation training of disabled men was a necessity. (Wikipedia)

84. Perpetuation of the 7th Battalion: 7th Battalion became 1st Battalion British Columbia Regiment (Duke of Connaught's Own Rifles.)
85. Attributed to Winston Churchill.
86. The car and driver cost him $10; he does not say whether he was able to recoup this from the *Province*, or whether it was just the price of becoming known.
87. Johnston, Derek, *A Personal Memoir*, p. 17.
88. It became a traditional invitation while they lived in Vancouver.
89. With no rain in July, these sometimes threatened houses along the shore of English Bay.
90. R.E. to Rufus, 4 May 1920, "I wonder if Miall will be of any help to Roy in his Department, he seems to have done very well."
91. Brigadier General Victor Odlum, CB, CMG, DSO (1880-1971) was seven years older than Rufus. He served in the Boer War with the RCR, became a journalist and was editor of the *Vancouver Daily World* from 1905. Though his father was a humble historian, he must have had family money — Odlum is unlikely to have become rich from the *World*. In WWI he went to France as a Major with the 7th Battalion, was spotted by Currie as a rising star, was fast-tracked and ended the war as a Brigadier-General. Brave as a lion, he would lead attacks with pistol drawn and was wounded in action three times. He and David Watson, GOC 4th Division, lent Currie money to enable him to avoid a charge of embezzling regimental funds. Odlum founded the investment firm Odlum Brown in 1923, was an MLA 1924-28, and owner of the *Vancouver Star* newspaper. Politically he was far right, virulently anti-Asian, and so anti-union that he closed down the *Star* rather than give in to employees who refused a pay cut. He was also teetotal, refused to allow troops a rum ration and was known to them as "Old Lime Juice."
92. *Victoria Daily Times*, 19 June, 1920.
93. *Daily Province*, 10 April, 1920.
94. Muriel Phelan, Mrs Freeman, Mrs Orchardson, Mrs Carter, Mrs Maxwell, Ivy Calloway.
95. Liberty League of BC was one of the three components of the Independent Party in the upcoming provincial election, the others being the Vancouver Ratepayers' Ass'n & the Women's Freedom League. The Liberty League took 10% of the vote, running 3rd behind the Tories in a huge field of which the nine most 'loony tunes' parties (combined) took only 3% of the vote. Fourteen soldier candidates ran for 3 different parties, taking between them 4.5% of the vote. The election was won by John Oliver's Liberals.
96. It was probably Steed's address to the Vancouver Canadian Club that first impressed upon Rufus the importance of the upcoming Washington Naval Conference. (*Province*, August 4, 1921).
97. Mr Toad was the motorcar-crazy character in Kenneth Grahame's *The Wind in the Willows*.

98. Originally Minoru Park (named after Edward VII's horse), it opened in 1909 as a horse-racing venue at Gilbert and the Westminster Highway in Richmond, BC. Renamed Brighouse Park (after WWI, after a local pioneer), it was also Vancouver's first airstrip.
99. The Washington Naval Conference of 1921 was a praiseworthy American attempt to prevent another arms race by reaching Great Power agreement on an acceptable ratio between navies.
100. In fact, Canada was not separately accredited but was part of the British Empire delegation, which also included Australia, New Zealand, South Africa, and India. The nine accredited powers were USA, China, Japan, UK, France, Italy, Netherlands, Portugal, and Belgium. Germany, Turkey, & Soviet Russia were not invited.
101. He must have had an arrangement with Cairns and Brown that he did not mention in his diary or letters.
102. This word was part of the normal lexicon at the time.
103. "Journalistic Minstrels of World at Washington — An Impression", *Daily Province*, 1 Dec, 1921.
104. He calls it "that circular room at the rear of the White House"!
105. Roy Brown retired in 1938.
106. *Daily Province*, 14 August, 1922.
107. The level of the Arrow Lakes was 12 feet lower and they were separated by the Narrows, which were just navigable.
108. The Kettle Valley Railway, opened 1915, connecting the towns of the Southern Interior and Kootenays with Hope and the Lower Fraser Valley.
109. Lamb, "Origin and Development of Newspapers", p. 59.
110. 639 Commercial Drive; it is currently (2012) being refurbished and turned over to the Vancouver East Cultural Centre.
111. *Daily Province*, 16 August, 1924.
112. "Amazingly" only because Dawson was later the brains behind appeasement and demonstrated a reluctance to criticize Hitler that Rufus could not have stomached. Dawson was a powerful intellectual, Fellow of All Souls, and proponent of Imperial Federation, a concept from which Canadian governments, and most thinking Canadians including Rufus, had moved away. His appeal for Rufus may have been his earlier career in South Africa where he likely knew Harry Lukin.
113. William George Murrin, born 1876 in Greenwich, Kent, England. He married Mary Jane Murrin in 1903 and they had had no children by 1911. An electrical engineer, by 1913 he had moved to Vancouver to join BC Electric and by 1917 was assistant manager of the BC Electric Railway. By 1929 he was president of BC Electric itself and remained so until he retired in 1946. His rise was probably influenced by his tough and unsentimental attitude to wage negotiations in the aftermath of the 1919 general strike, culminating in forcing wage reductions in 1922. From 1931 to 1960 he served on the board of the BC Commission providing

work for disabled veterans. From 1946 to 1953 he was a warden in Christ Church, cathedral of New Westminster diocese. He lived at The Gables, 2106 SW Marine Drive, Vancouver, and once had Emily Carr's *Trees in the Sky* hanging in his basement. He received an Honourary Degree from UBC in 1957.

114. Stuart, Sir Campbell, *Secrets of Crewe House.*
115. Johnston, Lukin, *Beyond the Rockies.*
116. Pacific Great Eastern Railway, incorporated 1912 — now BC Rail.
117. Soldier Settlement Board.
118. Odlum was a good friend to Rufus; like many of Rufus's friends he was a pretty extreme character and not to everybody's taste. See endnote 91.
119. Not mentioned in Chuck Davis's *Vancouver.* It was possibly near the foot of the modern gondola — itself at quite an elevation — and popular because the Second Narrows Bridge opened for cars in 1925 and the chalet/hotel at the top of Grouse Mountain, and road up to it, were not finished until 1927. Both hostelries were on the skids from 1928 when barge damage closed the bridge for four years. (http://www.vancouverhistory.ca/archives_grouse.htm)
120. Major James Skitt Matthews (1878-1970). He served with a British regiment in WWI but his grand obsession was city history. He probably lived on rents from his houses while he worked as (unpaid) city archivist. The position was formalized in 1933 but no archives building existed in his lifetime and he continued to own the collection. He left it to the city in his will on condition that they build an archives within a year — now the Major Matthews Building in Vanier Park.
121. Pacific Great Eastern, from North Vancouver, via Squamish, Pemberton, and Lilloet, eventually to Prince George.
122. Johnston, Lukin, *Beyond the Rockies*, p. 117.
123. The author and Val, Rufus's granddaughter, had a less extreme experience there in September 2009. While the north shore was again chilly and windy, they found the south beach bathed in sunshine, the sea calm, and a hundred loons feeding offshore.
124. These included: Graham Spry, Canadian Club secretary and broadcasting pioneer behind the future CBC; A.H. Sidgwick, English author and poet; Kenneth Lindsay, "a quaint, clever Englishman, a future Labour MP who spoke to the Ottawa Canadian Club on *The Significance of the British Labour Movement*; General Frank Sutton, British adventurer who lost an arm at Gallipoli, became a Chinese Nationalist general, and who was promoting a railway from Peace River to Vancouver; Gerry McGeer, Vancouver lawyer known as 'the man who flattened the Rockies' for winning freight rate concessions from Ottawa that made it economic to ship prairie grain out of Vancouver, of which city he was later mayor; Ralph Osborne Campney, Vancouver lawyer, first chairman of the National Harbours Board, a future Tory MP and Minister of Defence; Sir Robert Borden, "much aged",

Prime Minister 1911-20; General W. St P Hughes. GOC of 10th Brigade and Sam Hughes' brother; Willis O'Connor, ADC to Governor General Lord Willingdon who arranged lunch for Rufus as His Excellency's only guest at Rideau Hall; Governor General Lord Willingdon; and Wilson Southam, publisher of the *Ottawa Citizen*.

125. There was a Frank Cosgrave, aged 31, listed as a professor and a lodger in the house of the Vice-Provost of Trinity in the 1911 census, probably the same man. Was he perhaps one of his sister Joyce's in-laws?
126. *BC Bookworld* archive: http://www.abcbookworld.com/view_author.php?id=857.
127. William Garland Foster, editor *Nelson Daily News*, 1908 – 1914, Captain 54th Battalion, C.E.F., killed 14 Oct 1918 and another candidate for the friend who first kindled Rufus' appetite for journalism.
128. Godwin, *Eternal Forest.*
129. Godwin, *Why Stay We Here?*
130. Both the Hotel Buckingham and the Auberge du père Louis are still in business as of June 2012.
131. According to Derek, Cummings, in addition to possessing his stated virtues, was a pompous and cold-blooded man whom Grace Knowles detested. Rufus seems not to have noticed this throughout the years that they worked for him.
132. Their cat, Kiki, was mentioned in May and July in Rufus's diary but her arrival went unannounced — it must have been in early 1929.
133. Ex-UBC history prof whose material he had published in the Magazine Section, and who now worked for the ILO.
134. They had met in 1920 at the Imperial Press Conference in Ottawa.
135. Philipp Scheidemann had also been, briefly, the first President of the Weimar Republic.
136. Johnston, Lukin, *In England Today.*
137. The airport in Palma was built in the 1930s; during the 1920s airmail was delivered by seaplane.
138. Derek tells this story in his monograph, page 24, but I have taken his father's version where they differed on details.
139. Margaret Rutherford, 5 years younger than Rufus and Bee, was still at the start of her stage career (a late starter) and in 1930 acted with Epsom Little Theatre before doing a season in rep at the Oxford Playhouse. Bee probably knew her.
140. GBS, as he was known, was an intellectual celebrity with modern rock-star status.
141. St Stephen's was consecrated in 1218 on the traditional site where St Edmund, king of the East Angles, was crowned in 855.
142. For readers of *Lucky Alex*, the very same St Hubert airbase that Alex commanded in the 1950s.
143. *Daily Province* 2 Sept headline: "Labour Sunday Sermon Topic — Lukin

Johnston and J.S. Woodsworh Among Special Speakers" While Rufus was speaking at Christ Church, Woodsworth was speaking at First United Church.

144. Now the Brigantine Inn.
145. This could be wrongly deciphered, as his pencil was blunt — but Edmonton's population hovered around 50,000, having shrunk from a prewar 72,000 thanks to enlistment, hard times, and greener grass elsewhere. It was arguably still 'rural'.
146. *The Fortnightly Review* was a serious British literary and political magazine. The two issues of the magazine to which Rufus contributed also featured, *inter alia*, Aldous Huxley, G.K. Chesterton, and André Siegfried — exalted company.
147. Johnston, Lukin, *In England Today*, pp 90-95.
148. Johnston, Lukin, *Down English Lanes*, pp 52, 57.
149. The world of the British chattering classes is a small one. Dr Heckels' son Richard was my best buddy at Oxford, 1956-59. Richard and I kept in touch until his untimely death in 2008. While we were students, I visited Dr and Mrs Heckels — the doctor having recently retired — on several occasions at their house in Epsom.
150. Since September 1930 the Nazis, with 107 members, were the second-largest party in the Reichstag, though Hitler himself was not a member and was generally to be found at Party HQ in Munich.
151. When Brüning resigned in June 1932, Von Neurath was made Foreign Minister by von Papen, a position he continued to hold under Hitler until 1938. After World War II he was convicted of war crimes and spent 15 years in Spandau prison.
152. "Film shows Germany as underdog", *Daily Province* 1 Feb, 1932.
153. "In Germany Today", *Daily Province* 29 Feb 1932.
154. Christopher Isherwood describes a similar scene in a 'Communist dive' at that time. Isherwood's reaction was very different however: "it was all thoroughly sham and gay and jolly: you couldn't help feeling at home, immediately." *Goodbye to Berlin*, pp 191-92.
155. "In Germany Today", *Daily Province* 3 Mar 1932.
156. The Munich *putsch*.
157. "League's fate is linked with Far East clash; France & Germany may resign if conflict not halted." *Daily Province* 3 Feb 1932.
158. "Simon reveals big gulf in methods of disarmament", *Daily Province* 8 Feb 1932.
159. "Soviet Envoy Forecasts new War", *Daily Province* 11 Feb 1932.
160. Sir George Younghusband was a well-known, well-connected military blowhard, a sort of British Sam Steele — you name it, he was there — and his wife's sister lived in Qualicum. Beach, BC, and may have known Rufus and/or Bee.
161. Called Dominion Day until 1982 and later renamed Canada Day.

162. Derek had the day off work for having passed his Intermediate Accountancy exams.
163. The Bonn-Cologne autobahn begun 1929. Konrad Adenauer, then mayor of the city, opened it 6 Aug. 1932 — the Nazis had opposed its construction.
164. There was no reason why they should have recognized Linz as the birthplace of Adolf Hitler — few people outside of Germany then knew who he was, though Rufus was among them, of course.
165. Derek attached the group photograph to the back of the painting with his story of this 1932 encounter.
166. Dr Otto Rosenberg, a graduate of the University of Vienna, was secretary of the Austrian Bankers' Union. In this capacity he built a reputation as one of the ablest economic experts in central Europe and was consulted widely. After the Anschluss in 1938 he was expelled from Austria by the Nazis. (*Oshkosh Daily Northwestern* 13 Oct 1939).
167. Robert Best, an American and doyen of the international journalists in Vienna, who met nightly at the Café Louvre Stammtisch (reserved table) to chat and discuss the news. Its equivalent in Berlin was Die Taverne which Rufus would later patronize. www.academia.edu.
168. M.W. Fodor and his wife Martha. Fodor was born Hungarian but a naturalized Brit and correspondent for the *Manchester Guardian*. With Best, he led the Anglo-American journalist group at the Café Louvre and was considered the most knowledgeable of them all. No wonder that Rufus wanted to talk to him. www.academia.edu.
169. One reason why the journey of 150 miles from Vienna took 5 hours may have been the repair of Biatorbagy bridge outside Budapest. In September 1931 a terrorist's bomb had exploded on the bridge, derailing the Vienna Express and killing or wounding 150 passengers.
170. He flew in a Fokker FX1 monoplane.
171. Arthur Dowden later incurred the wrath of the Nazis at the Frankfurt Consulate in 1938 by his efforts to feed desperate Jews in the city — he was #90 on the Nazi blacklist for when they overran Britain!
172. Edward Benes was an influential figure at international conferences and became Czech president in 1935. He was forced to resign by Nazi pressure in October 1938.
173. Rennie Smith was the founding secretary of Friends of Europe, a British organization that published writings and speeches on European issues.
174. The memorial was unveiled 26 July 1936 by Edward VIII. Derek was there.
175. R.E. to Rufus, 5 Mar 1933. This was an astonishing thing for his father to have been reading — von Glaise-Horstenau was # 2 in the then-illegal Austrian Nazi party!
176. Rufus to F.N. Southam, 20 Mar 1933.
177. Noel-Buxton was a former Labour MP and minister who had been elevated to the House of Lords in 1930. He was an advocate of returning her African colonies to Germany and later an appeaser.

178. The Rev. William Charles Hawksley and his wife Julia Mary Anne Johnston, known as Sis. Hawksley held the living of Michelmersh, 1918-1934 where Sis travelled the parish in her pony and trap. Earlier Hawksley had been vicar of North Ormesby in Yorkshire.
179. Wickham Steed to Lukin Johnston, 26 Apr 1933.
180. Johnston, Derek, *A Personal Memoir*, p. 26.
181. H.S. Southam to Rufus, 23 Feb 1932.
182. It was actually October 24 — near enough; we can allow him artistic licence!
183. Rufus to Bee, Hotel Kaiserhof, Berlin, 27 Oct 1933.
184. Rufus never had a chance to discover just how reliable Robert Townsend Smallbones was. He was British Consul General in Frankfurt 1932-39. His courage, enterprise, and perseverance helped tens of thousands of Jews escape Germany after Kristallnacht. His most far-reaching contribution was the creation of a new type of entry visa. Coined the 'Smallbones Scheme' by the Home Office, it granted German Jews a temporary sanctuary in the UK, allowing them to wait in safety before travelling to the USA the following year once annual immigration quotas had been cleared. The scheme was kept quiet by officials to avoid parliamentary and press criticism, but it was estimated that it made possible the entry of an additional 48,000 Jewish refugees into Britain. With his deputy, Arthur Dowden (who helped Rufus in Bratislava in 1932), Smallbones worked tirelessly to process as many entry visas as possible.
185. Larson, *In the Garden of Beasts*, p. 160-61.
186. Charles J. Woodsworth (1909-2005) was the eldest son of the famous socialist J.S. Woodsworth (in 1935 founder of the CCF). Charlie started with the *Winnipeg Tribune* in 1932 which is how Rufus must have met him.
187. Norman Ebbutt had written in the *Times* in April: "Herr Hitler, in his speeches as Chancellor, has professed a peaceful foreign policy. But this does not prove that the underlying spirit of the new German is a peaceful one. Germany is inspired by the determination to recover all it has lost and little hope of doing by peaceful means. Influential Germans do not see ten years elapsing before the war they regard as natural or inevitable breaks out in Europe. One may hear five or six years mentioned." His warnings about the Nazis were largely suppressed by Geoffrey Dawson.
188. Larson, *In the Garden of Beasts*, p. 61.
189. Members of the Bund Deutscher Mädel or BDM, the girls' section of the Hitler Youth, the only girls' organization permitted.
190. Velten later became a sub-camp of the infamous Ravensbruck.
191. The descriptions of the trial and quotations are from Larson, *In the Garden of Beasts*, chapter 22.
192. Douglas Reed, born in 1895, a WWI fighter pilot with a badly burned face, was a complicated mixture — an anti-Semite who nevertheless vigorously

opposed Hitler and who quit *The Times* in 1938 because Dawson, the appeaser, wouldn't print his stuff. He wrote many books including *The Burning of the Reichstag* (1934) and *Insanity Fair* (1938).

193. The League-imposed constitution had to balance the 95% ethnic German population with Poland's need for a port.
194. Helmer Rosting (1893–1945) was a Danish theologian and diplomat who sympathized with the Nazis. During World War II he worked to support Denmark's Nazi occupiers and their anti-Semitic policies. After the liberation of Denmark he was arrested and questioned. Although he was released, he committed suicide a month later.
195. Elizabeth Montizambert (1875–1964) was a British author and journalist, famous for her book *Unnoticed London* (1922) and later for *Michael's London* (1936) for children, featuring an insufferable small boy. *Inter alia*, she wrote theatre reviews for a Canadian newspaper.
196. Rufus's diary entry has been combined with his letter to Bee for 6 Nov quotations.
197. Rhea Clyman, "BAD" or not, was a 28 year-old Toronto newspaperwoman working for the British *Daily Express* and some Canadian papers. Tough and intrepid, she had been expelled from the USSR for revealing embarrassing facts on the northern gulag and the Ukrainian famine. In 1938, as Munich correspondent for the British *Daily Telegraph*, she survived a plane crash near Amsterdam in which 6 other passengers died. Rufus evidently found her level of emancipation disturbing, if not distinctly threatening!
198. Mary Johnston's letter to Val Castle, 3 April 1991. Mary was Rufus's half-sister and Val's great-aunt. See family tree.
199. Göring claimed to speak some English. According to Brig-Gen. Robert I. Stack, Assistant Division Commander, 36th US Inf. Div, who took Göring's surrender in 1945, "he and I got out of our vehicles and von Brauschitz introduced us. Göring gave me the old German Army salute, not the 'Heil Hitler', and I returned it. I asked him if he wished to surrender and he said, "yes." We talked through my Sergeant-Interpreter although Göring said he spoke English but that he had not had much practice in the last five years. He did not wish to speak English as he might misunderstand or be misunderstood. http://www.kwanah.com/36division/ps/ps9277.htm
200. Larson, *In the Garden of Beasts*, p. 70.
201. Reports referred to are from these newspapers: *News Chronicle* 20 Nov 1933, "Passengers Lined up by Captain; *Daily Mirror*, 20 Nov 1933, "Lost Major Mystery"; *Daily Sketch* 1933, "Second Mystery of the Prague"; *Nottingham Guardian*, 20 Nov 1933, "Journalist Falls Overboard"; *Sunday Pictorial*, 19 Nov 1933, "Second Riddle of the Prague"; *Sunday Referee*, 19 Nov 1933, "Channel Steamer Mystery"; *Le Courrier de la Presse*, 20 Nov 1933.
202. Vernon Bartlett to 'Miss Johnston' in an undated letter, presumably when he was quite old — he died at 88 in 1983.

203. Johnston, Derek, *A Personal Memoir*, Appendix 8, p. 2.
204. Mary Johnston to her great-niece Val (Johnston) Castle, 3 Apr 1991.
205. Robert Keyserlingk in a letter of condolence and explanation to Bee, 20 Nov 1933.
206. Correspondence between R.E. and witnesses is not among his surviving papers and he or Derek probably destroyed it.
207. "Open Verdict on Former P&O Commodore, *The Straits Times* (Singapore), Saturday, 16 Sept 1933, p. 13, from which source all references to the inquest have been taken.
208. Website of the Greenock cemetery.
209. Bee's predicament was observed sympathetically by Katie Lukin, to whom she had been a good friend. When Katie died at 91 in 1945, she left Bee a small annuity.
210. Courses for foreigners.
211. The political union of Germany and Austria, which was the backdrop to the musical *The Sound of Music*. The Von Trapps were not alone among Austrians in opposing the Nazi takeover, which greatly strengthened Germany's strategic position *vis à vis* Czechoslovakia, the next item on Hitler's shopping list.
212. In 1933 the Southam stable included the following newspapers: *Calgary Herald*, *Edmonton Journal*, *Hamilton Spectator*, *Montreal Gazette*, *Ottawa Citizen*, Vancouver *Daily Province*, *Windsor Star*, *Winnipeg Tribune*.

Bibliography

Archives

- Provincial Archives of British Columbia. *Cowichan Leader*, 1911-1914.

Microfilm

- Vancouver Public Library. *Daily Province*. Microfilm.
- City of Vancouver Archives. Photographs.

Unpublished

- Cosgrave, Joyce. *The Way it Was*. Handwritten childhood recollections written in 1997 by Rufus's sister.
- Johnston, Derek L. *Edwin Harry Lukin Johnston, 1887-1933: A Personal Memoir*; 1978.
- Johnston, Nellie. Diary, 1893.
- King's School Canterbury register, 1859-1931.
- Photographs in private collections.
- Diaries of Lukin and Bee Johnston, family letters & other papers, all in the possession of the Johnston family.

Published

- Castle, Colin. *Lucky Alex, The Career of Group Captain A.M. Jardine*. Victoria, BC: Fighting Fit Publishing, 2000
- Dancocks, Daniel G. *Sir Arthur Currie, a Biography*. Agincourt, ON: Methuen, 1985.
- Davis, Chuck. *The Chuck Davis History of Metropolitan Vancouver*. Madeira Park, BC: Harbour Publishing, 2011.
- Morrison, Brad R. & Christopher P. Hanna. "Walter Cameron Nichol." *Dictionary of Canadian Biography*, Vol. XV (1921-1930) .
- *Encyclopedia of Saskatchewan*. http://esask.uregina.ca/entry/milling.html.

- Godwin, George S. *The Eternal Forest*. Godwin Books, 1994. Reprint.
- Godwin, George S. *Why Stay We Here?* Godwin Books, 2002. Reprint.
- Green, Valerie & Lynn Gordon-Finlay. *If These Walls Could Talk: Vancouver Island's Houses from the Past*. Victoria, BC: TouchWood Editions, 2001.
- Henry, Tom. *Small City in a Big Valley, the Story of Duncan*. Madeira Park, BC: Harbour Publishing, 1999.
- History of the *Times Colonist*. Victoria *Times Colonist*, January 2, 2008.
- Isherwood, Christopher. *Goodbye to Berlin*. Penguin Books, 1958.
- Johnston, E.H. Lukin. *Beyond the Rockies*. London and Toronto: J.M. Dent & Sons, 1929.
- Johnston, E.H. Lukin. *Down English Lanes*. London and Toronto: J.M. Dent & Sons, 1931.
- Johnston, E.H. Lukin. *In England Today*. Toronto, ON: McClelland & Stewart, 1931; and London, England: Heath Cranton, 1933.
- Lamb, Bessie. "The Origin and Development of Newspapers in Vancouver." MA Thesis, University of British Columbia, 1942.
- Larson, Erik. *In the Garden of Beasts*. Random House, 2011.
- Judd, B.C. "Maj.-Gen. Sir Henry Timson Lukin, KCB, CMG, DSO". *Military History Journal*, Vol 7, No 3(June 1987). South African Military History Society. http://samilitaryhistory.org/vol073bj.html
- Nagorski, Andrew. *Hitlerland*. New York: Simon & Schuster, 2012.
- O'Keefe, David R. *Great War Commands: Historical Perspectives on Canadian Army Leadership, 1914-1918*. Andrew B. Godefroy, ed. Kingston, ON: Canadian Defense Academy Press, 2010. Electronic download (pdf) regimentalrogue.com/library/great_war_commands_godefroy_htm
- Roy, Patricia. *A White Man's Province: British Columbia Politicians and Chinese and Japanese Immigrants 1858-1914*. Vancouver, BC: University of British Columbia Press. Google Books.
- *Wikipedia*. (for much of the detail in, and background of, this story!)

91st YEAR, No. 129. OTTAWA, CANADA, THURSDAY, NOV...

EXCLUSIVE TALK WITH HITLER BY CITIZEN WRITER

Reiterates Readiness To Enter Arms Negotiations But Only On Conditions Of Fullest Equality

Germany's Master Gives First Interview To Canadian Writer

To Correspondent of The Evening Citizen He Says Armed States Should Make First Move For Renewal Of Disarmament Discussions. Recalls His Meetings With Canadians in War Time, States Versailles Treaty a Danger, Asserts Training of Youth is Merely Educative and That Spirit of Discipline Must Be Kept Alive. Allows No Politics in Churches And Offers Canada Some of Undesirable Citizens He Has In Concentration Camps.

BY LUKIN JOHNSTON
Special Correspondent of The Evening Citizen
and Southam Papers. Copyright.

CHANCELLOR HITLER

BERLIN, Nov. 16.—Germany stands ready to consider favorably any invitation from the other great powers to recommence negotiations for disarmament or limitation of armaments. She does not care whether negotiations take place within or without the framework of the League of Nations. Her only condition is she will enter only on terms of absolute equality. She waits the call to Geneva or elsewhere. She believes the time has come when there is a general feeling somr new instrument should take the place of the Versailles Treaty.

Such were the unequivocal statements made to your correspondent by Chancellor Hitler in an exclusive interview here.

This is the first statement of Germany's future policy made since Sunday's monster referendum constituted Hitler absolute master of Germany.

First Interview to Canadian Newspaperman.

From the front page of the *Ottawa Evening Citizen*, Thursday, 16 November 1933. Allowing for the time difference, by the time subscribers started to read it, the writer, Rufus, may already have been dead.

Index

K

L

P

Q

R

Index of Military Units mentioned
(A bolded number indicates the presence of a map)

Colin Castle is a Canadian who was born in England in 1936. After wartime years at primary schools in Scotland and England, most of his schooling was at fee-paying boarding schools (similar to the one Rufus attended many years before). He left school at 18, spent two years in the British army in Berlin and three taking a history degree at Oxford. After trying several other careers he became a history teacher in 1961, and remained one until his retirement in 1998. He met his Canadian wife, Val Johnston, on a ski trip to Austria in 1964, and they were married in July that year in London, England.

Their early married life was in Westmorland, England, where their two sons were born. In 1969 they emigrated to Kelowna, BC, where Colin taught history and social studies in what is now West Kelowna — first at George Pringle Secondary, and then, for twenty-three years, at Mount Boucherie Secondary. Their daughter was born in 1971 and the three children grew up in the Okanagan. Colin and Val still rattle around happily in the family house beside the lake, often visited by their children and grandchildren who now live, learn and work in Victoria, Vancouver and Glasgow.

Apart from *Rufus*, Colin has written three books: *Lucky Alex*, a biography of Group Captain Alex Jardine (2001), *Canada's Story* — an (as yet) unpublished history of Canada for children; and a Family History of the antecedents and descendants of Allan Macdiarmid and Grace McClure, his Scottish grandparents.